Psychoanalytic Therapy and the Gay Man

Jack Drescher, M.D.

THE ANALYTIC PRESS

1998   Hillsdale, NJ   London

© 1998 by The Analytic Press, Inc.

Published by
The Analytic Press, Inc.
Editorial offices:
101 West Street
Hillsdale, New Jersey 07642

www.analyticpress.com

Index by Leonard S. Rosenbaum

Typeset by CompuDesign & Associates, Inc., Rego Park, NY

Library of Congress Cataloging-in-Publication Data

Drescher, Jack, 1951–
Psychoanalytic therapy and the gay man / Jack Drescher.
        p.   cm.
Includes bibliographical references and index.
ISBN: 0-88163-208-2
1. Gay men—Mental health.   2. Psychoanalysis and homosexuality.   I. Title.
        [DNLM: 1. Homosexuality.   Male—psychology.
        2. Psychoanalytic Therapy.   WM 611D773p 1998]
        RC558.3.D74 1998
        616.89'17'086642—dc21
        DNLM/DLC
    for Library of Congress   98-36101
                                                   CIP

Printed in the United States of America
10 9 8 7 6 5 4 3 2 1

CONTENTS

ACKNOWLEDGMENTS

This book was made possible by the efforts of previous generations of psychoanalysts and mental health professionals, both heterosexual and gay, willing to fight the psychoanalytic orthodoxy and dogma of their times. This book honors the memories of the late John Spiegel, Robert Stoller, Emery Hetrick, and A. Damien Martin. This book also owes a debt to Judd Marmor, Robert J. Campbell, Lawrence Hartmann, John Fryer, Stuart Nichols, Bertram Schaffner, Thomas Szasz, Melvin Sabshin, Norman Levy, Charles Silverstein, Richard Green, Richard Pillard, Richard C. Friedman, Richard Isay, Kenneth Lewes, James Krajeski, Terry Stein, and Robert Cabaj. In the battle against psychoanalytic theories and clinical practices that allowed social prejudices to masquerade as scientific and medical facts, they set in motion dramatic changes whose social impact is just beginning to be felt. Although the theoretical and clinical positions presented in this book may take issue with some of these esteemed colleagues, the transitional spaces created by their efforts made it possible for the disagreements we have to be thoughtfully and respectfully aired.

A study group with Barbara Miller, Catherine Stuart, Mark Siegert, Elena Skolnick, and Sarah Sternklar helped me develop some of my ideas regarding Sullivan's theory of dissociation that, in addition to a panel on dissociation at the 1995 Division 39 meeting in Santa Monica, eventually found their way into chapter 9. Another study group with Ann D'Ercole, Sandra Kiersky, Donna Orange, and Christina Sekaer helped me articulate some of my ideas presented in chapters 2 and 3. David Scasta, past editor of *The Journal of Gay and Lesbian Psychotherapy,* invited me to write a paper contrasting a contemporary analytic approach to treating gay men with traditional psychoanalytic attempts to convert homosexual identities. Some of the ideas in that paper, "Holding or Fixing," found their way into chapters 6 and 7. John DeCecco, editor of *The Journal of Homosexuality*, asked me to write a history of reparative therapies. That paper, "I'm Your Handyman," contributed to arguments made in chapter 6. A chapter entitled "Psychoanalytic Subjectivity and Male Homosexuality," in Bob Cabaj and Terry Stein's comprehensive *Textbook of Homosexuality and Mental Health*, contained arguments expanded upon in chapters 3 and 5 of this book. I wish to thank all my editors and study partners for their help.

I wish to thank the many friends and colleagues who have read portions of the manuscript as well as those who were willing to discuss my ideas during the preparation of this book. I am grateful for the especially thoughtful input of Susan Coates, Maggie Magee, and Diana Miller. I am also particularly thankful for the time and attention given to the manuscript by Richard Hire, Joyce Fisher, M. Luisa Mantovani, and Eli Zal. I would also like to thank Kenn Ashley, Mary Barber, Dixie Beckham, Laura Bernay, William Byne, Bertram Cohler, Ken Corbett, E. Gerald Dabbs, Charles T. Davis, Muriel Dimen, Thomas Domenici, Bruce Dorval, Jennifer Downey, Christopher Eldredge, Martin Stephen Frommer, Paul Giorgianni, Guy Glass, Deborah Glazer, Virginia Goldner, John Gosling, Jeffrey Guss, Adrienne Harris, Daniel Hicks, Lawrence Jacobson, Robert Kertzner, Susan Kolod, Golda Laurens, Ubaldo Leli, Ronnie C. Lesser, Paul Lynch, Joseph P. Merlino, Robert Mitchell, Attilio Mirenda, Sherry Ross, Ralph Roughton, Marcia Rosen, David Scasta, Roy Schafer, David Schwartz, Erica Schoenberg, Joanne Spina, Susan Vaughan, and Kathleen White for their time, conversation, encouragement, and feedback.

I also wish to thank those who offered me the opportunity to present my formulations about psychotherapy with gay men at various scientific meetings: Philip Bialer, Mark Blechner, Harvey Bluestone, Sheila Feig Brown, Marvin Drellich, Norman Haffner, Petros Levounis, Mary Alice O'Dowd, Charles Rizzuto, Eric Singer, and Steve Taravella. I am grateful for the appreciative responses my work has received at the meetings of The American Academy of Psychoanalysis, The Association of Gay and Lesbian Psychiatrists, Gay and Lesbian Analysts, the Gay and Lesbian Medical Association, Gay and Lesbian Psychiatrists of New York, the Group for Advancement of Psychiatry's Committee on Human Sexuality, The Institute for Human Identity, The New York County District Branch of the American Psychiatric Association, particularly its committee on Gay and Lesbian Issues, New York Gay and Lesbian Physicians, and the William Alanson White Psychoanalytic Society.

My time at the William Alanson White Psychoanalytic Institute has had a powerful impact on my thinking and psychoanalytic identity, not to mention providing me with a supportive and intellectually critical forum to present my work. I wish to thank Anna Antonovsky and Marcia Rosen for their early support. I am grateful to the Institute for awarding me its Lawrence W. Kaufman Award for my 1993 paper, "Psychoanalytic Attitudes toward Homosexuality." Carola Mann, and later James Meltzer, invited me to co-teach, with Christina Sekaer, a course in clinical work with gay and lesbian patients at White's Center for Applied Psychoanalysis. Miltiades Zaphiropoulos was an invaluable source of references to the work of Harry Stack Sullivan. I also wish to thank Joerg Bose, Philip Bromberg, Lawrence Epstein, John Fiscalini, Jay Greenberg, Amnon Issacharoff, Edgar Levenson, Marylou Lionells, Steve Mitchell, Nat Stockhamer, Donnel Stern, and Earl Witenberg for their direct and indirect contributions to my professional development and to my theoretical and clinical thinking. Leah Davidson and Ann Turkel have provided me with unique insights. Raul Ludmer's contributions are immeasurable and deeply appreciated.

This book honors the memories of Eric Cohen, Claudio Erbosi, Michael Frary, Ben Meiselman, Joseph Murdoch, Gerald Osofsky, Arte Pierce, Richard Sherwin, Ruen Stefnisson, and Michele Tombolani. A part of them lives on in this book.

I will be forever grateful to my editor, John Kerr, for his ongoing presence, insights, and contributions during the process of writing this book. I wish to thank Paul Stepansky and The Analytic Press for providing me with this forum to present my clinical work and ideas.

I am indebted to my parents for many things, but particularly for giving me the freedom to read anything I wanted and for buying that first manual typewriter. I deeply appreciate the love of Anne, Murry, Sol, Daniel, David, Rebecca, and Benjamin.

Finally, without the understanding, encouragement, and support of Nishan Kazazian, this book could never have been written.

1
INTRODUCTION

I have also realized that individual psychoanalysis and
sociology are, at base, essentially one field of study.

> Harold Searles, "Dual- and Multiple-Identity
> Processes in Borderline Ego-Functioning" (1977)

It is with a good deal of reluctance that the psychoanalyst undertakes to present a typology of behavior. . . .
But although we therefore feel that the setting up of
typologies is justified, it behooves us to be explicit
about the shortcomings inherent in any such attempt.

> Kohut and Wolfe, "The Disorders
> of the Self and Their Treatment" (1978)

Any attempt to turn a therapeutic discovery that
emerges from a relational context into a technique that
can be "applied" to other patients is an illustration of
what I believe to be the single most ubiquitous failing
in all analytic schools of thought as methods of therapy, and the shared blind-spot in each of their creators.

> Philip Bromberg
> "Speak! That I May See You" (1994)

Psychoanalytic Therapy and the Gay Man? When Paul Stepansky
of The Analytic Press suggested this as the title for my proposed book, I
immediately associated to Helen Gurley Brown. In the tradition of Freud,

whose theory of infantile libido ran counter to fin de siècle Vienna's prevailing beliefs about middle-class sexuality, Brown's 1960s book, *Sex and
the Single Girl*, had an oxymoronic quality that drew attention to her
time's cultural attitudes toward female sexuality. Since then, the sexual
emancipation of women has challenged traditional gender stereotypes
which inevitably led to the modern, cultural reevaluation of homosexuality. Today, a book that shows how a psychoanalytic psychotherapy can
affirm the sexual identities of gay men is part of that growing cultural
transformation.

It should be noted that *Psychoanalytic Therapy and the Gay Man* is not
just a book about doing psychotherapy with gay men. It is also a chronicle of the historical state of relationships between two controversial
cultural movements of the twentieth century: psychoanalysis and the
political struggle for gay rights. It would be an understatement to
describe the historical state of relationships between organized psychoanalysis and the lesbian and gay community as strained. What factors
led to that estrangement? Not only had American psychoanalysis
pathologized gay identities for many decades, but in the early 1970s,
psychoanalysts were among the most vociferous opponents of deleting
homosexuality from the American Psychiatric Association's official
manual of mental disorders (Bayer, 1981). Furthermore, with a few rare
exceptions, like the William Alanson White Psychoanalytic Institute in
New York City, organized psychoanalysis insisted that gay men and
women were unsuited to become psychoanalysts unless they converted
to heterosexuality (Socarides, 1995, p. 153). Those days are all in the past.
In the quarter century following the APA's 1973 decision, American psychoanalysis has undergone, and is still undergoing, rapid and radical
changes in developing theories and attitudes that can be therapeutically
helpful to lesbians and gay men. Across the country, even the most traditional psychoanalytic training institutions are now actively recruiting lesbian and gay candidates (Roughton, 1995). Most of these changes have
taken place in the last decade, but they have not been well publicized. As
a result, today's psychoanalytic theories and practitioners are still
regarded with suspicion and hostility in many segments of the lesbian
and gay community.

Why do I believe that this political history is relevant to psychoanalytic psychotherapy with gay men? In the postmodern world, personal
and political narratives are not easily separable. From its inception, psychoanalysis claimed privileged access to the meanings of homosexuality.
In fact, traditional psychoanalytic theories and attitudes, as they were
communicated in the training process, actually reflected cultural biases

against homosexuality. Because of this history, and the infantilizing and pathologizing attitudes that their theories subsequently fostered, many analysts found it difficult to consider alternative ways to think about homosexuality. I therefore believe that therapists have something to gain if they learn about the historical, political, and moral attitudes that surround the meaning of homosexuality. Not only will this allow them to understand the broader social implications of the clinical theories with which they work, it may also enable them to comprehend more fully the clinical narratives told by gay men in treatment. Of course, knowing something about gay patients is only part of the treatment. It is equally important for therapists to be consciously aware of their own feelings and attitudes toward gay men. And because I believe that psychoanalytically-oriented treatments are a significant research tool, Anne Fausto-Sterling's (1992) words are particularly relevant to therapists undertaking the exploration of gay patients' lives:

> We ought to expect that individual researchers will articulate—both to themselves and publicly—exactly where they stand, what they think, and most importantly, what they *feel* deep down in their guts about the complex of personal and social issues that relate to their areas of research. Then let the reader beware. The reader can look at the data, think about the logic of the argument, figure out how the starting questions were framed, and consider alternate interpretations of the data. By definition, one cannot see one's own blind spots, therefore one must acknowledge the probability of their presence and provide others with enough information to identify and illuminate them [p. 10].

In keeping with the above recommendation, I wish to state from the outset that this book is written by a gay male psychoanalyst. I work within an analytic perspective that sees the therapist as an agent of the patient, rather than as a representative of the patient's social milieu. In fact, I will explain and then argue against the positions of the psychoanalytically-oriented therapists, historical and contemporary, who overidentify with cultural expectations of traditional, gender conformity. I do not mean to suggest that therapists can or should ignore what are experienced by patients as social pressures to conform. The need to deal with external reality has always been part of the psychoanalytic model. However, Freud saw hysteria as a dissociative response to Victorian beliefs and attitudes toward human sexuality. His psychoanalytic method enabled his hysterical patients to take issue with sexual reality as it was defined in their time. Freud led the way by showing that only through the questioning of embedded cultural beliefs can analytic progress be made.

In addition to questioning sexual and gender conformity, I wish to name some of the other psychoanalytic values that inform this treatment approach. They include Winnicott's (1965) concept of the holding environment and Bion's (1967a) notion of containment. Both are therapeutic attitudes that create a setting in which a patient feels safe, respected, and accepted. In addition, I believe that Sullivan's (1954) detailed inquiry can teach a patient the value of curiosity. Curiosity can promote skepticism about authority, psychoanalytic or otherwise, as well as unravel what Sullivan referred to as the mystifications contained within authority's revealed truths. Curiosity can also foster integration by challenging a patient's dissociative tendencies. And, finally, I believe that awareness of and honesty about one's own fantasies, thoughts, and feelings are valuable and salutary, for both patient and therapist.

This book is primarily written for clinicians who have worked with gay patients, those who are currently working with them, or those who may have a desire to learn more about these men. However, I hope that this book will also be of some interest to anyone interested in learning more about psychoanalysis, psychotherapy, gay and lesbian studies, and queer theory. This book may also be of interest to any individual, regardless of his or her sexual identity, who is trying to understand the contemporary cultural debates regarding the meanings of homosexuality as our society tries to define a role for its lesbians and gay citizens.

Toward this end, I have tried to offer a glimpse of some developmental narratives that define some gay men's identities. Paradoxically, however, I cannot provide a singular definition of what it means to be a gay man. I do not wish to delimit the subject by defining it. In other words, I have not set out to write the definitive handbook about being gay. Gay male identities are not static entities because they vary according to time, place, and culture. The gay men of my generation are not like those of the generation before us, and younger gay men are different in other ways. For example, the distinguished anthropologist, Gilbert Herdt, along with the developmental psychologist Andrew Boxer, described a cohort system of four historical age-groupings of men in Chicago: (1) those who came of age after World War I; (2) those who came of age during and after World War II; (3) those who came of age after Stonewall and the period of gay activism around it; and (4) those who came of age in the era of AIDS (Herdt and Boxer, 1993). Their findings support my belief that all identities are culturally defined and that none of them can be captured by any one author's subjectivity, not even that of Herdt and Boxer.

Throughout this book, in discussing theories of homosexuality, I use quotation marks when the word "homosexual" is used as a noun. This is done to emphasize the point that being gay is not the same thing as being a "homosexual." The latter is a medical term that takes one aspect of a person's identity, his sexual attractions, and treats it as if it were the sum of his entire identity. In clinical practice, gay patients, like heterosexual ones, differ in temperament, personality, interpersonal relatedness, family background and cultural history. A therapist needs to remember that one is not just working with a gay man, but with a patient. It is the recognition and exploration of individual differences among gay men that should characterize a psychoanalytically-oriented treatment approach.

In trying to offer a meaningful, psychoanalytic way of working with gay men that respects individuality, ties past experiences to the present, and offers an increased awareness of their inner worlds and interpersonal relationships, this book tells what I think of as unofficial stories. My preference for this approach comes from the observation that official stories can obscure individuality. An official psychoanalytic story, such as the resolution of the Oedipus complex, will all too often legitimize only one path of development. Not only does this create a preferential developmental hierarchy, but in the hands of some psychoanalysts, official stories became authoritarian and disrespectful, as in Bergler's (1956) claim that "Homosexuals are essentially disagreeable people" (p. 228). Unofficial stories, on the other hand, can exist comfortably as nondominant narratives. They do not have to be imposed on everyone and, like countercultural narratives in general, their very existence subverts the official story's expectations of universality and conformity.

I also believe that this is not just a book about treating gay men. Freud took the idea of homosexuality and used it to make a case for his broader psychoanalytic concepts of bisexuality, libido, projection, paranoia, and narcissism (Freud, 1905, 1910a, 1911, 1914c). Conversely, psychotherapy with gay men touches upon many issues that are being contentiously debated in the modern psychoanalytic world. These include, but are not limited to, psychoanalytic epistemology; one-person versus two-person psychologies; the developmental influences of nature and nurture; the role of analytic neutrality; the very existence of neutrality; the role of subjectivity; the discovery of meaning versus the creation of meaning; the function of personal morality in clinical practice with implications for the influence of the therapist's beliefs on the conduct and outcome of a psychotherapy or analysis; the primacy of the Oedipus complex; the meaning of a developmental line; the nature of the unconscious; the uses of countertransference; therapist self-revelation; the psychoanalytic understanding of affects; and psychoanalytic pluralism.

I have made quite extensive use of quotes from the literature of gay studies, queer theory, psychoanalysis, sexology, religion, and reparative therapy. Paraphrasing does not always capture the tone of the original author's text and I often found that an author's tone played an important part in my affective experience of the material. If I call a particular psychoanalyst disrespectful, for example, it does not quite have the same effect as hearing, in his own words, the analyst's disrespectful tone. It is also my hope that in experiencing the wide range of authors' tones and the affective responses that they evoked, the reader may better approach the subjective experience of gay men. Thus, while reading the literature about homosexuality presented here, I invite the reader to hear the quotes as if he or she were a gay man. Listening to the voices quoted in this book was the closest approximation I could find to a gay man's subjective experience of his inner and external worlds. Those voices can be either soothing or harsh, accepting or critical; they will inevitably be contradictory. Although it was impossible to present the myriad attitudes toward homosexuality in one volume, the range offered here may provide therapists with some inkling of how gay men internally struggle to make sense of their same-sex feelings.

I have tried, perhaps unsuccessfully, to avoid sweeping recommendations and therapeutic prescriptions. Instead, my intent has been to illustrate a psychoanalytic attitude that is useful in understanding a particular life experience while recognizing individual variations within that experience. As a general rule, doing psychotherapy with gay men may entail more similarities than differences to the treatment of heterosexual patients. Consider the following patient, reentering treatment because of increased symptoms of depression and anxiety:

> **Patient:** I read *Darkness Visible* by William Styron. A friend gave me the book. He does an excellent job of describing the anxiety attack, the feeling that one is losing one's mind and going mad. In a sense it is comforting to know that someone else is going through it and yet worrying that this poor guy could not get out of bed and had to check into a hospital. He did get over it. He said if it happens once, it's likely to happen again. This is the fourth episode of depression I've had.
>
> **Therapist:** How do you feel about this being your fourth episode?
>
> **Pt:** Enough is enough. This is the first time I understand what it is. I had experienced it before without knowing what it was. The interruption of sleep, etc. I never did anything about it before.
>
> **Th:** You did come into therapy the last time you became depressed.

Pt: That's true. But this time I'm not suffering the breakup of a relationship. My feelings about Roger have passed. Now the depression is different. Now I'm questioning everything. What is debilitating is the feeling of worthlessness and inadequacy. It's kind of crippling. That's why I have the fantasy of working in a no-stress job. I have to eliminate stress or scale it back. I'm not sure if this high-powered career thing is a good thing for me. It's not making me happy. It's making me unhappy. In my state of mind right now, this pressure is crippling. I want to throw up my hands and say, "Screw it."

Without knowing the anatomical gender of this patient, the reader might not easily discern the patient's sexual identity. At this moment, in this particular session, the patient's concerns are indistinguishable from any of the issues that patients bring to therapy: emotional stress, difficulty with personal relationships, work relationships, or family relationships. And although an understanding of this patient's sexual identity will certainly be an important issue across the course of his treatment, it will not be the only subject talked about in therapy. It is difficult to quantify how much time is spent on issues related to gay men's sexual identities. And it would be yet another understatement to point out that the subject is rarely addressed in the psychoanalytic literature. My own clinical experience, in general, has been that approximately 10 to 15 percent of therapeutic time is devoted to discussing issues related to being gay. But having said that, it should be noted that a patient deeply engrossed in coming out will be highly focused on his gay identity for much of the time. Another patient, who may have been out for a long time, much less so. Therefore, it is not always possible to separate things out by percentages. Furthermore, a man's gay identity is linked to his multiple identities of child, parent, sibling, professional, patient, or citizen, just to name a few. So although a patient's gay identity is not necessarily the primary focus of treatment in many cases, its impact on the course of treatment cannot be overlooked.

This observation may escape a therapist who believes that treating gay patients requires no special knowledge. I have certainly heard therapists say, "I treat my gay patients just as I do my heterosexual ones." Laudable as this attitude may be, particularly within the context of psychoanalysis' historical animus toward gay patients, this belief ignores the fact that growing up gay is a different cultural experience than growing up heterosexual. There are specific issues that inevitably come up when a patient lives his life as a member of a sexual minority. One intention of this book is to explore, in a psychoanalytic context, how the larger world might look through a minority perspective.

My clinical approach is based upon my psychotherapeutic and psychoanalytic work with about one hundred gay men, and more than three hundred gay men seen in brief, office consultations, for a variety of reasons, since 1984. Although some of the patients I discuss are not gay, they have been included in this book because the issues they raised were relevant to the understanding of gay identities. While discussing these cases, I do not focus on frequency of sessions or whether the patient was seen face to face or on the couch. For the record, however, I see some therapy patients face to face, although most of them use the couch. Some patients came to treatment two or three times a week but most of them were seen once a week. Almost all of the patients entered treatment because they were in a crisis of some sort, usually accompanied by anxious and depressed feelings. None of them came seeking a didactic analysis. Several of the patients discussed in this book were only seen once or twice for a consultation. A significant minority were in treatment from six months to two years. The majority of the patients were in treatment for at least two years and some have been in treatment for as long as ten years.

Rather than presenting extensive case histories of individual patients, I have highlighted clinical and theoretical issues by relying either upon brief patient summaries or, more commonly, I have used edited transcripts of therapy sessions. The verbatim patient material was taken from process notes with over 40 patients, all of whom were told that I was writing a psychotherapy book. Although this may not give the reader the fullest sense of an individual patient, my goal was to cover a broad range of issues. The astute reader is likely to find both transferential and countertransferential subtexts contained in the clinical dialogues presented later. Sometimes these are commented on, but at other times they are not directly addressed. This does not mean, however, that they were never addressed. I am more than willing to acknowledge my own countertransferential blind spots, and I often had to do so when reviewing the clinical material after time had elapsed. But it is also important to note that in telling a story from one perspective, it may at times be necessary to leave out some of its narrative themes. So, although some of my reported interventions could and perhaps should have been different, I nevertheless elected to repeat what I actually said. This is not because I think my interventions were exemplary in any way, but for the sake of accuracy. I believe that intensive psychotherapy and psychoanalysis are complicated processes and that technical perfection exists only in manuals. And if, here and there, the reader picks up on my own biases, selective involvements, and selective inattention, I hope my attempt at clinical openness will serve as a constructive reminder that in one way or another we all hear material selectively.

In order to protect my patients' confidentiality, I have significantly altered many identifying characteristics such as family constellations, jobs, and relationships, as I tried to preserve the essence of the psychotherapeutic encounters. Further to protect confidentiality, the letters by which patients are identified change from chapter to chapter. In other words, Patient A is not the same person in every chapter. And finally, as this book went to press, I showed those patients who were still in treatment the material I planned to use.

All of the patients presented in the book are white, American-born men of differing ethnic and religious backgrounds. They live either in New York City or the metropolitan New York area. Some are native New Yorkers, but most moved to New York from other parts of the country. Patients ranged in age from 21 to 70. A significant minority are in their twenties but most are in their thirties and forties. Some are from lower middle-class or working-class families. Others come from either upper middle-class or wealthy backgrounds. Some patients were upwardly mobile and have managed to leave the social classes into which they were born; others have not. Some have experienced downward drift. Most of the patients are college-educated and about half of them have gone to graduate school. A few are in the mental health field, but most of them are not. Many patients had previous therapy experiences; despite my own therapeutic preference for nontechnical language, many of them were accustomed to using technical, psychotherapeutic terms and they often brought that language with them. Parenthetically, innumerable articles about mental health issues and homosexuality in *The New York Times*, *New York Magazine*, *The New Yorker*, and other sources were a great stimulus for many of the issues raised by my patients. I am deeply thankful to all of the patients who were willing to share their thoughts and feelings with me and I wish to acknowledge that I could not have written this book without their cooperation and trust. It is my hope that the generosity with which they shared their lives with me will be of some help to others.

2

DEFINING A GAY IDENTITY

The road that leads to a gay identity is often a slow
and difficult one, but it is not for any lack of gay desire,
or even necessarily of gay experience. It is because,
growing up in this culture, we are not exposed to stories and images that reflect that experience; we have no
words with which to name it. We must learn—or
invent—a vocabulary with which to call our gay selves
into being.

> Robin Metcalfe, "Halifax, Nova Scotia" (1991)

It was the first time I'd ever considered that gay might
not just be about whom we slept with but a kind of
sensibility, what survives of feeling after all the fears
and evasions of the closet.

> Paul Monette, *Becoming a Man* (1992)

It occurred to me that there were men—perhaps most
men—whom sexual labels failed.

> Darrell Yates Rist, *Heartlands* (1992)

A psychoanalytic approach to treatment strives to define an
individual's subjectivity through the use of language or interpretation. In
fact, for many psychoanalysts, interpretation is central to the analytic
process. Through the process of interpretation, the analyst attempts to
define or name what is going on. Defining, interpreting, naming: they all

have the uncanny ability to generate a sense of power or control over the subject matter named. Consequently, defining a gay identity is often a central issue in the psychotherapeutic encounter with gay men.

Marmor (1965) has noted that "one of the main difficulties underlying any discussion of the problem of homosexuality is that of definition. What, exactly, do we mean when we talk about homosexuality?" (p. 1). In fact, the task of defining what it means to be "gay" or the meaning of a "gay identity" is a complex, interpretative process. One might also reasonably ask what therapeutic purposes does such an inquiry serve? Or whose agenda is being served in undertaking such an endeavor? I strongly believe that helping patients in their ongoing attempts to define their gay identities can only be done by a knowledgeable therapist. If one is going to treat gay men, then one needs to have a sense of who they are. This is more than an issue of courtesy or respect, as important as those qualities will be to the therapeutic encounter. It is also a necessity of the work. One often finds that a gay patient comes into treatment following a lifetime of trying to make sense of his homoerotic feelings. Making sense of how he feels and finding a meaningful perspective for his feelings are all part of defining his gay identity. This is a process that begins well before the patient enters treatment, and defining one's homoerotic feelings is a developmental task, and for some, defining themselves as gay is a developmental achievement. Gay men, in the course of their treatment, will inevitably examine and reexamine themselves as gay men, just as they will go over many of their other identitites.

I have already asserted that a gay identity is not a synonym for being a "homosexual." So what does the patient mean when he says he is gay if he is not simply defining his sexual attractions? What does it mean to the therapist if he or she believes they are treating a patient who is gay? As this chapter will illustrate, patient, therapist, and therapist-patient definitions of gay will emerge at the interface between sociopolitical, psychological, and biological thought. As later chapters will show, any effort to define a gay identity will have a powerful impact on the conduct of a psychotherapy and may determine, for example, whether that identity is defined affirmatively (Isay, 1989) or in a denigrated manner (Nicolosi, 1991).

In order to work empathically and sensitively within this psychotherapeutic realm, therapists should recognize that there are differing aspects to defining gay. These various dimensions are interwoven, and as the clinical material in this chapter and throughout the book will illustrate, they are not always easy to isolate from each other. It is not possible to include all the definitions of gay in this chapter, and only some possibilities will emerge in psychotherapy with any particular gay man. The dimensions offered here should be thought of as artifacts of a process of trying to understand a complex whole by breaking it down into smaller components. The reader should therefore keep in mind that any one part of a person should never be confused with the entire individual.

The Dimension of Sexual and Romantic Attraction

The men who come for treatment in my clinical practice and call themselves gay usually mean that they are sexually attracted and romantically drawn to other men. They recall an awareness of these feelings from an early age, although they have often spent some period of time in their lives denying them. Some report an awareness of same-sex feelings at age four (Isay, 1989), while others recall the origins of these feelings in latency and adolescence. Still others only became aware of their homoerotic feelings in adulthood. As an adult, a gay man's attitudes toward homosexuality, either his own or that of others, may vary. Gay men's adaptations may range along a continuum that spans from living openly within a gay community to living among heterosexuals and completely hiding their sexuality from their friends, their family, and even from themselves.

Whether he is integrated into or isolated from a gay community, a man calling himself gay is invariably attempting, in part, to psychologically reframe his internalized prejudices against homosexuality in a more self-accepting way. For many gay men, this process of self-naming serves as an antidote for the experience of being labeled as unacceptable by others. All gay men have been raised with family and friends' expectations that they become heterosexuals. Many report feeling different from heterosexual peers and understood that their same-sex attractions presented obstacles in complying with the desires and aspirations of their heterosexual parents. As one patient put it, "We are the only minority group born into the enemy camp." Gay men, like the following patient, often recall childhood experiences that symbolized, to them, the cultural biases against homoerotic longings:

> **A:** I asked myself what made me feel so worn down. The answer is denying for twenty years that I was gay. I have known since I was four or five. For twenty years I kept saying "You are not, you are not." I spent twenty years denying what was in fact the truth and all that was required to keep that truth from myself and everybody else was working overtime. I would try to compensate for the things that might have been a telltale sign. That

would be part of the reason I'm so tired. There is a part of me that is emotionally exhausted. As a result, any relationships I had as a child or an adolescent were overshadowed by that. Never was I able to trust anybody. It wasn't my own craziness, but my sense of preservation; getting the message loud and clear that this was not the way to be. Having to mask it by having girlfriends.

I remember, before starting grammar school, a bunch of kids in my neighborhood had a club. There were more girls than boys. Boys younger than I was. I remember feeling part of that little group, a member of that club. There are pictures in the family photo album of us having club meetings. There was a kid named John. I remember me convincing him to get undressed, and all of us looking at him, and me being fascinated by his asshole. Nobody else was fascinated and then I felt very strange. For some reason, things changed after that. There's a picture of me the next year, with none of the kids from that club. Somehow I no longer belonged. I remember that episode with John. That's when I knew I was gay. His physical body fascinated me.

It was this patient's subjective experience that his interest and curiosity about another little boy's body eventually led to estrangement from his circle of friends. Whether this is how things actually occurred is, of course, an open question. Nevertheless, the revelation of same-sex feelings leading to rejection is a common associative link among gay men. And, complicating matters further, was this patient's immediate association to his other gender non-conforming behaviors in childhood:

A: I remember something else changed at that point. That I started to get another message. Another incident I remember was someone threw a pair of high heel shoes in a trash can. My friend and I dragged them out and walked up and down the driveway in those shoes. Then our mothers came out. I can't believe the reaction. They were so mortified. We were playing in the front yard. Up and down we pranced with the shoes. When our mothers found out, it was "Put those away, what are you doing? This is awful, I can't believe it, what's the matter with you? You are doing something that is so bizarre, it cannot be believed." I was crushed. We were having such a good time and then that response from my mother. I got "the look" and her words. The combination was a double punch. It flattened me out. How could having such a good time be bad? I felt gross. I felt dirty. Like when I looked at that kid's rear end. I felt disgusting. Somehow it was related. The same kind of feelings I remember in both cases. That I was disgusting. "What's wrong with you? Are you a pervert?" That seems to be a focal point of when the realization that I was different and wrong and dirty started to become a feeling that was inside of me. It was a realization that this was how people reacted to me. It was reinforced. Then it was my job to be careful not to let that happen again.

The patient associated his same-sex interests to gender-nonconformity, and in doing so drew attention to a complex issue. Although some might interpret a same-sex attraction as simply the love of men for men, male homosexuality is rarely considered to be a purely masculine affair. Instead, it is usually viewed from a cultural perspective that not only regards the relationships between men and women as the standard of relatedness but also defines the qualities of masculinity and femininity in heterosexual terms. As a result, male homosexuality gets defined in the language of femininity. In this heterosexual model, a boy's attraction to boys becomes inevitably lumped together with other girlish things that boys do not do and should not feel. Therefore, to understand what same-sex attractions mean to gay patients, one must know something about how all children come to learn the gendered meanings of human sexuality.

Gender Beliefs

Postmodern gender theorists, drawing upon the pioneering work of Foucault (1978), point out that the construct of *sex* "produces and renders intelligible all manner of sensation, pleasure, and desire as sex-specific. In other words, bodily pleasures are not merely causally reducible to this ostensibly sex-specific essence, but they become readily interpretable as manifestations or *signs* of this 'sex'" (Butler, 1990, pp. 94–95; also see Dimen, 1991; Butler, 1993; Fausto-Sterling, 1993). From this perspective, a single term, such as "sex," "woman," or "gay," embraces a multitude of topics, and therefore functions as a unifier of a number of potentially distinct discourses. This is commonly seen when cultural constructions of masculinity and femininity are internalized by patients and therapists, or incorporated into psychoanalytic and other theories as unexamined scientific facts. Freud (1914), for example, uses his era's concept of romantic love to support his concept of narcissism as intrinsically feminine:

> [The] comparison of the male and female sexes then shows that there are fundamental differences between them in respect of their type of object-choice. . . . Complete object-love of the attachment type is, properly speaking, characteristic of the male. . . . Women, especially if they grow up with good looks, develop a certain self-contentment which compensates them for the social restrictions that are imposed upon them in their choice of object. . . . Nor does their need lie in the direction of loving, but of being loved; and the man who fulfills this condition is the one who finds favor with them [pp. 88–89].

Breaking with Western cultural traditions and beliefs, modern sexology distinguishes a person's gender identity, or the sense that one is a man or a woman, from a person's sexual orientation, which refers to whether one is attracted to members of the same sex (homosexual), the opposite sex (heterosexual), or to both sexes (bisexual). These distinctions are derived from clinical experience and exposure to the varied subjectivities of transgendered and gay individuals (Stoller, 1968). However, because the general culture uses conventional heterosexuality and gender identities as its frame of reference, it conflates the differing categories of gender identity and sexual attraction. Examples of this cultural equation include the mundane belief that an attraction to men is a female trait or that gay men feel and act like girls. These are gender beliefs, as are beliefs about the kind of shoes men should wear or the kind of career a woman should choose. As the latter illustrate, gender beliefs are not confined to the realm of sexual attractions, for they concern themselves with almost every aspect of day-to-day life.

Although everyday gender beliefs are problematic for gay men, they are, of course, not alone in having to contend with them. Consider the following man in his late 20's who began treatment because of severe anxiety and psychosomatic symptoms after ending his heterosexual relationship of many years. His adult relationships, sexual experiences and masturbatory fantasies were exclusively heterosexual. However, he occasionally noticed the physical appearance of other men without any conscious sexual attraction, almost as if to say "Hey, he's a good-looking guy." Raised by parents whose intellectual and political philosophy included a doctrinaire belief in social and political equality of the sexes, as a child he was discouraged from male gender-stereotypical behavior, such as playing with toy guns. After beginning treatment, however, he became increasingly active in conventionally masculine pursuits that included hunting and contact sports. Coinciding with his increased interest in these activities was an increased focus in his therapy on what came to be called his internal coding system. As his treatment proceeded, he remembered that since early childhood, all activities, feelings, objects, and attitudes were classified as "M," "F," or "G," meaning male, female, or gay. Further along in his treatment, he offered a revised account of this system, saying that "gay," which meant something not stereotypically or conventionally male or female, was a later development: His original coding system contained M, F, not-M and not-F, and the latter two were fused into the category of "gay" as he grew older and discovered a word that offered potential explanations of these categories (see Whalen, Geary, and Johnson, 1990).

The following material came up a week after he reported a dream in which he was kissing a woman. He had the feeling, when he woke up, that he was in a therapy relationship with her. This made him wonder if there was some connection between the woman in the dream and his male therapist and he worried about the potential homoerotic meaning of the dream. The therapist had asked, in the previous session if, perhaps, being in therapy and getting help from a man stirred anxiety in him because the patient didn't know how to define himself in that kind of relationship.

C: The last thing you said, that I cannot expect nurturing or comfort from a man. It's strange being around men. Playing tackle football, it's one of the most macho sports. It is just strange hanging out with a lot of guys and doing something which is very aggressive. That is part of an ongoing experiment in what it means to be a man, or to be a male. Back to what we were saying last time, I think that is true. For my father, there wasn't this selfless nurturing about him. He was nurturing in terms of what he wanted me to do. He would cater to certain whims of mine and dissuade me from others. I have no memory of being encouraged to do sports, although as a kid I did get a little football uniform. I don't remember playing sports with my father. He bought me my first electric guitar when I was seven. When I wanted to be an architect, he got me drawing pens and triangles for Christmas. It was all genteel sports. I wanted to do karate and he wouldn't let me. But Tai Chi was OK. It was a nonviolent, passive, and defensive sport. What you said last session, something made me feel, "Like wow," and then we were out of time.

Th: What comes to mind?

C: The first thing that comes to mind was there was some element that was confusing about notions of sexuality in that statement. I have ascribed certain values that are for women only and I think nurturing is one of them. When we talk about the M, F and G thing, statements like that are confusing. They don't fit. It is a confusing pattern, is it M or F or G? It's not that simplistic. For a man to be nurturing does it make him a woman? Is it a gay relationship to be nurtured by a man?

Th: So my comment confused you?

C: It's almost like a fear of suddenly realizing that I was gay. I don't know why I have that. Comments like that make me wonder. I search for it in many ways. It can't be M because it has F attributes, so it must be G, that notion of being nurtured. Not having other relationships to compare it to. It's not like I can say I've had a nurturing relationship with a woman. I don't think I had that with anybody. This relationship is part of the confusion.

Th: You feel nurtured here?

C: Definitely.

Th: That creates difficulties in defining this relationship.

C: It doesn't fit into my model. I only had one successful relationship in the past four years and it seems to be ours. That is what creates the confusion about the M-F-G issue here.

Th: What about your feeling last week?

C: It made me nervous. It made me think, "Does this mean that I am gay?" This is a nurturing relationship and you are a man. That part is true. That I ascribed this sexual idea to the nurturing, that threw me off. That made me uncomfortable. Does this mean I'm gay?

Th: Many men define their maleness as not being able to accept nurturance from another man.

C: I have that belief. I do have this perception that in a relationship, the real nurturing comes from a woman. There is something feminine about it. That is the feminine side of my male friends who do that. That feeling that I've never been in a nurturing relationship.

Th: How does it make you feel?

C: Sad.

To repeat, gender beliefs are not just about sexual feelings. And it is rare, of course, to find any patient in treatment who doesn't have a personal theory about the meaning of his feelings, sexual or otherwise. Patients use their meaning-making systems to construct not only a sexual identity, but an entire identity. The heterosexual man above struggled with the gendered meanings of his desire for nurturance, and inevitably wondered whether that feeling defined him as masculine or feminine. These kinds of gender beliefs will similarly have a powerful impact upon the psychological development of gay men, although it should be noted that adult sexual attractions are not part of the early acquisition of a gender identity. But children who are spontaneously attracted to the other sex at an early age, and who grow up to be heterosexuals, feel no dissonance with the gender-coded language, at least in this sphere. However, in gay men who report an awareness of interest in boys or men at an early age, these feelings may conflict with their developing sense of gender. And that conflict, and the gender confusion it can foster, may be revisited when their feelings are eventually incorporated into their adult, gay identities.

Because of the linkage of gendered behaviors and sexuality, one often finds that gay men in therapy are frequently concerned that if they were to show feelings ostensibly having nothing to do with sexuality, they would be revealed as being different from other men. Their gender beliefs lead them to associate their same-sex attractions to a wide range of affects. And because they learn at an early age to hide their homoerotic feelings, they also learn to hide many other feelings as well. This was seen in a session with one gay man who was mourning the death of a friend from HIV, but was reluctant to show or talk about his feelings:

B: I'm sure others see how I'm feeling, but I don't like to think that they can.

Th: Why not?

B: I'd rather be different. I'd rather create a different persona. Not suffering. Not visibly suffering. Not visibly affected.

Th: Why do you need to create that persona?

B: I don't know. Why would it be bad to feel vulnerable? It feels weak to me. I don't like the idea of projecting weakness. I don't know why.

Th: What comes to mind?

B: It's feminine. It's not strong. It's weak.

Th: Feminine?

B: I'm very insecure about appearing feminine. The idea makes my skin crawl. I was thinking about that on the way over here. The whole process of what we are doing. Whether I want to change myself, get comfortable or somewhere in between. Do I want to get comfortable with the softer side of myself? I don't know the answer. I wish the softer side would go away.

Th: That softer side is something about yourself that you don't like?

B: Yeah, like being in the fifth grade and being called a pansy. It's weak and feminine and it singles you out. There's one thing about being gay, another thing about being flawed. There is an idea, not having to be lonely, indecisive or bitchy. I would think of them as feminine things or things that are not assets. When I called up my boyfriend, I wanted to be angry, but I didn't want to be bitchy. I don't know how I came across. I wanted to be mad, but I didn't want to appear to be wounded. I'm sure I came across as being wounded, but I didn't want that. Maybe I should tell myself that I should get comfortable with the idea of being wounded. It's not easy for me to say that. I have a real prejudice against that.

Th: Boys don't show their wounds.

B: Right. Except to lick them.

Th: Boys feel they have to tolerate pain and not show their feelings.

B: I wonder at what stage you have to stop doing that?

This man feared that showing anything that might be construed as "soft" feelings would reveal his despised homoerotic ones. Being a vulnerable boy could be translated to mean "I am gay." His gender beliefs were that vulnerability in relationships is a feminine trait, and so was his attraction to men. It is this common, cultural definition of homosexuality that can lead a gay man himself to question his gender identity, to question whether he is male or female. Gender beliefs therefore raise the question of how one learns the cultural and psychological meanings of gender.

Gender Acquisition

People may be born with an anatomical gender, but their psychological gender is a later, cognitive and affective acquisition. How that actually occurs is not known, although there is empirical data showing that it is a long process, as well as a complex one. Gender researchers believe that children can assign themselves to a gender by about 2¹/₂ years of age (Kohlberg, 1966; Fagot and Leinbach, 1985; Coates, 1992). Children make this distinction not simply out of awareness of anatomical differences between the sexes, but on the basis of superficial appearances such as clothing styles or long hair. This gender awareness is not a unitary category. For example, the work of Kohlberg (1966) distinguishes between an individual's gender stability and gender constancy. Gender stability "refers to an understanding that one's gender at birth will remain the same throughout life, that boys start out as boys and grow up to be men." Gender constancy is "a technical term that followers of Piaget use to refer to the child's understanding that external changes in appearance or activity do not change one's gender identity. For example, a boy must learn that even if he changes his physical appearance by putting on a dress or growing long hair, he will still be a boy" (Coates, 1992, p. 253). Another concept is gender role, "the overt behavior one displays in society, the role which he plays, especially with other people to establish his position with them insofar as his and their evaluation of his gender is concerned" (Stoller, 1968, p. 10).

In addition, there is a concept known as core gender identity (CGI), defined by Stoller (1985) as "a conviction that the assignment of one's sex was anatomically, and ultimately psychologically correct" (p. 11). For some gay men, CGI is a liberating idea, dispelling their own internalized cultural myths about the meaning of homosexuality. Gay men need not necessarily think or believe they are women or girls. Their sexual attractions can be independent of their sense of themselves as men and women. However, as useful as the concept of CGI may be to some clinicians and patients, it has also, it seems, become part of a psychoanalytic tradition that concretizes mental processes and functions, defining them as structures (Freud, 1926a). Some even elevate Stoller's "conviction" to the status of a metapsychological concept, calling it "a remarkably sturdy psychological construct, . . . a permanent label indicating that the self is male or female, . . . analogous to a cellular structure that has differentiated from a multipotential precursor" (Friedman, 1988, p. 231).

Nevertheless, the sturdiness of this construct is based upon some questionable biological and metapsychological beliefs. Consider Freud, who also resorted to a language of mental structures to describe mental processes, but when pressed about what he meant by structure, had nothing more to say than this: "I must beg you not to ask what material it is constructed of. That is not a subject of psychological interest. Psychology can be as indifferent to it as, for instance, optics can be to the question of whether the walls of a telescope are made of metal or cardboard" (Freud, 1926b, p. 194). Later ego-psychologists (Hartmann, 1958) likewise avoided troubling questions regarding "what" material by stressing the functions of the ego, all the while presuming that the structure is grounded in some hypothetical biological or autonomous substrate. To repeat, the elevation of function into concrete form has clinical uses. Yet this paradigm moves beyond its clinical utility when the functions of a structure are suddenly taken to mean that there exists a structure within the biological substrate. Such conceptual leaps ultimately explain nothing about the processes leading to the acquisition of beliefs about gender and one's own gender identity.

Stoller (1985), for example, relates the case of Jack, née Mary, assigned to be a girl at birth but found at age fourteen to have an intersexed or hermaphroditic condition and to be a genetic male. Mary/Jack was described as an unfeminine girl throughout her childhood. Her/his behavioral history, combined with the fact that Stoller found her/him "grotesque as a girl," and his impression of the "naturalness of her 'masculinity,'" led him to tell the 14-year-old girl

> to become a boy. "She" did. From that day on, I was with a boy. He
> had immediately known how to be one, not just how to buy the

appropriate clothes or get a haircut. Far more, he fit these accouter-
ments. To the present, he has been unremarkably, unaffectedly masculine [p. 67].

Proponents of CGI, in arguing that it is grounded in some biological
substrate, tend to focus on its presumed immutability. Stoller, for example, offers this case as a rare but provocative illustration of the way a biological CGI can overcome environmental influences. However, his data
is open to multiple interpretations, and it might reasonably be argued
that his case illuminates something else altogether. For it is no secret that
in learning the socially sanctioned attributes of their own gender, children must concurrently learn about the other gender, linguistically and
culturally defined as its opposite. This designation of genders as "opposites" obliges every child, regardless of anatomical sex, to learn something about the qualities attributed to both boys and girls (de Marneffe,
1997). Regardless of one's own gender, one knows something about the
culturally-determined behaviors of both genders. Thus, in all the years
that Mary/Jack was learning to be a girl, she also had to learn something about boys. Jack knew how to behave like a boy because Mary was
taught how *not* to be a boy at the same time she was being taught how to
be like a girl.

Money (1986) theorizes that "Identifications and complementation
each have their representation or schema implanted in the brain. One
is the schema of one's own gender status. The other is the schema of
the other gender status to which one must complement one's own"
(pp. 118–119). But we do not know where gender identities are coded in
the brain. Or if they are, whether they are coded as specific structures in
specific sites. However, even if there is a biological coding of gender
identity, behaviors for both genders still seem to be psychologically coded
together and reinforced by the external environment. Unlike Mary/Jack,
who was physically unremarkable as a girl until puberty, Money and
Ehrhardt (1996) note that in intersexed children born with ambiguous
genitalia, the attitudes of the parents have a strong effect on whether the
child accepts the gender category to which it has been surgically
assigned. "In those instances [where the child does not accept the category to which it has been assigned,] . . . it is common to find a history in
which uncertainty as to the sex of the baby at birth was transmitted to
the parents and never adequately resolved [within the parents' mind]"
(p. 153). In other words, at least with intersexed children, comfort with
their own gender appears to be based upon the parents' comfort and
acceptance of the child's gender. And to bring the subject of gender
acquisition back to the children who become gay men, when their child-

hood same-sex attractions do not conform to gender expectations, they too may come to feel uncomfortable with, or in some cases even to question, their own gender identities.

The Dimensions of Gender Stress and Gender Confusion

Those who do not conform to cultural gender beliefs raise many confusing and unanswered questions about how one develops a gendered and sexual identity. Stoller (1985), for example, revisits Mary/Jack who is no longer a 14-year-old girl, but a heterosexual, married adult man. About his memories as a young girl, Jack tells Stoller:

> I honestly don't remember. I can't honestly think that I thought of myself as becoming a mother or a grown woman. Toward the last, when I was in junior high school and had to wear dresses, there was a blond, good-looking boy, and I thought, "Gee, nobody like that would ever look at me." Those were the years when I was really starting to get mixed up; I didn't know what the hell I was supposed to do. On the one hand, I would think maybe I should try to make myself prettier. I bought lipstick. It never did anything for me, of course [p. 73].

At the time of that thought, Mary/Jack was a genetic male who had been raised to believe she/he was a girl. But how should one understand that 12-year-old person thinking about other boys looking at her/him? If Mary/Jack thought she was a girl, albeit an unattractive one, it is understandable that she might have been concerned about whether good-looking boys would look at her. But if she/he was "really" a boy, what exactly would such a concern mean? If she/he was attracted to boys, Stoller doesn't say. Before she/he was given permission to be a boy, was she attracted to girls? Did she ever think she was a lesbian? Again, Stoller doesn't say. And how does one understand the meaning of adult heterosexuality in a man raised as a girl until the age of 12? While Mary/Jack appeared to have finally opted for conventional heterosexuality, we are left to make sense of the confusing way she/he arrived there.

Gay men, like intersexed individuals, also challenge cultural beliefs about human sexuality. Although the origins of same-sex attractions are unknown, gender beliefs define these feelings as resulting from confusion about the differences between men and women. Even early psychoanalytic theories incorporated these gender beliefs. Freud defined male homosexuality as a feminine trait (1905, 1914c), possibly resulting from too much childhood exposure to women (1910a). Reflecting cultural biases, later psychoanalytically-informed theorists attributed homosexuality to gender confusion (Socarides, 1968; McDougall, 1980; Moberly, 1983a,b; Nicolosi, 1991). Certainly, there are gay men who grow up going through a period of gender confusion. But if and when one sees gender confusion in gay patients, it does not necessarily represent the cause of their homosexuality, whatever that may be. Rather, any residual confusion they may have usually stems from cultural beliefs about the meaning of homosexuality and gender they have learned. In other words, in some children who grow up to be gay, their gender beliefs about the meanings of homoerotic feelings cause them to question their own identities.

When Stoller gave Mary/Jack permission to be a boy, the unhappy girl apparently accepted his authority and did so. Clinical work with gay men also shows that a person's sense of being a man or a woman can involve processes that are entirely dependent upon attitudes from the external environment, although over more extended periods of time. Children must learn a psychological construct of gender that is based not solely on anatomy, but on myriad cultural and familial clues (Fast, 1984; de Marneffe, 1997; Coates, 1997). For example, the meanings of aggressivity in girls, or a lack of athletic interests in boys, can be internalized along a family or cultural model that codes these attributes as gender-specific.[1] Butler (1990) defines "gender itself [as] a kind of becoming or activity, and that gender ought not to be conceived as a noun or a substantial thing or a static cultural marker, but rather as an incessant and repeated action of some sort" (p. 112). So, rather than thinking of it as a rigid structure of the mind, a gender identity could be thought of as the accretion of experiences or interactions with the external and internalized gender-coding environment. That is to say that one's gender is an activity occurring in a relational matrix, rather than it being a biological or intrapsychic structure.

Seen from this perspective, boys who grow up to be gay are often *gender stressed*. This is a process that can occur over a protracted period of time, as early homoerotic feelings become linked to other gender-nonconforming interests, and as these boys come to realize that they are failing to meet the cultural and social expectations of their assigned gender. This is commonly seen in gay men who were sissies, denigrated for

---

1. Therapists commonly reframe their patients' perceptions that a particular feeling they have is gender-inappropriate when they tolerate or affirm a man's wish to cry or a woman's desire to assert herself.

their putative effeminacy (Crisp, 1968; Green, 1987). However, even gay men who were not gender nonconforming as children recall gender stresses in their attempts to integrate their same-sex feelings into a masculine identity. And gender stress can lead to gender confusion. Clinically, gender confusion can be expressed as "If I am attracted to boys, I must be like a girl." But it might also include responses like "I am depraved," "I will be alone" or "I have sinned." Such are the gender beliefs about transgressing gender boundaries. Gay men can scrutinize their own behaviors and emotional responses in attempts to understand how they conform to or deviate from heterosexual, gender expectations. For example, one gay man recalled, at age 15, a self-conscious awareness that he had what he called a "limp wrist." He anxiously believed that this behavior marked him as a carrier of both effeminacy and homosexuality. And he was ultimately successful in ridding himself of the gesture. But he notes, with some irony, that his brother, a heterosexual, married man with children, still walks around with a limp wrist, apparently untroubled by what the patient had perceived to be its stressful, stigmatized meanings.[2]

The Dimensions of Culture and Subculture

As gender beliefs illustrate, all definitions of gay are linked intimately to the cultures in which they are defined. Gay culture in the United States is not the same as in Holland (van Naerssen, 1987) or Italy (Pezzona, 1976), and the gay cultures in those latter two countries differ from each other. Similarly, within a broader gay culture there may exist different gay subcultures, each defined by a variety of shared experiences and interests. John Boswell (1980; 1994) and George Chauncey (1994) have documented the existence of historical homosexual cultures. However, contemporary gay cultures do not necessarily resemble those of the past:

> By the 1910's and 1920's, men who identified themselves as different from other men primarily on the basis of their homosexual interest rather than their woman-like gender status usually called themselves "queer." "Queer wasn't derogatory," one man active in New York's gay world in the 1920's recalled. "It wasn't like kike or nigger. . . . It just meant you were different." . . . Many queers considered *faggot* and *fairy* to be more derogatory terms, but they usually used them only to

---

2. Even boys who do not grow up to be gay may have similar fears about showing feelings or behaviors defined as feminine. However, their fear is that they might be mistaken for a sissy, i.e., a boy who can't compete, a mama's boy, etc.

refer to men who openly carried themselves in an unmanly way. It was the effeminacy and flagrancy, not the homosexuality, of the "fairies," "faggots," or "queens" that earned them the disapprobation of queers [Chauncey, 1994, p. 101].

How these men viewed themselves, and how the larger culture in which they resided viewed them, was deeply embedded within the social and historical context of their times. In fact, defining them as gay is an imposition of a modern identity upon those living in the past. The term "gay" only acquired cultural prominence in the years following the 1969 Stonewall riots (Duberman, 1994), and it is questionable that modern gay identities are entirely analogous to those of the same-sex cultures of earlier eras (Lauritsen and Thorstad, 1974). Illustrating these differences, for example, is the fact that in the era following World War II, homophile groups fought for the civil rights of homosexual men and women but many of them publicly accepted the belief of that era that homosexuality was a mental illness (Bayer, 1981). As opposed to the gay political organizations that emerged after Stonewall, these earlier political groups believed civil liberties should be granted to homosexuals *because* they suffered from a mental illness rather than a moral failing. A modern gay identity, on the other hand, may be more commonly based upon a belief that homosexuality is a normal variant of human sexuality, rather than a pathological one.

Chauncey (1994) highlights how the contemporary scientific classification of same-sex attraction and sexual behavior into homosexual, heterosexual and bisexual was not the cultural norm in earlier times. A man could be *normal* if he had sex with another man as long as he adopted the masculine, that is insertive, role, and if his outward appearance and behavior did not betray him as a *fairy*. That cultural belief is at odds with scientific models that catalogue sexual attraction and behavior into two broad camps of homosexuality and heterosexuality. Furthermore, even Kinsey's (et al., 1948) classification of sexual behavior along a continuum of exclusive heterosexuality (Kinsey 0) to exclusive homosexuality (Kinsey 6) imposed a scientific label or description of sexual phenomena that does not always coincide with an individual's subjective experience. Men who perform homosexually under conditions of incarceration and behave heterosexually in the outside would certainly take umbrage at the suggestion that they are homosexual or gay. Outside the penal system, in the world of male prostitution or "hustling," for example, the subjective definitions of gay and straight are often startlingly at odds with those of sex researchers and psychoanalysts. Green (1987) interviews a young man who sells sexual favors to an older man:

R.G.: If somebody were to say to you, "are you straight, are you bisexual, are you gay?" What would your answer be?

Frank: Straight. I wouldn't want anyone to find out ever. I don't think I could handle that.

R.G.: How about in your own mind?

Frank: I think I'm pretty straight. You can't really think you are straight when you are doing those kinds of things, you know. I think in my own head that I'm still straight, just for my own ego.

R.G.: Does seeing this guy interfere with your girlfriend in any way?

Frank: I got her completely convinced that I am his security guard. She has no idea, no suspicion. She knows he's gay and all that stuff. She has no suspicion about me. That's just the way I carry myself. Not like my [gay] brother—he's a dead give-away [p. 348].

Further clouding attempts at categorizing individual subjectivity, many men perform heterosexually within conventional marriages, while retaining primarily homosexual fantasies and they do not consider themselves to be gay (Buxton, 1994). And the anthropological work of Gilbert Herdt (1994) among the Sambia of Papua, New Guinea, demonstrates how culture-bound are Western words like "gay," "homosexual," and "heterosexual" and how they lack equivalent meanings in another cultural context:

Sambia heterosexual manhood emerges only after years of normatively prescribed and prolonged homosexual activities. . . . Seven-to-ten year old Sambia boys are taken from their mothers when first initiated into the male cult, and thereafter experience the most powerful and seductive homosexual fellatio activities. For some ten to fifteen years, they engage in these practices on a daily basis, first as fellator, and then as fellated. Elders teach that semen is absolutely vital: it should be consumed daily since the creation of biological maleness and the maintenance of masculinity depend on it. Hence, from middle childhood until puberty, boys should perform fellatio on other youths. Near puberty the same initiates become dominant youths. Ritual helps remake their social and erotic identity, the bachelors becoming the fellated partners for a new crop of ritual novices. And at the same time, youths and boys alike must absolutely avoid women, on pain of punishment. . . . This dual pattern—prescribed homosexual activities and avoidance of women—persists until marriage [pp. 2–3].

The Sambia make no distinctions between a "homosexual person" and a heterosexual one in the way these categories are understood in

Western society (Stoller and Herdt, 1985), underscoring the cultural constructions of these concepts. A Sambian's ritualized homosexual experiences are culturally normal and they are required steps for the development of a masculine identity. One simply cannot become a normal Sambian man unless one has ingested enough sperm.

In Western culture, children grow up exposed to cultural expectations that define all aspects of human identity and experience within a male/female continuum . A developing child is observed, evaluated, and judged within the culture's gender expectations. While there may be a biological dimension to the preferred activities of boys as opposed to those which girls choose (Fagot, 1974), the conflation of statistical norms with expectations of uniform gender-appropriate behavior (Fausto-Sterling, 1992) puts a strain on those children who do not spontaneously conform. Boys are more likely than girls to be stigmatized when they cross the gender line, particularly by other boys (Fagot, 1977).

Labeling a boy as feminine is not an objective description of a child's behavior. It must always be placed in a social context that includes the way in which his environment reacts to his behavior. In an example of this relational phenomenon cited earlier, a patient recalled the horrified reaction of his mother to his spontaneous play in high heels. A more complex example, grounded in linguistic usage, is Green's (1987) attempt to measure masculinity and femininity with an "Adjective Check List":

> This list consists of three hundred adjectives commonly used to describe a person's attributes. The individual taking the test indicates which adjectives from the list are accurate self-descriptions.
>
> The thirty-one men in our study who had been "feminine" boys, compared to the twenty-five who had been "masculine," scored higher on the scale of succorance, or being more apt to solicit sympathy, affection, or emotional support from others. Adjectives which contribute to a [feminine] score are *appreciative, demanding, emotional, immature, self-centered, self-pitying, submissive,* and *whiny*. Those that yield a [masculine] score include *aloof, confident, dominant, independent, indifferent, individualistic, mature, self-confident,* and *strong*.
>
> The men who had been "feminine" boys scored higher on abasement, or the tendency to express feelings of inferiority through self-criticism, quiet, or social impotence. Adjectives contributing to a [feminine] score include *anxious, cowardly, despondent, gloomy, retiring, self-punishing, spineless,* and *timid*. Those that [masculinize] the score include *aggressive, arrogant, boastful, egotistical, hard-headed, independent,* and *self-confident*.
>
> The men who had been "feminine" boys also scored higher on deference. Adjectives which contribute to a [feminine] score include *appre-*

ciative, cautious, cooperative, gentle, obliging, and *peaceable.* Those that
[masculinize] the score include *opinionated, tactless, aggressive, boastful,*
and *headstrong.*

The men who had been "feminine" boys tended to score lower on
dominance. Adjectives which contribute to a [feminine] score include
dependent, easygoing, fearful, lazy, mild, and *shy.* Those that [masculinize]
the score include *aggressive, ambitious, confident, determined, forceful* and
outgoing [p. 252].

Green's test categorizes broad ranges of human experience as either
masculine or feminine. However his work could be seen as an example
of the way in which genders are linguistically coded. The study actually
illustrates that so-called feminine men present with many more undesirable self-descriptions than do ostensibly masculine men. Green concludes that "our new data reveal that most of the psychological test
differences shown by our groups of homosexual or bisexual and heterosexual men are consistent with the effects of having experienced a stigmatized life style" (p. 258). Nevertheless, within the text itself he treats
these adjectives as inherent to femininity, rather than a social construction of gender:

> Subsequent to the development of the original Adjective Check List,
> separate "masculine" and "feminine" scales were derived. Of the three
> hundred adjectives, twenty-eight "masculine" items, and twenty-six
> "feminine" items were extracted, based on score differences between
> samples of "masculine" males and "feminine" females. Some "mascu-
> line" adjectives are *aggressive, autocratic, dominant, inventive, self-confident,*
> and *shrewd.* Some "feminine" adjectives are *considerate, dependent,*
> *excitable, frivolous, sensitive, timid,* and *worrying.*
>
> The twenty-two previously "feminine" boys who are now homo-
> sexual or bisexual differed slightly from the nine who are now hetero-
> sexual. There was a tendency for more "feminine" adjectives to be
> checked by the bisexual or homosexual men.
>
> Thus the Adjective Check List provides evidence of developmental
> continuity between cross-gender behavior in boyhood and sex-typed
> self-descriptions in manhood. It also suggests more "psychological
> femininity" for the homosexual men [Green, 1987, p. 253].

The men defined as feminine report self-denigrating adjectives indicating low self-esteem. These adjectives are then labeled as feminine,
almost as if they were intrinsic to femininity, when it is equally plausible
that this self-labeling is the psychological and social consequence of
being perceived as feminine. How one sees oneself is intimately related

to how one is seen by others. Rather than markers of femininity, these adjectives are markers of denigration. From this perspective, one might restate Green's conclusions this way: Thus the Adjective Check List provides evidence of developmental continuity between denigrated cross-gender behavior in boyhood and self-denigrating self-descriptions in manhood. It also suggests more self-denigration for the homosexual men.

Early, childhood curiosity about gender roles is frequently reported among many gay men who, because of their atypical desires, may question both themselves and others regarding gender categories. This curiosity may persist into adulthood, as reported by a gay male medical intern, perplexed by his hospital's requirement that a female nurse be present during his physical examination of women patients. Female physicians were not required to have a nurse present when examining male patients. As a gay man, he found it difficult to find a rationale for the nurse's presence other than blind obedience to hospital regulations. Exploring the issue further, he learned that as well as protecting female patients from unwanted sexual advances by male physicians, this arrangement protected male physicians from false accusations of sexual misconduct. The cultural beliefs underlying the hospital's policy assumed that doctors are heterosexuals, that men are more likely to take sexual advantage of their patients than women, and that women are prone to making false accusations against men. The policy did not recognize the possibility of same-sex attractions in a professional setting, aggressive female sexuality or the possibility of men being aggrieved by unwanted sexual advances from women. The gay physician ultimately arranged for a nurse's presence during examinations of male patients. This is a single incident, of course, but it is a useful example of the kind of engagement a gay man is likely to have had with cultural expectations. In growing up gay, an accretion of these kinds of interactions with the culture forces an ongoing reevaluation of cultural norms.

Similar difficulties in conforming to cultural expectations of gender roles may foster a naive, anthropological approach toward unquestioned cultural beliefs in some gay men. One example of this honed awareness is found in the satire of gay transvestite performers, who poke fun at both female and male gender roles when they cross-dress (Browning, 1994). The following patient notes that what is gay in one culture is not defined the same way in another and how certain "gay" behaviors are tolerated under restricted social circumstances in his own culture:

> **E:** Last session, I raised the subject of how men show their love for other men. I thought about that during the past week. Let me ask you a ques-

tion. Do you think men show their love for men different than men show it for women?

Th: It is awkward for a man to show love for another man.

E: A lot of that is cultural, in terms of Americans. I find Latin cultures attractive. As compared to American men, Latin men seem more relaxed in showing their affection for each other. Men kiss each other, throw their arms around each other, no one thinks twice about it being a problem.

Th: Different cultures are not better or worse.

E: I am making judgments about better or worse.

Th: Your sensibilities are not in synch with the culture in which you were raised.

E: It has to do with repression. My brother-in-law, for example. I'll kiss my mother and father and my sister. He'll look at me and say "Don't do that to me." It's not something that most men, at least in my hometown, are comfortable with. Even my father, as I watch him reach out, it's clear that it's awkward. Even myself, although it's gotten better over time. The first time that I started with my friends, kissing them on the street or hugging them, it was not something that was totally natural or comfortable. We do have this sort of bias in the culture. You're right, saying one culture is inferior to the other isn't necessarily appropriate. It's a judgment. Men don't know how to emotionally communicate or to pick up on signals from other people as well. That's a real problem. For me, it's a particular problem, not necessarily having to do with my sexual orientation, although some of what I feel may have something to do with that. What you were saying before, feeling out of synch with the culture. I would not feel totally comfortable with expressing affection for another man because of the way I would communicate it. I would like to openly show my affection for another man. The way I felt comfortable communicating it is one that was not accepted by the people around me. From early on, I learned it was not an appropriate way to deal with other men. As much as I was attracted to that way of expressing affection for another man, it would make me feel insecure about it. I also have a tendency to look down at that other way of men communicating.

Th: That other way of communicating?

E: The nonemotional, less tactile, less physical. How somebody like my father might communicate his affection for his sons or another man. It might be how men in our culture do that. It may be something like bonding ceremonies, everybody going out drinking or to a baseball game. As opposed to a more direct way like hugging or kissing. It's funny, I'm probably more aware of it as a gay man. I noticed at my sister's wedding, afterwards everyone went out partying. Once men have a few drinks, they do throw their arms around each other. Even men who say that men shouldn't be physical with other men.

Th: It does raise questions about nature and nurture.

E: What is inherent? I can think of some of those wedding bashes where some guy who is very attractive throws their arms around you and hugs you. As a gay man I find it attractive. Nobody says the next day, "Oh gee, I'm sorry I threw my arms around you. I was drunk." When you are in that situation you are fine.

As the above patient experienced it, the culture of his origin could not accommodate his overt wish to express affection for other men, and this had an impact on the development of his sexual identity. Heterosexual men, however, are offered opportunities to integrate their overt but unspoken sexual identities into everyday life. Because being a heterosexual is synonymous with being normal, its symbols, such as wedding rings, its rituals, such as wedding ceremonies, and its social behaviors, such as bringing one's wife to a professional event, are not necessarily construed as sexual. Gay men, because they constitute a sexual subculture, in fact many subcultures, make different adaptations to the heterosexual majority in defining their identity. As Russo (1987) commented, "People say that there can be no such thing as a 'gay sensibility' because the existence of one would mean that there is a straight sensibility, and clearly there is not. But a gay sensibility can be many things; . . . Gay sensibility is largely a product of oppression, of the necessity to hide so well for so long" (p. 92).

Because a gay identity is neither normal nor taken for granted, it is often jarring to many heterosexuals when they encounter one. In the coming out process, an individual may tell an intimate acquaintance or family member that he is gay. For many, this is the beginning of a process of psychological clarification and liberation. Many heterosexuals, hearing these revelations, experience the gay person as breaking a social taboo: he or she is talking about his sexuality in polite company. These interpersonal encounters exemplify a culture clash. The gay person is saying "My feelings are different from yours. I want you to understand who I am even though my feelings are different from yours." The heterosexual listener may be startled by the admission because they feel someone is talking about their sex life. There was some aspect of this cultural misunderstanding in the recent national debate over gays in the military: Lesbian and gay soldiers who wish to come out want to integrate their personal and professional lives. Their heterosexual compatriots don't want to know or talk about it because the subject makes them uncomfortable; some of them responded as if they thought gay people were asking for the right to have sex in public.

In major metropolitan centers, and perhaps in some smaller towns, gay is increasingly defined as a social identity. Gay civic organizations, churches and synagogues, charities, political organizations, etc., allow gay people to integrate their feeling of "otherness" within a larger community. These social structures often provide gay men and women with the opportunity to integrate their professional and sexual identities in the way that heterosexuals do. Unlike heterosexual social structures that have existed for many generations, comparable gay structures have only recently come into existence. The gay bar was the progenitor of these structures since it was historically the only place where a more open gay identity was permitted to be defined (Chauncey, 1994; Duberman, 1994).[3]

The quest for an accepting social structure is exemplified by the experience of one gay man who came out in middle age. After abandoning his closeted, pseudo-heterosexual identity, he is struggling to find a gay social identity. He hopes to find a gay group that will define him, and tries them on like new clothing. He struggles with his attempts to separate his need for non-sexual social relationships with his sexual desires, worried that his gestures of friendship will be mistaken for greater intimacy and concerned that people offering friendship might be looking for sex:

> **F:** I call someone because I'm lonely and I want to go out to a movie or dinner. If I've never gone out with that person before, they may think it's a date and I may not want it to be. But I called two people last night and told them that I wanted to get together with them. One I met in my reading group and I'll meet him for dinner, but I don't want to date him and I don't know what message he's gotten. I called someone from the Gay Father's group who is easy to talk to. He's been friendly to me. He seems relaxed as a gay man and he is fun-loving. I told him last night that I'm having a hard time adjusting and I'd like to talk; to have dinner and talk about what the experience has been, coming out as a gay father. He is very receptive to that. I trust that relationship. I'm not as trusting of the people I met at Alanon. Another acquaintance of mine goes to Body Electric, where men take their clothes off and rub each other. I don't trust that. There is SCA (Sexual Compulsives Anonymous) and I'm not sure I trust that. The guy I called last night goes to SCA. Part of the reason to call him

---

3. There are also some subcultures, such as those of the theater and the entertainment industry, which are not exclusively gay but have been more tolerant of their gay members than the culture at large. However, Russo (1987) has documented some of the limitations of that tolerance.

is an attempt to get to know him, to explore that. It's like work; something I have to do, need to do or I will be lonely. I stayed around after church on Sunday. They were having a social. I was seriously thinking of leaving and I said I can't, I have to hang in here. Then finally someone I know came over and talked to me.

Th: You are searching for a group that will define what kind of gay person you are.

F: Yes, and in three years it is not getting any easier. I think I have improved. I'm sticking with the reading group, with the Gay Father's group. They'll be having a party at my apartment. I felt Alanon got me out of my apartment and being with people serves a purpose. In addition to that, I hear things that I can connect with. When I hear other men talking about isolating and withdrawing from people, I know I'm not the only one who does that. Then I see people hugging each other and making friends and it looks good. I don't do well once the structured part is over and that's what happened after church. The structured part is singing with the choir, the social event afterwards was scary. Finally somebody spoke to me. Then the scary part again. I just have to get out.

The Idiosyncratic Dimension

As the above patient illustrates, it is difficult to construct a gay identity in social isolation. Nevertheless, some individuals present with very personal meanings of gay that are not immediately comprehensible to the therapist. Although ongoing psychotherapeutic work can tease out some of the shared cultural beliefs underlying idiosyncratic definitions, such work may take a long time. The following man illustrates how an individual with a complex and unique problem tries to make sense of his difficulties by availing himself of the language at hand. The patient reported a history of adult homosexual and heterosexual experiences, but at the time of the initial consultation was not involved with another person. He struggled with compulsive exhibitionism: he would get drunk on alcohol, then go out in the middle of the night and repeatedly practice a fall that "inadvertently" caused his pants to drop, thereby exposing himself to a woman passerby. Despite extensive practicing of his fall, he rarely exposed himself for fear that he would be arrested. But sometimes, if sufficiently intoxicated, he would expose himself. He believed this behavior meant he was gay. This idiosyncratic definition was eventually decoded years later during his treatment. He described a compulsive need to look at women who passed him on the street. Exposing himself to women was a way of making himself feel stronger. The strength he felt as an exhibitionist served as a tonic for the "weakness" he felt was implicit in feeling compelled to look at women. It was this definition of weakness that led him to define himself as gay. To him, gay was synonymous with being a weak man. This is a recurring theme and a variation on the cultural stereotype of the sissy, but in this case the patient's definition of gay had nothing to do with same-sex attractions. In fact, his adult homosexual experiences were primarily motivated by efforts to explore the *idea* of being gay, as he understood it, and they were not emotionally or sexually satisfying to him.

Another idiosyncratic meaning of gay was offered by a heterosexual man who had broken off his relationship of many years with a woman, and then subsequently learned she was in a relationship with another woman. He came to a session after attending a wedding reception where several gay couples were present. As he looked at the gay couples celebrating, he thought to himself "Maybe being gay will make me happy." However, he was not emotionally or sexually attracted to men, and exploration of this idea led to his literally defining gay to mean "happy," in the hope that being gay might offer possibilities for happiness that heterosexuality had not yet provided him.

Another man applies the label of gay to his own personal qualities, despite the fact that he shares these traits with other non-gay family members:

> **G:** The fact that I'm gay and my mother knows I'm seeing an analyst has made her curious about it, asking me when did I know I was gay. We talked a little bit about my father and the fact that he had this strong need to be liked. It's always been that way. He thought people would like him as a result of doing things for them. I said to her, "Isn't that an awful situation to be in, to need the approval of other people so much?" This neediness seems to show up in our family. Not so much in the females, but in the men. My brother also wants to please others, to have the approval of others, as I do. There's some streak that is coming from my father down to his sons that seems to want sanctions from other people or approval. We talked a lot about my desire to avoid confrontation and to avoid conflict. It shows up with my father and my brother as well. My mother has said on a number of occasions that my brother would do anything rather than have a confrontation with his wife. My sister-in-law has a sense of what she wants to do, but she's not an abrasive person at all. He [the brother] wants to avoid the conflict. In my mind, its not unlike the situations we talked about where I have these anxieties about confrontation. Being gay may add to that hesitation, but it may actually be a theme that is there in the family and is picked up by my brother as well.

> **Th:** Gay people are not the only ones who avoid confrontations.

> **G:** (laughs) Right.

The Stereotypical Dimension

In the analysis of the idiosyncratic definitions of gay, one often finds that they are based on stereotypical depictions of homosexuality. Stereotypes are broad cultural definitions that caricature or oversimplify an individual's qualities. For example, a stereotypical way to define gay is to call it a "lifestyle," rather than an identity. This is a linguistic usage that defines being gay as volitional, a choice as changeable as one's hairstyle or moving from the city to the suburbs. However, this stereotype is far removed from the subjective experience of gay men's sexuality. Person (1980) refers to an individual's subjective desire as a *sex-print*, which she analogizes to a fingerprint that is unique, idiosyncratic, and not subject to conscious choice:

> From the subjective point of view the sex print is experienced as sexual "preference." Because it is revealed rather than chosen, sexual preference is felt as deep rooted and deriving from one's nature. To the degree that an individual utilizes sexuality and to the degree that sexuality is valued, one's sexual "nature" will be experienced as more or less central to personality. To the extent that an individual's sex print "deviates" from the culture's prescription for sexuality, it may be experienced as even more central to identity [p. 620].

Dismissing the subjective experience of depth while focusing on the surface appearances of what it means to be gay is common in the general culture, and sometimes in therapy as well:

H: My best friend goes to Fire Island every summer. I think, "What a bunch of silly people." Is this what I have to aspire to? It seems totally shallow to me. And yet I wonder what am I reacting to here?

Th: What is depth?

H: It's kind of a tough question. When I was younger I always found silly boys sort of distasteful. I wondered how people could engage in silly club hopping. It seemed mindless to me, even when I was that age and in my twenties. I was not that interested. It was too much of a mix of people. But what is depth? I don't know that I require depth, identifiable depth. It's like the Supreme Court's definition of pornography. I can't tell you what it is, but I know it when I see it. I suppose what I am responding to is the overriding concern over appearances that exists in that segment of gay society. I know it isn't pervasive. I know everyone is not in gyms lifting weights all the time. I find that boring, even distasteful. I really don't know what percentage of gay male society that represents. I pass people coming out of gyms, wearing scanty clothes in the dead of winter, showing off their arms or legs or chest. There are hundreds of people and I think "When is the last time you read a book?" Why do people feel compelled to do this? A peacock thing. Something I don't like. People don't do it in Europe, but here I see people my age doing that, spending their lives in gyms. I find that distasteful. Where did that come from? Why would gay men fall into that thing to the degree they have? It shows a kind of superficiality. Why are they doing this? To make themselves into attractive sexual partners? I'm embarrassed by it. In the same way that an effeminate male embarrasses me. I don't want people to think this is what I'm really like. I feel guilty for feeling uncomfortable.

The patient himself does not fit the stereotype that he decries, and is critical of those who do. He believes that those who resemble the culture's stereotypical portrayal of gay men are responsible for the negative attitudes toward homosexuality in the larger culture. This attitude is not uncommon among members of a subculture who have assimilated into the majority culture; they are often uncomfortable with those who openly display their differences from the mainstream. From the therapeutic perspective, it is important to understand how gay men who resort to stereotyping other gay men are sometimes expressing something unacceptable about their own gay identities.

A significant experience in the development of a gay identity is the intense feeling that one is all alone, one of a kind, unlike anyone else in the world. Thus gay men often report an important developmental milestone, the revelation that there are "others like me," which can signal the beginning of both acceptance of one's homoerotic feelings as well as questioning the cultural message that homosexuality consigns the homosexual to the extreme fringes of society. Some gay men first learn that others like themselves are sick, perverted, or degenerate and that accepting their homoerotic feelings means an identification with a denigrated other. For others, like the tormented ugly duckling who grew up to discover he was a swan, discovering gay men like themselves sometimes offers hope and the possibilities of living a fuller life. However, some cygnets raised as ducks may appropriate "duck values" and believe that ducks are the better birds. The idea of having to live life as a gay man fills these individuals with great despair, because it runs counter to the pejorative definitions of homosexuality they have internalized. They may define gay to mean living without morality or hope.

The Decadent / Aesthetic Dimension

Paradoxically, stereotypes of gay men actually contradict each other: one is the image of the depraved homosexual, while the other is the homosexual aesthete. The following material, from a session of a professionally successful gay man, emerged after a dream in which associations led to the question of whether he was a deep, "spiritual" person or a "superficial" one.

The patient has a history of drug use and periodically struggles with his urges to get high. The combination of therapy and antidepressant medication led to a marked decrease in anxiety and in his desire to use drugs, although he recently experienced an increase in these urges. Those urgent feelings and his recent joining of a gay men's study group provide the subject material for questions about the meaning of his gay identity:

> **J:** Maybe I'm not intellectual, maybe I'm not part of the intelligentsia. But in the book club, without being arrogant, I think I am a very refreshing addition. I can feel the energy that the people feel for me. I know a lot of things and it comes as a surprise to people. We read *Maurice* by E. M. Forster. I've read a lot about him and it surprised me that no one knew anything about Forster. With all that I know, that suggests I should be able to integrate it in a more meaningful way than people who don't know.

> **Th:** You appear to be asking yourself if you are an intellectual because you participate in the study group. Earlier, you expressed concern that you could be perceived as superficial because you want to use drugs. There is a question of which desire represents your deeper side and which the superficial one. Perhaps you fear the intellectual side is superficial and the wish to get high feels deeper to you?

> **J:** (Silent) As you were speaking I felt that I'm always asking questions about who am I. I like the way you tied it in once with the idea of feeling like two different people. A thesis of the *Gay New York* book is that gay culture became refined to set itself apart, a way to be gay and not be chastised. Maybe a little bit, not consciously, a little bit of wanting to know things is to protect myself. It makes up for the defect of being gay. It's the compensating element. It helps me to some degree to think of this as a definitional struggle. Who am I really? Is the pleasure-seeking person the deeper part, the fundamental part, or am I the person who would like to know about things? I generally keep notes on our sessions and I like to go through the files. I keep a file of dreams. You say, "Find out who you are." Who I am is contained in those notes and letters. In the same way, when I look at my library it tells me who I am. All those things are forms of self-definition. I had that insight in therapy. I could reflect on myself to find out who I am, and come to respect and appreciate those elements.

> **Th:** The question you ask yourself is "If I am gay, am I cultured or am I depraved?"

J: It seems hard for the two to coexist. There is an element that rejects the person that I try to be. There is an element that seems inauthentic to me, the intellectual cultured person. One of the refreshing things about the book club is I'm getting social support for the idea that I am unusual in a positive way. And I'm just being myself. But it doesn't fit well, it doesn't feel comfortable either.

It can be clinically useful to help a patient see this struggle within himself. However, the patient's question about whether homosexuality represents depravity or refinement is an age-old one and the answer, even among psychoanalysts, depends upon the analyst. Freud, in his "Letter to an American Mother" (1935) noted, "Many highly respectable individuals of ancient and modern times have been homosexuals, several of the greatest men among them (Plato, Michelangelo, Leonardo da Vinci, etc.)." On the other side of the cultural debate internalized by the above patient is McDougall's (1980) contention that "the fact of being homosexual . . . confers no particular creative gifts on the individual. On the contrary, it would be more exact to say that certain gifted persons are capable of authentic creative work *in spite of* their disturbed sexual organizations and deviations" (pp. 176–177).

The Political Dimension

In a relational perspective, intrapsychic struggles to define oneself are commonly reflected in interpersonal struggles as well. In the postmodern perspective, interpersonal struggles are always linked to issues of power and authority. This is the political dimension of defining gay. Bayer's (1981) study of homosexuality and American psychiatry concluded that "the status of homosexuality is a political question, representing a historically rooted, socially determined choice regarding the ends of human sexuality" (p. 5). Many theories have been offered to support this view (Boswell, 1980; Altman, 1982; Abelove, Barale, and Halperin, 1993; Duberman, 1994; Sullivan, 1997). In fact, any discussion of the definition of gay is inseparable from social and political attitudes about same-sex relationships. However, Butler (1990) highlights the political difficulty of trying to define gay with her thoughtful analogy to "the political problem that feminism encounters in the assumption that the term *women* denotes a common identity" (p. 3). Nevertheless, Chauncey (1994) asserts that "in calling themselves *gay*, a new generation of men insisted on the right to name themselves, to claim their status as men, and to reject the 'effeminate' styles of the older generation" (p. 19). Kushner's (1992a) mythic portrayal of the late Roy Cohn, being told by his doctor that he has AIDS,[4] poignantly captures the subjectivity of a man who defines himself as a "heterosexual," because he wields political power and "homosexuals" do not:

> Your problem, Henry, is that you are hung up on words, on labels, that you believe they mean what they seem to mean. AIDS. Homosexual. Gay. Lesbian. You think these are names that tell you who someone sleeps with, but they don't tell you that. . . . Not who I fuck or who fucks me, but who will pick up the phone when I call, who owes me favors. This is what a label refers to. . . . Homosexuals are not men who sleep with other men. Homosexuals are men who in fifteen years of trying cannot get a pissant antidiscrimination bill through City Council. Homosexuals are men who know nobody and who nobody knows. Who have zero clout. Does this sound like me, Henry? . . . Roy Cohn is not a homosexual. Roy Cohn is a heterosexual man, Henry, who fucks around with guys [p. 45].

Issues related to power and politics invariably surface in this clinical work. In fact, as shown in the words of one psychoanalyst, sometimes issues of power emerge as counter-transferential responses within the therapist:

> Homosexuals are essentially disagreeable people, regardless of their pleasant or unpleasant outward manner. True, they are not responsible for their unconscious conflicts. However, these conflicts sap so much of their inner energy that the shell is a mixture of superciliousness, fake aggression, and whimpering. Like all psychic masochists, they are sub-servient when confronted with a stronger person, merciless when in power, unscrupulous about trampling on a weaker person. The only language their unconscious understands is brute force [Bergler, 1956, pp. 28–29].

Bergler's quote demonstrates how clinical and scientific theorizing is embedded within prevailing cultural myths. A passing familiarity with a wide range of political beliefs and assumptions about human sexuality are useful to clinicians who treat gay men. For example, some gay men

---

4. The AIDS epidemic has had a significant and tragic impact on the gay community. The meaning of AIDS to the shaping of gay identities is a complex subject, worthy of an entire book in itself. This impact of AIDS on gay men and their caretakers is touched upon in greater detail by many authors (Nichols and Ostrow, 1984; Shilts, 1987; Holleran, 1988; Monette, 1988; Bayer, 1989; Sontag, 1989; Kramer, 1994; Schaffner, 1986, 1990, 1996; Blechner, 1997; Merlino, 1997; Rotello, 1997).

define promiscuous homosexual activity as a revolutionary response to oppressive heterosexual mores. Rechy (1977) both embraces and embodies this philosophy in his book, *The Sexual Outlaw*:

> The promiscuous homosexual is a sexual revolutionary. Each moment of his outlaw existence he confronts repressive laws, repressive "morality." Parks, alleys, subways, tunnels, garages, streets—these are his battlefields. To the sexhunt he brings a sense of choreography, ritual and mystery—sex cruising, with an electrified instinct that sends and receives messages of orgy at any movement, any place. Who are these outlaws? Single men, married men; youngmen [sic], older ones; black, white; your brothers, your fathers; students, teachers, bodybuilders, doctors, construction workers, coaches, writers, cowboys, truck drivers, motorcyclists, dancers, weight-lifters, actors, painters, athletes, politicians, businessmen, lawyers, cops. What creates the sexual outlaw? Rage [p. 28].

Sexual revolutionaries use terms like "liberation" and "battle" to define their sexuality. At a different place in the political spectrum's debate about human sexuality, are gay men who reject Rechy's revolutionary subjectivity in favor of middle class values such as monogamy and adherence to social convention (Bawer, 1993). In another political place altogether are those men who reject their homosexuality completely. Nicolosi (1991) reports the following from a patient:

> I was totally into anonymous sex and never into relationships with people. And now I look back on it as a huge, huge waste of time and energy. What in the hell was I doing? If I focused my energy in more productive ways I think I'd be in a different place right now. I think I probably would be more productive, maybe more successful, happier. It took a lot of energy. When the time came to do it, it was exciting and impulsive. I just went and did it. Whatever the consequences at the moment, I figured I'd deal with them later. When I was involved in such an experience, I never thought about anybody else but me. I was just totally, totally engrossed in what was going on at the moment for myself [p. 124].

As one man's internal struggles illustrates, a gay man can struggle with the many political meanings of being gay:

> **K:** I occasionally get angry at myself, not for being gay, but at the world for the way it handles it. I'm a silently suffering victim of stupidity. So I get angry when I'm reading newspapers and watching television and see the stupid things that people say, people who are not gay. I suppose I can't

help personalizing that since they are talking about me. These idiots have no idea what they are talking about and they should be quiet.

Th: It's painful because what they are talking about is something you learned about yourself. Inside you may share those beliefs.

K: Yes, it goes in a circle here. The negativity that one encounters as a gay male is nothing we haven't felt ourselves. Having grown up and heard it so long, it is an effort to disbelieve it. Even when intellectually you can disbelieve it, the emotional scar is there. It's as if it were true what they are saying. I resent having that button pushed. Intellectually I can say it is nonsense but emotionally it is rubbing salt into the wound. And I wish that all of us could be ourselves without having to contend with criticism, with being called perverts, with being called sick people, with being branded the enemy that society has to mobilize itself against. It's not nice to hear that even if you don't believe it is true. It is constant from different quarters. Sometimes the voice is louder. I guess that is a response to coming out of the closet, trying to get our rightful place, to tell us that we are supposed to be quiet and ashamed of ourselves. When you stand up and say I am not sick, there is nothing unnatural about me, that establishes the whole chorus. In a sense we have provoked these people. We deserve to hear what they are saying. This does provoke the elements of society that are the most vocal and the most critical. That is to be expected, but it doesn't mean I like it.

This patient is concerned about a process of political demonization that has spawned stereotypes of an openly gay, radical subculture that co-exists with influential and wealthy, closeted elements (Socarides, 1998). Together, they threaten to undermine traditional values. These beliefs obscure the wide spectrum of diversity in gay men's actual political beliefs, ranging from Radical Fairies to the Republican Log Cabin Club. Another patient came into a session on a presidential Election Day. He is closeted and works at an executive level for a large corporation. He felt he could not support the Democrats' economic platform and had just voted for the Republican candidate. He presented himself both defensively and filled with guilt because of what he described as the abysmal Republican record in funding AIDS research. While in the voting booth he thought about a neighbor with AIDS and he ruminated about how could he, after the vote, look this friend in the eye. Responding to the patient's defensiveness, the therapist asked if he was anxious about telling the therapist about his vote. The patient had often speculated in the past about the therapist's "radical" gay political views. Perhaps he anticipated that the therapist would disapprove of his political stance. This question made the patient more overtly anxious. The therapist pointed out that since he was an openly gay professional, and the patient was not, it was obvious that they had their political differences. The therapist wondered if the patient's perception that the two of them were not in agreement on this political issue reflected the patient's own inability to accept any opinions that might be different from his own. The patient acknowledged the truth of this interpretation and became less anxious. His belief that he and the therapist were on different sides of a political issue contained an element of truth, but his fantasy about what that meant also obscured his deeper feelings of needing to be in control of the therapist, as well as his difficulties with feelings of separateness and difference.

Gay patients often define themselves as members of a minority group. In doing so, they use political metaphors drawn from their external reality. The need to understand the impact of external factors on a gay identity is illustrated by the surprised response of a heterosexual therapist leading a male psychotherapy group:

> About two-thirds into the session, one of the men brought up the topic of the 1994 political elections. I immediately considered the topic inappropriate, given the intense feeling level of the group at that moment. All that kept me from intervening was my knowledge of the person who had brought it up. Usually he is not emotionally tuned out. Nonetheless, I wondered what, in this very intimate engagement, he was running away from.
>
> To my surprise, the group took up this political question with considerable intensity. They were extremely angered and saddened by the elections which had brought a conservative (translate, "reactionary," "anti-gay") majority into the House of Representatives and the Senate. They saw the results as devastating on a local level, bearing extremely bad tidings for them. I had also been disappointed by the results, but on a more strictly intellectual level. I didn't really understand the group's concern. As I sat in my bewilderment, the men in the group tied this experience in with their intense experience of loneliness. They did not hear the election topic as differentiated from their previous sentiments. The elections stood as further proof that no one cared for them. It underscored their loneliness. . . . Politics and personal life are of one piece. To oppressed minorities, the course of political developments is a symbolic expression of how we feel about them personally [O'Leary, 1997, pp. 217–218].

Conclusion

This chapter has tried to show that defining gay is not simply a matter of applying a label nor is it a unitary entity. The essence of psychoanalytically oriented psychotherapies is to focus on the individual and labels, like diagnoses, can sometimes be helpful in this endeavor. However, they may also obscure the deeper meanings of an individual's language and subjectivity. A gay identity is not a stereotype, although patients who come into treatment may define themselves as gay using the term in idiosyncratic or stereotypical contexts. A therapist cannot define a patient as gay, but can talk about the many ways in which a gay identity is defined.

3

THEORIES OF THE ETIOLOGY
OF HOMOSEXUALITY

It is not for psycho-analysis to solve the problem of
homosexuality.

> Sigmund Freud, "The Psychogenesis of a Case
> of Homosexuality in a Woman" (1920)

Christ, how sick analysts must get of hearing how
mommy and daddy made their darlin' into a fairy.

> Mart Crowley, *The Boys in the Band* (1968)

The story of origins is thus a strategic tactic within a
narrative that, by telling a single, authoritative account
about an irrecoverable past, makes the constitution of
the law appear as a historical inevitability.

> Judith Butler, *Gender Trouble* (1990)

Theories of etiology try to explain causes and becauses. That
is to say, they seek to provide both explanations and an ontological rationale for the way things are. An example of one such tale is "In the beginning God created man." This origin story then goes on to relate the
subsequent creation of woman and, in the process, raises the issue of
whether being first made man the better of the two. Or could the case be
made that the later model improved upon the earlier one (de Beauvoir,
1952)? That is the lesson taught by another etiological story in which the
Great Spirit created man from clay. He underbaked his first attempt,

creating a pale, white man. The next attempt baked too long and came out dark, that is as a black man. The Great Spirit got man just right on his third try with the Native American.

How does a person's place in the developmental line of an origin story relate to his or her place in a social hierarchy? Who decides which position is better and which is worse? How does an etiological narrative serve an individual's need for self-definition as well as a culture's need to define itself? And how do individuals or cultures decide which values it prefers in making these decisions? These are some of the questions worth thinking about when listening to a theory of etiology.

The tales told by scientists take the form of hypotheses or theories. But claims of objectivity notwithstanding, like other stories, they too involve a measure of subjectivity. A scientific system of classification, after all, "is not a neutral hat rack; it expresses a theory of relationships that controls our concepts" (Gould, 1977, p. 114). These controls abound in discussions of homosexuality's etiologies when the subject is framed, as it often is, in terms of "nature versus nurture," "intrinsic versus extrinsic," or "biological versus environmental." Although these theoretical dichotomies have generated both provocative and thoughtful arguments, embedded within them are many unproven assumptions and inarticulated beliefs. When the latter are brought into clearer view, opposing arguments in these debates can surprisingly line up on the same side.

Presenting all the etiological narratives of homosexuality is beyond the scope of this chapter. Although some may categorically assert that they know the causes of both homosexuality and heterosexuality, the origins of human sexual attraction still remain an unsolved mystery.[1] Rather than offering a new etiological theory, this chapter offers a sampling of a range of theories from two perspectives. The first perspective shows how a theory often makes use of unidimensional constructs of homosexuality. In understanding the stereotypes that inform a theory's portrayal of homosexuality, the reader can see how one theory's "homosexual" may have little in common with those of another. After recognizing the culturally embedded stereotypes used in theory-building, the second perspective shows the unproven assumptions that form the basis of what I refer to as narratives of immaturity, pathology, and normal variants.

---

1. Criticisms of psychodynamic explanations are offered by Bell, Weinberg, and Hammersmith (1981), Friedman (1988), Isay (1989), and Gonsiorek (1991). For criticisms of biological explanations see Gagnon (1990), Byne (1994, 1997), Byne and Parsons (1993), Byne and Stein (1997), and Schüklenk, Stein, Kerin, and Byne (1997).

What necessitates this discussion of origin stories? I believe there are two very obvious ways in which etiological theories can have an impact upon the conduct of a psychotherapy. The first is that the therapist's own theory of homosexuality will inevitably be a distraction from listening to the patient. The other is that the patient's etiological theories, overt or subliminal, provide a valuable way to make sense of the cultural forces that can shape and define a gay patient's identity. And these are, after all, the themes to which a therapist must attend in the psychotherapeutic work. When a therapist learns to recognize the narrative forms presented as theories of immaturity, pathology, and normal variation, some of the moral judgments and beliefs embedded in each of them can become clearer to both the patient and the therapist.

The Yearnings of Urnings and Other Hypothetical Homosexuals

In the mid-19th century, Ulrichs (1864) hypothesized that some men were born with a woman's spirit trapped in their bodies. He believed these men constituted a third sex and named them *Urnings*. The term was derived from a speech in Plato's *Symposium* which told of the elder Aphrodite, a daughter of Uranus, who was conceived from the remains of his dismembered body. Because she had no mother and her birth involved no female participation, the Uranian Aphrodite, according to Plato, inspired the love of men for men, while the younger Aphrodite, daughter of Zeus and Dione, inspired the love of men for women.[2] But despite the fact that the concept of Uranian love had its roots in mythological parthenogenesis, Ulrichs nevertheless claimed that a man's sexual attraction to men was feminine: "The Urning is not a man, but rather a kind of feminine being when it concerns not only his entire organism, but also his sexual feelings of love, his entire natural temperament, and his talents. The dominant characteristics are of femininity both in his behavior and his body movements. These are the obvious manifestations of the feminine elements that reside in him" (p. 36).

The concept of Urnings rested upon the presumption that an attraction to men is a feminine attribute (Sedgwick, 1991). In fact, there are many stories defining the "homosexual" as one who loves like a woman (Freud, 1910a), while a lesbian is defined, conversely, as a woman who

---

2. Ulrichs designated the term *Dionings* for what we would today refer to as heterosexuals. It should be noted that Ulrichs' classification system predated the later concepts of homosexuality and heterosexuality (Bullough, 1979; Greenberg, 1988; Katz, 1995).

loves like a man (Freud, 1920; for discussions see Magee and Miller, 1997; Schwartz, 1998; Kiersky, in press). Labeling an attraction to men as a feminine trait is a popular belief and one found in many cultures. Its perennial appearance in the scientific literature clearly demonstrates the powerful hold of this binary concept on even the most creative of theorists. Yet, these theoretical attempts to understand the meaning of homosexuality in terms of male and female traits has led to the creation of many different "homosexuals" whose hypothetical nature is as hard to define objectively as are the concepts of masculinity and femininity. Homosexuality, masculinity and femininity, as the terms are frequently used, are often nothing more than an accumulation of projections and cultural stereotypes, not to mention a conflation of sexual attraction, sexual orientation, sexual identity, gender roles, and gender identity. And while some theoretical constructions of homosexuality may try to be flattering, most are not. In fact, reflecting cultural values, male homosexuality usually serves as the repository of many denigrating beliefs. A prime example of this is Western culture's disdain for femininity in men, embedded in concepts, discussed below, like Freud's (1923b) psychological passivity or Dörner's (1986) biological lordosis. And because homosexuality can mean many things to different people, discussions and disagreements regarding its etiology are often rendered meaningless, because different theorists are, in fact, describing different "homosexuals." A theorist will all too often depend upon the stereotypical assumptions about homosexuality's meanings that are embedded in everyday language. For example, in a search for a genetic marker of homosexuality on the Xq28 region of the X, or female chromosome, Hamer and Copeland (1994) resort to concrete, sexually dimorphic metaphors. A key concept in their hypothesis is the "crossover":

> But every once in a while . . . the X and Y chromosomes get jumbled up, and this little strip of DNA from a Y chromosome is "mistakenly" passed to a daughter (or a bit of the X goes to a son). That means boys are getting a tiny bit of "female" chromosome and girls are getting a bit of a "male" chromosome. This raised the intriguing possibility that a genetic crossover between the male and female sex chromosomes is related to the behavioral "crossover" between heterosexuality and homosexuality [p. 128].

Hamer and Copeland's theory draws upon several stereotypes of homosexuality. First, the "behavioral crossover" to which the authors allude assumes that an attraction to women is a male trait and an attraction to men is a female trait. That is a variation of the cultural belief that a male "homosexual" crosses over a gender boundary and acts like a girl. This, in turn, derives from another cultural belief that homosexual attractions deviate from a standard of relatedness based on heterosexuality. In this theory, the physiological antecedents of sexual attractions are hypothetically encoded in so-called sex chromosomes. The argument rests upon the semantic equation of two expressions of sexual attraction, one to men and the other to women, with two kinds of sex chromosomes, one male (Y) and the other female (X). That a boy, regardless of his sexual identity, also carries an X chromosome is irrelevant. That is because the authors speculate that homosexuality's origin resides in the second sex chromosome—the one that genetically separates the boys from the girls. This is, of course, based upon the mundane belief that a gay boy has feminine qualities.

This latter assumption has also generated theories of etiology that attempt to explain the so-called feminine behaviors of gay men. One typical example of culturally-defined femininity is the sexually receptive position. This form of sexual activity is usually ascribed to heterosexual women and, if male locker room humor is any indication, is also one that many heterosexual men find aversive. Cultural beliefs about the sexually receptive position may explain why etiological theories, in their focus on male effeminacy, rarely attempt to explain the homosexually insertive man's feelings, motivations, or behaviors. This selective inattention facilitates the categorization of same-sex pairings as substitutes for heterosexual ones, regardless of what those relationships may actually represent. Because sexual receptivity transgresses cultural norms, the man who acts the part of the woman, sometimes referred to as "the bottom," must be explained. The inserter, colloquially referred to as "the top," plays a presumably natural part, that of the man, and therefore requires little or no explanation. One explanation sometimes proffered for being on top is the absence of normal heterosexual outlets: "In the situational form of utilitarian homosexual behavior the unavailability of a partner of the opposite sex, in institutional settings particularly, such as war camps, prisons and other milieux, may cause an individual to seek temporary orgiastic satisfaction with a person of the same sex. This behavior is discontinued as soon as the situation changes" (Socarides, 1968, pp. 92–93). However, there is a paucity of theories to explain how a "situational homosexual" might actually enjoy same-sex activities, including sexual receptivity. To even propose such a theory would, of course, fly in the face of cultural expectations.

Some theorists have tried to avoid perpetuating stereotypes of homosexuality with caveats about generalizations (Ulrichs, 1864; Freud, 1905) or by referring to the "various homosexualities" (Bell and Weinberg, 1978; Marmor, 1965, 1980). Unfortunately, these warnings are often unheeded in attempts to make theoretical points. Furthermore, there are theorists whose reductionistic approaches create the erroneous impression of a single kind of homosexual, or of a typology of homosexuality, as in Bieber et al.'s (1962) assertion that homosexuality is always caused by "hidden but incapacitating fears of the opposite sex" (p. 303). Unfortunately, when trying to fit their patients' life stories into an etiological narrative, therapists may forget that they are dealing with real people, not hypothetical ones.

I Won't Grow Up—Narratives of Immaturity

In psychoanalytic theory, narratives of immaturity are frequently confused with theories of pathology. However, an inability to mature does not necessarily mean the same thing as being ill. While pathologizing theories treat homosexuality as deviant and abnormal, immaturity theories regard homosexuality as a normal step in the development of heterosexuality. They define same-sexuality as a passing phase to be outgrown on the road to adult (hetero)sexuality. In fact, the belief that homosexuality is something one outgrows may be consistent with the life experience of many heterosexuals. Kinsey et al. (1948) found that 48 to 60 percent of male subject groups reported homosexual activity in pre-adolescence but among men who went to college, 80 percent of them did not have later homosexual experiences. Thus, some heterosexual men may come to believe they have advanced beyond childhood homosexual activity but that adult gay men have not.

This everyday cultural perspective was invoked in a personal way in treatment by one gay man, distraught about a recent communication from his father. The patient, despite a lifetime attraction to men, had married and raised his children into adulthood. When they left home, he told his wife about his true sexual attractions and they subsequently divorced. He had recently written to tell his father he was gay, and had just received a letter that admonished him for his "childish behavior." The father explained that he too had had homosexual experiences as a teen-ager. But he added that he had put aside his "selfish pursuit of pleasure and taken on the responsibilities of marriage and a family." Of course, so had the patient, although his father was unable to comprehend his son's announcement as anything other than a childish act of selfishness.

Freud tells a tale of immaturity in a theory of instinctual bisexuality. In "The Three Essays" (1905), he described a sexual instinct, analogous with hunger, termed *libido*. This instinct was directed toward a sexual object for satisfaction and "the act toward which the instinct tends [is] the sexual aim" (p. 136). Ideally, the aim of the instincts were to be subsumed in the service of heterosexual relations between adult human beings. However this naturalization of adult heterosexuality meant that homosexuality or inversion was a "deviation in respect to the sexual object," as were pedophilia and bestiality.

Drive theory further distinguished these instincts from sexual acts. *Constitutional bisexuality* meant there was a certain component of *masculine* (active) as well as *feminine* (passive) *tendencies* rather than behaviors. Although bisexual tendencies were universal, some people were constitutionally endowed with more of one than the other. Freud believed life experiences, particularly traumatic ones, could have an impact on the development and expression of these innate instincts. Under normal or non-traumatic circumstances, the component instincts that determine one's final sexual object choice should be consistent with one's anatomical sex. That is to say an anatomic male should ideally express the masculine component instinct and obtain sexual satisfaction from women. However, even adult heterosexuals retained the homosexual component, albeit in sublimated form.

In Freud's model of normal development, instincts had to traverse two immature *psychosexual stages*, the oral and anal phases, before they were capable of attaining more mature expressions of sexuality. Adults who used other means to achieve sexual excitement, as in the acts of fellatio or receptive anal sex, were said to suffer from either *fixations* or *regressions* of libido. It was hypothesized that these latter activities were expressions of immature sexuality, as contrasted with mature forms of genital, (hetero)sexual expression: "The final outcome of the sexual development lies in what is known as the normal sexual life of the adult, in which the pursuit of pleasure comes under the sway of the reproductive function and in which the component instincts, under the primacy of a single erotogenic zone, form a firm organization directed towards a sexual aim attached to some extraneous sexual object" (1905, p. 197).

It should be stressed that "The Three Essays" did not specifically address homosexuality but instead laid out Freud's theory of sexual development as progressing from a polymorphously perverse state in infancy to a progressively constructed adult sexual condition. The concept of instinct embedded in "The Three Essays" was an elaboration of the model of the instinctual energies of the mind in Freud's "The

Interpretation of Dreams" (1900) which, in turn, was based on his ongoing clinical work with hysterics (Breuer and Freud, 1895; Freud, 1896a, b). The concept is also central to Freud's narrative of immaturity. In so-called normal people, perverse instincts were repressed and pushed out of consciousness. They could, however, emerge in dreams in disguised forms and were either forgotten (repressed) or consciously regarded as meaningless. In hysterics, the repressive mechanism did not function normally and the unacceptable instincts were in danger of entering consciousness. The hysteric transformed them, through displacement and conversion, into physical symptoms that symbolized the conflict between the instinct and a repressive agency, one whose functions were later attributed by Freud to the ego. Perverts, on the other hand, did not repress their instincts but enacted them because, unlike hysterics, their instincts were not in conflict with their egos. This was the basis of Freud's mathematically elegant claim that "neuroses are the negative of perversions" (1905, p. 165). This reasoning was also the basis of his assertion that homosexuality was not an illness (1935), at least not a psychoneurotic one, which Freud defined in terms of the symptoms that result from intrapsychic conflict (1926a). However, although homosexuality was technically not an illness, this unique, and somewhat idiosyncratic, psychoanalytic definition did not quite constitute a clean bill of health. For example, as Freud's narrative of immaturity imperceptibly merged into the pathological theories of later psychoanalytic writers, the absence of conflict in expressing perverse instincts came to be defined as a form of impaired ego function (for discussion see Lewes, 1988). Freud, nevertheless, saw homosexuality primarily as a developmental arrest, a fixation, or a sign of psychological immaturity.

Like other etiological theorists, Freud used stereotypes of homosexuality to buttress his story. He claimed, for example, that Leonardo da Vinci's homosexual identity resulted from an identification with his mother in which he took someone who resembled himself as a younger man for a love object (Freud, 1910a). In effect, this made da Vinci a man who loved like a woman, who in this case was his mother. Not only did this draw upon the aforementioned idea that a man's love for a man is a feminine trait, it also blamed Leonardo's close relationship with his mother for his homosexuality. That is to say, Freud's etiological theory evoked the stereotype of the mama's boy.

The idea of a mama's boy is one of many cultural beliefs that can shape a gay patient's feelings about his own homosexuality. Such a patient may feel incomplete, or think he doesn't measure up to a conventional, masculine ideal. This feeling is sometimes attributed to narcissism

(Freud, 1914c), a psychoanalytic concept that straddles the fence between narratives of immaturity and pathology. In some accounts, the narcissist's difficulties stem from insufficient quantities of parental responsiveness (Kohut, 1971). The psychologically stunted growth that theoretically ensues implies both immaturity and pathology. However, feeling deficient, regardless of one's sexual identity, could be alternatively understood as the result of chronic devaluation, or from having to hide parts of one's identity.

A patient discussed the wedding of a coworker. The event had made him uncomfortable, and he associated that feeling to being in a heterosexual environment where it was not generally known that he was gay. He contrasted the public celebration of marriage with his relationship of many years which he had kept secret from his professional colleagues. Although he had, in recent years, begun feeling more comfortable being "out" within a wider circle of acquaintances, he felt a "lack of completion" in his life. This brought to mind a dream:

> **A:** The image I have from the dream is unfinished nuclear reactors that are architecturally beautiful but an enormous expense with no output. There are three round hills curved with metal, the foundations for a reactor that is never completed. It tears up the land but is architecturally beautiful. I go up a set of stairs, wanting to go into Cuba. A Spanish guard answers the door and says, "What do you want?" I say, "El Presidente." He laughs and says, "You can't see Castro." Finally I get in. I go around the island, and there is a panoramic view of the reactors. It is thrilling to have gotten into the country, but it is still fairly closed.

The feeling reported in the dream was one of inadequacy, attributed at first to a lack of fluency in Spanish. This led to an association that the patient felt "unfinished" because he had no children and no wife. Castro represented, in his associations, an unfinished life. Having lived his adult life as a gay man, he felt he had not lived up to his heterosexual potential. In fact, narratives of immaturity imply that heterosexuality is grown-up and that gay men are not.

In his critical discussion of developmental models, Mitchell (1988) explains that "in employing infantilism as a basis for interpretation, we are using our image of the baby as a metaphor. The analysand is not literally a baby, but if we think of him in those terms, as wishing, fearing and experiencing like a baby—*we find meaning* and patterns in otherwise inchoate fragments of experience" (p. 128, emphasis added). Despite their clinical utility, metaphors of immaturity can sometimes leave a therapist with the impression of being an adult who is guiding a child. And it is also worth noting that in everyday conversation, calling someone immature may not be as offensive as calling them sick, but neither appellation is particularly respectful. Just as a narrative of immaturity rationalized the exploitation of non-European cultures as "the white man's burden," theories of homosexual immaturity are usually experienced as paternalistic, colonizing, or condescending by their subjects. And as many accounts in the psychoanalytic literature have shown (Lewes, 1988), gay patients who present with the belief that their homosexuality stems from immaturity are often quite successful at projecting and inducing identifications with their own condescending feelings in their therapists.

This tendency to denigratingly define oneself may explain why Harry Stack Sullivan's own homosexuality (Chatelaine, 1981; Perry, 1982; Ortmeyer, 1995) did not preclude him from defining it as immature. Although his psychoanalytic theories are rarely equated with those of Freud, and despite the marked differences in their views of human drives and development, both Sullivan and Freud believed that a normal, childhood phase of homosexuality was a necessary precursor to the development of adult heterosexuality. And both of them also held external events responsible for a gay man's purported developmental arrest. In contrast to Freud, Sullivan's (1953) Interpersonal theory replaces biological instincts striving for satisfaction with needs for interpersonal relatedness. These vary with age; as one passes through a series of developmental stages, different needs emerge:

> Needs for satisfaction include a broad range of physical and emotional tensions and desires. Many of these, such as needs for food, warmth and oxygen, pertain to the chemical regulation of the interaction between the organism and the environment, and thus concern the survival of the organism. Other needs for satisfaction pertain to the necessity for emotional contact with other human beings, beginning with a simple "need for contact" in the infant and proceeding, through the various developmental epochs, to needs for more and more complex and intimate relations with others [Greenberg and Mitchell, 1983, p. 91].

Sullivan believed the significant developmental epoch of homosexual expression was *preadolescence* and that it occurred between $8^{1}/_{2}$ and 10 years of age. This is when children's needs are no longer met entirely by their nuclear families and they begin to express the need for "playmates rather like oneself" (Sullivan, 1953, p. 245). Sullivan described this relationship as a *chumship* and called it a "manifestation of the need for interpersonal intimacy." Although it did not necessarily involve genital contact, other forms of closeness were possible. Sullivan did not see homosexual behavior during this stage as a problem:

> I want particularly to touch on the intensity of the relationship, because it is easy to think that if the preadolescent chumship is very intense, it may tend to fixate the chums in the preadolescent phase, or it may culminate in some such peculiarity of personality as is ordinarily meant by homosexuality—although, incidentally, it is often difficult to say what is meant by this term. Actual facts that have come to my attention lend no support whatever to either of these surmises. In fact, as a psychiatrist, I would hope that preadolescent relationships were intense enough for each of the two chums literally to get to know practically everything about the other one that could possibly be exposed in an intimate relationship, because that remedies a good deal of the often illusory, usually morbid, feeling of being different, which is such a striking part of rationalizations of insecurity in later life [1953, p. 356].

Sullivan asserted that: "Those [preadolescents] who had participated in mutual [homo]sexuality were married, with children, divorces, and what not, in the best tradition of American society. In other words, relationships of what might be described as 'illegitimate' intimacy toward the end of the preadolescent period had not conducted to a disturbed type of development in adolescence and later; the facts showed something quite different" (pp. 256–257). He hypothesized that those who ultimately became "homosexuals" as adults were members of the "outgroup, if only with respect to so-called mutual masturbation and other presumably homosexual activity which went on in this group of boys as preadolescent pals" (p. 256). That is, he thought the gay men had been unsuccessful in negotiating the preadolescent same-sex activity that led to normal heterosexuality. Perry's (1982) biography intimates that Sullivan's developmental theory reflected many of his own life experiences and that this is probably how he understood the origins of his own homosexuality. His theory of immaturity suggested that homosexuality in adulthood occurred when a boy lagged behind others his own age:

> One of the lamentable things which can happen to a personality in the preadolescent society is that a particular person may not become preadolescent at all promptly—in other words, he literally does not have the need for intimacy when most of the people of about the same age have it, and therefore he does not have an opportunity of being part of the parade as it goes by. But then this person, when preadolescence is passing for most of his contemporaries, develops a need for

intimacy with someone of his own sex and may be driven to establishing relationships with a chronologically younger person. This is not necessarily a great disaster. What is more of a disaster is that he may form a preadolescent relationship with an actually adolescent person, which is perhaps more frequently the case in this situation. This does entail some very serious risk to personality and can, I think, in quite a number of instances, be suspected of having considerable to do with the establishment of a homosexual way of life, or at least, a 'bisexual' way [1953, p. 258].

Sullivan's theory draws upon a belief that homosexuality is the result of an immature person's vulnerability to seduction by an older one. This too is a common cultural belief, and one that resonates with a gay man's memory of his own teen-age sexual experiences with a younger cousin:

B: The first person I had sex with was my younger cousin who was also having sex with girls. I remember thinking it odd that he could have sex with me and then go and have sex with girls. I saw my not having sex with girls as sort of a void. Since childhood, I don't have depth perception. Never having had it, I don't know what it is and I don't really miss it. That is how I viewed heterosexuality. I never had sex with women and I never had a desire for it, so I didn't miss it. But the first time I fucked my cousin, it ended our four years of having sex together. I remember thinking "What have I done? He might be gay now!" I looked at the world as if there is a toggle switch and you are either straight or gay. Until I was older I never realized there was a continuum. When I had sex with my cousin, I was having sex with someone who was straight and who was just fooling around. When I fucked him, I mentally thought I had thrown the toggle switch. He had been straight and now he was gay. I was thinking that as we finished having sex and my cousin said, "Next time we should use some lubricant because it will be more comfortable." I realized, to my horror, that I was not the first person to fuck him. But I believed he was becoming gay and I was making him that way. That caused me to panic and I avoided him for a whole year with no communication or explanation. His reaction, and I don't blame him, was that I had been intimate and had thrown him away now that I fucked him. I never realized how much he loved me until he told my aunt that I was the only person who loved him at that time in his life. What was ironic is that it hurt me so much to stop being intimate with him and I was trying to do the right thing. I've seen my cousin only once since then. He didn't want to see me after that. We met recently. He brought his son, I believe, so we couldn't talk privately. When his son went to the bathroom, I broached the topic of visiting his family. He said "No," because he didn't feel it would be safe for me to be around his sons. I didn't know what to say about it.

According to the theory shared by Sullivan and the patient, the cousin was more likely to become gay. This, according to the popular beliefs that underlie the theory, was due to the fact that the cousin was younger, and presumably more vulnerable to fixation, as well as from the fact that he was the sexually receptive partner. As it turns out, of course, things are much more complicated than cultural stereotypes permit, and it was the older, insertive boy who grew up to be gay while the younger, receptive one married and became an ostensibly heterosexual father.

Feed a Fever, Starve a Cold— Narratives of Pathology

While theories of immaturity naturalize same-sex experiences in early life, narratives of pathology define adult homosexuality as a disease or abnormal condition that deviates from biologically predetermined heterosexual development. These etiological theories, psychoanalytic or otherwise, are based upon several assumptions. The first is that adult heterosexuality is the normal, nondiseased state. The second assumption is that deviations from conventional gender role expectations are symptoms of the disease. And finally, these theories contend that some external, pathogenic agent traumatizes an individual and turns him from a straight path leading to normal heterosexuality. The external event can occur pre- or postnatally and may include intrauterine hormonal exposure, too much mothering, insufficient fathering, seduction, or a decadent lifestyle. As shown in both Freud's and Sullivan's theories, narratives of immaturity may also define a role for external trauma in precipitating homosexuality. However, they tend to view the resultant immaturity as a benign condition. Theorists of pathology, on the other hand, have a tendency to emphasize the potentially malignant meanings of homosexuality.

Krafft-Ebing's *Psychopathia Sexualis* (1886) was a 19th-century bestiary of sexual psychopathology which chronicled a wide range of sexual activities. In the degeneracy theory he espoused, man's higher nature was purported to be a product of his evolution, and perversions, like homosexuality, were illnesses that ran counter to nature's design. Homosexuality, either constitutional or acquired, was a symptom of "nervous degeneration." Even if one were presumably born gay, it was considered to be an inherited, degenerative condition that could be traced to the afflicted individual's family history. And as for those who were not born that way, "Careful examination of the so-called acquired cases makes it probable that the predisposition—also present here—consists of a latent homosexuality, or, at any rate, bisexuality, which, for its manifestation, requires the influence of accidental exciting causes to rouse it from its dormant state" (p. 247). Thus, even so-called acquired cases were presumed to result from a pathological, biological predisposition toward homosexuality which had been evoked by such factors as enforced abstinence or masturbation. There was no such thing as normal homosexuality in Krafft-Ebing's reasoning; even when it was innate, it was a congenital disease, not a normal variant of human sexuality. And homosexuality that was not caused by bad protoplasm was the result of socially unacceptable practices:

> Nothing is prone to contaminate—under certain circumstances, even to exhaust—the source of all noble and ideal sentiments, which arise of themselves from a normally developing sexual instinct, as the practice of masturbation in early years. It despoils the unfolding bud of perfume and beauty, and leaves behind only the coarse, animal desire for sexual satisfaction. If an individual, thus depraved, reaches the age of maturity, there is wanting in him that aesthetic, ideal, pure and free impulse which draws the opposite sexes together [p. 248].

Although Freud (1905) rejected degeneracy theory's etiological narrative, his psychoanalytic descendants echoed Krafft-Ebing by pathologizing homosexuality. Rado's (1969) theory, for example, was a major force in shaping these later psychoanalytic theories. It ordered life according to Darwinian principles of adaptation and defined an individual's psychological responses as either adaptive or maladaptive to cultural experiences. One could make compromises that were psychologically adaptive in one context but inappropriate in another:

> In adaptational psychodynamics we analyze behavior in the context of a biological organism interacting with its cultural environment. The human organism, like other living organisms, may be defined as a self-regulating biological system that perpetuates itself and its type by means of its environment, its surrounding system. From this it follows that life is a process of interaction of the organism and its environment. . . . In the theory of evolution, the crowning achievement of eighteenth- and nineteenth-century biologists, *adaptive value is a statistical concept which epitomizes reproductive efficiency* in a certain environment. This is strongly influenced by the type's ability to survive. Hence, "more adaptive" means more able to survive and reproduce [Rado, 1969, p. 4, emphasis added].

Rado's neo-Darwinian claim was that human psychology is intimately linked to reproductive survival which meant that nonprocreative sexual activity is maladaptive. This assumption also led Rado to reject Freud's theory of bisexuality (1940). Instead, homosexuality, or *homogeneous pairing* as he termed it, was entirely based on a deviation from the "male-female" design. Thus, two men seeking sexual intimacy with each other were engaged in a misguided, maladaptive attempt to mimic heterosexual encounters. Rado's "homosexual" was narrowly constructed of butch and femme stereotypes that made no distinctions between gender roles, gender identity and sexual attraction:

> What evidence enables me to assume that every homosexual act or homogeneous relationship is a statement of the male-female design? If male desires male, why does he seek out a male who pretends to be a female? Why does a male affect femininity if he wants to express a male's desire for a male? Why does a female turn to a masculine acting female if she is expressing the desire of a female for a female? How else can the crucial fact be explained that in male pairs one male impersonates a female and in female pairs one female impersonates a male? Sometimes evidence for the male-female pattern is deeply repressed, but I think it can be found with a thorough search. They are pretending to be a male-female pair. The male-female sexual pattern is dictated by anatomy [Rado, 1969, pp. 211–212].

Despite his theory's emphasis on cultural factors, Rado believed that biology, rather than custom, ultimately determined the mimicry of heterosexual gender roles in same-sex couples. That is to say, even the environmental factors that caused homosexuality could not overcome the biological drives to create some semblance of male-female pairs. Rado saw parental behavior as the pathogenic agent:

> Why is the so-called homosexual forced to escape from the male-female pair into a homogenous pair? . . . the familiar campaign of deterrence that parents wage to prohibit the sexual activity of the child . . . causes the male to see in the mutilated female organ a reminder of inescapable punishment. When . . . fear and resentment of the opposite organ becomes insurmountable, the individual may escape into homosexuality. The male patterns are reassured by the presence in both of them of the male organ. Homosexuality is a deficient adaptation evolved by the organism in response to its own emergency overreaction and dyscontrol [pp. 212–213].

Rado's theory was to have a far-ranging impact upon later psychoanalytic narratives of pathology. Bieber et al. (1962), for example, conducted a study of gay men in psychoanalysis and compared them to heterosexual analysands. Their study used Rado's assumption "that het-erosexuality is the biologic norm and that unless interfered with all indi-viduals are heterosexual" (p. 319) as its starting hypothesis and labeled "homosexuality . . . a pathologic biosocial, psychosexual adaptation consequent to pervasive fears surrounding the expression of heterosex-ual impulses" (p. 220). They then claimed to have discovered the homo-sexuality's causes through the analytic deciphering of their patients' narratives:

> The majority of H-parents [of homosexual patients] in our study had poor marital relationships. Almost half the H-mothers were dominant wives who minimized their husbands. The large majority of H-mothers had a close-binding-intimate relationship with the H-son. In most cases, this son had been his mother's favorite. . . . Most H-mothers were explicitly seductive, and even where they were not, the closeness of the bond with the son appeared to be in itself sexually provocative. In about two-thirds of the cases, the mother openly preferred her H-son to her husband, and allied with son against the husband. In about half the cases, the patient was the mother's confidant [p. 313].

The Bieber group claimed that a marital relationship in which the father's authority was undermined by the mother was a contributory fac-tor in causing male homosexuality. They found "the best interparental relationships," meaning those least likely to produce homosexuality, in those families where "father dominates but does not minimize mother" (p. 158). Despite its shortcomings, this theory does lend the weight of medical authority to a cultural belief that a father should be the head of his household. However, it is essentially the story of a boy who is closer to his mother than he is to his father, the stereotype of the mama's boy.

Blaming mothers for homosexuality is routine in the general culture and many patients seek explanations for their own homosexuality in sto-ries about family dynamics. One patient, after describing a fight with his mother, said she was always on the defensive with him because "I'm gay." The therapist wondered why that would make her feel defensive. The patient replied that his mother had always dominated his father and that was why he was gay: "She feels guilty because she made me gay." When the therapist said to the patient that the actual causes of homo-sexuality were unknown and still subject to debate, he responded with surprise. A few months later, he admitted that he always blamed his mother for the fact that he was gay and, subsequently, blamed her for his being HIV-positive. Further exploration revealed that blaming his mother for being gay represented his own unwillingness to accept his homosexuality. But when told that it was not a fact that his mother was responsible, he had to directly address his own unaccepting feelings. As he did so, he began to feel less angry with his mother and as a result, their relationship improved significantly.

Another patient, entering psychotherapy for the first time, also presented with a complex narrative of pathology that purported to explain why he was gay:

> **F:** Last week we were talking about my relationship with my father. The conflict between us, from the time I was very young, relates to his perception of what a boy should be. I was a bookworm and wanted to read rather than play sports. That conflict was there before I knew anything about my sexuality. We would fight about other things. All that got connected. There's this basic building block that is either missing or weak.

> **Th:** What is this building block?

> **F:** I think it's two things. One is a lack of confidence in my masculinity that I thought I had outgrown and put aside. I guess I didn't. The other thing, growing up, the people you naturally look to for approval, sanction, and guidance are your parents. Maybe because I had my mother's approval, I didn't realize it was important to have my father's approval as well. I could pull back from any conflict I had with him and fall back on the fact that my mother approved. So it was possible to avoid resolving that conflict with my father.

> **Th:** They had different goals for their children and showed their disagreements openly.

> **F:** Funny, when you mention that, a lot of their shared goals for their children fell on me as the firstborn. My mother may have been projecting into me things that she wanted from life or in her relationship that my father wasn't providing. One example is when I was about twelve, my mother took me to my first opera. She liked opera a lot but my father despised it. She took me to the opera so she would have someone to go with. She wanted to share that and put it on me.

> **Th:** Did you experience that as a burden?

> **F:** Not at all! I loved the opera. She was also the one who encouraged me in theater in high school. That could have been the beginning of the conflict. My father still hates to go to the theater and my mother drags him. If it's something light with a lot of music and dancing, that's OK. His approach was he didn't want to think. He had enough problems in the course of the day and he didn't need to spend his evenings being challenged. He really didn't like the opera or theater and my mother was encouraging me to do both. Not only was this something he didn't care

for, but something he didn't consider particularly masculine. Being masculine had to do with sports and things of that nature. I think he has mellowed over the years, but when we were growing up, expressing emotions was definitely something feminine. I can remember him getting angry at us and usually I would cry and crying was not masculine. He would say something like "Don't be such a baby," or "Be more of a man!" When I was growing up I was emotional. I did cry. My mother saw nothing wrong with that. From her standpoint it was perfectly OK to go to her and talk about a problem and cry.

Th: Your father may have been struck by the fact that you were more interested in your mother's values than in his, and they didn't share the same values.

F: Hmm, interesting. A lot of the values that she had and my father had, from a perspective of this day and age, were not things that were feminine and masculine. The fact that they were her values and not his, my sharing of those values made me less masculine. That makes the battles over me playing sports make more sense. If that what was going on in his head— these things that were very masculine, were clearly things my mother didn't share. My mother has no interest in sports. Doing sports would pull me back into a more masculine camp.

Psychoanalytic theories, of course, are not alone in pathologizing homosexuality. Consider, for example, the biological work of Dörner (1972, 1986, 1989; Dörner et al., 1975, 1991). An endocrinologist studying rat behavior, he presents animal models of sexual behavior as paradigms for human homosexuality. He hypothesizes that sexually dimorphic differences in rat brains govern so-called male and female behaviors. For example, mounting another rat, the male's usual position in copulation, is regarded as a biological, masculine behavior whereas presenting for mounting, in a position called *lordosis*, is defined as biological, feminine behavior. By experimentally altering hormone levels of genetic males in the first day of life, castrating them so they would not produce normal androgen or male hormone levels, he creates lordotic male rats who allow themselves to be mounted by other males. Conversely, "masculinized" female rats, given male hormones in the early days of life, are more likely to mount other females when they became adults. In Dörner's construction of same-sexuality, the lordotic male rat is defined as "the homosexual rat." Yet he does not say what one should call the unaltered male rat who is doing the mounting (Byne, 1994). In fact, Dörner's model, like many others, illustrates the cultural attitude that it is only the receptive male whose homosexuality must be explained, while a male who mounts other men is simply normal and does not require much explanation.

Despite a lack of evidence that rats offer a viable animal model for approximating human sexual psychology, Dörner generalizes from his research to hypothesize an etiology for human homosexuality. Since endocrinological studies have shown that there are no hormonal differences between adult male heterosexuals and gay men, he ascribes hormonal influences to a critical period of development in early life. He speculates that the hypothalamus is either masculinized or feminized during the prenatal period. This area of the brain is presumed, by some, to control sexuality, in part because in some species hypothalamic nuclei are truly sexually dimorphic, that is, they are of different sizes in males and females (LeVay, 1991, 1993).

Dörner goes on to speculate that maternal stress during pregnancy leads to a reduction in the normal exposure of the male fetus's developing brain to testosterone, or androgenization, leading to what he calls a female-differentiated brain. However this is a finding that has never been directly verified *in vivo*. In search of men with female-differentiated brains, Dörner tested gay male volunteers with injections of estrogen, a so-called female hormone. Estrogen and leutenizing hormone (LH) are interrelated in a hormonal feedback mechanism that involves the hypothalamus. A *positive estrogen feedback* was defined as an initial drop in LH levels followed by an increase in LH levels after estrogen injection. He reported a positive estrogen feedback in gay men similar to the one seen in (presumably heterosexual) women, and it was a response that differed from those of heterosexual male controls. Others (Gooren, 1986a,b), however, have failed to replicate Dörner's feedback responses and his work and reasoning have many detractors (Gooren, 1990; Byne, 1994; De Cecco and Parker, 1995; Magee and Miller, 1997). Nevertheless, the claim that gay men have feminized brains is a compelling story, and compelling stories do not necessarily require much verification to be repeated and treated as scientific facts (Fausto-Sterling, 1992). That explains why psychosurgery was actually performed on gay men in Germany in the 1970s based on Dörner's assertion that "Neuroendocrinologically determined male homosexuality can be brought to far-reaching regression [reversal] in adult animals through surgical lesions of a female erotic center located in the central hypothalamus" (cited in Herrn, 1995, p. 42). However, as Herrn has noted, "This led to severe personality disturbances in those so altered. Only on the basis of strong protests . . . were these inhuman practices halted" (Herrn, 1995, p. 42). But like earlier medical experiments in which male "homosexuals" were treated with male hormones to make them more masculine, that is, less homosexual, these surgical procedures were essentially the result of concretely applying gender stereotypes to human brains.

In addition to his endocrinological manipulations, Dörner cites research showing that prenatal stress produced bisexual behavior in adult male rats. He goes on to hypothesize that prenatal stress was responsible for the development of homosexuality in adult human males. He conducted a retrospective study of German men born in "the stressful period" during and shortly after World War II and found "more homosexuals" were born in that time. He also compared histories of 100 "bi- and homosexual men" with 100 heterosexual controls regarding stressful events during their mother's pregnancies and found greater reports of stress in the prenatal histories of the former.

The evolution of Dörner's theoretical reasoning shows how difficult it is to tread the slippery slope between the narratives of normal variants, discussed below, and theories of pathology. His early work (Dörner et al., 1975) offered a relatively unambiguous pathological point of view. Not only was homosexuality a result of maternal stress in pregnancy, it might be a preventable condition: "Theoretically, a preventive therapy of sexual differentiation disturbances could be accomplished during these critical prenatal organizational periods" (p. 7). Ten years later, moreover, Dörner was still saying "sexual deviations appear to be avoidable, at least in part, by preventing prenatal stressful events and/or abnormal levels of sex hormones and neurotransmitters during a critical period of sex-specific brain differentiation" (1986, p. 19). He drew analogies with diabetes mellitus studies that show children are at greater risk for developing the illness if their mothers had diabetes during pregnancy: "In view of these data, we have predicted for many years that a genuine prophylaxis of diabetes mellitus may become possible by preventing hyperglycemia in pregnant women and hence hyperinsulinemia [with subsequent adult diabetes] in fetuses and newborns" (p. 21). He evoked the concept of *teratogens*, agents causing birth defects, and with a novel metaphor, extended the concept beyond the physical domain into the psychological:

> Our request for many years that teratology of structures, i.e., teratomorphology, should be supplemented by teratology of functions, i.e., teratophysiology, *teratopsychology* and even teratoimmunology, appears to be of outstanding practical relevance for preventive medicine. I am convinced that many developmental disorders and diseases can be prevented and that the capabilities of body and mind can be improved by avoiding and/or correcting abnormal levels of systemic hormones and/or neurotransmitters during critical developmental periods of the brain [Dörner, 1986, pp. 24–25, emphasis added].

Several years later, however, while retaining the pathological aspects of his theory, Dörner appears to rethink the logical consequences of the teratopsychological view. This appears to be a response to criticisms from those who believe homosexuality is a normal variant of human sexuality. He creates a complex classification system that includes distinctions between something called healthy homosexuality "without desire and need of therapy" and unhealthy outcomes leading to homosexuality "with desire and need of therapy, somatic pseudohermaphroditism, or transsexualism" (Dörner, 1989, p. 17). Dörner vainly struggles in the attempt to salvage a pathological theory by denying its own logical conclusions. He does so by offering a somewhat unusual definition of normal:

> Stressful social events are general attributes of healthy human beings. Consequently, homosexuality caused by . . . early social events [i.e., maternal stress during pregnancy], as we have found, can no longer be considered as illness and should be canceled as soon as possible in the WHO classification of diseases. The more so as there is no desire and need for therapy in homosexuals without specific complications. Furthermore, the complete tolerance and acceptance of bi- and homosexualities as natural sexual variants should be recognized as soon as possible by the WHO, UNESCO and World Church Council as well. . . . Our experimental and clinical studies of the past two decades suggest that genuine bi- and homosexuality per se may be considered as natural, biopsychosocial, gene and/or environment-dependent sanogenetic and not pathogenetic developmental processes of the brain, which are mediated by hormones and/or neurotransmitters [Dörner et al., 1991, pp. 146–149].

Dörner's work raises the issues of what is healthy and what is unhealthy. Similar questions plagued the American Psychiatric Association (APA) in its controversial 1973 decision to delete homosexuality from its *Diagnostic and Statistical Manual—Second Edition (DSM—II)* (American Psychiatric Association, 1968). In order to find a middle ground between pathological theories and those of normal variants, the *DSM-II* coined the diagnosis of *sexual orientation disturbance*:

> This category is for individuals whose sexual interests are directed primarily toward people of the same sex and who are either bothered by, in conflict with or wish to change their sexual orientation. This diagnostic category is distinguished from homosexuality, which by itself does not constitute a psychiatric disorder. Homosexuality per se is a form of irregular sexual development and like other forms of irregular

sexual development, which are not by themselves psychiatric disorders, is not listed in this nomenclature of mental disorders [quoted in Bayer, 1981, p. 128; also see Krajeski, 1996].[3]

A Solomonic solution, like the APA's, is one way to find a balance between narratives of pathology and normal variants. Friedman (1988), on the other hand, takes a different tack. His psychoanalytic narrative begins with a pathological event but he immediately takes the story in a direction of tolerance and acceptance. It should be noted that Friedman (1976a,b, 1997; Friedman and Downey, 1993, 1994) is an early challenger of psychoanalytic orthodoxy's stigmatization of homosexuality (cf. Bieber, 1976; Socarides, 1976). But Friedman, like Dörner, also believes some types of homosexuality are prenatally caused by deficient androgen exposure in the womb that causes a subsequent disturbance in the development of a masculine gender identity in young boys. Overtly effeminate homosexuality, he believes, results from this "feminine or unmasculine self-concept" independent of family constellations: "A strong case can be made for the hypothesis that a feminine or unmasculine self-concept during childhood is not only associated with the emergence of predominant or exclusive homosexuality in men, it is the single most important causal influence" (p. 74). However, the pathological, prenatal condition corrects itself in adolescence, leaving the affected individual's gender identity repaired, although an attraction to the same sex remains as a residual effect. In other words, an effeminate gay man's attraction to men was a feminine trait which grew out of an early gender identity disturbance and this residual same-sex attraction persisted into adulthood, even after the gender identity disturbance managed to correct itself.

Although some studies have shown childhood gender nonconformity to be a strong correlate of adult homosexuality (Bell, Weinberg, and Hammersmith, 1981, p. 76), it is not a universal trait in the development of a gay identity. Furthermore, attempts to frame boyhood effeminacy in the language of pathology are criticized by those who see it as a normal developmental step for some gay men (Sedgwick, 1991; Corbett, 1996, 1997). Nevertheless, Friedman's theory is unique among narratives of illness in its attempt to make the case that the biological immutability of homosexuality makes it unwise to try changing it with psychotherapy.

---

3. The *DSM-III* (American Psychiatric Association, 1980) later changed this category to "ego-dystonic homosexuality" in 1980 and then dropped that category in 1987 in the revised *DSM-III-R* (American Psychiatric Association, 1987). In the DSM-IV (American Psychiatric Association, 1994), the category of Sexual Disorder Not Otherwise Specified still includes "persistent and marked distress about sexual orientation" (p. 538).

By strategically locating the hypothetical trauma within a prenatal period of abnormality, Friedman then exhorts the analysts of an earlier generation to cease their search for the psychodynamic causes and cures of homosexuality.

Given their ubiquity in the culture, narratives of pathology are prevalent in psychotherapy. A gay man may link physical deformity, illness, and homosexuality. One patient began a session talking about feeling ashamed and embarrassed. This led to an association to a congenital anatomic deformity of his leg that had been cosmetically repaired with surgery when he was an adolescent. He then associated to his mother, who knew the patient was gay but who disapproved of his homosexuality:

> **J:** My mother's theory about my homosexuality is that I am gay because of my leg and my perception of my body. That it is a low self-esteem kind of decision, not based on a biological thing. Her logic is that homosexuality is about low self-esteem.

> **Th:** Your mother doesn't think much of homosexuality.

> **J:** That's her theory about it. It's hard to argue with that logic when someone believes that.

> **Th:** Since she holds homosexuality in low esteem, she believes the homosexual must hold himself in low esteem.

> **J:** Her theory is that all gay men are ugly. (The patient and therapist both laugh.) She would be surprised.

I Am What I Am—Narratives of Normal Variants

There are narratives that regard homosexuality as a *normal variant*, a phenomenon that occurs naturally and which is not a sign of illness or pathology. Normal variant theories, in an ongoing dialogue with narratives of pathology, criticize psychiatric and medical practitioners for drawing unwarranted conclusions from the patients who present for treatment of their homosexuality. As Kinsey (et al., 1948) noted, "the incidence of tuberculosis in a tuberculosis sanitarium is no measure of the incidence of tuberculosis in the population as a whole; and the incidence of disturbance over sexual activities, among the persons who come to a clinic, is no measure of the frequency of similar disturbances outside of clinics" (p. 201). Evelyn Hooker's (1957) innovative study supported Kinsey's assertion. She did her work at a time when psychoanalytic theories that pathologized homosexuality predominated among

American mental health practitioners. At the time she did her research, homosexuality was characterized as a quasi-psychotic disorder with global disturbances in mental and social functioning (Bergler, 1956). To test that claim, Hooker gave projective tests to 30 matched pairs of *non-patient* gay men and heterosexual male controls. "Blind" judges scored test results for psychopathology and were unaware of their subjects' sexual orientations. The gay men who were not in psychoanalytic treatment showed no evidence of greater psychopathology than the heterosexual controls, findings consistent with a normal variation theory.

As one patient tells it, the normal variant has its own biological rationale:

> **G:** I thought I was born gay. I knew I liked to watch guys on TV. I never thought "I liked men." I just accepted it. But when I was 14, I felt I had to get this fixed. I didn't know anyone who was gay. I saw an episode of *All in the Family* with a man in drag. I thought, "Is that what I am going to turn into?" He may not have been a homosexual, but that is what it meant to me. After I told my mother I was gay, I heard her on the phone, asking my grandmother what she did wrong. Now I'm sure it's my destiny.

> **Th:** What do you now think is the cause of your homosexuality?

> **G:** I think there's a gene that skips a generation. My Dad's brother was gay. I think it's genetic. I'm sure in some people they can go both ways. Something in their life pushes them one way or the other.

Themes of normal variants, such as Ulrich's (1864) Urnings, claim that gay men may be born different, but they are born natural. Left-handedness is often used as an analogy in these stories. Is left-handedness a disease or a normal variant? Today, the presence of left-handedness in a minority of people is not defined as an illness, although being left-handed may have disadvantages. In the past being left-handed did lead to social opprobrium; the word *sinister* is derived from a Latin root connoting the left side. And historically, analogous to gay men, left-handed children were often treated as if they were abnormal and cured of their antisocial habit by forcing them to write right-handed.

What differentiates the normal from the abnormal? Who decides? Is normal a synonym for a statistical mean? If not, how can it be declared normal—except by assertion? We find such a declaration in the writings of a normal variant theorist like Havelock Ellis (1938), a 20th-century pioneer of sexology. Like Freud, Ellis believed in bisexuality and that all sexual variations "must at some point include the procreative end" (p. 147) in order to be considered normal. *Deviations* were defined as heterosexual or homosexual activities that replaced "the desire for coitus," that is they deviated from reproductive goals. He implied the term was a neutral one and not a judgment of the activity. In Ellis's nosology, "not normal" was not a synonym for illness, and homosexuality was seen as inborn and natural:

> We seem justified in looking upon inversion [homosexuality] as a congenital anomaly—or, to speak more accurately, an anomaly based on congenital conditions—which if it is pathological, is only so in [the] sense that pathology is the science not of diseases but of anomalies, so that an inverted person may be as healthy as a color-blind person. Congenital sexual inversion is thus akin to a biological variation. It is a variation doubtless due to imperfect sexual differentiation, but often having no traceable connection with any morbid condition in the individual himself [p. 228–229].

A later, influential theorist of normal variants was Alfred Kinsey (et al., 1948), an insect taxonomist who brought a new scientific methodology to the study of human sexual behavior. After interviewing thousands of people about their sexual histories, he wrote "a report on what people do, which raises no question of what they should do, or what kinds of people do it" (p. 7). His approach was based on Darwin's (1859) observation on the evolutionary importance of variations within a species. He treated sexual behaviors as one of many possible variations within the human species, like hair or skin color. In his model of normal variants, there were six statistically significant ways for a man to achieve sexual climax or orgasm. He did not attempt to judge one form of sexual expression, or *outlet*, as superior to others on the basis of greater statistical frequency. Sexual outlets in men included, "self-stimulation (masturbation), nocturnal dreaming to the point of climax [wet-dreams], heterosexual petting to climax (without intercourse), true heterosexual intercourse, homosexual intercourse, and contact with animals of other species [bestiality]. There are still other possible sources of orgasm, but they are rare and never constitute a significant fraction of the outlet for any large segment of the population" (p. 157).

Kinsey both drew attention and objected to dichotomous thinking in sexuality research: "It would encourage clearer thinking on these matters if persons were not characterized as heterosexual or homosexual, but as individuals who have had certain amounts of heterosexual experience and certain amounts of homosexual experience" (p. 617). He reported 37 percent of the male population he surveyed had some homosexual experience leading to orgasm between adolescence and old age. This included individuals in "every social level, in every conceivable occupation, in cities and on farms, and in the most remote areas of the country" (p. 627). He challenged the stereotypes of homosexuality that abounded in the psychiatric literature of his time: "The homosexual male is supposed to be less interested in athletics, more often interested in music and the arts, more often engaged in such occupations as bookkeeping, dress design, window display, hairdressing, acting, radio work, nursing, religious service, and social work. The converse to all these is supposed to represent the typical heterosexual male" (p. 637). He reported that men who had homosexual experiences at one time in their lives may act heterosexually at other times, and vice versa. Some men engaged in homosexual and heterosexual acts during the same period of time:

> For instance, there are some who engage in both heterosexual and homosexual activities in the same year, or in the same month or week, or even in the same day. . . . The world is not to be divided into sheep and goats. Not all things are black nor all things white. It is a fundamental of taxonomy that nature rarely deals with discrete categories. Only the human mind invents categories and tries to force facts into separated pigeon-holes. The living world is a continuum in each and every one of its aspects. The sooner we learn this concerning human sexual behavior the sooner we shall reach a sound understanding of the realities of sex [p. 639].

Kinsey's 7-point scale categorized variations along a spectrum of sexual possibilities. At one end was the Kinsey 0, the man who was exclusively heterosexual and had never had an orgasm as a result of physical contact with another man or been aroused by someone of his own sex. At the other end was the Kinsey 6, the individual whose physical contacts and psychological responses were exclusively homosexual. The ratings of 1 to 5 represented different degrees of bisexuality with the Kinsey 3 being equally homosexual and heterosexual in both behavior and/or psychological attraction. Yet, despite his forceful opposition to dichotomous thinking, Kinsey nevertheless succumbed to it. His scale, although wider in its scope than other classification systems, and intended to address only the issue of variability, created a homosexuality/heterosexuality continuum that implicitly polarized human sexual experience.

Cross-cultural studies offer another way to test hypotheses about what are normal variants of human sexuality. Ford and Beach (1951) compared the sexual activities and beliefs of almost 200 cultures, in addition to the sexual activities of primates and other mammalian species. Their approach attempted to sort out biological aspects of sexuality, presumed to be universal in all societies, from social components expected to vary from culture to culture:

> Human societies appear to have seized upon and emphasized a natural, physiologically determined inclination toward intercourse between males and females, and to have discouraged and inhibited many other equally natural kinds of behavior. We believe that under purely hypothetical conditions in which any form of social control was lacking, coitus between males and females would prove to be the most frequent type of sexual behavior. At the same time, however, several other types of sexual activity would probably occur more commonly than they do in the majority of existing societies. . . . Interestingly enough, the picture [among animals] does not differ greatly from that presented by the cross-cultural evidence. In all infrahuman animals, heterosexual intercourse is the most frequent form of sexual behavior. To be sure, autoerotic and homosexual activities occur among animals, but they are less numerous than coitus despite the absence of cultural restrictions [p. 19].

It is possible that ethological studies have applicability to the understanding of human homosexuality. However, they do undermine traditional naturalistic arguments that homosexuality is not natural, meaning it does not occur in nature (Coleman, 1995). Ford and Beach also reviewed the status of homosexuality in 78 cultures. Twenty-eight societies, including the United States, disapproved of homosexuality. Forty-eight cultures approved of some forms of homosexuality. One group, the Tswana of Africa, disapproved of homosexuality in men and approved of it in women. Cultures that disapproved of homosexuality commonly reported that homosexual behavior was absent or rare or carried on in secret. In those societies, homosexuality was stigmatized from childhood on into adulthood by ridicule and punishment, and sometimes even the death penalty.

Two patterns predominated in those cultures that approved of some forms of male homosexuality. In the first, men who played the gender role of women, including the role of "wife," were known as *berdaches* (Williams, 1986). Their societies defined them as "the homosexual" because they adopted a female gender role. However, much like Dörner's mounting male rats, the man that the berdache married was considered normal by his culture. The second prevalent model of culturally sanctioned homosexuality was one in which homosexuality is part of the ritual of initiating younger men into adulthood (Herdt, 1994). In many cultures, the same-sex relationship between an older man and a younger boy, as was found in ancient Greece, is considered an integral part of the rites of passage.

In recent years, analytic writers have attempted to incorporate normal variant themes into psychoanalytic theory and practice. Isay (1989, 1991, 1996) has the historic distinction of being the first psychoanalyst to write in this area as an openly gay man. He attributes homosexuality's causes to unelaborated constitutional factors and describes the dilemma of a normative homosexual adaptation in a heterosexual world:

> I have come to believe that at ages three, four, five and six some homosexual children assume opposite gender characteristics in order to attract and sustain the attention of the father. These are usually such attributes as sensitivity, gentleness, and a lack of interest in aggressive sports. Some homosexual children may also seem noticeably feminine in manner, dress and behavior. I believe that they develop these characteristics for the same reason that heterosexual boys may adopt certain of their father's attributes, in order to attract, first the mother's interest and later, someone like the mother [Isay, 1989, p. 19].

Isay's approach is to reinterpret earlier psychoanalytic findings. He rejects the contention of Bieber et al. (1962) and Socarides (1968) that distant fathers contribute to the development of homosexuality in their sons. According to Isay, homosexuality is not caused by withdrawn fathers. Instead, fathers who sense their sons' innate same-sex attractions will anxiously withdraw from their own future gay child. In actuality, his alternative theory deftly illustrates that the psychoanalytic unconscious can be a projective screen open to multiple interpretations by analysts holding differing views of human development.

Although gay patients may present with a belief that homosexuality is a normal variant, those stories are usually a later, cognitive acquisition. A patient who has these beliefs often holds them in a tenuous relationship with more affectively charged narratives of pathology and immaturity acquired earlier in life. Such was the case of a patient who sought a consultation after being treated by a psychoanalyst for more than twenty years. Many of those years were spent trying to "cure" the patient of his homosexuality. The patient had been married when he began treatment, but was now divorced and identified himself at the time of the consultation as a gay man. He explained why the therapy had ended. During a session in which the patient spoke of the possibility that his homosexuality might be genetic in origin, he said the analyst called him "stupid." He left the office in an agitated state and the analyst subsequently called him at home to express concern about what had happened. The patient explained that he was upset because "You called me stupid." The analyst proceeded to clarify his statement and told the patient, "I didn't say you were stupid, I said the idea was stupid." The patient responded, "Well, it's the same thing, isn't it?"

When asked what he found so distressing about his interaction with the previous therapist, the patient had several associations. At one level, he felt the analyst had been rude and had called him stupid. But there was something more troubling to him. It had taken the patient a long time to reevaluate the theory of pathology that had, in part, motivated his earlier wish to change his sexual identity. He was now more comfortable with the idea that his homosexuality might be considered normal. Like many people today, he believed that if homosexuality has a genetic or biological origin, and that "gay people are born that way," then being gay should be considered normal. And if homosexuality was biologically normal, then it was not necessarily a bad thing. However the patient's newly-acquired belief in normal variant theory also co-existed with his much older theory of pathology. Whatever the analyst's motive for denigrating the biological, normal variant theory, the patient experienced it as an attack on his belief that being gay was good. He heard the analyst align himself with internalized, self-critical aspects of the patient that condemned his own homosexuality.

The Moral Underpinnings of Etiological Theories

As the above patient's experience illustrates, embedded within etiological theories are stories about the impact of homosexuality on the social order, on an individual's worth within that order, or the relationship between homosexuality and the intent of a higher force. A higher force may include God, other deities, spiritual beings, nature, or evolution. These tales offer instruction about what is valuable and what is devalued. Among the key words in the morality tales that underlie etiological theories are "social benefit" and "social harm," "good and evil," "health and illness," "adaptive and maladaptive," "holy and sinful," or "mature and childish."

Although moral concerns are more routinely ascribed to religious narratives, scientific theories of homosexuality are just as likely to be based upon the personal beliefs and values of the theorizer. And while some may assert that their opinions are grounded in objectivity or neutrality, a theorist who believes that homosexuality is a scientific issue and that its meanings lie outside the realm of morality maintains those convictions in opposition to cultural beliefs that define homosexuality as immoral. In fact, the assertion that homosexuality is a scientific issue, and not a moral one, is in itself a statement embedded in personal beliefs about science, religion, and human sexuality.

The moral themes embedded in narratives of immaturity are a case in point. In the 19th century, and even in the 20th, many scientists regarded human history as a progressive unfolding, a constant, linear flow of accumulated knowledge, with successive generations inexorably marching on to ever-increasing enlightenment and progress. One lesson to be learned from narratives of immaturity was that one could grow up to fulfill one's adult potential and become something better. In Freud's work, the resolution of the Oedipus complex (1924) was the sine qua non of adult development. It was only by achieving this step that one identified with the parents, gave up infantile sexual wishes, and came to accept reality. In other words, Freud explained how to attain the psychological status of an adult. But embedded in this descriptive stance was a very real sense of moral judgment. Adulthood required the mature exercise of one's sexual responsibilities:

> Since normal intercourse has been so relentlessly persecuted by morality—and also, on account of the possibilities of infection, by hygiene—what are known as the perverse forms of intercourse between the two sexes, in which other parts of the body take over the role of the genitals, have undoubtedly increased in social importance. These activities cannot, however, be regarded as being as harmless as analogous extensions [of the sexual aim] in love relationships. They are ethically objectionable, for they degrade the relationships of love between two human beings from a serious matter to a convenient game, attended by no risk and no spiritual participation [Freud, 1908, p. 200].

For Freud, treating sex as a childish game was immoral because it lacked "spiritual participation." Astonishing as such an assertion from an avowed atheist (Freud, 1927; Gay, 1987) might be, it is a rather prosaic example of the commingling of science and personal values. Freud's opinions about homosexuality could be similarly judgmental. Wortis, during his 1932 analysis with Freud, asked him why people shouldn't express both aspects of "bisexuality":

> Normal people have a certain homosexual component and a very strong heterosexual component. The homosexual component should be sublimated as it now is in society; it is one of the most valuable human assets, and should be put to social uses. One cannot give one's

impulses free rein. Your attitude reminds me of a child who just discovered everybody defecates and who then demands that everybody ought to defecate in public; that cannot be [Wortis, 1954, pp. 99–100].

It is worth noting here that Freud responded to his patient as if he were an unruly child, rather than a sick patient. In fact the moral judgments embedded in narratives of immaturity are somewhat different than those of narratives of pathology. For example, religious theories of the 18th century condemned homosexuality only to be later replaced by the pathologizing medical theories of the 19th (Szasz, 1974b; Konrad and Schneider, 1980). Yet theories of immaturity comprised a category that was neither religion's sin nor medicine's disease. By maintaining that homosexuality could be a normal part of the heterosexual's own experience, this paradigm was more inclusive and compassionate. It was an approach that allowed for the possibility that a gay man might sufficiently mature and become a heterosexual, if he was sufficiently motivated and if he received adequate adult, meaning heterosexual, guidance.

In the 20th century, theories of immaturity have become increasingly important to religious thought. They provide a way to deal with homosexuality that is more compassionate than historic religious traditions of outright condemnation or execution (Moberly, 1983a). Some religions have adopted a modern moral imperative to "love the sinner but hate the sin." A gay man does not have to be automatically ejected from his religious group and can even be embraced in the hope that he renounces his homosexuality. This is one point made in a brochure advertising the organization Courage and EnCourage, an ex-gay ministry that tries to convert homosexuality to heterosexuality through religious means:

> Homosexuality is not the word of God—nor is it usually a person's choice. Homosexuality is an aspect of *underdeveloped sexuality* resulting from no one simple factor. *Homosexuality of itself is not a sin—it does not make a person sick or perverse. Homosexual acts, however, are wrong*—and do not lead a person to deeper life in Jesus Christ. . . . We are not the cause of our loved one's homosexuality but we are responsible to help them live and grow as Catholic Christians. Reparative *growth* to a fuller possession of heterosexuality is possible for those so motivated. This is never easy or overnight—it demands serious commitment to emotional and spiritual growth. It is not to be forced on anyone but it is a viable option.

The religious adoption of Freud's narrative of immaturity by the Roman Catholic church strongly illustrates how etiological theories make the strangest bedfellows:

The existence of a close link between emotions and sexuality and their interdependence in the wholeness of a personality cannot be denied, even though these two things are diversely understood. In order to talk about a person as mature, his *sexual instinct* must have overcome two *immature* tendencies, *narcissism* and homosexuality, and must have arrived at heterosexuality. This is the first step in sexual development, but a second step is also necessary, namely "love" must be seen as a gift and not a form of selfishness. The consequence of this development is sexual conduct on a level that can be properly called "human" . . . *Sexual maturity represents a vital step in the attainment of psychological adulthood* [National Conference of Catholic Bishops, 1982, p. 167, emphasis added].

Like theories of immaturity, narratives of pathology also contain underlying values, most often seen in the tendency to use illness as a synonym for immorality. However despite the claims by pathologizing theorists that their models are scientifically objective, the relationship between any physical illness and these theories is entirely metaphoric (Szasz, 1974a). For example, the deficiency model in medicine attributes physical symptoms to the absence of an external substrate required for normal growth and development. Typical examples of such illness are vitamin-deficiency diseases, like scurvy and rickets. Inadequate quantities of Vitamins C or D can have damaging, even lethal physical consequences. Moberly (1983a), a fundamentalist Christian therapist who defines homosexuality as an illness, takes literary liberties with this model and proposes that as a child, a gay man lacked a good relationship with his father: "the homosexual . . . has suffered from some deficit in the relationship with the parent of the same sex. . . . Any incident that happens to place a particular strain on the relationship between the child and the parent of the same sex is potentially causative" (pp. 2–3). Unfortunately, Moberly cannot objectively define an ideal parental-child relationship. Unlike a vitamin, the nature of this particular nutrient is entirely subjective. In addition, her theory rests upon a model of an inscrutable unconscious whose operations are not only subjective, they are apparently immune to classification. Her post hoc reasoning offers parents few useful guidelines on how to supply adequate psychological nourishment to their child or to prevent homosexuality:

> The common factor in every case [of homosexuality] is disruption in the attachment to the parent of the same sex, however it may have been caused. Whatever the particular incident may be, it is something that has been experienced as hurtful by the child, whether or not intended as hurtful by the parent . . . it must be emphasized that this

relational defect may not be evident, or not more than partially evident to appearances. At the conscious level an adjustment may be made that leaves few or even no signs of disturbance. The family relationships of a homosexual may in a number of instances seem to be good, indeed, in such cases they are good at a certain level. This is not an objection to the present hypothesis, since what we are speaking of is intrapsychic damage at a deep level, much of which may not be overt or conscious. Similarly, it may not always be readily evident what led to the deficit in the first place. The cause may not be readily recognized, or recognized for what it is [p. 4].

Narratives of immaturity and pathology often wear their morality on their sleeves. In contrast, theories of normal variants, often presented as scientific, neutral, or objective, are more circumspect about declaring their underlying moral beliefs. These narratives prize rational and logically derived solutions more than emotional or spiritual ones. For example, condemnations of homosexuality based upon literal interpretations of the Bible fall within the latter category and are treated as products of ignorance, prejudice, or superstition. Theorists of normal variants also have a view of the social order that sees potential value in individual variation:

Until the extent of any type of human behavior is adequately known, it is difficult to assess its significance, either to the individuals who are involved or to society as a whole; and until the extent of the homosexual is known, it is practically impossible to understand its biologic or social origins. It is one thing if we are dealing with a type of activity that is unusual, without precedent among other animals, and restricted to peculiar types of individuals within the human population. It is another thing if the phenomenon proves to be a fundamental part, not only of human sexuality, but of mammalian patterns as a whole [Kinsey et al., 1948, pp. 610–611].

In accordance with their scientific beliefs, normal variant theorists feel society should tolerate individual differences, including those involving sexuality, because the evolutionary plan is not fixed and increased variations *add* to the richness of life (Gooren, 1990). Witness Kinsey (et al., 1948) taking umbrage with social exhortations for sexual conformity:

The publicly pretended code of morals, our social organization, our marriage customs, our sex laws, and our educational and religious systems are based upon an assumption that individuals are much alike sexually, and that it is an equally simple matter for all of them to confine their behavior to the single pattern which the mores dictate. . . .

> Even the scientific discussions of sex show little understanding of the
> range of variations in human behavior. More often the conclusions are
> limited by the personal experience of the author [pp. 197–199].

In its treatment of homosexuality, sociobiology (Wilson, 1975) can
be read as an evolutionary morality tale that hypothesizes how social
benefits are provided by gay people. It begins with the assumption that
homosexuality's ongoing presence in populations, despite cultural stigma
and a "homosexual's" lack of self-reproduction, suggests a biological origin of adaptive value. As it is built upon stereotypes of homosexuality,
the fact that gay people can and do reproduce is irrelevant to this theory's narrative thread. It is a story that can only be understood by looking at two of its underlying biological analogies: sickle-cell anemia and
the altruistic behavior of social insects.

Sickle-cell anemia is a genetic condition present in individuals who
have two autosomal recessive genes (SS) for a type of hemoglobin that
causes red blood cells to have an abnormal or sickle-shape that leads to
many damaging medical complications. The condition can be debilitating, yet sickle-cell trait persists in many populations, despite it's maladaptive or illness-causing potential. Its persistence, however, may be due
to the prevalence of malaria, an infectious disease endemic to areas
whose populations show the sickle-cell trait. In fact, individuals who are
heterozygous (designated HS), bearing a dominant gene for normal
hemoglobin and a recessive gene for the abnormal hemoglobin of sickle-
cell anemia, are more resistant to malaria than the homozygous dominant (designated HH) who has normal hemoglobin and no sickle-cell
trait at all. However, in malarial zones, the so-called healthy individual
(HH) is at greater risk than the sicker heterozygote (HS). Illustrating
nature's aversion to the clear-cut distinctions so prized by human beings,
the same gene (S) that causes debilitating illness in one setting (SS) can
afford an adaptive measure of protection and greater health in another
(HS). Analogously, genetic homosexuality should lead to extinction
since gay men are "less likely" to reproduce. But if the hypothetical gay
gene offered some adaptive value, like sickle-cell trait, that could explain
its continued presence in populations.

This leads to another analogy, one drawn from studies of social
insect species, such as bees and wasps, in which many members of the
colony do not reproduce themselves but may derive a genetic benefit in
helping their queen reproduce. The feeding of the fertile queen and the
care of her young by non-reproducing workers is defined as *altruistic*
behavior. According to this theory, because workers share some of the
genetic traits of their queen, they have a reasonable likelihood of contin-

uing their own genetic line by providing scarce resources to the queen and her offspring. This phenomenon, referred to as *kin selection*, could be called a genetically selfish solution masquerading in the guise of altruistic behavior.

The next step in this line of reasoning is the theory of *homosexual altruism*. It hypothesizes that a gene causing homosexuality, while interfering with the individual's own reproductive capacity, may guarantee him a measure of genetic success even if he is incapable of reproducing himself. The "homosexual" increases the likelihood of passing on his own DNA by taking care of the children of his reproducing siblings. Having an increased number of caretakers per child would be likely to increase the child's reproductive success and favor transmission of the homosexual gene. Unsurprisingly, Wilson's altruistic "homosexual," like his counterparts in theories of immaturity and pathology, is also constructed from stereotypic gender roles (Dickemann, 1995). In this case, being a gay man is defined as being a helper, rather than a hunter. That is to say he fits the stereotypes of a man who is not as athletic as other men or as one who is interested in domestic or other feminine pursuits:

> The homosexual members of primitive societies may have functioned as helpers, either while hunting in company with other men or in domestic occupations at the dwelling sites. Freed from the special obligations of parental duties, they could have operated with special efficiency in assisting close relatives. Genes favoring homosexuality could then be sustained at a high equilibrium by kin selection alone. It remains to be said that if such genes really exist they are almost certainly incomplete in penetrance and variable in expressivity, meaning that which bears of the genes develop the behavioral trait and to what degree depends on the presence of modifier genes and the influence of the environment [Wilson, 1975, p. 555].

The projection of modern social stereotypes onto hunter-gatherer societies does have a narrative appeal. In fact, the writer Edmund White (1991), exploring aspects of gay culture in the United States, actually did find a gay "helper":

> Oh, that's my play son. I guess that's a Southern expression. He's a neighbor boy I'm helping to raise. When his parents can't buy him something, I pitch in. I pick him up after his job as a dishwasher at midnight and bring him home. I teach him things and take him places. I also have a play daughter. She's just fifteen and she got pregnant, so now I have a play granddaughter as well [p. 246].

Today, biological theorists argue on the side of nature and assert that phenomena which occur in nature are normal and good (Fausto-Sterling, 1992). In the past, however, Thomas Aquinas argued from the naturalistic point of view and claimed that homosexuality was not a part of nature and therefore sinful and bad (Boswell, 1980; Pronk, 1993; Coleman, 1995). A contemporary secular belief that the presence of a phenomenon in nature removes it from the realm of morality is strongly opposed by religious conservatives. Instead, they compare homosexuality to murderous feelings or the genetic trait of alcoholism. Although the latter may also be part of the natural order, their expression must be controlled to maintain the social order.

Conclusions

As this chapter has shown, attempts to explain the origins of same-sexuality all too often rely on a homosexual straw man to make a case for immaturity, pathology, or normal variation. Each of these approaches contains a moral narrative about the harm or benefits of homosexuality. The search for homosexuality's origins is part of an ancient and venerable tradition in philosophy, literature, science, and psychoanalysis. However, before getting tangled in questions of etiology in psychotherapy, therapists would do well to familiarize themselves with the literature on this subject. Hopefully, this chapter will leave the reader with a feeling of uncertainty regarding the actual state of knowledge in these areas, and with an understanding that the causes of both homosexuality and heterosexuality still remain a mystery. Yet, ignorance of etiologies can lead to other kinds of knowledge. And although it may not lead to a definitive conclusion about the true origin of a particular patient's homosexuality, a willingness to tolerate our current lack of knowledge may help the therapist to generate narratives that are sufficiently helpful and internally consistent to a patient.

For any particular patient, an etiological theory is likely to have a personal meaning and an affective charge. Often, different etiological viewpoints can be expressed by a single patient:

Th: What do you think causes homosexuality?

K: I think there is something of nature in there [Ellis, 1938; Kinsey, et al., 1948]. I can think of myself having gay impulses and gay fantasies before the most seminal event of my life when I was 10 and my father died [Freud, 1905]. I remember being fascinated by male anatomy, fooling around with the boy across the street before he died. There was a theory that loss of a father figure [Bieber, et al., 1962] or dominance of a father figure [Freud, 1923a] made a boy gay. It makes some intuitive sense that having suffered that loss and being predisposed to an interest in boys, that may have helped [Freud, 1910a; Stekel, 1922]. I may have been consciously trying to fill that void when my father died. But my sensory titillation has always come from males, not from females [Friedman, 1988; Isay, 1989]. It's an interesting thing, I was always a sensitive child. I have to wonder what the connection is between sensitivity and what we call feminine characteristics, and the tendency of people with feminine characteristics to become gay [Ulrichs, 1864; Green, 1987]. Do we search for the other [Rado, 1969]? The image that strength is intrinsically attractive to those who don't have it [Moberly, 1983a; Nicolosi, 1991]. Is it a need to be taken care of? The argument is that it clearly is a powerful dynamic that is not at all susceptible to choice, impervious to my volition [LeVay, 1993; Hamer et al., 1993; Hamer and Copeland, 1994]. I don't know why anyone would choose to be gay in a society like ours [White, 1994]. There also seems to be a lot of evidence among monozygotic twins raised in different households and a large coincidence of homosexuality among them [Bailey and Pillard, 1991]. Maybe I'm predisposed to my inkling that there is some nature. I've been thinking about sexual compulsives because a lot of my friends are. It seems to be that sexual compulsivity stems from a sense of hatred in being gay. It mutates into a sense that is unworthy of intimacy or commitment from another [Nicolosi, 1991]. This is one quarter intuition and three quarters the way people act. In my experience they have been really dysfunctional and tried to get into committed relationships and they feel smothered [Socarides, 1968].

A therapist who authoritatively claimed to know the definitive etiology of homosexuality would have great difficulty entering the wider dimensions of this patient's experience. A *knowing* approach would prevent the therapist from appreciating how etiological narratives primarily serve as vehicles for other issues. For example, a gay man asking "What is the cause of homosexuality?" may simply be asking "Why do I feel different from everybody else?" As a result, focusing on homosexuality's etiology is not necessarily the most meaningful way to conduct a psychotherapy. One might reasonably ask how psychotherapy would unfold if a therapist were to spend inordinate amounts of time with a heterosexual patient searching for the origins of those sexual attractions. Yet such time-consuming endeavors are quite widespread in psychoanalytic treatments of gay men. It is only by recognizing the often irrational underpinnings of the analytic search for origins that allows the focus of treatment to shift from finding the causes of homosexuality to helping patients understand what it means to them to be gay.

This alternative approach in psychotherapy with gay men can have interesting results. Patients, like therapists, try to resolve important issues they cannot understand by filling in the "gaps" (Sullivan, 1954). All theories fill their gaps in actual knowledge by extrapolating from the data and generating hypotheses. There is nothing wrong or unusual about doing this. It is how we make sense of the world. One unfortunate consequence of today's politicized debate about homosexuality is that rather than engaging in a complex discussion of shared ignorance, there is a taking of sides and a resort to reductionistic dichotomies of nature versus nurture. The politics of scientific debate is an interesting social phenomenon and worthy of study in itself, but it is not particularly useful to clinicians or patients. The work of therapy can only be advanced by acknowledging the gaps in our own knowledge. In this way, curiosity can emerge, true learning can take place, and one may see something new about the patient that neither he nor anyone else has seen before.

4

THERAPEUTIC MEANINGS OF ANTIHOMOSEXUALITY

During the sixties, as I spoke to audiences about the unfairness of the prevailing attitudes [toward homosexuality], I was stunned by the severity of the reaction. In Chicago, I needed an escort to get from a radio station to my hotel. Later, in Baltimore, a caller to a radio program threatened my life and was encouraged by the interviewer. In New Jersey, a bomb threat emptied out a church in which I was to speak. . . . In 1967 I coined the term homophobia to describe this irrational reaction.

George Weinberg, *Society and the Healthy Homosexual* (1972)

Violence against lesbians and gay men is not a new problem. People who call themselves gay or whose sexual partner is of their own gender have long been subjected to physical brutality.

Herek and Berrill, *Hate Crimes* (1992)

Thou shalt not lie with mankind, as with womankind: it is abomination.

Leviticus 18:22

In all likelihood, a gay man will come into treatment having endured some experiences of ostracism, shaming, rejection, and perhaps even violence. The bases upon which these experiences will have been rationalized by those who perpetrated them will vary. Furthermore, the ways in which these experiences may have been internalized, and rationalized by a gay man will vary as well. It is highly probable that a therapist treating a gay man will also have been exposed to the cultural attitudes that led to the enactment and rationalization of these experiences, and will therefore have to contend with their internalized aspects. In the course of psychotherapy with a gay patient, the gay therapist is likely to draw upon personal experiences in this arena in trying to explore what such experiences mean to the patient. If the therapist is not gay, the gay patient's experience of antihomosexuality will inevitably force the therapist to reexamine the belief systems with which he or she was raised (Marmor, 1996).

This chapter addresses how cultural attitudes leave a psychological imprint on a gay man, how they affect his own self-acceptance, and the ways in which this can emerge in treatment. It should be noted at the outset of this discussion of the therapeutic meanings of antihomosexuality that it is the rare member of society who has not been exposed to some degree of antihomosexual bias that is both culturally normative and embedded in other value systems. Accordingly, this chapter also examines some of the value systems that seek to rationalize antihomosexual bias, as well as looking at how the experiences that arise on the basis of these attitudes re-emerge in the consulting room.

Homophobia

Some authors, using the language of science, have hypothesized that the cultural denigration of homosexuality is the result of biological processes that insure reproductive survival (Socarides, 1994). However, the theoretical assumptions that biologize antihomosexual attitudes have been thoughtfully challenged (Kinsey, Pomeroy and Martin, 1948; Ford and Beach, 1951; Wilson, 1975; Foucault, 1980; Bayer, 1981; Butler, 1990; Gonsiorek, 1991; Fausto-Sterling, 1992; DeCecco and Parker, 1995; Cabaj and Stein, 1996). And although fundamentalist readings of religious documents attribute religious animus toward homosexuality to the unambiguous commands of a higher deity (Moberly, 1983a; Harvey, 1987; Coleman, 1995), modern scholars and religious figures have suggested alternative interpretations of that traditional antipathy (Boswell, 1980; Pronk, 1993; Helminiak, 1994; White, 1994).

Another perspective is that of social constructivists, who offer alternatives to the essentialist and religious explanations of antihomosexual attitudes. Just as some authors have argued that the meanings of any sexual activity are culturally and psychologically elaborated (Rubin, 1982; Butler, 1990, 1993; Dimen, 1991, 1995; Schwartz, 1993, 1995, 1996; Schoenberg, 1995; D'Ercole, 1996; Lesser, 1996), data regarding antihomosexuality's manifestations support the view that it, too, is a socially constructed phenomenon. In a constructivist view, male homosexuality's cultural meanings may differ from those of female homosexuality, and one person's understanding of female or male homosexuality may differ from those of other individuals in the same culture (Chodorow, 1996). Thus, Ford and Beach (1951), in their aforementioned cross-cultural study, found that American society "disapproves of any form of homosexual behavior for males and females of all ages. In this it differs from the majority of human societies" (p. 125). They noted that in 64 percent "of societies other than our own for which information is available, homosexual activities of one sort or another are considered normal and socially acceptable for certain members of the community" (p. 130). They reported societies approving of homosexuality in men that did not necessarily approve of same-sex relationships between women, and vice versa. Why one culture denigrates same-sex feelings and relationships, while another chooses to treat it with religious reverence, is unknown (Herdt and Boxer, 1993; Herdt, 1994). However, Ford and Beach found no evidence of universal, antihomosexual attitudes as some psychoanalytically-informed authors have implied (Rado, 1969; Kardiner, 1956; McDougall, 1980; Nicolosi, 1991; Socarides, 1994).

Whatever its cause, the cultural disparagement of same-sex activities and feelings, in this culture and others, is both long-standing and widespread. However, scientific and clinical studies of antihomosexual attitudes are a relatively modern endeavor. Weinberg (1972) is generally credited with inventing the term *homophobia*. He defined *external homophobia* as the irrational fear and hatred that heterosexuals feel toward gay people and *internal homophobia* as the self-loathing gay people felt for themselves.[1]

---

1. It should be underscored that there has been a paucity of mainstream psychoanalytic articles about homophobia. For example, the term only appears in the *Journal of the American Psychoanalytic Association* for the first time in 1983 (Poland), and only as a passing remark in an unfavorable review of Marmor's *Homosexual*

The 150-year history of psychiatric diagnosis is one of constant additions and deletions to the diagnostic nomenclature (Bayer, 1981). To some, these changes represent a gradual accretion of scientific understanding. However, diagnostic changes may also represent the ways in which changing cultural values define psychiatric disorders. This is certainly the case in Weinberg's formulation, which transposes the medical model in a novel way: If same-sex attractions are not a mental illness, then perhaps intolerance of homosexuality might be considered one instead. Although Weinberg appears to believe that homophobia is a psychiatric disorder, the perspective of his writing ingeniously demonstrates how a 20th-century theorist can construct a clinical syndrome in the same way that 19th-century scientists created a disease called homosexuality (Greenberg, 1988; Katz, 1995). Weinberg suggested several origins of homophobia: the religious motive, the secret fear of being homosexual, repressed envy, and the threat to values. His etiological formulations were meant to be a psychodynamic counterweight to the then-prevailing psychoanalytic theories of close-binding mothers and distant or hostile fathers hypothesized to cause male homosexuality (Freud, 1910a; Bieber et al., 1962; Socarides, 1968). Weinberg's work has been followed by an ever-expanding literature devoted to studying intolerance of homosexuality. Herek (1984) expands the etiological discourse and attributes nine factors that cause individuals to have "negative attitudes toward homosexuality." These include: (1) having little contact with lesbians and gay men; (2) a lack of homosexual experiences of one's own; (3) perceiving one's own community as unaccepting of homosexuality; (4) residing in areas where homosexuality is not acceptable; (5) being older; (6) being less educated; (7) identifying oneself as religious or as belonging to a conservative religion; (8) being less permissive about sexuality in general; and (9) expressing high levels of authoritarianism.

Weinberg's contribution has had an enormous impact on the postmodern discourse of homosexuality generally, and is noted every time an antihomosexual writer feels obligated to deny being homophobic. Routine denials of homophobia and bigotry are now part of the discourse of mental health professionals who still cling to the theory that

---

Behavior (1980). The historical equation of homosexuality with psychopathology may explain the analytic discomfort with the concept of homophobia. This assumption is supported by the observation that as organized psychoanalysis accepted the normal variant paradigm in the early 1990s (Roughton, 1995), the term concurrently entered mainstream psychoanalytic journals as a subject worthy of clinical discussion (Isay, 1991; Moss, 1992, 1997; Blechner, 1993; Lesser, 1993; Schwartz, 1993; Friedman and Downey, 1995).

homosexuality is an illness. Consider Nicolosi's (1991) contention that "many who use the term [homophobia] neglect to acknowledge that without being 'phobic' about it, it is quite possible to reject the gay life-style within the framework of one's own values . . . it is simply a nonacceptance of the [gay] life-style as a viable and natural alternative" (p. 138). This kind of assertion was unheard of in an earlier era, when curing homosexuality was characterized as a purely medical or scientific endeavor (Bergler, 1956; Bieber et al., 1962; Socarides, 1968, 1978; Ovesey, 1969; Hatterer, 1970). Nicolosi, however, argues that he does not suffer from a psychiatric disorder called homophobia. Instead, he believes his intolerant attitudes are expressions of his innate self and values. He refutes his homophobia, although not his antihomosexuality, by adopting a position that oddly parallels the beliefs of gay men who also declare that they do not suffer from an illness, homosexuality, but that they are only expressing their own values, or even more, their true selves.

One of homophobia's most powerful currents is felt in the cultural equation that commonly identifies homosexuality with effeminacy. A gay man can be physically indistinguishable from a heterosexual one. Yet the conflation of homosexuality with effeminacy is widespread and a common expression of antihomosexuality is the contempt displayed toward men who adopt behaviors or attitudes that are culturally designated as feminine. Chauncey (1994) suggests that these antifeminine attitudes became prevalent in the late 19th century when "middle-class men began to define themselves more centrally on the basis of their difference from women . . . to define themselves in opposition to all that was 'soft' and womanlike" (pp. 114–115). Nevertheless, there have always been men who challenged those values. Quentin Crisp (1968), an Englishman marked by effeminate behavior since childhood, defiantly chose to flaunt his differences in the first half of the 20th century:

> I was from birth an object of mild ridicule because of my movements—especially the perpetual flutter of my hands—and my voice. Like the voices of a number of homosexuals, this is an insinuating blend of eagerness and caution in which even such words as "hello" and "good-bye" seem not so much uttered as divulged. But these natural outward and visible signs of inward and spiritual disgrace were not enough. . . . I wanted it to be known that I was not ashamed and therefore had to display symptoms that could not be thought to be accidental. . . . I began to wear make-up [p. 28].

The social contempt of male effeminacy, evocatively described in Crisp's autobiography, is also found in the psychoanalytic literature. The following authors' technical language barely conceals their disdain for the effeminate subject:

> The effeminate male is thought to be "like" a female in certain ways: voice, intonation, gesture, posture, and other behaviors. The patterns of behavior associated with effeminacy in males, however, are not typical of women. Exaggerated shrugging, "wrist-breaking," lisping, hand-to-hip posturing, effusiveness, and so forth, when observed in women appear to be bizarre rather than feminine. When these gesture-voice affectations are taken on by effeminate males, the motoric pattern does not suggest freedom of movement but gives the appearance of constriction and inhibition since the movements are confined to small arcs in space; they are directed inwardly toward the midline of the body rather than away from it [Bieber et al., 1962, p. 188].

The low social status accorded to such individuals leads some parents, fearful that their children will grow up to be gay, to seek professional treatment for their effeminate sons. The parental struggles to come to terms with a son's effeminacy have generated emotional arguments. Richard Green's (1987) *The Sissy Boy Syndrome* is a prospective study that tracked the development of a group of gender-atypical boys into adulthood. In addition to displaying unconventional gender behavior, like preferring to play with dolls, most of these boys also reported the wish to be a girl. Seventy-five percent of the children Green studied grew up to be gay (p. 370). However, most of these boys were diagnosed as having childhood gender identity disorder (GID) and, as such, are not representative of most children who grow up gay who did not have childhood GID. In his report, Green defends the decision of parents who had their children treated, not only to change their effeminate behavior, but to prevent adult homosexuality:

> Should parents have the prerogative of choosing therapy for their gender-atypical son? Suppose that boys who play with dolls rather than trucks, who role-play as mother rather than as father, and who play only with girls tend disproportionately to evolve as homosexual men. Suppose that parents know this, or suspect this. The rights of parents to oversee the development of children is a long-established principle. Who is to dictate that parents may not try to raise their children in a manner that maximizes the possibility of a heterosexual outcome? If that prerogative is denied, should parents also be denied the right to raise their children as atheists? Or as priests? [Green, 1987, p. 260].

Certainly, other clinicians have emphasized that the treatment of the anxiety, depression, and family stress associated with GID does not necessarily require prophylactic measures against adult homosexuality (Coates and Wolfe, 1997, p. 468). Thus, from another perspective, Green is criticized for rationalizing parents' homophobia in their attempts to prevent adult homosexuality in effeminate boys (Mass, 1990). Sedgwick (1991), for example, finds him

> obscenely eager to convince parents that their hatred and rage at their effeminate sons is really only a desire to protect them from peer-group cruelty—even when the parents name *their own* feelings as hatred and rage. Even when fully one-quarter of parents of gay sons are *so* interested in protecting them from social cruelty that, when the boys fail to change, their parents kick them out on the street. Green is withering about mothers who display any tolerance of their sons' cross-gender behaviors [pp. 162–163].

Parents, of course, do have the right to transmit their own values to their children. And it is the fortunate parent indeed whose child chooses the vocation or religion preferred by the parent. However, when mental health professionals and parents join the social chorus of derision, presumably for a boy's own good, one can appreciate how being labeled effeminate at an early age can entail great suffering. Furthermore, the prophylactic treatments of homosexuality may produce predictable results. Consider Green's presentation of a young man, initially brought into treatment for boyhood effeminacy, who eventually claimed a heterosexual identity at the age of twenty-one. After years of treatment that encouraged him to adopt conventional, masculine behaviors, the successfully treated ex-sissy now shares his parents' homophobic values and stereotypes. As he tells Green (1987):

> If somebody comes up to me for advice, I can advise them . . . it [gay life] is not a good scene. I don't know any [stable] gay couple . . . the ones that get along are vicious little motherfuckers. I see old gay men that are just so lonely and unhappy, and they try so hard and they get so much rejection, and everybody's got that little thing about hiring gay people. There's one in my apartment building right now . . . he is so pathetic . . . and I really felt sorry for him [pp. 216–217].

It should be repeated that childhood effeminacy is not a pathognomonic feature in the development of a gay identity. Not all gay men have histories of childhood effeminacy, although many of them recall being afraid and even terrified that they might have been so perceived. Some, however, may recall the childhood thought that being attracted to a man was, in itself, a feminine quality. Corbett (1996), for example, quotes a gay man's paradoxically-gendered adolescent fear that having "an erection in the locker room would [mean] to be seen as a girl" (p. 450). Isay (1989) and Corbett (1993) have both described distancing by fathers from sons who are not considered to be sufficiently masculine. And many gay men do recount common childhood events as disdainful, paternal judgments of their gender identity. One patient told of a fight with an older brother who broke his nose. He ran into the house, bleeding and howling in pain. The patient remembers being yelled at by his father for "screaming like a girl." He was rebuked for this unmanly behavior, although his brother was not chastised for hitting the patient. In retrospect, the patient always believed that his brother was let off easily for "butching me up."

Such experiences of being shamed for perceived effeminacy may persist into young adulthood and they are certainly not restricted to gay men. Yet, consider the patient who shamefully tells of a letter of recommendation that made reference to his effeminate manner of speaking:

A: The professor wrote, "Despite an unusual quality to his voice, A is regarded by his colleagues as a regular guy." I can remember being puzzled by that. He said he had to say something negative, or the reference wouldn't seem credible to someone who was reading it. It doesn't sound like a big deal, but it was. He was someone I really respected. That was the first time I ever thought about my voice. It is also when I lost my voice.

Th: What do you mean?

A: It hurt me. Like I said, "I lost my voice." I felt self-conscious when I spoke.

Th: What did you think he meant by that comment?

A: (On the verge of tears) I knew what he meant. He was saying that I sounded effeminate. I knew he was saying that I was gay but that I was seen by my classmates as a regular guy. It felt like an attack, even though the rest of the reference had nice things to say. For me, that colored the entire reference. That comment is the only part of the letter that I remember. He was head of the department, very intelligent and very brilliant.

Th: The professor was intelligent and brilliant but not very tactful.

A: I guess he tried to word it as tactfully as he could.

Th: The essence of a successfully tactful comment should be that its recipient is not offended by it.

A: I thought, "Maybe it is me. Maybe I'm reading more into it than is there." Maybe he convinced me he had to say something to make me more credible. Even though I was ashamed to give that as a reference, I did. I would go on interviews knowing that the interviewers had read this. (He grabs himself and his whole body shudders) Oh God, this is awful.

The patient's near-apology for the professor's motives suggested that he was engaging in a defensive strategy. Some therapists, upon hearing their patients report the accumulation of a lifetime of homophobic attacks, unsympathetically describe gay men as "injustice collectors" (Bergler, 1956; Nicolosi, 1991). Their countertransferential attitude assumes that the grievances of gay people are either unjustified or exaggerated, or that gay people are too touchy and unforgiving. It is an attitude reinforced by an antihomosexual belief that lesbians and gay men have only themselves to blame for the ongoing experiences of hatred and prejudice with which they must contend on a regular basis. However, this patient, shuddering, suddenly experienced the actual intensity of his emotional responses. He had felt shamed by the letter. He had despairingly blamed himself for "reading more into it" rather than consider the possibility that the comment about his voice, regardless of the professor's actual motives, could be reasonably construed as hurtful. Furthermore, the patient's anxious confusion about the meaning of the letter caused him to participate in his own shaming every time he submitted it as a reference. It should be noted that in the developmental histories of many gay men, unintentional homophobic comments and attitudes of parents, teachers or other admired figures are commonly treated as both reasonable and normal. When a respected figure makes a hurtful remark in the guise of a helpful interaction, the subject of the assault may frequently believe his emotional responses are exaggerated and may become anxiously confused about the accuracy of his perceptions.

Th: That is quite a reference. "He talks like a faggot but he's OK."

A: That's really what he was saying. "He is a faggot, but he's a regular guy."

Th: Do you feel how hurt and angry you are?

A: (Deep sigh, followed by a tone of resignation) He was the head of the psychology department. He was also a minister, liked by everybody. He had a good sense of humor. He gave the spiel in class how homosexuality is wrong. I felt he was so wise. He knew I respected him. I've toyed with the idea of writing him a letter and telling him a different position on homosexuality. I thought about that, but then I thought, "He's too old." But every time the college sends me alumni stuff, I remember that letter and throw it in the garbage.

While some gay men are indeed effeminate, the equation of male homosexuality with effeminacy ultimately falls under the rubric of stereotyping. In stereotypical thought, all members of a group are perceived to have similar attributes (Allport, 1954). For example, all WASPS drink gin martinis, or all Jews are avaricious. For those who organize their experience through stereotypes, meeting someone who does not conform to their expectations does not disprove the rule. This is commonly expressed with a left-handed compliment, such as "Oh, you are not like other black people."

In addition to effeminacy, homophobia can be expressed in other clichés or caricatures of sexual identities. Common stereotypes of gay men include sexual promiscuity or compulsivity, a talent for the arts, a lack of courage, and a life doomed to loneliness. One contemporary homophobic stereotype is that gay men are mostly young, affluent, and politically represented beyond their numbers. This way of "perceiving gay people [as white, middle class, and male] allows one to ignore that some of us are women *and* people of color *and* working class *and* poor *and* disabled *and* old" (Smith, 1990, p. 101; also see Kertzner and Sved, 1996). Such a caricature of the gay community also underlies the Supreme Court's minority opinion defending Colorado's discriminatory Amendment Two.[2] Justice Scalia claimed that "because those who engage in homosexual conduct tend to reside in disproportionate numbers in certain communities, have high disposable income and of course care about homosexual-rights issues much more ardently than the public at large, they possess political power much greater than their numbers, both locally and statewide" (*New York Times*, 1996). The justice's resort to stereotypes can be contrasted with the more complex, political shadings of urban gay life in liberal New York City, as the following patient expresses his chagrin that many of his friends do not quite fit Justice Scalia's portrait of the politically active gay man:

> **B:** I feel defensive with my friends. Some of them are affluent. No one is rich, but no one is wondering where their next trip to Europe is coming from. I'm hearing people speak as if they were under siege. These nice gay friends who live in condos on Central Park West are agreeing with Rush Limbaugh. I say, "Wait a minute guys. Be careful. Remember there are people who hate gay men and want us dead. The next thing you know you are talking about family values, which means get us; get gay men." As I

---

2. In 1992, a referendum was passed in the state of Colorado that denied municipalities the right to offer civil rights protections to lesbians and gay men. This effectively nullified gay rights laws passed in some Colorado cities. The referendum was found unconstitutional by the Supreme Court in 1996 in the case of Romer v. Evans (Greenhouse, 1996).

pointed out to them, these are the people who believe that gays are the causes of social decay. I don't understand why my good friends are talking like this. What I'm hearing is a right-wing philosophy. None of these friends do anything for political causes. None of them give money to gay causes.

Th: Your friends don't just have a gay identity, they appear to have a conservative, white, upper-middle-class identity as well. In that role, they identify with the group in power.[3]

B: That's exactly it. I have problems with their not giving. I don't know why I should be friends with them.

A defensive resort to stereotyping is, of course, a human frailty which transcends sexual identities. Thus, conversely, caricatures of heterosexuality may emerge in a gay man's stereotyped fantasies of straight men. One patient began a session talking about a dispute with his work supervisor. As he related their exchange of words, he parenthetically described his boss as a "big, stupid straight man." When asked what that meant, he said he imagined his boss thought of the patient as a "weak, gay man." This then led to associations regarding the qualities and relative merits of being straight or gay. According to the patient, straight men were more self-assured but, in fact, their confidence was simply due to their tendency to be "dense." Furthermore, their insensitivity to others was the quality that allowed them to be more assertive. This patient experienced himself as bitchy—by which he meant effeminately angry—and tentative about asserting himself. He imagined the contempt in which his boss held him. When asked if he really believed that was what his boss thought, he said "No, that's what I think of myself." In this case, the stereotype of "the straight man" represented a complementary expression of the patient's internalized homophobia.

Gay men can sometimes stereotype heterosexuals in other ways. For example, "breeders" is a pejorative term some gay men use to ridicule heterosexual fecundity (Shilts, 1982); it mirrors the contempt embodied in the majority culture's denigrating stereotype of gay men as either sterile eunuchs or sexually promiscuous hedonists. In clinical work with gay men, a caricature of people's gender and sexuality may represent complementary expressions of internalized homophobia, although it may have other meanings as well. This observation is also true of patients who are not gay, and a therapist who is sensitive to the defensive use of

---

3. Closeted gay conservatives who defy cultural stereotypes have written quite revealing autobiographies (Bauman, 1986; Liebman, 1992; White, 1994).

stereotypes is better prepared to understand both their meanings and their counter-meanings in the therapeutic encounter.

Heterosexism

When gay patients feel themselves to be different, they sometimes attribute this sense of otherness to not being like heterosexuals. One patient presents an idealized view of "normal people," by which he means heterosexuals:

C: I'm rather envious of normal people.

Th: What do you envy?

C: Being able to be comfortable. Being able to relax. Being smug. Smug is comfortable. Being able to assume that you are right, and that you deserve it and that it is good. There, end of story.

This patient's stereotypes are based upon a widely-held belief system that regards heterosexuality as normal and natural and treats gay people as outsiders who are not. The same basic belief can be found in an essay by Joseph Wilson, a professor of public policy:

Nor does it seem plausible to me that a modern society resists homosexual marriages entirely out of irrational prejudice. Marriage is a union, sacred to most, that unites a man and a woman together for life. . . . Societies differ . . . scarcely at all over the distinctions between heterosexual and homosexual couples. The former are overwhelmingly preferred over the latter. The reason, I believe, is that these distinctions involve the nature of marriage and thus the very meaning—even more, the very possibility—of society [1996, p. 163].

In an argument against same-sex marriage, Wilson asks the reader to ponder not only the nature of marriage, but of society as well. In fact, it is the framing of the questions in the language of the *normal* and the *natural* that is an essential component of *heterosexism* (Morin and Garfinkle, 1978), looking at the world from a point of view that naturalizes and idealizes heterosexuality and either dismisses or ignores a gay subjectivity. Within a heterosexist perspective, gay people's lives are sometimes "banalized as lifestyles" (Rich, 1986, p. 241). Other common expressions of heterosexism, to name a few, include valuing heterosexual relationships above homosexual ones, an intensely felt opposition to gay parenting, regardless of the gay parent's actual qualities, and the belief that lesbians and gay men are unsuited for certain jobs. Heterosexist attitudes are pervasive in western cultures and place gay people in an awkward, and sometimes painful position of disproving cultural assumptions about homosexuality.

Interestingly, modern scientific theories that naturalize homosexuality and define it as a normal genetic variant are, in part, an outgrowth of the tendency, which is intrinsic to heterosexism, to define that which is good or normal as natural or occurring in nature. For example, the sociobiologist Edward O. Wilson's (1975) homosexual altruism argues that homosexuality serves a higher, evolutionary purpose. But it makes this case by bringing homosexuality in line with family values, albeit in evolutionary terms: the perpetuation of the human species by nonprocreating adults who add their resources to help rear the children of their siblings. Wilson's contemporary, sociobiological theory draws upon the analogy of "altruism" in hive species, such as bees, to argue that homosexuality is normal. In this way, the concept of adaptive value serves as a handy moral argument that refutes *peccata contra naturam*, that is, a sin against nature.

For millennia, the animal kingdom has served as a perennial source of metaphors regarding people's untamed, and therefore true natures. In earlier eras, homosexual activities were defined as unnatural because it was believed that, with rare exceptions, nonhuman species did not engage in them. In the ancient world, the hare and the hyena were uniquely considered homosexual in the animal kingdom and were thus metaphorically associated with nongender conformity (Boswell, 1980).[4] However, ethological research has amply demonstrated numerous examples of homosexual activity in other species, both in nature and in captivity (Ford and Beach, 1951). Unsurprisingly, as a consequence of the modern era's knowledge, some contemporary religious beliefs now equate the expression of same-sex behavior in humans with our other "beastlike" behaviors that must be carefully controlled if society is to function properly. Thus, antihomosexual attitudes can always find rationalizations in the theories of the historical epoch in which such beliefs arise.

What is true for the culture in general is also true for psychoanalysis. From its earliest days, psychoanalysis has wrestled with heterosexist essentialism. Freud's collected writings contains elements of both essentialist and constructivist approaches to heterosexuality. However in "The

---

4. Hares were believed to mount each other anally and, in some accounts, to grow a new anus each year. Hyenas were believed to change their anatomical gender every year, and were therefore capable of playing both the male and female role in their sexual relations.

Three Essays," heterosexist reasoning predominated as Freud defined an adult's attraction to a member of the other sex as the apex of psychosexual maturity (1905, p. 197) and defined perversions and homosexual inversion as deviations from the normal sexual object and aim of adult heterosexuality. Subsequent analysts, such as Rado (1969), naturalized heterosexuality to an even greater degree than did Freud. Furthermore, many psychoanalytic texts list "sexuality" in the index as a synonym for heterosexuality while assigning homosexuality to a category of its own. More recently, however, analysts have begun to draw attention to the neglected, social constructionist possibilities inherent in psychoanalytic theory (Lewes, 1988; Chodorow, 1992; Domenici and Lesser, 1995).

Psychoanalysis's heterosexism is, of course, embedded in the cultural values from which its theories are derived. In Western culture, most books, plays, movies, and print and television ads contain naturalized depictions of heterosexuality. "Boy meets girl, boy loses girl, boy gets girl" are common elements of a heterosexist script. Although it is not necessarily motivated by fear or hatred, heterosexism, in the experience of many gay men, is frequently antihomosexual. Bruce Bawer (1993) is a conservative, gay cultural critic who writes for publications like *The Wall Street Journal*. In his book, he tells of attending a close friend's wedding at which he was to toast the bride. He demonstrates how ritualized indifference to gay people can be painful:

> There is nothing like a wedding, moreover, to remind a gay couple that they live in a society whose institutions don't recognize their orientation or acknowledge their relationship. Almost every element of a wedding ceremony, from the bachelor party and bridal shower to the procession and the tossing of the bouquet, is organized along gender lines and assumes the heterosexuality of the participants . . . at the picture-taking ceremony, the wedding party posed for every possible combination of photographs: the bride and her family, the groom and the bridesmaids. . . . Last of all came the "couples" pictures: portraits of each of the ushers and bridesmaids with his or her significant other. . . . But one couple was excluded. As it happened, the list that had been given to the photographer did not include the name of the [gay] couple in whose home the bride and groom had met—Chris and me. . . . Later the groom took me aside and told me that he'd just realized the photographers hadn't taken our picture; he said that he'd put our names on the list and that there must have been a mistake. I wanted to believe this [pp. 260–261].

Another gay man describes a different, rather commonplace experience of heterosexism:

E: Last night my lover and I went out to dinner for Valentine's Day. The restaurant was overwhelmingly filled with straight people. I was extremely uncomfortable and felt vulnerable. Surrounded by straight couples, exchanging flowers and gifts, I felt like an anomaly. I even felt a little estranged from my partner during dinner. There was one young couple sitting next to us. The music they were playing was romantic and the guy kept singing to his girlfriend. I listened to the words of this love song, about a man loving a woman. There are all these songs about men loving women and women loving men.[5] The heterosexual world constantly celebrates itself. No wonder gay people have such a hard time. Gay love is not celebrated in that way.

The Moral Condemnation of Homosexuality

Heterosexism does not necessarily imply malice or ill will towards lesbians and gay men. Idealizing oneself does not necessarily require denigration of those who are different. Nevertheless, heterosexism's naturalistic arguments, sometimes implicitly, and at other times explicitly, tend to equate the non-heterosexual with the immoral and can rationalize the condemnation of same-sex feelings and behaviors (Coleman, 1995). The moral condemnation of homosexuality treats homosexual acts as intrinsically harmful to the individual, to the individual's spirit, and to the social fabric. Those who condemn same-sex activities believe that the tradition of philosophical, legal, and religious opposition to homosexuality are, in and of themselves, sufficient reason to forbid its open expression in the modern world. This was the reasoning of the Supreme Court majority that upheld the state of Georgia's right to ban same-sex acts in the 1986 case of Bowers v. Hardwick. They stated that their decision did "not require a judgment on whether laws against sodomy are wise or desirable" but was based on the "ancient roots" of proscriptions against consensual homosexual activity and a long-standing condemnation of those practices in "Judaeo-Christian" moral and ethical standards (quoted in Group for the Advancement of Psychiatry, in press). Their decision justified the censure of homosexuality in the present because it has been censured in the past, and argued that antihomosexual laws are permissible because they have always existed.

Some critics of these moral condemnations of homosexuality attribute them to simple homophobia. However, the commentator, William F.

---

5. It is no small irony that many heterosexual love songs have been written by closeted gay men like Cole Porter, Noel Coward, and Elton John, just to name a few.

Buckley, in a letter to a long-time friend and political associate who came out, demonstrates that antihomosexuality stemming from moral beliefs is psychologically complex:

> I understand the pain you have felt. . . . My affection and respect for you are indelibly recorded here and there, in many ways, in many places. But you too must realize what are the implications of what you ask. Namely, that the Judaeo-Christian tradition, which is aligned with, no less, one way of life, become indifferent to another way of life. . . . Is it reasonable to expect the larger community to cease to think of the activity of homosexuals as unnatural, whatever its etiology? . . . How, exercising toleration and charity, ought the traditional community treat the minority? Ought considerations of charity entirely swamp us, causing us to submerge convictions having to do with that which we deem to be normal, and healthy? It is a vexed and vexing subject, and your poignant letter serves to remind us of the pain we often inflict, sometimes unintentionally, sometimes sadistically. . . . You are absolutely correct in saying that gays should be welcome as partners in efforts to mint sound public policies; not correct, in my judgment, in concluding that such a partnership presupposes the repeal of convictions that are more, much more, than mere accretions of bigotry [reprinted in Liebman, 1992, pp. 260–261].

Some authors (Weinberg, 1972; Herek, 1984) have noted that individuals with antihomosexual attitudes may regard same-sex behaviors as a threat to their cherished values. Within that context, a 1996 federal law outlawing homosexual marriages is unself-consciously referred to as The Defense of Marriage Act (Sullivan, 1997, pp. 201–203). Those who morally condemn homosexuality claim they do so out of love for something else. In Sullivan's (1953) theory, a person's identity is constructed of affectively-laden markers, some of which must be excluded from conscious awareness. The affectively-laden markers of identity that can be consciously acknowledged, are called *good-me* and *bad-me*. Most gay men grow up with an absence of alternative, affirmative meanings of same-sex attractions (good-me). At the same time, they may incorporate denigrating stereotypes of homosexuality into their identities as bad-me. Although bad-me can be dissociated, it can also be brought into awareness, albeit with anxiety and shame. But Sullivan called those feelings and identifications that were unacceptable to the self and could not be consciously acknowledged *not-me*. Gay men often report histories of having dissociated from homoerotic and other feelings by defining them as not-me and excluding them from consciousness. The dissociated markers of not-me consist of words, symbols, memories or sensations that would induce anxiety if acknowledged by the self. Thus not-me is outwardly projected because acknowledging it leads to feelings of dread and terror. For some heterosexual individuals, a moral condemnation of gay men provides a solution to an intrapsychic conflict: "I protect my own non-gay identity by projecting and then condemning any trace of my own homosexuality." Support for this dissociative method of heterosexual identity formation is found in the common belief that anyone who speaks favorably of gay men and women may be secretly homosexual themselves. Yet, although some heterosexuals dissociatively reject any homosexual or homoerotic feelings or identifications, the growing number of them who accept gay people make it unlikely that a rejection of homosexuality is obligatory for the creation of a heterosexual identity.

Antihomosexual moralizing frequently appears in the clinical setting with gay men in the form of internalized moral condemnations. The following patient's dream illustrates how these attitudes can perpetually lie in judgment of a gay man. Again, we see how it can lead to "losing one's voice:"

> **G:** In the dream, I was sitting in a family room. I had some friends and my family there and also some people I didn't recognize. We were sitting and chatting. All of a sudden this alligator or crocodile springs out of an archway or doorway. The alligator runs by me, goes and butts its head against the door. Someone in the room said that's what he does when he's going to snap. Then he turns around. I suspected he was coming for me. I pulled my legs up from the ottoman I was sitting on so he couldn't get me and then I lost my voice.

> **Th:** What comes to mind about the dream?

> **G:** The first thing that comes to mind is my sense of isolation, being unable to communicate with those around me, especially emotionally. A sense of bewilderment about why they don't notice it or think it's odd. In a weird way, it makes me think of victimization. I wonder how I knew it was coming for me? In my dreams I don't think bad things happen to other people. I'm the one who has got the problem.

In addition to losing his voice in the dream, the patient spontaneously associated to victimization, and perhaps an unspoken feeling about being a gay victim:

> **Th:** What do alligators bring to mind?

> **G:** Monsters, dinosaurs, reptiles. Reptiles scare me. Violence, evil in a way. There is something about an alligator's eyes that appear evil, like a snake's eyes.

The therapist heard these further associations to evil as aspects of moral condemnation and then provided an association of his own:

Th: Alligators make me think of Lacoste shirts, a stereotypical gay costume of the 1970s.

G: That makes me think of my own feelings of alienation from the gay community. I do think there are many parts of it that are evil. The gay world is soulless. I mean it is entirely focused on the incidental, the aesthetic, the moment, the perfect pecs, the chiseled face, the biggest dick, the hottest go-go boy, the best dancing tune, the newest club. It's just dripping with superficiality. That, to me, is spiritually bereft. To me, it is ignoble. It sets man closer to the beasts than to the gods. I'm really coming to despise it quite thoroughly.

The patient's moralizing soliloquy resonated with the therapist's earlier association and echoed the sentiments of Green's (1987) ex-sissy. These self-loathing, condemnatory feelings may be quite common, even in men who have been living with a gay identity for a long time. However, the intensity of the patient's judgmental response was somewhat, if not entirely, surprising to the therapist. The patient had never previously spoken in such a derisive manner about being gay, and had been living as an openly gay man for almost a decade. He had actively participated in the wide range of social activities in the gay community. Yet, he emotionally defined "the gay world" as if he were an antihomosexual preacher, cognizant only of its most stereotypical and pleasure-seeking elements and extremely disdainful of them.

It is not unusual for patients, whatever their sexual identities may be, to adopt a self-condemning tone as a way to force themselves to behave in one way or another. In this case, the patient's demands upon himself to live a more meaningful life had become enmeshed with a critical judgment of his homosexuality. As his treatment proceeded, his rigid and stereotypical attempts to define the meaning of being gay were gradually disentangled from his other expectations of himself. After several months of treatment, he began exploring other aspects of his likes and dislikes and the earlier self-condemnations of his sexuality had diminished. This was made possible by treating the patient's critical demands of himself respectfully, and not just as an internalization of external authority. This approach eventually allowed his own wishes to emerge in a more differentiated way. One consequence of psychotherapeutic work, however, was that he decided to quit his high-paying job. Secretly, if not unconsciously, he detested the work he was doing but could not admit it to himself:

G: I'm coming to the conclusion there's nothing wrong with being unconventional. It's tough to get over the fact that society likes conformity. That's just not me, that's all there is to it. Rather than berating myself for that, I wonder what is wrong with me for not embracing that?

Th: What comes to mind?

G: I don't want to work. If I do, it will have to be something low stress that doesn't take everything out of me. Ever since I quit the job, I've been wrestling with what to do. Do I go back to school? Do I go to Key West and wait tables? I've always thought of my career as how I would define myself and my contribution to humanity. I'm reevaluating my understanding of the world. One should turn a liability of being unconventional into an asset and just embrace it. There's always that part of me down deep in my heart that says I wish I were normal, whatever normal is. At any rate it feels right. It definitely feels much better than any of the other options.

The patient was in an ongoing struggle and wavered between acknowledging his own wishes and pressuring himself to conform to conventional expectations. This could be understood as the intrapsychic representation of the moralizing demands of the socializing process. In Winnicott's (1960b, 1962) terms, his true self was struggling with internalized demands of the external environment. Earlier in treatment, this was a discussion about what it meant to be gay. Here, it was framed in terms of whether or not he should work in a conventional setting.

Th: What has been the resistance to embracing the option of not being normal?

G: Certainly it's not going to set me up for a life on easy street and not for a long time. Something in me says I can't worry about that anymore. One way or another I will eat.

Th: The fear that you won't eat sounds like your anxiety.

G: There are these things that scare you so much, you have to stare them down. When I think about it rationally, I'm not going to starve. It's overblown, my anxiety. The things that are important to me that I really want to go after, they do not involve money, other than the bare necessity. I want to maximize time and if that means relative indigence, I need to divest myself of the expectations and the conformism that is expected by the world. Say "No, I'm going to do it my way." Construct my world in my way. It's going to be idiosyncratic and that is OK. Somehow it doesn't sound as momentous as it feels.

Nevertheless, the patient's anxiety about being gay was still linked to his anxiety about making unconventional life choices. There is always a risk associated with revealing one's true self and wishes.

Th: What are your doubts about this decision?

G: Sticking out, drawing attention to myself. Maybe taking risks. Taking risks always scares me. It's connected with that nervousness, new things scare me a lot.

Th: What scares you about new things?

G: I don't know. The only thing that occurs to me is some sort of residual shame or guilt at being gay. When I became conscious of being gay, I always wondered if I was being judged. Meeting relatives, one has a consciousness that one is different, that one is not what one is expected to be, that one is not approved of. I was always thinking, "Do they know? Can they tell?" I think that made me very reluctant to meet people, very nervous about new situations. I don't have a problem with new ideas, or taking trips or things like that, I only have a problem with meeting new people. Places don't judge you, people do. It makes me angry. This is totally unnecessary and wanton bigotry on the part of other people.

Th: It sounds like the bigotry is inside you.

G: It's internalized, I'm sure. It's a constant battle. Is one ever done coming out? Feelings, like you say, are very cagey things. Even though one can be convinced intellectually that there is nothing to be ashamed of, a lot of that damage is done by the time one comes to that intellectual realization. That is how one discovers how deep it is over the years.

To avoid being judged at an early age, this patient adopted a veneer of conventionality. He entered treatment with a growing awareness of dissatisfaction with his life. His more conscious, initial focus was his disaffection with being gay, and he initially condemned the "superficial gay lifestyle." He did so by evoking stereotypes to which he and his immediate social circle did not conform. The therapist understood the patient's moral condemnations of gay men as a defensive attempt to ward off anxiety associated with revealing his own desires. The therapist did not tell the patient to refrain from the use of denigrating stereotypes. Instead, together they explored the patient's narrow, emotional definition of what it meant to be gay. As they did so, the patient was able to link a more conscious feeling of dissatisfaction with his sexual identity to his less conscious feelings about a job that provided a high degree of conventional status but also high stress and no personal satisfaction. The therapist was unaware of this associative link when they started treatment because the patient initially presented himself as both comfortable being gay and satisfied with his job.

Another patient's internal struggle in coming to terms with his same-sex feelings was described in terms of internalized, condemnatory religious beliefs and metaphors:

H: I've always felt the need to justify my existence. I'm only half human. It's a feeling that I am the outsider.

Th: Half human is a powerful image.

H: I read articles and I see shows on television about gay people who supposedly have relationships. I ask myself, "How much of that image is true?" How are we trying to make it look this way, but it's not really that way. Deep down inside, I bought the whole concept of what the heterosexual church taught me.

Th: You don't believe gay people are capable of living whole lives?

H: I guess I don't. When I meet gay people who have lives, I think they are superficial. For me, to be gay is to be half a person. You can't be a whole person. It's like two sides to my feelings. Part of my feeling is I believe that homosexuality is a sin. The other part of me says I don't believe a person can change their sexual orientation.

Th: Have you tried to change your sexual orientation?

H: Yes, in a way. I dated girls a couple of times. I always thought I should get married. I even thought about becoming a priest. That would be trying to become a whole human being.

Th: What have you experienced that convinces you that being gay is half human?

H: I don't know, a lot of gay marriages. It seems everyone I know, their relationships are transient, or screwed up.

McWhirter and Mattison (1984) have commented that "heterosexual and homosexual people alike have been taught by religion and society that the inability to maintain a lasting relationship is indicative of personal failure. For heterosexual persons these failures generally are believed to result from interpersonal relationship problems. For homosexual persons the failure to maintain an ongoing relationship was ascribed, more often than not, to their homosexuality" (p. xiii). The patient, in fact, was having difficulty with relationships. He used a broad religious indictment of homosexuality to explain his own personal difficulties in that area:

H: I feel that a gay person can do the friendship thing, but he can never have a relationship. Gay relationships are immature. I guess I bought the baggage.

Th: This emotional reaction influences the way you approach all your relationships with other gay men. Part of you throws yourself into gay life while part of you says gay life is not workable.

H: That's where I fall into my hopelessness. I tried to lead the heterosexual life of dating women and felt I was bending myself into someone I'm not. Then I went into the opposite direction. I became gay and there's a lot of things there that bother me and I feel, "How can I live this way?" So then I start pulling into myself. I wallow in my self-pity of regrets and pain I caused other people; pain I caused my family.

Th: You are arguing with yourself and use your relationships with other people to settle the debate for you.

H: I always saw myself as a failure, so if I make a choice, if it's something I come up with, then its going to fail anyway. I have to find somebody who is a reputable source that can say who I really am.

The patient experiences a conflict between his homosexual feelings and his inability to accept them. How to therapeutically proceed in this patient's struggle can hinge upon a therapist's own feelings and beliefs about homosexuality. Therapists who try to rid patients of their homosexuality can use their authority to buttress the rejection of homosexual feelings. Patients who seek an authoritative voice to settle their internal conflicts may find their way to these therapists. However, the therapist who takes such a position may undermine the patient's ability to settle the internal struggle for himself. As this patient described his first visit to a Greenwich Village church that was affirming of lesbians and gay men, he illustrated the value of allowing an internal struggle to emerge into consciousness in a way that gives all of his feelings a voice:

H: The church has a mostly-gay congregation. I saw a lot of gay couples, some gay men my own age, single and in couples. It was very disturbing. I had mixed feelings about it. I regret that I didn't grow up in a church like this. But I also had a deeper feeling of outrage about the liberalism of that church. This shouldn't be. I was taught that a woman should never be allowed to give a homily and here a woman was doing it. I separate my gayness from my religion. Going to discos and drinking and being gay was bad. I was not prepared for this kind of openness, even though I'm looking for a social group in which to participate. What would my parents think of that place? Not that I would ever bring them there. Part of me is interested in pursuing this further as a way to meet people. Part of me is in terror that I won't be able to manage it. I'm too judgmental.

The patient had not yet appreciated that he had already brought his parents to that church, or at least his internalizations of their moral condemnations. Despite his intellectual understanding of this struggle, he finds it difficult to integrate his religious beliefs with the idea of being a gay man. He emotionally believes that religion and heterosexuality represent his potential for goodness and that being gay means he is bad. Thus, the concept of a gay congregation is an anxiety-producing oxymoron.

The patient articulated the wish that an outside source securely define his identity, heterosexual or gay, for him. Early in the unfolding of this patient's sexual identity, he might have wanted such a confirmation one way or the other. At another time, however, he might have reacted differently. In this session, if the therapist were to have said to this patient, "I think you are gay," it is conceivable that the patient would have experienced the affirmation of his homosexuality with either suspicion or the same outrage he felt in the gay church. The patient alone can authentically define himself as gay; it is his struggle for his own identity. At times this conflict may be framed in terms of whether the patient is heterosexual or gay. However, among many men who feel that they are gay, the struggle is often between their homoerotic and homophobic feelings and the role of the therapist is to help the patient contain, tolerate, and hopefully, integrate them.

Love the Sinner, Hate the Sin

Sustaining a therapeutic process in which a patient's inarticulated moral condemnations of homosexuality can emerge requires more than just a passing acquaintance with overt antihomosexual attitudes. It should be noted, for example, that in their more subtle forms, moral condemnations of homosexuality include an attitude such as "loving the sinner and hating the sin." In earlier historical eras, religious as well as secular authorities condemned sodomites to eternal damnation and even sometimes to physical torture (Boswell, 1980; Plant, 1986; Herek, 1990; Herek and Berrill, 1992). The 19th-century invention of the homosexual, and the subsequent creation of the heterosexual (Katz, 1995), caused a paradigm shift (Kuhn, 1972) in modern religious debates about same-sexuality. Science and medicine's redefining of homosexuality, as well as the growing number of openly gay and lesbian voices, had an enormous impact on religious attitudes. In contrast to traditional sharp distinctions between good (i.e., monogamous sex within the sanctity of marriage) and evil (i.e., the sins of sodomy, onanism, and extramarital sex), religious authorities were forced to integrate accumulating scientific data regarding the presumptive etiologies and naturalness of homosexuality.

They also had to contend with the spiritual needs of a growing number of gay people, as well as those of their families. Several religious denominations, adopting a normal variant model, openly embraced lesbian and gay worshipers. Integrity, for example, is "a group of gay, lesbian, bisexual and transgendered Episcopalians and their families and friends" (Hynes, 1997, p. B1) who are welcomed by and meet within Episcopal churches. And some organized religious groups have admitted openly gay men and women as priests, rabbis, and ministers. However, that has not been the majority approach. Many contemporary, antihomosexual religious authorities have instead chosen to embrace the homosexual but not the homosexuality. *Choice* is a charged word in moral debates about homosexuality. Antihomosexual authorities believe one chooses to be "a homosexual" despite prohibitions against it. Gay people believe they choose to act on their homoerotic feelings in order to avoid the choice of suffering in the closet. However, the wide variance in accepting or condemning homosexuality demonstrates another dimension of the idea of choice: The official interpreters of religious doctrines also appear to be making choices. Further complicating matters, some religious authorities have accepted the normal variant model (Coleman, 1995) while others cling to the illness model (Harvey, 1987). However, although the presence of homoerotic desires may not necessarily be considered a sin, both Coleman and Harvey, like the relative of the patient below, consider acting upon the feelings as sinful:

> **J:** My uncle tells me how much he loves me while giving me the impression that he finds my homosexuality loathsome. I left him a message that I'd be visiting my cousin. If my uncle doesn't want to see me, he won't answer or he'll say no. Then I won't feel this compulsion to be with him, even though not seeing him makes me feel guilty. Am I cutting myself off from my family? At the end of my message, I said, "I hope to hear from you." I hope he calls and says "I'd like to see you." If he doesn't, I'm not going to put myself in a position where I feel he is condemning me.
>
> **Th:** How does he condemn you?
>
> **J:** He sends me religious tracts. He'll tell me things like "I hate your homosexuality, but I love you." Now that I've been coming to therapy, it's interesting to notice that a lot of the judgmental things he was saying before, I wasn't really paying attention to them.

Another patient struggled with how to live an openly gay identity and maintain a relationship with a relative who morally condemned his homosexuality:

K: My sister used to be good about not talking about religion. We got alone fine until the AIDS scare got going. She said that gays deserved AIDS, and that being gay was against God's will. I got rather upset. I always knew the church could be hateful.

Th: They love the sinner but not the sin.

K: It gets into that, but if you don't consider it a sin, how can you stop sinning? They probably want me to go into shock therapy. They think I'm living a life of sin and not doing anything to change it.

Religious beliefs that disapprove of homosexuality constitute substantive, ongoing themes in psychotherapy with some gay patients. Many of these themes are intertwined with issues regarding family relationships, particularly in gay men who have had strict, fundamentalist, or orthodox religious upbringings. Because they may no longer be participating in religious activities, they are often estranged from their families. However, they often remain deeply concerned about the moral implications of being gay and about their alienation from their co-religionists. The following patient expressed his contempt toward religion in a way that could be understood as defensively reflecting back the moralizing condemnations of his church:

L: Over the weekend I bought two more videos. I almost take a certain delight in the fact that I am using the money I used to give to the church to buy pornography. I'm angry about the church. I don't feel comfortable there.

Despite his conscious pleasure at thumbing his nose at the church, he struggled with guilty feelings about his behavior and attitudes:

L: However, buying and looking at videos also helps me with not socializing with people, it helps time go by. I thought the other day, "I really should try the Monday night meeting of SCA [Sexual Compulsives Anonymous]." But why should I go to that group when I'm already in therapy and why can't I deal with the issue of gay videos in therapy?

This patient's struggle with contradictory feelings sounded like he was arguing with himself. He was able to feel both the pleasure of his sexual activity, masturbating while watching pornographic videos, and the shame of what he believed to be its sinful nature. He felt the pleasure of being his own person and the fear that being such a person made him an outcast. His anxiety began to mount in the session. He was not sure which troubled him more, his resentment toward his church or his disapproval of his isolated, sexual activities:

Th: You do not wish to go to SCA where you will be asked to put yourself in the hands of a higher power.

L: It is hard to do. I tried reading theological books. Last night I was looking for one that might help. (Tearful) Something I can put in my mind that will help.

Th: This is not about SCA. It's about God. You have no faith in Him.

L: No, and I haven't for years. And I didn't pray at all. I stopped, because I felt there was nothing out there. I was thinking that the sex is my religion. That is what I do on Sunday mornings, I go buy pornographic videos. It is the first time I have not belonged to a church since I was 10 years old. So I have no church membership now.

The patient did not know how to integrate a religious identity with a sexual one and was envious of and mystified by a friend who appeared to have done so:

L: He makes me a little bit nervous. He talks so openly about sex and it's really almost embarrassing, how open he is. He belongs to a church where he's an elder now. He talks about all kinds of sexual activities and he's matter-of-fact and graphic. The sexual activities he discusses are what I have fantasized about for a long time. (Astonished tone of voice) Here is someone who talks about it. It is a little bit embarrassing to hear a person say, in a group setting, sexual things that I think should be kept secret. He's connecting with his church, so it made me think, maybe I can connect the two.

Despite the anxiety it evoked, the patient entertained the possibility of integrating his conflictual feelings:

L: I had to get rid of God because He was unhealthy for me. I believed I was unacceptable to God as a gay person. That is what I was taught, that is what I heard. Not that I was personally unacceptable, but that gay people were. (Exasperated tone of voice) I can't go anywhere with this. I've said it all before.

Th: You still believe that you are unacceptable to God.

L: I am continually reaffirming that belief by getting gay videos. Now I'm getting ones with younger guys. That's even more of a way to feel that I'm not OK. Because it's not OK for someone my age to be sexual with younger guys. This is intellectualizing. I can't get to the feeling.

Th: You were crying earlier.

L: About not being able to connect with God.

Th: How does it feel to be disconnected from God?

L: Last night I didn't want to feel dirty and shameful. I would like to be sexually available and emotionally available to someone. I want to feel good about myself. Somehow I think connecting with God or religion will help me feel that way. I looked for any book that I could find on my shelf. I've been trying to find something that speaks to me.

The patient believed his capacity to relate to others was connected to his religious faith. Without his faith, the patient believed he was incapable of forming relationships. In fact, such feelings and attitudes are not uncommon in individuals who grow up in religious communities where social and religious activities are deeply intertwined. The patient also believed that integrating his internal contradictions was a form of hypocrisy, connoting not only an unspoken criticism of the friend discussed earlier, but also his transferential apprehension about the therapist who was obviously biased in favor of integration and therefore an object of suspicion:

L: I don't want to be a phony. For so many years as a church-goer, I felt like a phony and I pretended. I don't want to go through the motions of something I don't believe in.

Th: What emotions are related to the part of you that doesn't believe in God?

L: It's anger, loneliness. (Tearful) Loneliness makes me feel tearful.

Th: What's the connection between loneliness and the part of you that doesn't believe in God?

L: I thought of being a fluke in creation. A fluke in the universe. A mistake.

Th: How do you mean that?

L: Being gay. The reason I'm alone is because I'm gay. That's the reason I'm not with my family. And when I was trying to make religion work, I was trying not to be gay. As my life went on, and it felt like a losing battle, God was my way out of being gay. For me, personally, there has always been a very strong streak of self-hatred and self-loathing. I still feel that. (Angry tone of voice) I take my fist and slam it against the wall. saying "Fucking, fucking, mother-fucking. " Instead of saying "Holy, holy, holy Lord God almighty," it's more like "Fucking, goddamned Almighty, heaven and earth are full of shit." I feel rage when that happens. I suppose I have to keep a lid on it. It's not acceptable. I have to keep control.

The patient believed he could not maintain his religious convictions and be a gay man at the same time. He regarded with suspicion those religious denominations and institutions that provided opportunities to do so. He also regarded the therapist with suspicion, although he was too reserved to say so at this point in his treatment. His emotional dilemma resulted from his belief that he had to choose sides, that his contradictory wishes and feelings could not be integrated. This was consistent with his own religious denomination's stand on homosexuality which said he must choose between a gay identity and a religious one. He used his anger and contempt to keep in check the religious feelings he now deemed unacceptable. Having spent much of his lifetime using moral condemnations to submerge his gay identity, he now used a similar dissociative mechanism to keep his religious identity submerged. He did so through the articulation of curse words, blasphemies and expressions of contempt for his God and his religion. But only through articulating all aspects of his identity was there any hope that the patient could more comfortably find a way to bring his disparate "parts" together.

Enactments of Moral Condemnation

In the case of the previous patient, an intrapsychic dimension of morally condemning homosexuality was illustrated. At other times, a patient's discomfort with his own sexuality is told through the narrative of an unaccepting, moralizing relative, friend or acquaintance. In these cases, the patient's lack of self-acceptance is projected onto someone else. The following patient is contemplating coming out to his father. One can listen to the imagined account of the father's responses as projections of the patient's own internalized judgments. The exploration of someone else's imagined responses may make a patient more aware of his own lack of acceptance:

Th: What do you imagine is your father's objection to your being gay?

M: He looks to the church to provide him with guidelines. That's where he looks to for information. No rules, no morality. You've got strong condemnation.

Th: What is the nature of your father's condemnation?

M: He still believes in the concept of sin and afterlife. By being gay, I am sinning and risking my afterlife, risking condemnation.

Th: What exactly would his words be?

M: It's so foreign to me.

The patient's experience of his father's words as "foreign" is a clinical presentation of a dissociated feeling:

Th: It may not be entirely foreign. It may be something you don't usually think about.

M: If he actually expressed it, he would say that, "It's a sin and that it's against God's law," and that by doing homosexual acts I'm risking damnation, risking going to hell. And that even if it's a very strong inclination or orientation on my part, I need to bring that under control. God gives people tests or puts challenges in their way and they are supposed to rise to those challenges. My sister's alcoholism, for example, is a problem presented by God that you need to face, rather than giving in to it. Despite what I say my views are, I see how much baggage I am still carrying around with me from my religious upbringing. For anyone to say something like that, there is a piece of me in those attitudes. Even though it may be suppressed, it believes that being gay is a sin. Sin is something to be concerned about.

Th: What are your feelings here?

M: What I come back with is that being gay is wrong. That piece of me saying, "It is wrong," and yet I continue to follow though on my sexuality. This certainly eats away at any sense of self-worth or self-confidence.

This patient's projection of self-condemnation simply led to his distancing himself from his family. At times, however, more dramatic events may ensue when a family member participates in the patient's dissociative processes. Another patient decided to forego the Christmas holidays with his family. He had wanted to use the visit as an occasion to come out to his parents but did not feel he could do so in person. Because he was uncomfortable about hiding his gay identity, he decided to avoid the family altogether. The therapist, however, wondered why the patient felt he had to come out in their presence. The patient replied that his sister had dissuaded him from writing to tell them he was gay. She insisted that if he told them, he had to do so face to face. The therapist was curious why the patient accepted her counsel on this matter. Telling his parents he was gay was something he found difficult to do. Doing so in person, as his sister suggested, appeared to be an arbitrary obstacle to the process. Since he had previously told the therapist that his sister did not accept his homosexuality, why would he take her advice on how to come out to his parents?

Surprisingly, the patient revealed he had also come out to his brother who had not rejected him. The therapist wondered how his brother felt about the patient staying away during the holidays and whether he agreed with the sister's advice. This prompted the patient to call his brother who angrily disagreed with the sister's suggestion. Eventually, the patient wrote his parents a coming out letter. They were polite and confused about the meaning of his homosexuality, but they strongly expressed their love and acceptance of their son.

A patient's internal world is filled with numerous identifications, feelings, and attitudes. This patient's internal attitudes and contradictions regarding his sexual identity are embodied by the external attitudes of his sister, his brother, and his parents. Patients present one point of view and selectively inattend (Sullivan, 1956) to the others in attempts to maintain a dissociated state. In this way, their anxiety-producing emotional conflicts are not consciously experienced. The patient was able to share his sister's disapproval with the therapist but dissociated himself from his other sibling's acceptance. By asking the patient what his brother thought, the therapist was not telling him to call the brother, although that was the enactment that ensued. The therapist invited the patient to look at the dissociated possibility of self-acceptance and to bring those feelings more directly into consciousness. In this way he would have to integrate the possibility of acceptance with the more conscious feeling that his being gay was unacceptable. In projecting his own lack of acceptance into his sister, she, in turn, enacted this aspect of his feelings for him. The ensuing interactions between the patient and his sister can be understood via the mechanism of projective identification.

The varied presentations of moral condemnation appear to be derived from complex motivations and there are both interpersonal and intrapsychic aspects to this particular presentation of antihomosexuality. As important as it is in the work with gay men, it should be incumbent upon a therapist doing psychotherapy with any patient to be aware of his or her own moral beliefs. By maintaining such an awareness, a patient's enactments can be interpreted to further the therapeutic process. And by paying attention to enactments that primarily stem from the therapist's own countertransferential judgments, the therapist may yet help the patient find his own moral center.

It is also worth noting that a well-trained analyst should not see anything unusual about dealing with any patient in this manner. One might reasonably assert that these are the kinds of interventions analysts routinely make in clinical practice with all patients. However, one point worth underscoring here is that psychoanalytic theory and practice historically regarded gay patients as different from others. As Mitchell (1981) noted, "[psychoanalytic literature] seems to reflect the position of those with a proverbial axe to grind in relationship to homosexuality, viewing it as something out of the ordinary, posing unique technical problems and requiring a departure from the traditional analytic process" (p. 63). Eissler (1953) described deviations from the analyst's interpretive stance as *parameters*. He believed non-analytic interventions, like telling a patient to expose himself to a phobic situation or warning the patient that acting out would lead to terminating analysis, were necessary for treating conditions such as phobias and social delinquency, among others. These were some of the parameters used to treat homosexuality, conceptualized as a phobia by some (Rado, 1969) and a sociopathic disorder by others (Bergler, 1956). Gay men in analytic treatments were often encouraged to date women or told that treatment would be terminated if they engaged in homosexual activity (Ovesey, 1969). It is worth noting that the use of parameters in treating gay men was a reflection of psychoanalysis's own moral discomfort with and condemnation of homosexuality.[6] In the absence of that moral condemnation, one does not need parameters to treat gay men and analysts can resume their usual standards of analytic technique in treating them.

Antigay Violence

Intellectual, legal, and moral arguments abound at one end of the antihomosexual spectrum. At the other end are society's more violent expressions of intolerance. Invariably, not everyone is capable of distinguishing "homosexuals" from their homosexuality. Just as gay men experience same-sex attractions as intrinsic to their identities, gay-bashers usually treat them as if that were the case. The problem of antigay violence is widespread and in 1990 the federal government passed a law ordering a study of hate crimes, including attacks on gay men and women, the first time a federal civil rights law covered sexual orientation (Schmalz, 1992).

Gay-bashing is a common form of violence in which gangs of young men descend upon neighborhoods where gay people meet. Armed with bats, clubs, or other weapons, they attack anyone they believe to be gay:

> Suddenly the door burst open and a very large man rushed in, bleeding profusely. He was naked from the waist up, bleeding from his arm, shoulder and head. . . . "They got to us. Two men with baseball bats. . . . They bashed us." . . . The bashers, it turned out, had calmly

---

6. Two studies, MacIntosh (1994) and Friedman and Lilling (1996; also see Lilling and Friedman, 1995), use self-reports from psychoanalysts regarding their attitudes about homosexuality. Both studies conclude that the majority of responding analysts do not themselves hold antihomosexual views. Nevertheless, a significant number of respondents in both studies believed that their colleagues held antihomosexual views.

asked for "the manager" [of the lesbian and gay community center] and singled him out for attack. . . . The assailants had entered . . . and clubbed several people [Herdt and Boxer, 1993, pp. 86–87].

Rist (1992) relates a gay-bashing incident with many tragic dimensions. A closeted young man, Rob, upon graduating from high school, organized a private party for three gay friends. After his brother and a friend, Steve, found out about the gathering, they

> decided to launch a guerrilla attack against Rob and the other three discovered homosexuals. Dressed in military fatigues, the two boys stormed the beach house . . . roughed up Rob's friends, burned Rob's hand with a high-voltage police stun gun, and broke his nose with a five-cell steel police flashlight. Still, the greater horror was what happened afterward. [The brother and Steve then went] to "out" Rob in front of his parents. A terrible row ensued. Rob had spent what seemed like a lifetime concealing his desire for men from his father. Now all of the frantic hiding counted for nothing. . . . Rob jumped in his car and fled for days. When he returned he was carrying a machine gun. . . . At his trial he insisted that he had only wanted to frighten Steve . . . but when he confronted him . . . his brother's good buddy only taunted him again, and Rob raised the gun and massacred him [p. 434].

Violent acts may not create power, but they often announce where power lies. Some religious authorities have ominously warned, "When civil legislation is introduced to protect behavior to which no one has any conceivable right, neither the Church nor society at large should be surprised when other distorted notions and practices gain ground, and irrational and violent reactions increase" (Congregation for the Doctrine of the Faith, 1986, paragraph 10; reprinted in Herek and Berrill, 1992, pp. 90–91). Similarly, implicit threats of violence from the more-powerful majority were heard in the controversy surrounding the "Jenny Jones Murder Case." The producers of the *Jenny Jones Show* invited Jonathan Schmitz to appear on their television talk show to meet a secret admirer. To his chagrin, the admirer turned out to be his gay male neighbor, Scott Amedure. Schmitz killed Amedure three days later. In one report of the incident, a psychoanalyst discussed the murder with the press and faulted

> both the media and the gay rights movement for the Jenny Jones incident. . . . To turn the world upside down and say it doesn't matter if we are homosexual or heterosexual is folly . . . to ask for total acceptance and enthusiastic approval of homosexuality as a normal and

valuable psychosexual institution is truly tempting social and personal disaster [C. Socarides, quoted in Dunlap, 1995a].[7]

The analyst's quoted remarks illustrate how the increasing publicity and documentation of gay-bashing incidents has provoked the open articulation of previously unspoken cultural beliefs. One is that violence is an excusable response to an unwanted sexual advance from a gay man. Another is that gay people are responsible for provoking any violence that ensues if they come out. Others, however, do not blame the victim and contend that antigay violence is the inevitable outgrowth of the unexamined and unstated beliefs implicit in homophobia, heterosexism and moral condemnation. They argue that those who marginalize homosexuality are either directly or indirectly responsible for the brutality against gay men and women (Rechy, 1977; Shilts, 1982; DeCecco, 1985; Herek and Berrill, 1992).

Leaving the unanswered question of antigay violence's origins aside, a gay patient in treatment will always have legitimate concerns about potential physical attacks. Many adolescents perceived to be gay by their peers have reported physical attacks (Hetrick and Martin, 1988; Herdt and Boxer, 1993). The following patient associated his adult work difficulties to the memory of being assaulted and tormented in high school:

N: I remember getting beat up in the halls in high school. It's a feeling of being out of control. A feeling of being worthless, a feeling of having no value. A feeling of being exposed. At work, I feared my colleagues would expose my lack of technical knowledge. I always fear being humiliated in public in front of my peers.

Th: Why do you think you were beaten and humiliated in high school?

N: I was an easy target. I wouldn't fight back. If I did, it got worse. I would get hit even harder. I didn't know how to respond. I want to say there was nobody there for me. I remember my parents driving me to school because I was afraid to go on the school bus. If that happened today, the parents would complain and say, "My child is being harassed." I don't know why that didn't happen.

Th: Why do you think nobody stepped in?

---

7. Most damaging to a patient's self-esteem is the therapist who blames the victim of violence. As this remark demonstrates, some psychoanalysts have moved toward positions that parallel those of religious denominations that blame gay men and women for provoking the violence they experience.

N: The thought that came into my mind was, "What made a village idiot a village idiot?" That's the way it is. A certain part of it is inertia. If this kid didn't want that to happen, he could take the initiative and change it. If he's not pulling himself up why should anyone help him.

Th: It's hard to imagine someone of your intelligence as a village idiot.

N: Part of it revolves around being gay and knowing that those feelings were totally off-limits.

Th: What do you mean?

N: I knew instinctively that telling somebody I had gay feelings would be a total disaster. I felt it would be another weapon in the arsenal to humiliate me. When I grew up, it was never even mentioned, and when it was, it was mentioned derogatorily. I always thought of myself as different. I wasn't a jock. I wasn't into the rough and tumble. I was always a loner.

Antigay violence is believed to be an underreported phenomenon because its victims are often reluctant to come forward. The above patient was typical of the many children who are reluctant to share with parents and teachers the antihomosexual taunts that accompany the gay-bashing. Another patient explained why adult victims of a violent, anti-gay attack may be unwilling to denounce their assailants as well:

P: I used to go to this park where gay men go to cruise, but sometimes just to talk. One day, I saw two teenagers chasing a guy. As they ran past me, I yelled at the kids to stop. They came up to me and one of them had a knife. The one with the knife took my watch. The other one told me to give him my wallet. When I said I'd give him my money if he let me keep the wallet, he hit me on the head with his fist and said "Give it to me." I gave up my wallet and all my papers. One of them took the knife and stabbed me in the leg so I couldn't chase after them.

Th: What happened after that?

P: I limped to my car and drove to an emergency room. I told the doctors I had been mugged, but I didn't tell them where or the exact circum-stances. When I got home, I lied to my parents about where the incident had happened. They wanted me to go to the police and report it, but I refused. I said I was upset and just wanted to forget the whole thing. I couldn't tell anyone what happened because I was embarrassed. I felt guilty. Even though I had tried to stop them from hurting that other guy, I felt like I had done something wrong. I guess I had. I was there and part of me felt that I had no business being there in the first place.

It is reasonable for therapists to acknowledge the everyday dangers gay men face or may have faced. If a gay man has been assaulted, the experience is internalized and working through that trauma will inevitably be part of the therapy. Even if they have not been assaulted themselves, gay patients are sensitized to the ways in which members of the dominant culture, either in positions of authority or on its margins, feel they can make threats and do as they please. A psychotherapist can be most helpful by being sensitive to patient anxieties regarding antigay violence, as gay patients can be retraumatized by denying or minimizing the extent to which the phenomenon colors their lives and affects their self-esteem.

Conclusions

This chapter reviewed some presentations of antihomosexual attitudes and the impact they can have on the social and psychological development of gay men. Perhaps one day, if society becomes more accepting of homosexuality, clinicians will work with gay men who are more accepting of themselves. In today's world, however, doing psychotherapy with gay male patients requires a therapist to be aware of how antihomosexual attitudes are often associated with feelings of helplessness, shame, victimization, exploitation, and rage. Trying to make sense of the meanings of antihomosexuality will inevitably have an impact on the development of a gay man's self-esteem and his life experiences, family relationships and temperament will all contribute to how they affect his self-concept or identity. And to repeat, in this culture, antihomosexual attitudes are ubiquitous and, consequently, no one is free of them, not even therapists. This obliges therapists to understand and be aware of the ways in which these attitudes have had an impact on the development of their own identities. This can help a therapist come to a greater empathic appreciation of the impact of such attitudes on a gay man.

5

PSYCHOANALYTIC THEORIES OF HOMOSEXUAL DEVELOPMENT

It is self-evident, I suppose, that I am conspicuously taking exception to the all-too-prevalent idea that things are pretty well fixed in the Jesuitical first seven years. This idea has constituted one of the greatest problems for some anthropologists who have tried to translate psychiatric thought into anthropologically useful ideas. The anthropologists have noised at them from all sides the enormous importance of infantile experience—meaning experience certainly under the age of eight. Yet one of the most conspicuous observations of an anthropologist working anywhere is that children of the privileged, who are raised by servants, do not grow up to be like the servants. That is a little bit difficult for an anthropologist to reconcile with the tremendous emphasis on very early experience.

Harry Stack Sullivan, *The Interpersonal Theory of Psychiatry* (1953)

In the father's specific contributions to his son's psychosexual development, the father should be a male model with whom the son can identify in forming masculine patterns in a specific cultural milieu. An affectionate father through his warmth and support provides a reality denial for any retaliatory expectations the son may have for harboring sexually competi-

tive attitudes. The father who promotes an identification with him will ordinarily intercede between his son
and a wife who may be [close-binding], thus protecting
the boy from demasculinization. Such a father does
not default his paternal role out of submissiveness to
his wife.

Irving Bieber et al., *Homosexuality* (1962)

The overextrapolations of Bieber, with their untenable
implications of universality, have created clutter in a
field in which their data regarding, for example, close-
binding mothers and distant fathers might, if modestly
treated, have clear usefulness in the understanding of
some aspects of development in some gay men. In a
similar vein, but probably even worse, the energetic
pseudocertainties of Socarides about pre-oedipal and
oedipal development have probably created flawed data
and misinformation from which it will take scientific
objectivity some time to reemerge.

Graeme Hanson and Lawrence Hartmann
"Latency Development in Prehomosexual Boys" (1996)

As was observed in the previous chapter, many gay men recall
painful childhoods in which they were exposed to antihomosexual biases
while simultaneously being subjected to expectations of heterosexual
normativity. Not only does doing psychotherapy with gay men draw a
therapist's attention to the power and ubiquity of these cultural beliefs
and experiences, it also highlights the ways in which these attitudes have
shaped psychoanalytic theory. Psychoanalytic developmental theories,
particularly those that try to explain the causes of homosexuality, uncan-
nily reflect the social prejudices of the culture. The most common example of this is psychoanalysis' appropriation of the culture's standard
definition of a "normal boy" to mean one who is attracted to girls. Thus,
to the extent that they tend to explain male homosexuality from this perspective, analytic theorists have neglected other subjective possibilities.

These include the observation that a masculine identity can actually be consistent with an attraction to boys. Or that a boy's attraction to another boy may altogether exclude the concept of femininity. Or that labeling one's own spontaneous homoerotic feelings as feminine may in fact be a developmental achievement in itself, one that occurs much later than a conscious awareness of the actual feeling.

There are many ways in which theories of homosexuality's etiology can have an impact upon the developmental experiences of gay men. Moreover, there exist both fanciful and serious theories regarding the "causes and becauses" of homosexuality. Some etiological theories are known only within certain disciplines, while others have entered into and become popularized by the general culture. Gay patients will have inevitably read or been exposed to these theories, which, in various ways, have either caused these men to be mystified or stigmatized, or, in some cases, have actually served to anchor some part of their gay or homosexual identities. The focus here, however, is on psychoanalytic theories in particular, not only as systems of interpretation, but on the ways in which they reflect and express unexamined cultural beliefs that both naturalize heterosexuality and denigrate homosexuality. In addition to the traditional biases in analytic theories, this chapter also explores the theoretical strategies of more recent, affirming psychoanalytic approaches to homosexuality.

It would be unfair, of course, to single out psychoanalytic theories as the only ones that rely upon heterosexual models of normativity. Certainly, psychoanalysts are not unique in offering theoretical assumptions that depend upon defining male homosexuality as a feminine trait (see for example Dörner, 1986; Green, 1987; LeVay, 1993; Hamer and Copeland, 1994). Nevertheless, it is important to emphasize this issue in regard to psychoanalytic theories since analysts regularly find themselves in clinical situations that other sex researchers do not. After all, it is one thing to label posthumously a man's hypothalamic nucleus as "feminine" at autopsy. It is another thing altogether to countertransferentially impose a therapist's own restrictive gender definitions on gay patients in ways that recapitulate painful developmental experiences of childhood and retraumatize people seeking help.

Because analytic theories inevitably affect therapeutic listening, the impact of a therapist's etiological theory in doing clinical work with gay men cannot be underestimated. For example, one consequence within psychoanalysis of normalizing heterosexuality was that a gay man's developmental history could only be framed as abnormal. Many theorists have implied that they understand how normal human development unfolds, even though conflicting models of psychoanalytic developmental theory made it difficult, if not impossible, to reach a consensus on how one becomes an average heterosexual (Freud, 1905; 1908; Sullivan, 1953; Hartmann, 1958; Blos, 1962; Winnicott, 1965; Bowlby, 1969; Kohut, 1971; Segal, 1974; Mahler et al., 1975; Greenberg and Mitchell, 1983; Fast, 1984; Stern, 1985; Tyson and Tyson, 1990). Despite such broad theoretical diversity, a common characteristic of psychoanalysis' developmental literature is a paucity of theories that might account for a normative, nonpathological gay male identity. Psychoanalysts and other theorists, with few exceptions (Morgenthaler, 1984; Friedman, 1988; Lewes, 1988; Isay, 1989), do not envision such a line of development. Instead, they conceptualize same-sex attractions as the result of some failure to acquire the psychological equipment required to stay on the path toward an expected, and a preferred, heterosexual outcome.

These theories do not necessarily require pathological models of homosexuality. Freud (1905), for example, did not pathologize homosexuality, he juvenilized it. One implication of his theory was that the presumably mature, genital analyst could potentially use the analytic situation to show the immature, pregenital, homosexual analysand how to leave childish pursuits behind. As generous as such an offer may appear at face value, if a therapist sees homoerotic attractions as a conscious or unconscious resistance to growing up, this may consciously or unconsciously rationalize therapeutic attempts to effect sexual orientation conversions (Duberman, 1991). Mitchell (1988) alludes to this countertransferential phenomenon of psychoanalytic theory and praxis in his concept of infantilism, that is, thinking about the patient as a metaphorical baby. Of course, as many a denigrated borderline patient can attest, the clinical tendency to treat patients as developmentally immature is not restricted to gay men. However, theoretical infantilism is often accompanied by therapeutic condescension (Drescher, 1997a) toward gay men, if not outright hostility, that often parallels the culture's denigration of homosexuality. McDougall's (1980) description of the "neosexual inventor," among whom she includes gay men, typifies such a condescending analytic attitude:

> The neosexual inventor is able to maintain the unconscious fantasy that the genital organs of his parents are not complementary to each other, and that he is in no way excluded from their eventual sexual relationship. In other words, the child has exchanged the oedipal myth, rooted in the socio-biological structure, for a private sexual mythology running counter to the cultural discourse. From this point on, his psy-

chosexual life will develop in conformity with this new model of sexuality, even though he will recognize intellectually that his is a fictitious primal scene. It is evident also that the creator of this fiction will find himself engaged in a continual battle with external reality. To realize that "one and one makes two" is not in itself a profound intellectual acquisition, but he who, in spite of the evidence to the contrary, calculates on some other numerical system, is going to encounter difficulties wherever he goes; he will have to make constant personal adjustments. The false arithmetic of perverse sexuality is not always entirely limited to the sexual relationship; it may color the understanding of human relations in general with the concomitant risk of precipitating moments of psychotic confusion [pp. 194–95].

It is worth noting that theorists like McDougall, in trying to present their biases as objective truths, rhetorically use mathematical analogies to elevate their own subjective narratives to the level of hard facts. This is a time-honored psychoanalytic tradition seen in Freud's (1905) previously cited but highly creative and original claim that "neuroses are . . . the negative of perversions" (p. 165). And the positively and negatively valenced Oedipal complexes (Freud, 1924) were early forerunners of McDougall's own arithmetic metaphors. From her perspective, she sees a heterosexual, mathematical design in nature. And, in her view, attempts to live outside the norms of heterosexuality are akin to courting psychosis—which is defined as denying the fact that one (man) and one (woman) equals two (a heterosexual couple).

In addition to infantilism, and the implicit condescension toward patients that it engenders, Mitchell has also criticized psychoanalysts who reason by genetic fallacy (Hartmann, 1960), and make "the equation of a behavior with its origins, or the assumption that a behavior originating out of conflict is inevitably forever linked to conflictual difficulties" (Mitchell, 1978, p. 258). It is, however, understandable how psychoanalysts are easily lured into this intellectual morass. There is, after all, an element of truth in McDougall's contention that it may be folly to attempt to live one's life in violation of cultural expectations and norms. Gay men often do face many interpersonal difficulties in their lives for that reason alone. However, McDougall's position does not accurately reflect the subjective experience of many gay men and fails to account for the actual developmental difficulties that they may face. In fact, finding oneself in opposition to the beliefs and biases of a powerful majority can often lead to marginal experiences that are frequently a prelude to future difficulties in living. Growing up to be gay means eventually having to challenge unproven cultural assumptions about what is innate about human sexuality. But contrary to McDougall's beliefs, it is not a psychological inability to accept the reality of heterosexuality with which gay men must contend. Instead, more commonly, they face the unaccepting attitudes and unwarranted expectations of the heterosexuals among whom they are raised: their families, their neighbors, their employers, and their peers, and sometimes the mental health professionals they seek out for psychotherapeutic assistance.

Heterosexual Normativity

One of the most difficult developmental tasks faced by gay men and women is the culture's demand for heterosexual performance. These demands have an enormous impact on gay people's lives at every level of the social order:

> Among developmental scientists it is still widely assumed that the normal and natural condition of sexual development is heterosexual. The evolution, functions, and outcomes of sexual development are still largely perceived as taking shape from the "natural fact" that desire for the opposite sex and reproduction guide all human affairs. Thus the occurrence of same-sex desire and action has been seen in negative terms. Homosexuality during adolescence has been explained by attributions to a variety of negative causes: to sexual abuse and seduction (typically imposed by an older perpetrator on a younger "victim"); to social learning through the associative pairing of sexual gratification with a same-sex dyad, often in situations of antisocial behavior, delinquency, and other forms of psychopathology; and to the lack of opportunities or restricted options for heterosexual outlets [Herdt and Boxer, 1993, p. 177].

Herdt and Boxer are describing the influence of heterosexual biases on developmental theories in general. But until recently, most psychoanalytic theorists of development likewise focused on heterosexual outcomes as the only desirable or positive possibility.[1] The theoretical biases of these analysts drew upon Freud's (1905) 19th-century interpretation of Darwinian evolution (1859), as it was transformed by Rado's (1969) mid-20th-century adaptational psychodynamics. Psychoanalysts com-

---

1. Alternative approaches to gay identities and relationships have been proffered by nonanalytic clinicians and social theorists (Weinberg, 1972; Tripp, 1975; Silverstein, 1981, 1991; McWhirter and Mattison, 1984; Stein and Cohen, 1986; Berzon, 1988; Coleman, 1988; DeCecco, 1988; Hanley-Hackenbruck, 1993; Hancock, 1995).

monly believed that normal development leading to procreative capabilities required identification with the sexual attractions of the same-sex parent and desire for an object of the other sex. This was referred to as the positive Oedipus complex. The fact that many lesbians and homosexual men could and did reproduce, despite an absence of attraction to the other sex, was irrelevant in this nosology. Freud (1923b) believed that "maleness combines the factors of subject, activity and possession of the penis; femaleness takes over those of object and passivity" (p. 145). In adopting this model, psychoanalysis not only naturalized the heterosexual paradigm, it also perpetuated the popular linkage of male homosexuality with a denigrated effeminacy. Blos (1962), for example, presents a theory of male homosexuality that sees it as both heterosexual development gone awry as well as the result of traumatic, feminizing experiences:

> In the boy three preconditions favor the channeling of genital sexuality into a homosexual object choice during puberty. One is a fear of the vagina as a devouring, castrating organ; we recognize in this unconscious concept a derivative of projected oral sadism. The second precondition resides in the boy's identification with the mother, a condition which is particularly apt to occur when the mother was inconsistent and frustrating while the father was either maternal or rejecting. A third precondition stems from the Oedipus complex which assumes the form of an inhibition or restriction summarily equating all females with mother and declaring introitus to be the father's prerogative [Blos, 1962, p. 105].

Many analysts have relied upon formulations like these in treating gay patients and have regarded them as genetic truths. Yet, Blos's etiological conclusions draw upon unanalyzed cultural assumptions, shared by analysts and patients alike, that have uncritically found their way into psychoanalytic formulations. In fact, embedded in each of Blos's three psychodynamic explanations are some common denigrating attitudes toward and beliefs about what it means to be a gay man: that he is a coward who fears women (Rado, 1969); that he is too close to his mother or a mama's boy (Freud, 1910a); and that he is an impotent competitor when compared to real, heterosexual men (Freud, 1923a). And it is these popular images, among others, that suffuse much of psychoanalysis' developmental literature. Tyson and Tyson's (1990) approach, for example, tries to integrate a range of differing, developmental models in psychoanalytic theory: psychosexuality, object relations, cognition and gender, to name a few. Nevertheless, despite the apparent complexity of the theoretical material they present, they too evoke the cultural belief that although one starts out a mama's boy, one must later give that up to become a man: "During the first two years the boy's major relationship is usually with his mother or female caregivers who provide him with his first role model . . . the boy, in order to establish a male gender role, must switch his identification from mother to father. It is the boy's successful disidentification with his mother that is crucial to his finding a firm sense of masculinity" (pp. 282–283). They then go on to say:

> Usually the little boy gives evidence of experiencing libidinal longing toward both parents (positive and negative oedipal strivings), and he may picture himself in a male or female role in relation to either of his parents. The boy's negative oedipal position in which he pictures himself consciously as feminine is usually shorter in duration than the positive position. This is commonly understood to result from his castration anxiety; if he were to persist in attempting to take mother's place and in identifying with her gender role—thus in fantasy becoming female—it would entail the loss of his precious penis [Tyson and Tyson, 1990, pp. 286–287].

The Tysons say a boy's attraction to his father means he "pictures himself as feminine." This assertion implies that a boy's same-sex interest is feminine, a common cultural belief about male homoerotic feelings. However, a boy's attraction to his father may initially have nothing to do with concepts of masculinity or femininity, although the feeling may later be labeled as such by the external environment (Chodorow, 1996). The feeling of attachment to father may come first, and its cultural and personal meaning regarding the boy's gender much later (de Marneffe, 1997; Coates, 1997). But in their psychodynamic formulations, the Tysons are not averse to equating male homosexuality with other denigrated cultural stereotypes as well. They further contend that to develop fully the negative oedipal complex, and to achieve a homosexual identification, the boy must imagine himself to be castrated, evoking the image of a gay man as eunuch. The eunuch is, of course, a variation on the impotent competitor, who in some cultures may even guard the heterosexual's wives and concubines.

Like many analysts, the Tysons treat the nuclear family as the template upon which appropriate models of gender are or should be constructed. A boy must become like the father who sired him. And, drawing upon Stoller's (1985) theory that gender identity disorder (GID) in boys is caused by a blissful, maternal symbiosis, a theory disproved by contemporary GID clinicians (Coates, 1992; Bradley and Zucker, 1997), the Tysons apparently also believe that maternal attitudes and behaviors may cause effeminacy, and subsequent homosexuality, in boys:

> The difficulty in counteracting identifications with the mother when no father figure is available was exemplified when one three-year-old was psychologically evaluated. On successfully pointing to all body parts on a picture of a small boy, his single mother reached under his shirt and insisted he point to his "boobies." She explained that the flowery jacket he was wearing was a hand-me-down from a friend's little girl and wasn't he lucky—it fit! About his long curls, she admitted they made him look like a girl, but they were so pretty she hated to cut them [Tyson and Tyson, 1990, p. 280].

Ostensibly, this is simply a clinical example of a disturbed mother who exemplifies, for the Tysons, how one should not raise boys. However, embedded in their text is the implication that the masculinizing role of the father is to tell the boy that he does not have "boobies," to prevent the child from wearing a girl's hand-me-downs, and to make sure the child gets his hair cut regularly. Furthermore, they do not clearly spell out what exactly was this child's "difficulty in counteracting identifications with the mother when no father figure is available." They provide no other clinical data, either about the mother, or about the child, or about the psychological tests he was undergoing. Is the boy's behavior effeminate, or is he, to the obvious chagrin of the Tysons, simply being dressed as a girl? Is this a boy who wants to be girl, that is to say a child with GID? Again, they do not say, although they point out that it was the mother, not the child, who drew attention to his "boobies." And despite having such a disturbed and disturbing mother, the child did "successfully" point to all of a boy's body parts on the test. Rather than clarifying and proving their theoretical point, which is that boys need a father or male figure to develop a masculine identity, this vignette instead invites the reader to share the authors' own disdain for the mother who is raising a mama's boy.

The Tysons write within a traditional psychoanalytic model that hypothesizes the existence of biological antecedents to one's sense of psychological gender. In their model, a boy's psychological attraction to his father would derive from a feminine or bisexual biological drive. Fast (1984), on the other hand, is a more innovative theorist who assumes both boys and girls must learn the attributes of their respective genders as part of normal development. She does not believe that children adopt the behaviors attributed to their anatomical gender solely on the basis of biological factors. She asserts that children are not just polymorphously perverse, they are also polymorphously gendered and that one must learn to become either a boy or a girl:

> As with other differentiations, gender differentiation is hypothesized to begin with the recognition of a limit. It begins as the boy gradually becomes increasingly aware of the meanings of sex difference. He notices that some capacities and attributes (expressed in self representations or as identifications) that he had assumed for himself cannot be his. They are the prerogatives of women. The genital differences between males and females determine the limits he must recognize. His typical reaction is a sense of loss or deprivation, although objectively no loss of attributes or capacities has occurred. However, the loss is actual, in that self representations embodying desired capacities and attributes must be given up as possibilities for himself. He may respond with protest, denial of sex difference, and so forth. Such reactions are usually transient [p. 52].

Fast, highlighting one aspect of the social construction of gender, believes that environmental influences, such as the mother's handling of the child, can shape a child's sense of gender and his understanding of femininity and masculinity. Yet, she, like the Tysons, also reasons from a heterosexual subjectivity that defines bisexuality as a "gender-inappropriate orientation" and a "developmental incompleteness in the move from a narcissistic to an object-related elaboration of masculinity and femininity, one that signals disturbance in both the individual's gender identity and in his or her perception of and relation to other-sex persons" (p. 93). In fact, one can read Fast's work as a heterosexual, feminist theory that tries to widen the gender options available to heterosexual women, although not those of gay men. Consequently, she too writes as if all boys are expected to develop a putative masculine identity which is synonymously defined as a heterosexual one.

Like traditional analysts, Fast places a great importance on the developing child's psychological responses to learning the anatomical distinctions between the sexes (Freud, 1925). As a consequence, in her heterosexual model of gender development, a boy must presumably learn to accept that sexual receptivity with a man is a female prerogative. And a boy must also learn that seeking out a male figure to satisfy one's affectionate and sexual longings is unacceptable. Fast, however, does draw attention to the difficulties encountered when one tries to make sense of a traditional Freudian belief regarding masculine development:

In this formulation all developmental influences in the boy's preoedipal period are seen as tending toward the establishment of his masculinity. Anatomically, the boy is male. His instinctual aims, when arise in the phallic period, are masculine. His first relationship (to his mother), by its cross-sex character, predisposes him to heterosexuality. In his experience there is only one sex, the male one. He uncritically assumes that everyone is, like himself, altogether male and masculine [Fast, 1984, pp. 48–49].

The belief that the mother-son dyad serves as a template for later adult, male heterosexuality is a recurring—albeit unproven—theme of psychoanalytic literature. Boys are presumed to attach heterosexually to their first object, the mother. Conversely, the infant girl's relationship to the mother is a homosexual one. She is presumed to have the more difficult task of learning to become a heterosexual by shifting her attachment from the mother to the father (Freud, 1920). Here, psychoanalytic drive theory uses the metaphor of *sexuality* to mean that phenomena observable in infants and children are the hypothetical antecedents of adult heterosexual behavior and that attachment is intrinsically sexual (Freud, 1905). However, other than its metaphoric quality, the heterosexuality implied to exist between an infant boy and his mother may, in fact, be totally unrelated to adult heterosexuality. Morgenthaler (1984), who writes within Freudian traditions, critically notes that: "Psychoanalysis discovered infantile sexuality as the expression of the polymorphous perverse sexual predisposition of man. However, it cannot refer solely to this discovery in order to explain mature sexual behavior, for no linear correlation exists between infantile sexual instinctual impulses and adult sexual modes of expression and experience" (p. 71).

Paradoxically, the theoretical construction of infantile heterosexuality in early male development coexists with another psychoanalytic hypothesis that infant boys believe everyone has a penis (Freud, 1923b). In other words, the theory also asserts that the subjectivity of the young male child is actually that of a homosexual male who believes the object of his affection, his mother, possesses the same anatomical endowment that he does. The reader who finds these discrepant perspectives confusing and unsettling is not alone. Is the male child to be defined as a heterosexual based on his physical, anatomical differences with his mother of which he is supposedly unaware? Should he be defined as homosexual because of his subjective belief that both he and his mother have a penis? Part of the difficulty in sorting out these contradictions stems from an ambiguous use of the terms heterosexuality and homosexuality. Do these categories refer to physical or psychological relations or, upon closer examination, are physical and psychological meanings being used interchangeably? Do adult heterosexual and homosexual relationships really have any direct correlation, other than linguistic ones, to the early mother-child relationship? Although psychoanalytic practice does require that a therapist tolerate contradiction and ambiguity in a patient's clinical material, this listening stance should not justify resorting to an illogical psychoanalytic theory. For as de Beauvoir (1952) wryly observed, "The psychoanalysts have had no trouble in finding empirical confirmation for their theories. As we know, it was possible for a long time to explain the position of the planets on the Ptolemaic system by adding to it sufficiently subtle complications" (p. 49).

Teleology

Some theories of heterosexual normativity rely upon underlying explanatory systems that account for heterosexuality by its final causes. Yet as Bowlby has noted, all teleological theories are scientifically suspect:

> A teleological theory is one that not only recognizes that an active biological system, whether physiological or behavioral, tends in a species' environment of adaptedness to result in a predictable outcome that is usually of value to the species, but accounts for its reaching that outcome by supposing that in some way the outcome is itself an immediate cause of the physiological reaction, or of the behavior, that leads to it. "The bird builds a nest to have somewhere to rear young" is a teleological statement when it carries the meaning that a bird needs to have somewhere to rear young and that such need causes it to build its nest. And because such a theory entails supposing that the future determines the present through some form of "finalistic causation," it lies outside the realm of science. . . . The puzzle has always been to understand how an action which has such predictable and useful results can be the effect of causes conceived in terms that are compatible with hard-headed science [Bowlby, 1969, pp. 124–125].

"People are heterosexual to have children" is a teleological statement in that it assumes the outcome of sexual reproduction is the cause of heterosexual attractions (Gooren, 1995). In "Three Essays on the Origins of Sexuality," Freud (1905) added a footnote ten years later that showed his awareness of the effects of such reasoning and warned that heterosexuality "is not a self-evident fact based upon an attraction that is ultimately of a chemical nature" (p. 146). Freud retained the footnote in subsequent versions as he struggled between essentialist and constructivist positions.

Lewes (1988) underscores this often-neglected Freudian position and Chodorow (1992) has also taken up the same point with her reminder that heterosexuality may also represent a compromise formation. Yet, despite their own objections to teleological reasoning, both Freud and Bowlby resort to it. Their own subjectivities led them to assume a purpose for human sexuality, that is, a heterosexual object choice leading to reproduction. Schafer (1995) draws attention to the role of teleology in psychoanalytic thought:

> I would say that in his theorizing Freud was looking backward from the teleologically prescribed endpoint of Darwinian sexual development. We can anticipate this conclusion from the word pregenital, for that word implies that one is speaking of matters that the individual ought to get beyond. . . . The word pregenital . . . is closely allied to the word preoedipal, even though it does establish a somewhat different center of interest. I maintain that "preoedipal" is also a teleological, implicitly moralistic term. It naturalizes a normative development that has been, from Freud on, usually understood in the sense of the positive oedipal, the crystallization though not the culmination of heterosexual development [pp. 195–196].

Despite his thoughtful footnote, as we have already seen in the actual text of "The Three Essays," Freud declares "The final outcome of the sexual development lies in what is known as the normal sexual life of the adult, in which the pursuit of pleasure comes under the sway of the reproductive function and in which the component instincts, under the primacy of a single erotogenic zone, form a firm organization directed towards a sexual aim attached to some extraneous sexual object" (1905, page 197). And Bowlby (1969) himself waxes teleological when he compares homosexuality to the military concept of friendly fire:

> An example of a system or rather integrate of systems that is in working order but not in functionally effective working order is the integrate responsible for sexual behavior in an adult who is a confirmed homosexual. In such a case all components of behavior may be performed efficiently but, because the object towards which they are directed is inappropriate, the functional consequence of reproduction cannot follow. The integrate not only has a predictable outcome, namely sexual orgasm with a partner of the same sex, but is so organized that the outcome is achieved. What makes it functionally ineffective is that for some reason the system has developed in such a way that its predictable outcome is unrelated to function. Were a similar error to have crept into the design of a radar and predictor-controlled

anti-aircraft gun, it might lead to the gun's firing efficiently but aiming so that it always destroyed a friendly plane and never an enemy one [pp. 130–131].

Both Freud and Bowlby were, in many ways, men ahead of their time; but in other ways, both were embedded in the social conventions of their own eras. Neither, of course, could have envisioned contemporary social phenomena such as gay men who marry women to have children, gay men who adopt children or find surrogate mothers willing to be inseminated (Patterson and Chan, 1996), or lesbians mothers who adopt or reproduce through artificial insemination or by asking a male friend to impregnate them (Kirkpatrick, 1996). And even if they had, the belief that one is supposed to be heterosexual in order to reproduce remains a powerful one, not only in the general culture, but in psychoanalytic theory as well.

Preoedipal Homosexuality

Psychoanalytic theory has struggled with an embedded heterosexual normativity based upon teleological assumptions as it tried to make sense of those individuals who did not conform to this ideal. This is most evident in Freud's (1924) belief that the positive resolution of the Oedipus complex was the central developmental task for all human beings. Although "positive" was originally intended in a mathematical sense, its normative dimension cannot be overlooked. So central was the belief in the Oedipus complex to his thinking, that questioning its universality in human development was akin to challenging the foundations of psychoanalysis itself (Freud, 1914b; Jones, 1961; Kerr, 1993). Sexual and psychological maturity were defined as identifying with the parent of the same sex, renouncing one's longings for the parent of the other sex and then ultimately seeking an adult, heterosexual partner of one's own.

The psychoanalytic imperative to heterosexually resolve the Oedipus complex became a procrustean bed into which homosexuality could only fit through a process of either juvenilization or pathologization. Freud and later psychoanalysts ultimately came to explain the "homosexual's" nonconformity with the expected Oedipal outcome by focusing on "preoedipal" aspects of development. Based upon Freud and Abraham's (1924) theory of psychosexual stages, analysts looked to the possible unfolding of events occurring in the years prior to the resolution of the Oedipus complex. Thus, homosexuality was commonly attributed by psychoanalysts to traumatic experiences that either arrested development (the individual never reached the positive Oedipal stage) or caused a regression (the individual reached Oedipal development but went back to an earlier psychosexual stage due to some trauma). If a gay man preferred sexual acts, such as placing his penis in a mouth or anus, or in his own hand, or in another person's hand, these were thought to represent the satisfaction of infantile, pregenital wishes. Infantile behaviors, of course, could be practiced by either heterosexuals or homosexuals (Freud, 1908) and were sometimes referred to as forepleasure (Freud, 1905), or the satisfactions that come before the main event. But in the psychoanalytic theory of immaturity, genitality, or inserting the penis in the vagina, is the main event and is the concrete representation and expression of a mature human sexuality.

A significant, corollary belief to pregenital sexuality and the psychoanalytic centrality of the Oedipal complex was a technical emphasis on interpreting clinical data from patients in developmental metaphors ascribed to the first five years of life. "If the memory which we have uncovered does not answer our expectations, it may be that we ought to pursue the same path a little further; perhaps behind the first traumatic scene there may be concealed the memory of a second, which satisfies our requirements better and whose reproduction has a greater therapeutic effect; so that the scene that was first discovered only has the significance of a connecting link in the chain of associations" (Freud, 1896b, p. 195). This belief also informed Freud's (1899) concept of screen memories, which hypothesized that significant early childhood events are obscured by later, sometimes apparently insignificant memories. Screen memories "are compromise formations like parapraxes or slips and more generally symptoms" (Laplanche and Pontalis, 1973) and therefore subject to analysis. One consequence of an interpretive stance that telescoped significant developmental phenomena into the first five years of life was that the oral, anal, and genital psychosexual stages were regarded as the most significant analogies through which all later experiences were defined. And consequently, much of the psychoanalytic literature on homosexuality primarily preoccupies itself with oral and anal explanations for the difficulties in living experienced by gay men (Lewes, 1988). In these formulations, analysts concern themselves with the developmental period before the ages of three to five. Combined with a belief that the subsequent years are only a latency period, analysts have a theoretical bias toward the formative effects of early life experiences that may lead them to diminish the relative importance of later ones:

> The literal interpretation of the term latency period to mean that these years are devoid of sexual urges—that, sexuality is latent—has long

ago been superseded by an acknowledgment of clinical evidence that sexual feelings expressed in masturbatory, voyeuristic, exhibitionistic. and sadomasochistic activities do not cease to exist during the latency period. However no new instinctual aim appears at this stage. What does change in the latency period is the growing control of the ego and the superego over the instinctual life. . . . This shift is substantially promoted by the fact that "object relations are given up and replaced by identifications" (Freud, 1924). The shift in cathexis from an outer to an inner object may well be called an essential criterion of the latency period [Blos, 1962, pp. 53–54].

Because of metapsychological beliefs like these, that no new instinctual aims emerge after the first five years of life, and that patient descriptions of later trauma are actually screens for earlier ones, many psychoanalysts are skeptical about interpreting postoedipal memories at face value. They believe that a deeper analysis, one which finds traces of the later memory in stages leading up to the Oedipus complex, is both necessary and more psychoanalytically meaningful (Freud, 1914b). Certainly, as any analyst can attest, careful attention to the multiple meanings of a memory is clinically useful in the treatment of any patient, regardless of sexual identity. However, Spence (1982), among others, has shown how studies of memory may not support these historic psychoanalytic assumptions. He makes the point that narratives in psychoanalysis may not actually emerge from memories at all but may instead be shared constructions of the analyst and patient. Stern (1985) makes a similar point:

In contrast to the infant as observed by developmental psychology, a different "infant" has been reconstructed by psychoanalytic theories in the course of clinical practice (primarily with adults). This infant is the joint creation of two people, the adult who grew up to become a psychiatric patient and the therapist, who has a theory about infant experience. This recreated infant is made up of memories, present reenactments in the transference, and theoretically guided interpretations. I call this creation the *clinical infant*, to be distinguished from the *observed infant*, whose behavior is examined at the very time of its occurrence [p. 14].

In addition to the problem of reconstructing memories that emerge in analysis, data from contemporary infant research also raises significant challenges to the assumptions that typically underlie preoedipal explanations of homosexuality. In the Freudian model, attachment to the mother was linked with the oral phase. Bowlby (1969), drawing upon the work of Lorenz (1953), emphasized that attachment did not necessarily depend upon feeding behaviors or putative sexual drives (Goldberg, Muir, and Kerr, 1995). Bowlby's work throws into question a host of psychoanalytic assumptions about the "orality" underlying gay relationships. Similar questions are also raised regarding Socarides' adaptation of Mahler's (1975) developmental model of separation and individuation, in which he claims homosexuality is a "resolution of the separation from the mother by running away from all women" (1968, p. 60). He believes that the homosexual is, in fact, caught between psychological fusion or symbiosis with the mother and the early phase of attempting to separate from her. This preoedipal assumption unflatteringly locates a gay man's character structure at a developmental level somewhere between those of a psychotic individual and a borderline personality disorder. Although Socarides treats Mahler's theory as a proven fact of normal development, Stern's (1985) concept of an *emergent self* questions the unproven assumptions of Mahler's developmental and, by extension, Socarides' preoedipal theory as well:

> The idea of a period of differentiation that is subjectively experienced by the infant as a form of merger and dual-unity with the mother is very problematic, as we have seen, but at the same time it has great appeal. By locating at a specific point in lived time those powerful human feelings of a background sense of well being in union with another, it gratifies the wish for an actual psychobiological wellspring from which such feelings originate and to which one could possibly return.
>
> Ultimately, this kind of notion is a statement of belief about whether the essential state of human existence is one of aloneness or togetherness. *It chooses togetherness, and in doing so it sets up the most basic sense of connectedness, affiliation, attachment, and security as givens.* No active process is needed for the infant to acquire or develop towards this basic sense. Nor is a basic attachment theory with purposeful moving parts and stages a necessity. Only a theory of separation and individuation is required to move the infant on developmentally, which Mahler goes on to provide.
>
> Attachment theory does the opposite. It makes the achievement of a basic sense of human connectedness the end point, not the starting point, of a long active developmental course involving the interplay of predesigned and acquired behaviors [pp. 240–241, emphasis added].

Stern contends that contemporary infant research based on attachment theory does not support Mahler's model of symbiosis preceding separation. And sex researchers outside psychoanalysis also offer data more directly at odds with preoedipal theories. Bell, Weinberg and Hammersmith (1981) questioned 979 homosexual and 477 heterosexual men and women about their early family relationships. Their results did not verify the smaller, psychoanalytic study of Bieber et al. (1962) which claimed that homosexual men had dominating mothers and withdrawn or hostile fathers:

> Thus, contrary to certain theoretical models, unusually close mother-son relationships in general do not appear to be important in accounting for the development of homosexuality among the men in our study. In other words, some boys who have this kind of relationship with their mothers may, for whatever reason, go on to become homosexual, but such cases appear to be the exception rather than the rule. It should be remembered that over half of the homosexual respondents did *not* report this kind of maternal relationship. Thus, neither unusually close nor unusually negative mother-son relationships can be considered important in the development of homosexuality among our male respondents [Bell, Weinberg, and Hammersmith, 1981, p. 45].

Unfortunately, an analytic conviction that the gay patient's intrapsychic and interpersonal difficulties are of preoedipal origin frequently results in a denial of the ways in which later experiences are important to an individual's development and dynamics. In fact, some analysts (Bergler, 1956) adopted a theoretical and clinical stance that dismissed the subjectivity of the adult gay man by denying the impact of their painful, traumatic encounters with antihomosexual attitudes. And such a stance also overlooked the possibility that these later, traumatic experiences may have had greater explanatory power than preoedipal theories did in explaining the adult, interpersonal difficulties of gay patients. Although some psychoanalysts argued that a gay man adopts a homosexual orientation as a result of fantasized beliefs about human sexuality and relationships, it may be more theoretically parsimonious to argue that gay patients' fantasies about the meanings of their sexual feelings strongly resonate with cultural prejudices about homosexuality. That is to say that as gay men were growing up, they internalized the culture's antihomosexual symbolism as a way to explain their own same-sex feelings. Or, it may be the therapist who, when confronted with a gay man's responses to these prejudices, goes looking for a supposedly deeper meaning. Consider the following session with a gay man who was reflecting on the painful fact that he had not recently heard from a man he was dating:

A: Martin and I had a hard time getting together for the first couple of weeks. He'd say he was working late or wasn't feeling well. My sense is that is really what is going on. I can remember there was a time when I would have turned that all around. I would wonder, "Is he really working late? Is he not interested? Is he seeing someone else?" This time I said to myself "That sounds right." If it's not what is going on, he has his reasons for not getting together. My attitude is the same at work, where things are going relatively well. My boss knows I'm gay. He's very supportive. I'm getting involved in some good projects and stepping into a role that is exactly what I want. All that has made me feel more comfortable in dealing with people professionally. In negotiations, I'm finding myself more able to think on my feet and less panicked. There haven't been any major confrontations. I'm not really sure what will happen when there is really a conflict with somebody. The other night I got a call to represent the agency where I do volunteer work. This is exactly the sort of thing I like doing, being involved with organizations like this one and being out front. I was thinking about the time when I would be more panicked about being out front for a gay organization, or even joining a gay group.

Th: What would panic you?

A: I was thinking about when some friends who were trying to get me involved in a gay political group. That was when I was still working at my previous job which was a pretty homophobic place. What the organization was doing was appealing, but I was worried what would happen if someone at work knew I was involved in work like that. I'm involved in a conservative, corporate community. A friend of mine, in a similar situation, was interested in working for the gay agency where I volunteer now. But he panicked about anybody at his job knowing he was involved in something like this. They had been instructed never to contact him at work and to only call him at home. A secretary slipped up and called him at work and he practically freaked out. He stopped coming to meetings after that. That is how I used to feel. The fear that someone at work may find out is still there but it does not drive me as much as it did years ago.

Th: What is the anxiety about people finding out?

A: On a rational level, I'm not sure what I have to be worried about.

Th: And on the anxiety level?

A: It's not so rational. It's not that you will lose your job. It's an anxiety about abuse, or confrontation.

Th: What comes to mind?

A: Well, whether its rational or not, somebody yelling something at you. "You faggot" or something along that line. Rationally, in the circles that

I'm traveling in, even if someone is thinking that, they probably wouldn't say that to your face. But the images coming up are that. Or gossiping behind your back that, "Oh well, A is gay" and being dismissive of anybody who falls into that category. That's what comes to mind when I think about that anxiety.

Th: Who is doing the yelling and the dismissing?

A: It doesn't have a particular face, but it's definitely male. The image is male figures, not female figures. This goes back to something I talked about before: people internalizing prejudices. Women internalize prejudices about women, blacks internalize prejudices about blacks, gays internalize prejudices about gays.

How do developmental theories affect how a psychoanalytically-oriented therapist listens to this material? For example, is the patient's sensitivity to rejection due to an early, preoedipal narcissistic vulnerability (Freud, 1914c)? Is this the same narcissistic vulnerability that caused his homosexuality or are the two traits independent variables? Is the patient simply an overly-sensitive injustice collector (Bergler, 1956)? Does this patient fear paternal reprisals and castration for desiring his mother (Blos, 1962) or does he fear social opprobrium for being gay? Might not growing up gay in a heterosexual world expose an individual to experiences that heighten a pre-existing narcissistic vulnerability? Are gay men postoedipally traumatized by rejecting experiences that lead to either regressive behaviors or dissociative tendencies? Where should a therapist focus the psychotherapeutic work with such a patient?

Any theory that does not account for the impact of early experiences on adult behaviors is not likely to be considered a psychoanalytic one. It is a central tenet of psychoanalysis that early relationships affect the nature and quality of later ones. And it should be emphasized that the analyses and meanings of early, dyadic experiences are as clinically useful to gay men as they are to heterosexual patients. However, an unfortunate consequence of the psychoanalytic emphasis on preoedipal explanations of homosexuality are the sometimes well-intentioned, and at other times ill-considered attempts to convert gay patients into heterosexuals. For these patients and therapists, the goal of analysis is to help patients resolve the preoedipal difficulties they presumably experienced in the early, dyadic relationship with the mother. If this can be done, the patient might take a further developmental step, enter the Oedipal triangle, and achieve heterosexuality. Although the obstacles along this theorized path can be both arcane and tortuous, it is believed by some that once gay men understand, in preoedipal terms, *why* they are homosexual, they stand a chance of getting back on the path to heterosexuality.

Unfortunately, the theoretical designation of the positive resolution of the Oedipal complex as the universal key permitting entrance into mature adulthood inevitably led to psychoanalysis' denigrated, hypothetical homosexual, endlessly caught up in a metaphoric cycle of immaturity and regression.

Oedipal Homosexuality

Although preoedipal theories of homosexuality predominate in the psychoanalytic literature, in recent years, some theorists have attempted to redefine affirmatively the Oedipal meanings of homosexuality within the traditional psychoanalytic canon. Rather than throw out the Oedipal baby with the bath water, these newer psychoanalytic formulations attempt to integrate existing psychoanalytic theories of development with the growing cultural belief that homosexuality is a normal variant of human sexuality. Greenberg and Mitchell (1983) refer to this strategic approach toward psychoanalytic theory as *accommodation.* Analysts with an accommodationist bent do not dispute the primacy of the Oedipal metaphor but instead claim that homosexuality can occur as a normative resolution of the Oedipus complex. Thus, Lewes (1988), Morgenthaler (1984), and Isay (1989) all pose respectful challenges to mainstream psychoanalytic theory without challenging its central dogma. They present normal variant theories of the Oedipus complex's resolution that make the case for a "mature" homosexuality. Lewes (1988), for example, takes the aforementioned psychoanalytic tradition of mathematical metaphors to creative heights. He charts a dozen possible oedipal outcomes, six of which are heterosexual and the other half homosexual (p. 83). He elaborates upon Freud's theory of the negative Oedipus complex in which the boy identifies with his mother and seeks an object resembling his father. Lewes hypothesizes remarkably complex but mathematically elegant interactions between "instinctual aims," "identifications," and "object choices." Lewes's creation of a narrative for oedipally neurotic (that is, normal or higher functioning) homosexuals is a theoretical developmental step that elevates gay men out of the preoedipal muck and mire of immaturity and pathology. It also illustrates the contortions theorists may perform to locate themselves in the center of an unquestioned belief in Oedipus.

> It is not accurate to speak of "normal" or "natural" development in the case of the Oedipus complex, since these terms suggest an orderly efflorescence of possibilities inherent in the individual before he enters

the oedipal stage. The mechanisms of the Oedipal complex are really a series of psychic traumas, and all results of it are neurotic compromise formations. Since even optimal development is a result of trauma, the fact that a certain development results from a "stunting" or "blocking" or "inhibition" of another possibility does not distinguish it from other developments. So all results of the Oedipus complex are traumatic, and, for similar reasons, all are "normal." Some are more pathological than others, but the reason for considering them so cannot be derived from the operations of the Oedipus complex. Those writers who think otherwise ignore the traumatic origins of even optimal results and, in effect, disguise a moral judgment about what is "natural" as a pseuodobiological argument [Lewes, 1988, p. 82].

With a different theory, but with a similar proclivity for accommodation, Morgenthaler (1984) explains the dynamics of neurotic homosexuals within an Oedipal framework that avoids pathologizing them:

Neurotic homosexuality can be termed a regressive adaptation that prevents an oral regression. It serves the defense and is the expression of the repression of the Oedipus complex. The incest wish and castration anxiety provoke a regression that rests on two fixation points— one is sado-anal; the other, phallic-narcissistic. The castration anxiety chases the homosexual from one level of regression to the other, while the incest wish finds gratification in either one or the other libido positions. The two libido positions, the sado-anal and the phallic-narcissistic, can be interchanged with the greatest ease. The homosexual fixation is found in this double track of the regression procedure. The homosexual cannot do without it, because of the threat of a further regression. This regression to oral fixations would lead to a complete dissolution and disintegration of the ego [p. 34].

Morgenthaler and Lewes both demonstrate how the dynamic unconscious can be, in fact, a blank screen upon which analysts project multiple theories and interpretations. Their Oedipal formulations of neurotic homosexuality can be contrasted with the equally intricate metapsychological constructs of theorists with whom they disagree. Ovesey (1969), for example, writes from an adaptational (Rado, 1969), pathological view of homosexuality and offers an alternative explanation regarding the relationship between castration anxiety and homosexuality:

The child will abandon important gratifications to insure dependency status. A good example is infantile sexuality. Here, excessive parental discipline confronts the child with two great dangers: physical punishment and the withdrawal of love. The former is frequently extended in fantasy to imply bodily mutilation (castration) and death; the latter means loss of dependency. In either case each is a threat to survival and the child responds with the emergency emotion of fear. This fear may be so great as to force a partial or complete withdrawal from sexual activity. Later, as the child grows, any sexual situation will revive the earlier fear, and an inhibition of normal sexual behavior is established. This inhibition of healthy function by fear in response to an imagined danger is the core of the neurotic process.

Such an inhibition is the take-off point for a homosexual adaptation. The person reacts with such intense fear in relation to a heterosexual object that he fails in heterosexual performance. His sexual need, however, continues unabated and is diverted to a "safer" object. This object is a homosexual one, and it derives its added safety from the reassuring presence of the penis, which allays the patient's castration anxiety. Homosexuality, in this light, is a deviant form of sexual adaptation into which the patient is forced by the injection of fear into the normal sexual function [pp. 20–21].

As is often found in political debates, opposing factions may use the same words but imbue them with different meanings. Here, for example, Ovesey, unlike Morgenthaler and Lewes, does not define neurotic as normal. Like Socarides (1968), he uses the term to mean that homosexuality is a curable neurosis rather than an untreatable developmental arrest. Discrepancies like these, which are common in the analytic literature, undermine the credibility of the universality of the Oedipus complex, particularly when even the advocates of this theory are unable to agree among themselves about the complex's actual meaning.

Postoedipal Homosexuality

Postoedipal theories are relatively rare in the psychoanalytic literature and are mentioned here for the sake of inclusiveness. A postoedipal theory of homosexuality does not necessarily have to deny the importance of early developmental issues. For example, Friedman (1988) believes that intrauterine factors biologically cause a preoedipal gender dysphoria that is the precursor for adult homosexuality. However, a postoedipal developmental stage explains why adult gay men do not have a gender identity disorder:

As I see it, during adolescence and young adulthood the capacity for abstract reasoning and theorizing increases and the person's social world greatly expands. In addition, the meaning of the categories masculine and feminine change. Despite the existence of a homosexual script, self-labeling can change to accommodate a masculine label. According to this model, many boys become homosexual in a preadolescent environment in which they felt unmasculine and remain homosexual after they learn to view themselves as masculine. A large number of homosexual men thus seem to leave behind the childhood psychopathology associated with gender disturbance. In these individuals, superego and ego ultimately evolve normally despite childhood gender-self impairment. It is possible that, using Kohut's terminology, key transmuting internalizations occur in these individuals, but later than normal and long after homoerotic fantasies have become differentiated. With such internalization comes self-repair: the self is no longer perceived as damaged and self-esteem regulation is internalized and normalized [p. 243].

Friedman's locates the causes of homosexuality within the womb—homosexuality is not just preoedipal, it is actually prenatal—thus undermining the arguments of preoedipal theorists who use their own hypotheses about family constellations to justify psychotherapeutic conversions of sexual identities. His theory further defines homosexuality as originating from a pathological process, a gender identity disturbance, that eventually corrects itself postoedipally. Thus, later developmental experiences can overcome the difficulties presumed to appear in the first years of life. Friedman's theoretical strategy is more subversive than an accommodationist reliance upon the negative resolution of the Oedipal complex. Like Rado and Bowlby, he uses scientific research outside of psychoanalysis to buttress his own arguments. These findings, however, are presented as a harder, and therefore purer, truth than the softer science which characterizes psychoanalytic inquiry. Appropriately, this stance ultimately leaves the worth of purely psychoanalytic findings open to question. As Friedman notes,

> As Freud acquired more experience with psychoanalysis, however, he tended to justify his assertions about scientific matters not only on the basis of superior insight but also because he and his colleagues were using a method of treatment and research that no one else had access to. At times, the complex and evolving psychoanalytic method was treated as if it were an invention like the microscope or the light bulb. The "discoveries" of psychoanalytic research were reported in the form of "conclusions" based on personal observation [p. 53].

Coming from an entirely different perspective is Sullivan's postoedipal theory of homosexuality and its placement of the significant developmental epoch of homosexual expression, "preadolescence," between eight and a half and ten years of age. Sullivan believes it is a time when boys show "a specific new type of interest in a *particular* member of the same sex who becomes a chum or a close friend" (1953, p. 245) and describes these relationships as *chumships*. In this developmental model, homosexual behavior between boys of the same age is normal and expectable. It was also not a predictor of adult homosexuality but rather just a part of the normal process of learning about other people's bodies. However, Sullivan believed that a chumship between a preadolescent boy and an older, adolescent boy could traumatize the younger boy and be a postoedipal cause of homosexual feelings and arousal patterns that persisted into adulthood.

Sullivan's theoretical approach attempts radically to undermine the Freudian canon by developing a psychoanalytic approach based upon social theory (Perry, 1982; Greenberg and Mitchell, 1983; Lionells, et al., 1995). His resort to juvenilization illustrates further that a developmental theory's timing of the acquisition of homosexuality can be independent of the theorizer's belief about its potential valued or denigrated meanings. And finally, that Sullivan himself was a closeted man who lived with a homosexual lover (Chatelaine, 1981; Perry, 1982; Ortmeyer, 1995) serves to highlight the ways in which the social denigration of homosexuality can be internalized by a gay man himself.

The Invisible Gay Adolescent

One unfortunate result of the psychoanalytic emphasis on the preoedipal meanings of homosexuality has been the field's neglect of gay teenagers. The invisibility of gay adolescents in the psychoanalytic literature stems from another, unproven analytic assumption: that adolescents are too young to have a fixed gay identity. This is actually not the case of many gay men who recall strong, same-sex attractions from an early age. Many teenagers can and do identify themselves as gay (Martin, 1982; Hetrick and Martin, 1988; Herdt and Boxer, 1993). Usually, parents only learn about their children's same-sex feelings at a much later age than when they initially emerged. Puberty can sometimes provoke the first public "coming out" of these feelings, for example, when an anxious and confused child tells his parents about being attracted to other boys. At other times, the parent learns about these feelings inadvertently, as when they find the child in a compromising position or discover a cache of nude male photographs. One parent reported the discovery of gay web pages listed in their fifteen-year-old son's Internet bookmarks. These discoveries often lead to a "heterosexual panic" in the family and an increased

scrutiny of the child. Often, the child is taken to a mental health professional and sometimes even hospitalized. A classical example of these
parental responses was seen in Freud's (1920) treatment of a young,
homosexual woman. Although Freud noted that she was not ill and had
no symptoms, she did, however, attempt suicide as a result of being
intensely caught up in a struggle with her parents to give up her homosexual infatuation with another woman (Harris, 1991). Further illustrating psychoanalysis's selective inattention to gay teenagers is the absence
of any significant literature that addresses the problem of suicide among
them. (For nonanalytic discussions of this problem, see Bell and
Weinberg, 1978; Hetrick and Martin, 1988; Hendin, 1992; Herdt and
Boxer, 1992; Remafedi et al., 1998.)

Fraiberg's (1961) treatment of a male adolescent troubled by his
homosexuality is illustrative of the psychoanalytic bias that ignores and
may even do harm to gay teenagers. Her encouragement of her patient's
heterosexual activities, and discouragement of his homosexual ones, led
to his sexual experimentation with a female prostitute followed by a subsequent avoidance of contact with members of either sex. Fraiberg
thought it was most important to keep her patient from finding "a homosexual partner to whom he was bound through love" (p. 107). In Fraiberg's
view, the teenage boy's sexual experimentation with a prostitute was still
considered a superior option to his forming loving attachments with
another man. Ironically, Fraiberg's work with this patient ultimately led
him to attempt to find a solution to his sexual dilemma that echoed a
rather common cultural belief about how to "cure" homosexuality. (See
Isay, 1996, for a more detailed discussion of this case.)

Of course, there are children who do have homosexual interests in
adolescence that do not necessarily lead to an adult, gay identity (Kinsey,
Pomeroy and Martin, 1948). And perhaps it is this phenomenon that
contributes to the psychoanalytic presumption that all children are heterosexual until proven otherwise. But in their attempts to avoid a non-
heterosexual outcome, psychoanalysts have rationalized coercive
conversions of gay teenagers. And in their efforts to save any potential
heterosexual they may encounter, psychoanalysts sometimes seem willing to inflict damage upon the self-esteem of the children who eventually
grow up to be gay. The latter are frequently traumatized by treatments in
which a therapist communicates the expectation that the child would be
better off if he conformed to heterosexual expectations. Jay, for example,
was a patient I treated as an adult who was in treatment as a child and
adolescent with a psychoanalytically-trained therapist. When Jay was fifteen, he told his therapist he was gay. The therapist explained to Jay that

homosexual feelings were normal in adolescence and just because he had them did not mean that he was gay. The therapist also said that he himself had "bisexual" feelings as a young man but he was now happily married with a wife and children of his own. He strongly urged Jay not to discuss this with his parents, as he believed that coming out to them might undermine Jay's eventual ability to develop a firm, heterosexual identity.

However, as treatment proceeded, Jay's therapist was repeatedly pressed by the parents who wanted to know if their son was gay. The therapist repeatedly told them that Jay was not. When Jay eventually did come out to his parents at age eighteen, he did so over the objections of his therapist. The parents were angry at the therapist because they had been led to believe that the treatment would prevent such an outcome. Coming out inevitably led to the end of a treatment relationship that had lasted many years. Jay felt the therapist did not support him for who he was, and the parents felt they had been deceived by the therapist. Jay, reentering treatment in his early twenties as a self-identified gay man, welled up with tears when he told this story and didn't wish to speak of his feelings about the previous therapist. When contacted regarding the details of Jay's treatment, that therapist explained that the patient had always been confused about his own identity, that he had very serious psychological problems, and that he was only defining himself as gay as a way to avoid dealing with these more serious problems.

This therapist's approach to Jay was not unusual. A psychoanalytic unwillingness to see gay teenagers, supported by many unwarranted theoretical assumptions, renders them invisible. Often, this invisibility is, in part, linked to the wishes of the parents who bring their children into treatment. Parents often have a strong desire for heterosexual progeny who resemble themselves and who will not live outside their beliefs and values. They will sometimes designate a shamanistic psychoanalyst to provide the role of male guide when the usual methods believed to inculcate masculinity and heterosexuality have failed. That some psychoanalysts believe they should provide this masculinizing function reflects not only their theoretical biases, but their ignorance of human sexual diversity and about normal gay male development as well (see Corbett, 1996).

The Observed Gay Man

Clinicians treating gay male patients may find themselves in the unenviable position of sorting out the complex frames of reference created by the standard preoedipal and oedipal narratives. Given the wide range of narrative possibilities, it is unclear that listening to a patient's material through a filter of theory is always helpful:

> **B:** The first dream, which I don't remember, left me with an all-alone feeling of being abandoned and everybody not liking me, including my [female] friend Bobby to whom I felt a strong attraction. She doesn't like me. Then, in the second dream, there was some girl teaching me this game. It wasn't a game but something to do. She is fearful and disgusted by me but feels sorry for me and is trying to teach me the game. I can see by looking in her eyes, her dislike for me now. It was something I did in the first dream that made everyone hate me. I fucked something up. Is it being gay? I don't remember.

The first two dreams, both describing uncomfortable dyadic relationships with a woman, might easily be interpreted to have preoedipal meanings. The patient goes on, however, with dream material about his paternal relationship that could be linked to oedipal issues:

> **B:** Then the final dream which was fresh in my mind. I feel like shit, very depressed, unloved and unwanted. My Dad comes home, finds me watching TV and asks why didn't I fix this remote gadget. He showed me this remote and told me he wanted it fixed. Now I remember the object but I don't know what I'm supposed to do with it. He starts screaming. I start to cry. I tell him I'll do it right away, after dinner. He is angry and has to punish me. He pushes me on my side and lightly slaps me on my butt. I said, "What is that for? I'm sorry. I fucked up. I didn't get it done. Why did you have to hit me? What did that prove?" All hell breaks loose. My Mom is there. I try to explain that I am in therapy now and that is why I want to discuss this situation. "Why did you hit me? Is this your way of proving you are a tough guy?" I'm afraid of really being hurt and I'm afraid of saying this to him. I get up the nerve to say "You were a lousy father" and I remember, in the dream, trying to come up with an analogy. I said "I hated you more than glass in my eye or glass in my penis." When you think of it, what are the two worst feelings? He is sitting at the dinner table and picks up a large pair of scissors. I'm afraid he will throw them at me. By saying it I hope he won't and I open the door, only halfway. Then I wake up.
>
> I figured the first question was how did I feel in the dream. I felt this is an important dream. Do I need to do this in reality? I hope not. It felt good to stand up and present my case. I was angry. I was hostile. I felt a lot of hostility towards me. I was fearful. There was a lot of crying and a lot of screaming on both our parts. Getting back to the penis and what that might bring up. There was a shower incident in my youth. I took a shower with my father and it was the first time I saw his penis. I was seven or eight years old. It wasn't unnatural, but being a gay kid, there

was something about seeing this penis for the first time. And then it was almost at eye level.

It should be noted that in his account of an early childhood memory, the patient thinks of himself as having been gay at the age of seven or eight.

Th: How did it make you feel to see your father's penis?

B: I guess it was awkward. It felt strange to be in the shower with him at the same time. I had never done that before. I think it means you will tell me to confront my father about his parenting skills.

Th: Perhaps you have opinions about his parenting skills?

B: I do. I remember thinking more and more as a child how I hated my father. I wished he was dead. Why couldn't he leave? I wished him dead. I felt that a lot in my childhood. The criticism, the yelling, the screaming, the constant yelling between him and my mother and my siblings. We were all idiots. We couldn't do anything right. There was this constant bickering that he and my mother had. As a kid seeing all this anger coming from him, I always thought, "Why can't he be dead? Mom and I can do fine. We don't need him." I remember wondering why didn't Mom divorce him? I never understood why she stayed with him. I've been thinking about these things recently. The dream gave me the opportunity to get it out in the open.

Historically, psychoanalysis' preoedipal formulations focused on the "causes" of homosexuality. A gay man's low self-esteem, for example, might be attributed to his difficulties in acquiring ego strengths during that early period of development. Within the confines of the oedipal narrative, this dream, considered in all three parts, might be interpreted as either a preoedipal identification with the mother (Freud, 1910a) or a regressive inhibition to avoid oedipal conflict and aggression (Freud, 1923a), or both. Castration and competition metaphors abound in support of an oedipal interpretation. What is a therapist to do?

I would suggest that treating this gay man is best accomplished when the therapist first begins by acknowledging the patient's subjectivity in growing up to be gay. In this case, the patient never quite mastered the rules of the heterosexual game. He is expected to operate the way his father does, but his equipment doesn't seem to work according to the expectations of father, mother, or anyone else. Something is wrong with him and no one can show him how to make things work properly. His parents lacked the ability to explain how to make sense of not only his homoerotic feelings, but of all his feelings. People don't like him, not only because of what he feels, but because he cannot do what is expected of him. This has left him feeling alone, criticized and incompetent. He never mastered the role of heterosexual boy to which he had been assigned at birth and into which he was supposed to develop. Not surprisingly, an individual's incompetence in the heterosexual arena does not easily or automatically translate into competence in gay relationships. Thus, this man came into treatment seeking help in working on finding a gay relationship because he felt incompetent and inadequate to that task as well.

Conclusion

The traditional psychoanalytic developmental literature's perspective on homosexuality as failed heterosexuality was based on cultural beliefs that psychoanalysts shared with patients and their families. As part of this cultural bias, the historic privileging of data obtained from antihomosexual psychoanalytic narratives led to the creation of developmental myths now known to be at odds with data from other sources. Psychoanalytic approaches that described the psychological and interpersonal difficulties of gay men in preoedipal terms were frequently reductionistic and often removed from the actual reported experiences of gay men. And preoedipal theories of homosexuality were primarily used to explain interpersonal difficulties that developed in the postoedipal era.

The cultural belief that one is supposed to be heterosexual in order to reproduce is a powerful one. In fact, homosexuality is always inappropriate when reproduction is the teleologically reasoned goal of human sexuality. This belief is not confined to psychoanalysts, although some (Socarides, 1994) claim the ubiquity of this belief across cultures "proves" homosexuality is pathological (by the same reasoning, the ubiquity of a belief in God across cultures would prove the existence of a higher being). Contending with cultural constructions of masculinity and femininity is a major stressor for men who grow up to be gay. That is why the psychological and interpersonal difficulties of gay men who come into treatment are often more comprehensible when viewed as adaptations to later life experiences rather than preoedipal ones.

Contemporary psychoanalytic clinicians should be able to incorporate data from other fields that conflict with traditional psychoanalytic explanations of homosexuality. One valuable achievement of psychoanalytic growth and understanding *is* the ability to tolerate mutually contradictory ideas. Rather than insisting on the veracity of psychoanalytical narratives that simply recapitulate antihomosexual cultural beliefs, clinicians need to acknowledge the present uncertainty in our understanding of the origins of human sexuality. To avoid retraumatizing gay patients in treatment, the principal therapeutic goal should be to help them understand how they make sense of their homoerotic affects, rather than assuming one can determine why they are gay. In doing so, a psychoanalytically-informed treatment can help gay patients come to understand the meanings that they, their families, and their culture attribute to homoerotic attractions. In the analytic exploration of the way these meanings have been internalized, new and respectful meanings may ultimately emerge.

6

REPARATIVE THERAPIES

We refused most emphatically to turn a patient who puts himself into our hands in search of help into our private property, to decide his fate for him, to force our own ideals upon him, and with the pride of a Creator to form him in our own image and see that it is good . . . we cannot accept (the) proposal either—namely that psycho-analysis should place itself in the service of a particular philosophical outlook on the world and should urge this upon the patient for the purpose of ennobling his mind. In my opinion, this is after all only to use violence, even though it is overlaid with the most honorable motives.

Sigmund Freud, "Lines of Advance in Psycho-analytic Therapy" (1919)

There is no point telling people who have difficulties that they are ill.

Donald W. Winnicott, *Talking to Parents* (1957)

No man should be yoked by any stereotyped notion of idealized maleness or a single way of life. Every man has to be the kind of man that he can be within the limitations of his past, his present, and what he can envision as a future for himself.

Lawrence J. Hatterer
Changing Homosexuality in the Male (1970)

As opposed to psychosurgery, electroshock, or various aversive behavioral techniques, there are some practitioners who offer psychotherapeutic treatment approaches for gay men which make the claim that they can substantially alter a patient's sexual identity and/or sexual attractions. One leading contemporary figure in this group is Joseph Nicolosi (1991) who terms his particular approach to changing sexual orientation "reparative therapy." In recent years, the term has come into general usage among laymen and mental health professionals. Properly speaking, reparative therapy refers to his work and to that of his predecessor, Elizabeth Moberly (1983a,b). Reparative therapy is so-named because it is based upon a developmental theory that claims a "failure to fully gender identify" with male figures leads to a "deficit in sense of personal power. Homosexuality is understood to represent the drive to repair the original gender-identity injury" (Nicolosi, 1991, p. xvi). Reparative therapy claims to repair the deficit that leads to homosexual activity.

Although Nicolosi presumes to change homosexuality, and to be able to do so while working within a psychoanalytic frame of reference, he is not alone in claiming that a psychoanalytically-informed psychotherapy can bring about this change in some people. In fact, he joins a list of practitioners dating back several decades, prominent among whom are Bieber (et al., 1962), Socarides (1968), Ovesey (1969), Hatterer (1970), Moberly (1983a,b), and Siegel (1988). These practitioners, in turn, are informed by other theorists, some of whom have already been discussed, who did not necessarily offer a sexual conversion therapy per se, but who did proffer psychoanalytic formulations as to the etiology of homosexuality (Rado, 1969; Khan, 1979).

This chapter concerns itself with those theorists who offer a definitive treatment strategy to change homosexual attractions and who, for convenience's sake, are grouped together under the rubric of reparative therapies. Different practitioners have differing ideas as to the meaning of homosexuality and how to "cure" it through psychoanalytic psychotherapy. However, what these theories have in common with each other, and with the approach taken by Nicolosi, is a model of psychotherapy that presumes to be psychoanalytically-informed, and thus to exist on the same practical basis as conventional psychoanalysis or psychoanalytic psychotherapy. This chapter questions these claims on the basis of my belief that psychoanalytic treatment is voluntary, respects the individuality of the patient, and seeks to provide relief through means other than suggestion, coercion, or indoctrination. Firstly, however, this chapter draws attention to the kinds of theories reparative therapists employ, their tenuous connection to either Freud or contemporary psychoanalytic theory, as well as to the embedded moral judgments that these theories contain. In proffering these discussions, which are occasionally quite pointed, it is not my intention to denigrate the good faith of the therapist or theorist with whom I disagree. I also do not wish to question either the motives or posttreatment reports of patients who have sought these treatments and who feel they have benefited from them. On the contrary, my goal is to open up a discussion that moves away from polarizing categories and to illustrate what psychotherapeutic approaches, when viewed through a relational paradigm, can and cannot accomplish.

Toward that end, though it will involve some repetition from earlier chapters, this chapter begins by critically reviewing some common features of the psychoanalytic theories that inform reparative therapy. It also explains the history and meanings of the values that lead to that therapeutic approach. The motivations of patients seeking reparative therapy, the majority of whom do not respond to these treatments, are also discussed. Reparative therapy's aversive side effects have been insufficiently documented and to that end this chapter also offers some anecdotal reports of patients who have unsuccessfully undergone these treatments. Finally, I believe that reparative therapy practices distort mainstream psychoanalytic theories and practices, and, in explaining how they do so, I raise some ethical questions about them.

Reparative Therapy's Etiological Theories

It is instructive to begin with Freud's own position on the etiology and treatment of homosexuality. One important thing that Freud did was to imagine an alternative to essentialist and functionalist views of sexuality as uniform in development and leading inevitably to heterosexuality and procreation. It is this latter view, widely shared in the culture, that motivates many gay and homosexually-identified men to spend years in therapy or analysis trying to find out what caused their same-sex attractions. The questions of etiology that surround their homosexual attractions arise from the perspective that treats heterosexuality as nature's default setting. Freud (1905), in questioning that assumption, in a previously-mentioned footnote added "the exclusive sexual interest felt by men for women is also a problem that needs elucidating and is not a self-evident fact based upon an attraction that is ultimately of a chemical nature" (p. 146). Some contemporary analysts have recently revived Freud's idea that the etiology of heterosexuality is also a mystery to explore (Lewes,

1988; Chodorow, 1992). In fact, in some of his writing and theorizing, Freud believed heterosexuality to be as much of a mystery as homosexuality. Either mystery could only be solved by taking developmental vicissitudes—here modern relational theorists would say a constructivist approach—into account.

But Freud was not always consistent with himself, and more than once succumbed to making various etiological claims. For example, in "Three Essays on the Origins of Sexuality" (Freud, 1905), he claimed to have found an organic substrate for inversion: man is innately bisexual and, in the absence of psychic repression, it is possible for his homosexual instinct to be expressed in adulthood. The repressive agency hypothetically charged with preventing such expressions was a developmental achievement, and its absence in adult inverts allowed expression of their sexually immature instinct. Almost twenty years later, Freud's repertory of etiological tales had grown to four (Freud, 1910a, 1911, 1920, 1923a). Since then, psychoanalysts have crafted many more theories explaining homosexuality's causes. (For critical discussions of those theories see Lewes, 1988; Hopcke, 1989; O'Connor and Ryan, 1993; Domenici and Lesser, 1995; Glassgold and Iasenza, 1995; D'Ercole, 1996; Drescher, 1996a; Lesser, 1996; Magee and Miller, 1996a, 1997; Orange, 1996; Lingiardi, 1997; Schwartz, 1998; Kiersky, in press; Kiersky and Gould, in press.) The lure of making further etiological discoveries continues to exert an understandable, if methodologically faulty attraction for many a clinician. Somewhere at this moment, a therapist is certain that he or she is discovering the origins of a patient's same-sex feelings, and may be writing a case for publication about another new cause of homosexuality, or is presenting such a case at a clinical conference to professional colleagues.

Methodological debates aside, the search for etiological explanations is a misleading guide to the conduct of a psychotherapy. Rather than discovering origins, psychoanalysis is better suited to decipher meanings. Inevitably, an analytically-informed treatment must contend with the patient's meanings, those of the therapist, as well as the interplay between them. The therapist cannot truthfully answer the patient who asks "Why am I a homosexual?" However, he or she can answer, or at least address, a different question: "What does it mean to the patient if he is a 'homosexual?'" as well as another question: "What does it mean if the patient wants to know what causes homosexuality?" From this perspective, the meanings of the extant psychoanalytic literature of etiologies can be seen altogether differently. It is a catalogue of the many explanations used to encompass meanings, often denigrated meanings, of same-sex feelings to patients, to their families, to their cultures, and to their therapists.

In this context, it is quite striking that the group of thinkers who are referred to here as reparative therapists uniformly introduce etiological formulations into their discussions of treatment, not only with their colleagues, but also with their patients. In general, reparative therapists claim that a psychoanalytic understanding of human nature reveals adult homosexuality to be either a developmental arrest, or a result of traumatic, psychological conflict. The attractiveness of these theories to men who are deeply troubled by their homoerotic feelings should not be underestimated. Just as the psychoanalytic literature's etiological repertoire subsumed multiple meanings of homosexuality, similar meanings, most often denigrated ones, are quite regularly the motivating force that drives patients to seek reparative treatments. The stage is thus set for the patient's meaning-making system to become interdigitated with the reparative therapist's etiological theory in ways that may well foreclose a deeper exploration of what troubles him.

The reparative therapy view can be strongly contrasted with Freud's original one, that homosexuality is simply a nonconflicted, if developmentally immature, normal deviation. That theory leaves open the possibility that a patient may actually like his or her homoerotic feelings. In "Psychogenesis of a Case of Homosexuality in a Woman" (1920), Freud documented the case history of his self-consciously benighted attempt to change a lesbian's sexual orientation. His patient was an eighteen-year-old Viennese girl who had developed an intimate relationship with an older woman. After she attempted suicide because her father criticized her scandalous behavior, the parents brought the young woman to Freud for psychoanalytic treatment. They wanted him to change her sexual identity.

> Unfavorable features in the present case were the facts that the girl was not in any way ill (she did not suffer from anything in herself, nor did she complain of her condition) and that the task to be carried out did not consist in resolving a neurotic conflict but in converting one variety of the genital organization of sexuality into the other. Such an achievement—the removal of genital inversion or homosexuality—is in my experience never an easy matter [Freud, 1920, p. 151].

To reiterate, Freud (1905) saw deviations from adult heterosexuality as a nonconflictual expression of the instincts. Because this patient had no intrapsychic conflict, there was nothing to treat. Freud believed there was as little possibility of effecting a sexual orientation change in his lesbian patient as there was of converting a heterosexual woman into a homosexual one, noting that "except for good practical reasons the latter is never attempted" (Freud, 1920, p. 151).

To refute this therapeutic pessimism, reparative therapists integrate neo-Freudian theories into the Freudian canon. Reparative theories disagree with Freud's etiological hypotheses while otherwise claiming allegiance to mainstream analytic principles. Socarides' (1968) theory of homosexuality, for example, retains Freud's original language of instincts and psychic structures but goes on to describe a homosexual, neurotic conflict that Freud had never envisioned: "The perverted action, like the neurotic symptom, results from the conflict between the ego and the id and represents a compromise formation which at the same time must be acceptable to the demands of the superego. . . . [T]he instinctual gratification takes place in disguised form while its real content remains unconscious" (Socarides, 1968, pp. 35–36). Homosexual acts, perverted actions in Socarides' nomenclature, would in principle reveal an underlying conflict. Further, an examination of that conflict should obviate the need to retain the symptom. What Socarides asserts is not merely that homosexual men have conflicts, nor that their sexual lives may be caught up in those conflicts in various ways, but that some hitherto unexamined conflict is the very cause of the homosexual act.

Socarides' theory, interestingly, implies that Freud had not seen the instinctual conflict because it was too well disguised. Yet Socarides did not prove that homosexuality arose from an unconscious, intrapsychic conflict. Unconscious, intrapsychic conflicts are metapsychological abstractions that can only be understood inferentially. Like any interpretive stance, this model has value only insofar as it leads to productive engagement with the patient, its ultimate validity necessarily having to be supported by extraclinical research. However, coming from a perspective that naturalized heterosexuality, Socarides did not have to prove anything. He only needed to construct a meaningful case for his particular vision of unobservable, unconscious processes.

Socarides' etiological theory derives, in part, from Rado's (1969) adaptational psychodynamics, a post-Freudian approach that rejected many early psychoanalytic concepts, including that of innate bisexuality: "I know of nothing that indicates that there is any such thing as innate orgastic desire for a partner of the same sex. . . . Homosexuality is a deficient adaptation evolved by the organism in response to its own emergency overreaction and dyscontrol" (Rado, 1969, pp. 210–212). Socarides similarly rejects innate bisexuality. Where Freud saw a psychic disposition, Socarides, like Rado, saw an illness. However, unlike Rado, Socarides retained enough elements of Freud's theory to avoid the accusations of psychoanalytic heresy that plagued Rado (Glover, 1957; Roazen and Swerdlow, 1995). Socarides dressed up Rado's pathological, adaptational model of homosexuality in the language of Freud's drives and structures.

Nicolosi is another reparative therapist who claims psychoanalytic allegiance. However, though ultimately derived from the Radovian tradition, his etiological theory adopts the language of D. W. Winnicott (1965). Nicolosi claims that a homosexually-identified man's true self is constituted of hidden aggressive feelings that have become linked to his heterosexual desire. In other words, because he hides his aggression, a homosexually-identified man cannot express his innate heterosexuality. If a reparative therapy patient learns to express his hidden aggression more directly, his true, heterosexual self will emerge. In other words, this approach teaches the homosexually-identified individual to express his angry and sexual feelings "like a man."

Unlike Nicolosi, Winnicott claimed no knowledge of his patients' true selves. He pointedly remarked that the true self was private and unknowable (Winnicott, 1963). Nicolosi's generic "true self" has more in common with Bieber's (et al., 1962) earlier contention that "everyone is a latent heterosexual" (p. 220) than it does with Winnicott. Bieber's work in turn, like Socarides', is derived from the theories of Rado: "This study provides convincing support for a fundamental contribution by Rado on the subject of male homosexuality: A homosexual adaptation is a result of 'hidden but incapacitating fears of the opposite sex'" (Bieber, 1962, p. 303). Which is to say that everyone begins life as a heterosexual until they are derailed by overwhelming trauma, seduction, or conflict.

Some reparative therapists exhume and embrace psychoanalytic concepts long put to rest by contemporary analysts. Among the questionable psychoanalytic premises that inform reparative theories are instinctual drives, drive-based theories of identification, and the conflation of sexual attractions with gender identity. Siegel (1988), for example, resurrects the drive concept and develops it into a near-mystical definition of narcissism: "an energy" that allows individuals to adapt to "the reality of life, what I have called *Lebensbejahung*, the cathexis of life" (p. 21). Nicolosi's drive-based theory of identification draws upon equally mystical premises:

> The boy does not yet understand that his emerging interest in father comes from a primal affinity based in their shared masculinity. . . . He desires to be received and accepted by his father, and that fragile emerging masculine identity, receiving its only impetus from instinct,

must be reflected in their relationship. . . . This beautiful and mysterious match is the union of an inner need and an outer reality [Nicolosi, 1991, p. 27].

Paradoxically, reparative therapists emphatically reject innate bisexuality, an intrinsic part of Freud's original drive theory of identification. In Freud's theory, libido could cathect itself to a person of either sex. The process of identification begins with a libidinal detachment from a cathected object. The ego is ultimately constructed of the accumulation of abandoned object cathexes, which could be of either gender, in line with libido's innate bisexuality. A person's sexual attractions to others was determined in large part on the basis of an identification with the sexual desires of either one parent or the other (Freud, 1910a, 1914c, 1917, 1923a; Butler, 1990, 1995). Identification with the same-sex parent led to heterosexuality. Identification with the other-sex parent was the path toward homosexuality. Freud's instinct theory rests upon an assumption that a man's attraction to men is a female trait. A boy who likes boys is not masculine because he likes the same thing his mother likes (Freud, 1910a).

For Freud, however, the innate bisexuality of the libido meant that both same-gendered and other-gendered identifications were part of normal development, although some of these identifications were pushed into unconsciousness later in life. For example, alongside the positive Oedipus complex, one could also expect to encounter a negative one. Reparative therapists, by contrast, in rejecting bisexuality, are forced into the theoretical position that a predominant and organizing identification with the other-gendered parent's desires can only come about as a result of unusual family constellations. More particularly, they theorize that not only must the family constellation have been unusual, but its impact on the child was traumatic. However, the statistical data on gay people's families cast serious doubt on the psychoanalytic claim that male homosexuality is uniformly produced by a particular family constellation (Bieber, et al., 1962; cf. Bell, Weinberg, and Hammersmith, 1981). Nevertheless, reparative therapists commonly describe the mothers of gay and homosexually-identified men as overbearing, possessive of their children, undermining of their husbands, interfering with father-son relationships, symbiotic, or as having poor boundaries. The fathers of homosexual sons are described either as totally absent, negligent, evaders of bonding experiences with their sons, emasculated dupes of their shrewish wives, or as sadists: "The family of the homosexual is usually a female-dominated environment wherein the father was absent, weak, detached or sadistic. This furthers feminine identification. The father's inaccessibility to the boy contributed to the difficulty in making a masculine identification" (Socarides, 1968, p. 38).[1] These are the psychoanalytic variations of the popular belief that mothers turn their sons into sissies and that only fathers can show their sons how to be men.

A Relational Approach to Identification

Because the sexual and aggressive drives are the foundation of drive theory, such a theory ultimately defines all human identifications in the language of sex and aggression. In contrast to this reductionism, relational theories of identification do not privilege an identification with a parent's sexual orientation over other identifications (Sullivan, 1953; Racker, 1968; Stern, 1985; Bollas, 1987; Mitchell, 1988; Ogden, 1990). In this approach, identifications are the meanings attributed to the affectively-charged interactions that take place throughout the life cycle. It should further be noted that a relational approach to issues of identification is as useful in the treatment of gay patients as it is in the treatment of heterosexual ones.

A gay man came into treatment because of difficulties he experienced in coping with his responsibilities. He and his lover of more than twenty years owned a successful business together, but when the lover became ill, the patient had to do most of the work. He was constantly concerned about his lover's health, but intermittently resentful of the many burdens he had to shoulder alone. This man had many losses throughout his life. At eight years of age, his three-year-old sister died of a sudden illness . When he was fourteen, his father developed emphysema and then died of respiratory failure three years later. In those last years of his life, the father was physically disabled and unable to work. As a result, this man's mother did all the work in their family-owned business. She was contemptuous of her husband's infirmity and expressed those feelings in front of their children. When he was 25, the patient's 22-year-old brother committed suicide. His mother died shortly afterwards from complications of hypertension, in part exacerbated by her poor compliance with her medications and diet. His maternal grand-

---

1. Socarides' theory preceded knowledge of his own son's homosexuality (Nagourney, 1995; Dunlap, 1995b). If he is correct, his words are a startling self-indictment. If he is wrong, they illustrate the tragic frame of mind of parents who blame themselves for causing their children to be gay.

mother, who lived with his family until her death, had also had hypertension and had been noncompliant with her diet.

Reparative theory would assert that the mother's denigration of the father interfered with this gay man's "masculine identification" and contributed to his homosexuality. It would claim that he is primarily identified with his mother, who also had a disabled spouse. From a relational perspective, identifying with a parent's sexual orientation could be analogized to identifying with a parent's manner of expressing anger. However, a person's character is not defined by his anger, nor does one usually think of anger as a symptom. The same can be said about a sexual attraction. Like the expression of anger, an attraction is not simply a drive. Instead, it usually represents a complex form of relatedness.

When he suddenly developed a physical illness, the patient became aware of his own wish to be taken care of by others. Prior to his illness, he had never been able to openly acknowledge that wish. In part, wishing to be cared for symbolized an identification with his mother. She also yearned for her husband's care after he was too ill to provide her with any. The father's more blatant need of the mother's care was treated as a sign of his weakness. The mother's wish to be cared for was expressed in loud, angry contempt for the father. This gave the illusory impression that she was emotionally stronger than his father and that she didn't really need care. In order to express directly his need for care and attention, the patient had to overcome the fear that to do so meant he was weak. After he began directly asking for help, he discovered his previously unconscious identification with his father. Awareness of this paternal identification was accompanied by an increase in his self-esteem, but not a change in his sexual attractions.

In a relational model, the parental relationship serves as an internalized standard by which a person measures their own relationships, as in "I would never want the kind of relationship my parents had," or "I hope my marriage works as well as my parents' did." A person is likely to identify with the role each parent played in their interactions with him. For example, this gay man's mother ambivalently gratified the grandmother's tragic self-destructiveness. She did so by arguing that the grandmother shouldn't have salty foods, but would then relent and give them to her. This gay man identified with his mother's ambivalent relationship to the grandmother. And, when his mother became older and infirm, he too gave in to her pleas by allowing her to eat foods which were not in her prescribed diet. Now, he occasionally wishes that his lover would let him cheat on his own diet. At other times, he complains that the lover is not scrupulously controlling him. This conflicted enactment of love, caretaking, and aggression is a complex identification that traverses three generations and two anatomical genders.

In addition, the lover's henpecking supervision of the patient's eating habits brought to mind the vigilant, but futile care his sister received before her untimely, childhood death. This gay man has, of course, identified with her helplessness as well as what he experienced as the incompetence of her caretakers. He also identified with his younger, heterosexual brother and blames himself for the suicide. He feels he should have been able to prevent it. His ongoing worries about his depressed lover's potential for suicide represents a reaction against his own aggressive feelings. But there is also an identification with his brother as a tragic victim, and with his sister-in-law, whom he blames for precipitating his brother's death. In the work of his analysis, this gay man was to discover that he played many parts in his relationships, sometimes several of them with the same person. The multiple identifications seen in this man are poorly captured, indeed not acknowledged as possible, in any of the prevalent reparative theories.

The theories of identification found in reparative theories typically blur imperceptibly into gender stereotypes. Again, this can be contrasted both with contemporary relational psychoanalytic theory and with Freud's own ideas. Bisexual drive theory designated activity and passivity as the psychological manifestations of innate masculinity and femininity, respectively (Freud, 1915a). For contemporary theorists, social forces, rather than biology, dictate whether feelings and behaviors are designated as either male or female. Yet, while drawing upon cultural definitions of masculinity and femininity, reparative therapy's drive theory of identification equates psychological gender with biological anatomy. In line with prevailing cultural beliefs, it defines masculinity and femininity as mutually exclusive entities. It also treats gay men as if they were stubborn children who refuse to choose between them: "Many homosexual men still hold onto [an] infantile wish to be both male and female, expressing it through androgyny and occasionally bisexuality. There is sometimes an idealization of women celebrities—Judy Garland, Barbra Streisand, Marilyn Monroe, and Bette Midler, for instance—and even an impersonation of such women in humorous projection of a particular man's feminine ideal" (Nicolosi, 1991, p. 30). Reparative therapists reify and idealize strict gender categories. Masculinity is good, insofar as it conforms to one's anatomical gender. It is bad when it doesn't. Unfortunately, this approach to treatment does not take into account that the therapist who denigrates a man's feminine identifications is also denigrating the man. Denigrating a patient's identifications should alert a therapist to signficant countertransference problems (Winnicott, 1947).

Reparative Therapy's Morality

In promulgating their theories of immaturity and pathology, reparative therapists incorporate and strongly identify with society's antihomosexual traditions and values. Those who disagree with reparative therapists counter their arguments with normal variant theories. The latter believe that diversity of sexual expression can be regarded as normal and that it should be treated respectfully. However, both sides on this debate often appear as if they believe scientific objectivity can provide the fair and unbiased answers that will conclusively settle the issue. In framing the debate solely as a scientific issue, which it is not, both sides sidestep the moral assumptions and beliefs that are fueling this controversy.

All individuals must adapt or respond to social demands for conformity. In the process of adaptation, some people lose sight of their own identities, needs, and wishes as they conform to the demands being made upon them by others. Psychoanalysis tries to help a person find a balance between his needs as an individual, and his need to be part of a larger social order. For people who have lost sight of their individuality in trying to satisfy their social needs, psychoanalysis needs to address these individuals accordingly.

Based on their case reports, reparative therapists do not appear curious about patient individuality. They unquestioningly accept society's belief that everyone is supposed to be heterosexual (Rado, 1969, p. 210; Bieber, et al., 1962, p. 220; Socarides, 1968, pp. 5–6; Nicolosi, 1991, p. 5; van den Aardweg, 1997, p. 21). As a result, rather than asking their patients the psychoanalytic question, "Who are you?" their approach raises an altogether different question: "What happened to the heterosexual you were supposed to become?" As stated earlier in this book, science and psychoanalysis have yet to provide the definitive proofs of the hypothesis that everyone is supposed to be a heterosexual as a developmental necessity. And, in any case, neither science nor psychoanalysis are capable of deciding this question as a moral issue. Therefore, the embedded moral certainty of reparative theories necessarily originates from other sources, sources which are only masked by the use of scientific rhetoric.

In this respect, reparative theories are not unique. In Western culture's shift from traditional religious to modern scientific thought, many of its ancient moral beliefs were never abandoned. Instead the language of science appropriated and perpetuated earlier religious beliefs and moral prescriptions (Szasz, 1974b). For example, the religious belief that man is the pinnacle of God's creation was translated into the belief that Homo sapiens is a superior example of animal evolution. The assumption of man's superior position in the animal kingdom was not questioned. Only the theories that explained how he arrived there were.

In the realm of moral theory, the ascent of scientific assertions about man's innate nature has led to previously unimagined distinctions regarding the sphere of individual responsibility. Traditionally, an evil thought was considered to be equal to committing a sin. In the modern era, ethicists now routinely distinguish between the thought, which can be seen as natural and inevitable, and the deed. In the realm of sexual behaviors and feelings, some religious denominations concede that homosexual attractions may not be under an individual's conscious control. As a result, the homosexual thought may not necessarily be sinful. But they do believe the act of homosexuality is morally wrong. Similarly, some modern theologies analogize homosexuality with other sinful practices, such as murder, alcohol abuse, and adultery. In doing so, they occasionally make recourse to scientific explanations of behavioral tendencies while maintaining their discourse in an overall moral frame. From this perspective, one might have a genetic predisposition to alcoholism, but one can still choose not to drink. These same theologians employ a similar morality that defines homosexual behavior as a moral choice. One chooses to act or not to act on homoerotic feelings. One can choose not to act upon one's homosexual feelings and remain in the closet. A homosexually self-aware person can choose celibacy. *Choice* is the linchpin concept of a moral theory of behavior.

How do scientific certainties and pseudo-certainties become intertwined with a moral bias against homosexuality? The theology that regards homosexuality as sinful or immoral is complex and a review of it is beyond the scope of this chapter (Moberly, 1983a, b; Harvey, 1987; Coleman, 1995; cf. Boswell, 1980, 1994; Pronk, 1993; Helminiak, 1994; White, 1994). However, in lieu of that discussion, the phenomenon can be illustrated as follows. The religious teachings of St. Thomas Aquinas contain the seeds of moral disapproval and condemnation of homosexuality as a sin against nature, as well as a sin against reason. This conception later flourished in scientific and medical theories as a vehicle for introducing moral judgments into what ought to have been judgments of facts:

> In sins according to nature (*peccata secundum naturam*), the sin is determined as being "contrary to right reason": for example, fornication,

rape, incest, adultery, sacrilege. The lack of conformity to right reason is common to all sexual sins.

In sins against nature (*peccata contra naturam*), the sin contains an *additional* aspect; it is not only against reason but it is also inconsistent with the end of the venereal act, i.e., the begetting of children: e.g., masturbation, bestiality, homosexual activity, contraception [Coleman, 1995, p. 76].

Sins against nature, according to Aquinas, place a sinner "in conflict with our ultimate end, the supreme good, God himself" (Coleman, 1995, p. 76). Religion has argued, and still does, that God has a plan for both man and nature. So do some scientists. Indeed, there is already a scientific tradition in this regard. In 19th-century degeneracy theory, we see an early transition between the religious paradigm of unnatural acts and the new, scientific theory of evolution. Degeneracy theory substituted a religious belief in God's will, with a scientific belief in an intentional, evolutionary design. It reified Victorian morality and sexual standards as the superior products of Nature's evolutionary design:

The propagation of the human race is not left to mere accident or the caprices of individuals, but is guaranteed by the hidden laws of nature which are enforced by a mighty, irresistible impulse. Sensual enjoyment and physical fitness are not the only conditions for the enforcement of [natural] laws, but higher motives and aims, such as the desire to continue the species or the individuality of mental and physical qualities beyond time and space, exert a considerable influence. Man puts himself at once on a level with the beast if he seeks to gratify lust alone, but he elevates his superior position when by curbing the animal desire he combines with the sexual functions ideas of morality, of the sublime, and the beautiful. . . . The episodes of moral decay always coincide with the progression of effeminacy [homosexuality], lewdness and luxuriance of the nations. These phenomena can only be ascribed to the higher and more stringent demands which circumstances make upon the nervous system. Exaggerated tension upon the nervous system stimulates sensuality, leads the individual as well as the masses to excesses, and undermines the very foundations of society, and the morality and purity of family life. The material and moral ruin of the community is readily brought about by debauchery, adultery and luxury. Greece, the Roman Empire, and France under Louis XIV and XV are striking examples of this assertion. In such periods of civic and moral decline the most monstrous excesses of sexual life may be observed, which, however, can always be traced to psychopathological or neuropathological conditions of the nation involved [Krafft-Ebing, 1886, p. 23–27].[2]

"The jump from biological value to social value is the crux of human morality" (Szasz, 1965, p. 136). Yet this emphasis on nature's design was later incorporated into psychoanalytic theory as well, most notably in Freud's claim of the hierarchical superiority of genital sexuality (Freud, 1905, 1908). However this latently Thomistic element in Freud's work was greatly exaggerated by Rado's adaptational school. Like degeneracy theory, the adaptational psychoanalytic tradition saw a linearly progressing biological evolution. This unproven assumption then formed the basis of an equally hierarchical and cultural evolution:

> Cultures, in general, advance in the following ways: from bigotry, dogmatism, and regimentation to freedom of conscience, thought, inquiry, expression, teaching and learning; from violence to peaceful cooperation marked by equitable human relationships and readiness of the members to compose their differences; from government by coercion to government by consent of the governed; from rigidly centralized control with little local independence to a sound balance between centralized control and local independence; from a rigid hierarchical stratification of society (castes) to a complete vertical mobility fostering individual initiative and productive effort and enterprise, and the creation of equal opportunity for all [Rado, 1969, p. 5].

Consistent with this orderly arrangement of both society and man, the Radovian tradition regards evolution as if it were an anthropomorphic force that expects every individual to survive and procreate. The

---

2. Degeneracy theory also held that moral degeneration, often defined in terms of permissive, excessive, or deviant sexual activity or experimentation, led to neurological degeneration and psychiatric illness. In the service of this view, they invoked archeological and anthropological examples as they understood them. Thus, fallen civilizations of great achievement served as moral and scientific warnings for modern societies. However, turn-of-the-century portrayals of decadent, morally degenerate cultures often had little to do with the complex historical, sociological, and anthropological factors that lead to a civilization's growth and decline. Freud, in his criticism of degeneracy theory, noted aptly that "inversion was a frequent phenomenon—one might almost say an institution charged with important functions—among the peoples of antiquity at the height of their civilization. . . . It is remarkably widespread among many savage and primitive races, whereas the concept of degeneracy is usually restricted to states of high civilization" (1905, pp. 138–139).

evolutionary mandate of survival dictates that couples must be monogamous and have stable, long-term relationships. This is required for the rearing of children into adulthood. Thus, the adaptational school pathologizes homosexuality, heterosexual promiscuity, and short-term relationships because these activities are perceived as threats to the nuclear family's survival:

> Sex morality is not an arbitrary set of rules set down by no one knows who, and for purposes that no one understands, but is what man found expedient in his long evolutionary march, his social evolution. . . . If we find a culture, such as our own, that not only has survived but has to its credit the highest accomplishments ever recorded for man, then the patterns of morality—or the mores by which it governs the relations of the constituents to one another—must have a high degree of effectiveness . . . at the time sex custom entered recorded history, it already was more or less settled. Monogamy, for example, was an established custom in the Homeric legends[3] . . . we can assume that "human nature" has certain constant features and that human interaction, within certain limits, can be predicted on the basis of man's biological make-up. . . . What is more certain is that in man the capacity for love is more extensive owing to the fact that human infants need the proximity of protecting parents for a longer period than do any other mammals. This dependency is the nucleus about which the emotion known as love develops [Kardiner, 1956, pp. 22–31].

As Freud (1927a) and many others have conjectured, man created God in his own image. Modern man appears to have done the same with evolution. Reparative theories are not alone in using the language of evolution to clothe their own moral beliefs. Questions of social benefit and social harm, and of health and illness, are reframed in terms like adaptive and maladaptive, developed and undeveloped, mature and immature, and evolutionary fit and unfit are their moral code words. A hundred years after Krafft-Ebing, Socarides reprises his moral pronouncements, albeit in the guise of a psychoanalytic theory:

> Psychoanalysis reveals that sexual behavior is not an arbitrary set of rules set down by no-one-knows-who for purposes which no one understands. Our sexual patterns are a product of our biological past, a result of man's collective experience in his long biological and social

---

3. Kardiner, here, appears to be selectively inattending both the intimate, homosexual bond between Achilles and Patroclus and the central importance of that relationship to Homer's *Iliad*.

evolutionary march. They make possible the cooperative coexistence of human beings with one another. At the individual level, they create a balance between the demands of sexual instinct and the external realities surrounding each of us. Not all cultures survive—the majority have not—and anthropologists tell us that serious flaws in sexual codes and institutions have undoubtedly played a significant role in many a culture's demise [Socarides, 1994].

The reader should not assume, however, that reparative theorists are, as a group, disingenuous, forever hiding behind a scientific, evolutionary rhetoric. In fact, in recent years, some reparative theories have directly acknowledged their underlying religious origins: "Traditionally, the Christian faith has regarded homosexual activity as inappropriate, as contrary to the will and purposes of God for mankind . . . it seems to the present writer that one may not avoid the conclusion that homosexual acts are always condemned and never approved. The need for reassessment is not to be found at this point" (Moberly, 1983a, p. 27). In the same vein, Nicolosi (1991) is open about his connection with the world of pastoral counseling and his book is dedicated to a priest who founded an ex-gay ministry (Harvey, 1987), although most of his references are to psychoanalysts.

Nicolosi's theory of the father-son relationship evokes Christian mysteries of the heavenly Father and Son: "For the rest of his life, the homosexual tries to figure out his father. For him, both father and masculinity remain elusive and mysterious. If father was hostile and antagonistic, then he becomes a *confounding mystery*. If father was emotionally distant and inadequate, then he becomes a *longing mystery*" (p. 49). Similarly, his idealization of heterosexual relationships and denigration of gay ones can be read as the language of psychoanalysis in the meter of religious antihomosexual intolerance:

Each one of us, man and woman alike, is driven by the power of romantic love. These infatuations gain their power from the unconscious drive to become a complete human being. In heterosexuals, it is the drive to bring together the male-female polarity through the longing for the other-than me. But in homosexuals, it is the attempt to fulfill a deficit in wholeness of one's original gender.

The inherent unsuitability of same-sex relationships is seen in the form of fault-finding, irritability, feeling smothered; power struggles, possessiveness, and dominance; boredom, disillusionment, emotional withdrawal, and unfaithfulness. Although he desires men, the homosexual is afraid of them. As a result of this binding ambivalence, his same-sex relationships lack authentic intimacy.

Gay couples are characteristically brief and very volatile, with much fighting, arguing, making-up again, and continual disappointments. They may take the form of intense romances, where the attraction remains primarily sexual, characterized by infatuation and never evolving into mature love; or else they settle into long-term friendships while maintaining outside affairs. Research, however, reveals that they almost never possess the mature elements of quiet consistency, trust, mutual dependency, and sexual fidelity characteristic of highly functioning heterosexual marriages [Nicolosi, 1991, pp. 109–110].

Romantic love is neither a scientific nor a psychoanalytic concept. Neither is "complementarity," a spiritual term that Nicolosi alludes to here as "the drive to bring together the male-female polarity." A more sophisticated approach, at least on the surface, is that of Socarides, whose reading of Freud has alerted him to the possibility that the choice of object may not be innate. And yet, contradicting himself, Socarides mixes psychoanalytic theory with cultural prescription and clothes it all in evolutionary design:

The homosexual often asks if there is not some kind of genetic or hormonal factor, innate or inborn, which accounts for his condition. Homosexuality, the choice of an object of the same sex for orgastic satisfaction, is not innate. There is no connection between sexual instinct and the choice of sexual object. Such an object choice is learned, acquired behavior; there is no inevitable genetic or hormonal inborn propensity toward the choice of a partner of either the same or opposite sex. However, the *male-female design* is taught and exemplified to the child from birth and culturally ingrained through the marital order. This design is anatomically determined as it derives from cells which in the evolutionary scale underwent changes into organ systems and finally into individuals reciprocally adapted to each other. This is the evolutionary development of man. The male-female design is perpetually maintained and only overwhelming fear can disturb or divert it [Socarides, 1968, pp. 5–6].

The attentive reader will note how the argument of the preceding paragraph heads in the direction of gender. Gender definitions often figure prominently in the discourses of reparative theorists; here too, one regularly encounters a mixture of cultural, moral and scientific idioms. Thus, for example, Nicolosi relates "complementarity" to his notion of femininity, and sees the absence of both as characteristic of same-sex relationships between men:

Women bring stability and complementarity into a love relationship. Without the stabilizing element of the feminine, and the stimulation of her complementary physical and emotional makeup, men are generally unable to sustain sexual intimacy and closeness [Nicolosi, 1991, pp. 117–118].

The gender stereotyping which one continually encounters in this literature attributes to men and women an almost-mythical nature on the order of the most rudimentary cultural notions. "It is in man's nature to be a hunter. Women, being essentially nurturing, are born to be mothers." Few people ever measure up to these stereotypes. In fact, an inability to do so is often one of the reasons people give for starting psychotherapy. Ideally, providing a therapeutic environment ought to entail a respect for a patient's deviation from conventional standards of masculinity or femininity, as well as for the patient's sexual feelings, fantasies and behaviors. But the issue of creating a therapeutic environment goes beyond discussions of gender or sexual behavior; it involves respect for the individual as an individual, quite apart from all stereotypes. The issue of respect has been explicitly addressed by the American Medical Association (AMA) as a general principle of medical ethics: "A physician shall be dedicated to providing competent medical service with compassion and respect for human dignity" (reprinted in American Psychiatric Association, 1993, p. 3). And the extension of this principle to gay and lesbian patients has also been explicitly addressed. The AMA has called for "nonjudgmental recognition of sexual orientation by physicians" with "respect and concern for their [patients'] lives and values" (reprinted in Hausman, 1995, p. 18). Astonishingly, reparative therapists, through the voice of their official organization, have explicitly balked at this: "One wonders how reasonable it is for the AMA to mandate respect (rather than simply tolerance) for every person's 'life and values'" (National Association for Research and Treatment of Homosexuality, 1994). This leaves hanging the issue of tolerance. Consider the following statement by Nicolosi which draws a clear line about how far either tolerance or respect should go:

The Gay Liberation Movement began in 1969 with protests at the Stonewall Club in New York City. Now into its third decade, this movement makes two distinct demands: *Tolerance* [and] *Approval*. . . . These two arguments are frequently blurred and represented synonymously. For there is a faulty assumption that if society is tolerant and respects an individual's right to pursue the gay life-style, it must go one step further to equally value that life-style, as well as the homosexual condition. Although we must respect individual rights, we as a society still have a responsibility to inquire: "What is healthy?" For the past twenty years, the Gay Liberation Movement has been demanding not only the right to political and social equality, but an endorsement of normalcy [Nicolosi, 1991, pp. 131–132].

It is the lack of respect that is most problematic in reparative theory. It allows these therapists to employ psychoanalytic terminology as a veil that thinly disguises their contempt for same-sex relationships. The result is a discourse that defines the meaning of same-sexuality to the therapist while foreclosing the possibility of exploring its meaning to a homosexually self-aware man. Consider the following:

> There is no empathic affective reciprocity in the male homosexual relationship. Each partner is playing his part as if in isolation with no cognizance of the complemantariness of a sexual union, as if the act were consummated in "splendid isolation" with the other person merely a device for the enactment of a unilateral emotional conflict. . . . The imagery accompanying the homosexual act between males is total fantasy without relevance of the other except as a device. This is a masturbatory equivalent and highly narcissistic. . . . There is no reality awareness of the partner or his feelings; the contact is simply epidermal, mucous and anatomic. . . . The "welfare emotions," those arising from pleasure, are conspicuously absent: joy, love, tenderness, and pride. . . . This is the enactment of the fundamental nature of their object relationships: relating to part objects, not whole objects [Socarides, 1968, pp. 135–136].

The reparative therapy literature sometimes reads as a bestiary of stereotypes, as in the following statements by Socarides: "Homosexuals rarely participate in athletics or competitive sports because of childhood fears of being different from other boys" (Socarides, 1968, p. 136). "Some young men do it [engage in homosexual activity] to advance their careers. Some actors, for example. They have made it into the movies by going to bed with directors or producers who prefer same-sex" (Socarides, 1995, p. 18). "In some homosexuals, their lifestyles are intimately connected with their careers. Some 90 percent of the men in New York's fashion world are homosexuals" (Socarides, 1995, p. 103).

There is another troubling repercussion to reparative therapists' belief that homosexuality always exists outside the range of healthy or normal human function. They find it difficult to accept the view of both the American Psychiatric and American Psychoanalytic Associations that homosexuality is a normal variant of human sexuality. This lack of acceptance informs their treatments: "But viewing my patients through the lens of psychoanalytic thinkers and clinicians soon showed me that allowing myself to be seduced into perceiving female homosexuality as a normal lifestyle would have cemented both my patients and myself into a rigid mode that precluded change of whatever nature" (Siegel, 1988, p. xii). Reparative therapists find the increasingly public stance of lesbian and gay mental health field professionals particularly nettlesome:

> We've been under assault by a small coterie of gay doctors inside the profession, but we're trying to stand firm in our convictions that we can help homosexuals who want to be helped—despite loud and sometimes very obnoxious insistence on the part of gay activists that they don't need help. . . . For years, we psychoanalysts didn't knowingly allow homosexual doctors into our training institutes unless they went through analysis for their homosexuality. In 1991, under a great deal of political pressure, we passed a resolution at a meeting of the American Psychoanalytic Association that allowed them entry. Then they demanded more; they wanted to become training analysts without first undergoing analysis of and treatment for their condition, and, when we refused, they actually succeeded in getting the ACLU to send a letter to the president of our association, threatening a lawsuit. The cost of fighting such a suit would have run into seven figures. Because of the cost, we capitulated—to sexual politics and legal coercion. We sacrificed our scientific integrity, and let them in, without insisting that their homosexuality be subjected to the same rigorous analysis that other candidates get for their heterosexuality [Socarides, 1995, pp. 153–154].

Insofar as reparative theory views homosexuality as pathognomonic of serious psychopathology, then the logical implication is that lesbian and gay mental health professionals suffer from a severe psychiatric condition that impairs their ability to function as physicians, psychiatrists, or as therapists. The belief harkens back to the historical era when openly gay men and women were not permitted to train in the mental health professions (Drescher, 1995; Martin, 1995; Isay, 1996; Magee and Miller, 1997).

The Patients Seeking Reparative Therapy

Let me return briefly to the assertion of Socarides above that in a training analysis, a gay candidate does not have his homosexuality "subjected to the rigorous analysis that other candidates get for their heterosexuality." This misses the point, and does so in two ways. First, heterosexual candidates, and heterosexual patients in general, are never asked to explain or account for their desires *qua* desires, nor are they usually subjected to inquiries based on the premise that their desires are symptomatic of conflict, trauma, or serious psychopathology. Heterosexual desire itself is treated as normal, although the timing of its appearance and the use that the patient makes of it may be questioned. Had the same treatment been accorded to gay candidates and patients, there would have been no problem. This did not occur. There is another, more important issue being elided by Socarides' summary statement: Coming to terms with a homosexual or gay identity in a culture that still has enormous difficulty accepting it as a normal variation requires psychological adaptations that are not necessary for coming to terms with a heterosexual identity.

The complexities involved in establishing a gay identity require a therapist to be tolerant, respectful, and sophisticated regarding sexual matters. They do not require, in my view, an abandonment of the principles and techniques of a psychoanalytic approach. That is to say, the different kinds of subjectivities one may encounter in working with gay men can be understood and appreciated within the language of such concepts as hiding and revealing (Winnicott, 1960b, 1971), awareness and unawareness (Sullivan, 1953, 1956), or of self-acceptance and nonacceptance (Kohut, 1971). These and other concepts are useful insofar as they facilitate the discovery of individual meaning. What the therapist has to contend with in a patient with same-sex feelings is that his understanding of his own sexuality will, in part, be shaped by the meanings attributed to them by a predominantly heterosexual world. The possibilities of individual meanings are innumerable, yet experience suggests certain patterns that might be useful to delineate. Toward that end, let me try to describe some broad concepts that may provide clinicians with an initial basis for entering into the subjectivity of a man with same-sex feelings.

A closeted man is unable to acknowledge to himself that he has homoerotic feelings and fantasies. In popular usage, "closeted" may refer to a person who is actively engaging in homosexual acts but is concealing them. That is a behavioral perspective and it is one that is sometimes accurate at that level. However, from the retrospective accounts of many gay men, the experience of being in the closet is often more psychologically complex. The feeling of same-sex attraction is often unacceptable to conscious awareness or integration into the individual's public persona. It must be hidden from the self as well as from others. A closeted individual may not act on the feeling at all, or he may do so only in a dissociated state (see Sullivan, 1956, pp. 169–179, for a classic description). Strictly speaking, these feelings are not unconscious, as in the concept of latent homosexuality, but they are out of awareness and only sometimes accessible to consciousness, at certain times or in certain situations. Subjectively, a closeted man may tell himself he really does not have same-sex feelings, or, if he is aware of the feelings, he hopes they have some other meaning besides homosexuality.

The *homosexually self-aware man* acknowledges to himself the existence of his homoerotic feelings and attractions. Irrespective of how comfortable he is with them, he recognizes their homosexual meaning. Here again, subjectivities and behaviors may vary from individual to individual. A man may choose not to act on the feelings or, if he does, may act on them in a secretive way. Some behaviorally closeted men are homosexually self aware and some are not. Some homosexually self-aware men consider the possibility of accepting and integrating these feelings into their public persona. Others withdraw from these possibilities in various ways. For example, a homosexually self-aware man may choose to be celibate as a way of binding his anxiety and avoiding what, for him, would be a problematic identity.

A man may define himself as *gay* when his sexual feelings are homoerotic and he is prepared to act on them and reveal them so that his sexual identity is known to others. Defining oneself as gay requires some level of self-acceptance. Some gay men may choose to come out to family or intimate acquaintances. Others may come out to people they have met in the gay community and keep their gay identity separate from the rest of their lives. Note that this way of thinking about a gay identity recognizes the role of self-definition as part of the process. From the therapist's perspective, a man is not gay because others consider him to be gay, but because he defines himself as gay. Gay men most often describe the experience of feigning heterosexuality as stressful. However, some may relish the deception.

The expression "He is gay but he doesn't know it" is an external perspective that offers very little insight into an individual's subjectivity. Such a phrase could describe a closeted man who is truly unaware of his homoerotic feelings; it could just as well describe a homosexually self-aware man who knows he has these feelings, but is trying to prevent others from knowing he has them; and finally, it could describe a gay man who is out to a limited circle of individuals, recognizes his own sexual feelings, but is selective about revealing them.

Yet a different subjectivity, one that does not have a common cultural definition as yet, is that of the *non-gay-identified* man. This man is aware of his same-sex feelings and may have even acted on them, but he cannot or will not accept any meanings that might naturalize them. He may have experimented with the possibility of being gay, but he has no wish to come out any further. Having found the heterosexual marginalization of gay life unbearable, he may reject his homoerotic feelings and choose assimilation at any cost. Such a man may seek to change his sexual orientation. In his effort to disidentify with his homoerotic feelings and activities, which he experiences as Sullivan's (1956) not-me, he may refer to himself as either "ex-homosexual" or "ex-gay." In many ways, this is a new cultural subjectivity. For these men, it is first and foremost a question of identity.

These different subjectivities should not be thought of as existing on a developmental continuum or as being associated with more or less psychopathology. Furthermore, they are not mutually exclusive; there is overlap between them and differing motivations within them. They are offered as a way for the clinician to begin thinking about the importance of an individual's meaning-making system in defining a sexual identity. In assessing an individual from this perspective, a clinician should take into account four domains used in meaning-making. The first is the quality of the desire. The second is the awareness of the desire. The third is the acceptance of the desire. The fourth is the conclusions drawn about one's identity on the basis of the first three domains. A man in prison may experience being aware and accepting of same-sex desire, and act on it, but may not draw any conclusions vis á vis his sexual identity from the experience. The same can be true of the man who defines his homosexual desire and actions as "just fooling around."

It should also be emphasized that this way of thinking about sexual identities does not see them as either diagnostic or immutable. The subjectivities outlined above are shaped by individual and cultural factors. There is a wide range of psychosocially constructed attitudes and responses that a man may develop toward his own homosexuality. A homosexually self-aware man may come out, identify himself as gay, but then regret that decision and return to his earlier practices of hiding. Another man may choose a nongay identity, seek reparative therapy, but then later decide to accept his homosexual feelings and come out. These various possibilities for changing subjectivities can sometimes lead to odd therapeutic encounters:

> **A:** During my last year in college, a talk show on TV had some people on who were Aesthetic Realists. They would say they could change homosexuality to heterosexuality. I thought, "That might help me change." I was unhappy about being gay. All my friends were straight. My family was

homophobic. I played around with a couple of guys growing up, but they all had girlfriends. I felt like the odd man out. There were no gay bars in our town. My college was very conservative. I feel embarrassed talking about this.

Th: What's embarrassing about it?

A: It felt like a sneaky, cheesy thing to have done. I went for treatment once a week and I was supposed to think about what I thought. To get at the flawed examples in my thinking.

Th: Could you give me an example of what you mean by flawed thinking?

A: I would say, "I don't know why you have your office down here in such an ugly part of town." They said, "Look at its potential. Look at its possibility." They charged $35 a visit. I went for four or five months.

Th: How did you experience the sessions?

A: I had a gut feeling it wouldn't work. I felt picked on, under siege. They really didn't change any of my views. What I believed was ugly, stayed ugly. I was seriously thinking of not telling you about it. I'm so ashamed of it. But I know I get the most benefit from telling the most embarrassing thing. It makes me mad and sad that I spent all those years in the closet, rather than enjoying the best years of my life. I lived in utter doubt and self-loathing. Those people validated that I should have felt that way. I wondered if those other guys had really changed. Their attitude seemed forced to me. The whole experience seemed like Chinese herbs rather than medicine. They said, "A dick is made to fit into a pussy. Yin and yang." They never used those exact terms, but that was the general idea. In a nutshell, "God made Adam and Eve, not Adam and Steve." That is what they were all about. It was all scary to me and very sad and hopeless. I went there thinking, "This is a cure. This is a fix." But I still stayed in the closet three more years after that experience.

Th: Did you make any friends in the group?

A: No, but I used to cruise this guy who was there at the same time I was in the waiting room. I would look at him but he never looked back. If he had, I would have probably looked away.

The homosexual subjectivities outlined above have no exact heterosexual equivalents. Having to hide one's interest in the other sex is usually not intrinsic to forming a heterosexual identity. A *heterosexually-identified man* is most likely to identify himself as *normal*. Even if a heterosexually-identified man engages in a homosexual act, he may do so without ever identifying himself as gay. The subjectivity of a sexual identity is shaped by culture and language, often with little or no regard to prevailing scientific or psychoanalytic categories of sexuality (Drescher, in press).

These subjectivities can intersect in many ways with the wish not to be gay. And by the same token, they can intersect with the wish to seek reparative therapy. In their own way, some reparative therapists are aware of these varieties of subjectivities and what they may augur for the success of the treatment they are actually offering:

> The homosexual who has a feminine identification and accepts his homosexuality usually identifies himself socially as a homosexual. He openly enters into "gay life," socializes mostly with other homosexuals, and often lives with a homosexual partner. It is doubly difficult for homosexuals of this kind, who are intimately involved in homosexual society, to give up their homosexuality. Not only must they learn to relate to women sexually, but also they must sever established social ties and start anew in heterosexual circles. Most are ill suited for this task and have no desire to undertake it. They are confirmed homosexuals and remain so. Only a few in this group apply for therapy. Their prognosis is usually poor, and their motivation for treatment should always be suspect. The outlook is much better for the homosexual who keeps his homosexuality hidden, practices it surreptitiously, and identifies himself socially as a heterosexual. This, of course, occurs only in homosexuals whose masculine identification is so strong that they struggle against their homosexual inclinations [Ovesey, 1969, p. 112].

The homosexually self-aware man may believe that fostering a heterosexual social identity will expand his freedom of movement. Ironically, maintaining that identity can feel like a prison whose cells are constructed of society's unrelenting demands for heterosexual normativity. This sometimes leads to living an "as-if" heterosexuality, in which a homosexually self-aware man adopts an outward appearance of a heterosexual life. He may try dating women or may even marry one. That is what Mel White, a filmmaker, writer, and ghostwriter for conservative Christians like Jerry Falwell, did before he came out years later to become dean of a gay church:

> Although I longed for an intimate relationship with a man, when the wedding vows were made that next day and the service finally ended, it was a woman standing at my side. It wasn't Darrel or Gordon or Ted who wore my wedding ring or kissed me before the applauding crowd of family and friends, it was Lyla. It was to her that I pledged my life-long love and loyalty. Now looking back, was that a cruel trick I played? Was it a terrible mistake for both of us? Was I really in love

with someone else and not in love with Lyla? . . . I married Lyla because I loved her and wanted to spend the rest of my life in her company. And I wasn't afraid to marry her because I believed my conservative Christian friends and family who said or implied or somehow managed to convey to me the following dangerous misinformation: "If you're struggling with homosexuality, a good woman will take care of it." It was the lie that led to so many of the joys and sorrows that followed for both of us [White, 1994, pp. 86–87].

A homosexually self-aware man may seek reparative therapy out of a legitimate wish to live as a heterosexual in a heterosexual world. Unable or unwilling to accept his homoerotic feelings as either normal, natural, or moral, he seeks to bolster his self-esteem interpersonally, through reflected appraisals (Sullivan, 1972). The environment from which he seeks support includes his family members and friends, his co-religionists, his professional colleagues and his therapist. A perfect example of this is the experience of an analyst in training in an era only recently passed:

Persons who were actively homosexual were not accepted for training at psychoanalytic institutes. . . . Since I was making an effort [in six-times-a-week psychoanalysis] to rid myself of homosexual fantasies and to disinhibit my heterosexuality, I believed I could be accepted and decided to apply for psychoanalytic training. Three senior analysts interviewed me. . . . [They] saw my eagerness to spend one hour every day labeling myself as neurotic as a sign of emotional health. . . . I did not look or act like all homosexuals were assumed to appear or behave—effeminate, odd, or in some other way unconventional. It was for these reasons, I believe, and because I was not "acting out" my sexual fantasies, that [they] did not consider me to be homosexual and I was accepted for training [Isay, 1996, p. 20].

A fear of being old, lonely, and sexually desperate is often presented as a reason to seek out a "cure" for homosexuality. Or a man may report dissatisfaction with his forays into what reparative therapists call "the gay lifestyle." This usually refers to the periphery of the social environment, like cruising areas, or public spaces, where men can have anonymous sex with each other. A patient may have gone to a gay bar or club and been put off by what he saw there. For many men, this is a first point of entry into the larger gay community. But for some men, it is the only gay community they will ever know. The patient who seeks reparative therapy may have met other men in cruising areas and bars who feel

equally marginalized. After an unsuccessful, anxious, or degrading experience, and lacking any social supports, a man may feel he has good reason for not wanting to be gay:

Therapist: Why don't you want to be gay?

Client: Well, one main reason is that I really do want to get married and
have kids. I know the gay life-style leads to loneliness. I know a lot of people that are like that and are very unhappy, that are alone late in life. . . .
For me I think I got involved in it because I just needed to be close to
somebody and this was always there. Someone was always coming on to
me and sometimes I just let it happen. . . . During the time of my high
school years I was shy and at that time, I had no social friends that were
homosexuals at all. I had a sort of a girlfriend. . . . She had a lot of gay
friends. The first time I was exposed to them it seemed that they had
something that I was looking for . . . it was the sociability. They were so
outgoing. Like, "Oh wow, they're gay." So I just started going out to the
nightclubs. . . . I always liked going out and dancing and just having fun.
That's one of the reasons, the social aspect of it. . . .

Therapist: What kind of guys were you trying to meet?

Client: Back then? I think . . . just somebody basically who would like to
go out and have fun and talk and all that. Lately I've been feeling down in
the dumps—it comes out sexually, lots of fantasies, lots of crap . . . masturbation and pornography. I used to go into restrooms and you know,
look at guys, but not lately. It's something I'm ashamed of [Nicolosi, 1991,
pp. 223–232].

Some gay men have documented their unsuccessful attempts to find a
cure for homosexuality:

For . . . years, I read and memorized biblical texts on faith. I fasted and
prayed for healing. I believed that God had "healed me" or was "in the
process of healing me." But over the long haul, my sexual orientation
didn't change. My natural attraction to men never lessened. My need for a
long-term, loving relationship with another gay man just increased with
every prayer.

After months of trying, my psychiatrist implied that I wasn't really
cooperating with the Spirit of God. "He is trying to heal you," the doctor
said, "but you are hanging on to the old man and not reaching out to the
new." After that, my guilt and fear just escalated.

In fact, the doctor was wrong. He had promised me that if I had
enough faith, God would completely change my sexual orientation. I was
clinging to that promise like a rock climber clings to the face of a cliff. You
can imagine how confused and guilt-ridden I became when my homosex-

uality stayed firmly in place and the new heterosexual man I hoped to become continued to elude me [White, 1994, p. 107].

Men who tried to change their sexual identities, and then failed to do so, recall it was a painful and humiliating experience:

B: I met a guy last night. He is good looking and a pretty outgoing person. He told me had gone through a long struggle of accepting himself. He was even in the ex-gay movement. He said it was a disaster. The ex-gay ministry tried to take gay men through spiritual energy and prayer and exorcism to try and make them heterosexual. He doesn't know anybody who's actually been through the change. He is accepting himself more. He was very interested in my experience of trying to change. I told him about being in therapy with a psychiatrist, who was not homophobic, but who bought into the old school of trying to change homosexuality. My experience was very painful and it didn't work.

Th: What happened?

B: I used to think I was gay because my mother was a dominant, pushy, bossy woman who turned me against women. That's what I used to think before I came out as gay.

Th: Where did you hear that?

B: When I was in college and trying to figure out what homosexuality was, that was what I was picking up; that I was blocked. My mother blocked me in adolescence, and I would have become heterosexual if it hadn't been for her pampering and messing around in my life and development. I believed that until 1989, because I didn't want to read anything or know anything about homosexuality. I didn't want to believe that I was gay and I didn't want to look at it or face it. I honestly never thought that I was gay from birth, or in utero or age five or six. That never entered my mind. If I had thought that might be true, then it meant I couldn't reverse it. I would have to deal with it.

Th: So blaming your mother for causing your homosexuality in adolescence left you with the option to change?

B: The first psychiatrist I had certainly allowed it. I told him these things and he never said anything to the contrary. In some ways, I thought he, as a professional, should have pointed me toward some book, some resource, some information that I didn't have.

Th: Your first psychiatrist gave you what you wanted.

B: Not entirely. Well, I guess he did. He heard me saying, "I don't want to be gay." And so he was taking that at face value. He did say that, "You probably will never get rid of these feelings altogether, and they will come and go, but you don't have to do anything about them. You don't have to act on them." That wasn't really working, because I went through a whole year of buying men's magazines with naked women in them. I would try to build up my sexual energy by looking at pictures of women and fantasizing about them. I went a whole year doing that and got more and more frustrated. By the end of the year, I got some male magazines again and I felt like I really failed. It was kind of hopeless. I got depressed and more depressed. In fact, I was depressed the whole time. I felt hopeless. I felt suicidal. The worst depression I've ever had was somewhere in there. I went to that psychiatrist for four years and only stopped after he retired.

A partial reparative therapy success is the man who still has same-sex feelings but remains celibate, rather than "acting out" on them (Harvey, 1987, pp. 145–146). Reparative therapists often recognize the difficulty, if not impossibility, of changing sexual orientation: "Reparative therapy is not a 'cure' in the sense of erasing all homosexual feelings" (Nicolosi, 1991, p. xviii). This would be consistent with the observation that many heterosexually-identified inmates who engage in same-sex activities do not lose their sexual attractions to women (Socarides, 1968). Nevertheless, some apparently successful reparative treatments end with accounts of the patient getting married and hopefully, fathering children (Ovesey, 1969; Trop and Stolorow, 1992; cf. Mitchell, 1981). In fact, some analysts take extraordinary pride in the putative conversion of their patients to heterosexuality:

> In my third year of analysis my future wife and I became engaged. My analyst, who had never called me by name in our sessions because he felt it would interfere with the perception of his neutrality, enthusiastically congratulated me. And although he was on vacation at the time, he sent a warm telegram to the synagogue on the occasion of our marriage the following summer [Isay, 1996, p. 19].

The disjunction between partial and total success creates a serious difficulty in assessing what is truly transpiring in reparative therapy and whether it deserves to be considered a psychoanalytic form of treatment. In agreeing to help a homosexually-self-aware patient become a heterosexual, a reparative therapist embarks upon a strange therapeutic venture: It becomes unacceptable for the two of them to acknowledge that the patient's homoerotic feelings might be authentic. Therefore, the patient must actively reassure the therapist that he wants to change, and at the same time must hide his wishes not to change:

> Most homosexuals who come to the psychiatrist . . . state unequivocally that they wish to become heterosexual. Obviously, this is the

group with the best prognosis, but their declaration cannot always be taken at face value. What the homosexual patient consciously claims he wants is not infrequently contradicted by his hidden unconscious desires, which become apparent only after he has gone into treatment [Ovesey, 1969, p. 109].

When therapists take sides in a patient's internal struggle to establish a sexual identity, they run the risk of reinforcing dissociative, rather than integrative tendencies. The risk is compounded in a treatment predicated upon an unproven theory that a gay man's major difficulty is a failure to establish a relationship with a benign, paternal figure. For then the stage is set for the analyst, in overt and covert ways, to encourage the patient to identify with the analyst's attitudes and values and to view resistances to the analyst as reenactments of some original traumatic disidentification.[4] It is besides the point that the therapist undertakes such a task with the best of intentions and feeling only good will towards his client. When surveying the literature of reparative therapy, however, one finds that these and other possible obstacles in the way of providing respectful care within a psychoanalytic framework are either not recognized or ignored. This leads to many clinical practices that most analysts and psychoanalytically-oriented psychotherapists would find unusual or frankly unacceptable. And it is to these that I now turn.

Reparative Therapy Practices

Reparative therapists necessarily reinforce social expectations for heterosexual normativity—this is intrinsic to their endeavor as they define it. Ovesey (1969), using a disease model, makes this explicit: "Those who lack conviction that homosexuality is a treatable illness, but believe instead that it is a natural constitutional variant, should not accept homosexuals as patients" (p. 119).

---

4. This possibility is compounded when the therapist himself is narcissistically invested in achieving a transformation of the patient's sexual orientation. Here, one can only quote Freud's (1912) warning about the dangers of seeking too hard for dramatic cures: "the feeling that is most dangerous to a psycho-analyst is the therapeutic ambition to achieve by this novel and much disputed method something that will produce a convincing effect upon other people. This will not only put him into a state of mind which is unfavorable for [the analyst's] work, but will make him helpless against certain resistances of the patient, whose recovery, as we know, primarily depends upon the interplay of forces in him" (p. 115).

Then, by his own account, he brings this model into the initial session:

> As the patient was giving his history and registering his complaints, the therapist asked him why he did not list homosexuality as one of the symptoms he wished to have corrected. The patient seemed bewildered. It had never occurred to him that homosexuality was a neurotic symptom, nor that one went to a psychiatrist to have it cured. His brother, a homosexual like himself, was also in psychoanalysis, and his analyst felt homosexuality was an inherited way of life that could not be altered and hence was of no particular therapeutic interest. The therapist stated unequivocally that he could not agree with this position, since he considered homosexuality a psychiatric illness which could be treated by psychotherapeutic means [Ovesey, 1969, p. 128].

Ovesey practiced at a time when homosexuality was considered a psychiatric illness (Bayer, 1981). In more recent years, reparative therapists have gone beyond the illness model and appeal to social consensus. In the process, they disdain moral relativism as providing an unsatisfactory basis for treatment. Nicolosi (1991) has made this stance overt in presenting his own treatment philosophy:

> In the 1960's, the humanistic movement then influenced psychology into a new but disguised version of moral authority. Its new reliance was on the gauge of feelings to assess morality. This popular movement of the sixties and seventies opposed the psychological tradition and preached emotional openness, spontaneity, and loyalty to oneself. Growth was no longer seen as a product of intelligence and problem-solving, but rather was viewed solely in emotional terms. "Feeling good about yourself" became the litmus test of good behavior, a sort of bastardized moral sense. This humanistic psychology rejected much of the rationalism of the psychoanalytic tradition. It introduced instead the soft sentiment of full acceptance of the person, as he is, without expectations [pp. 16–17].

Such a treatment philosophy not only abhors the sexual relativism of normal variant theories, but it also demands of the therapist that he possess a certain level of conviction. Expecting the patient to join the therapist in adopting certain values is also made explicit in the reparative therapy literature. Nicolosi, for example, believes "effective treatment takes its direction from a shared value system between client and therapist (1991, p. 17)." He further believes:

Those who seek reparative therapy do not blame social stigma for their unhappiness. Many have looked into the gay life-style, have journeyed what became for them a "via negativa," and returned disillusioned by what they saw. Their definition of self is integrally woven into traditional family life. They refuse to relinquish their heterosexual social identity. Rather than wage war against the natural order of society, they instead take up the sword of an interior struggle [Nicolosi, 1991, p. 5].

Here the reader may question whether such generalized attitudes truly influence the conduct of the treatment, and if they do, how so? Consider the following vignette provided by Nicolosi on how to conduct an initial interview:

Therapist: Have you ever had relationships with guys that weren't homosexual?

Client: Sure. Although I must admit, I wish I felt more comfortable about making friends.

Therapist: Male relationships are very important. Do you ever notice— let's see if this is true for you—some guys say it's true. When they are feeling bad or weak about themselves, or having had a failure or disappointment, that's when they seem to sexualize other guys more. When they are feeling good and secure and confident about themselves and they have their life in order and things are going well, the sexual preoccupations diminish. They can look at a nice-looking guy but not have sexually compelling feelings for them. Does that describe your feelings?

Client: Yeah. I guess that's actually true [Nicolosi, 1991, p. 232].

The therapist has succeeded in putting an issue—male relationships—on the treatment agenda. This is a prelude to an interpretation. The following is from the same initial interview:

Therapist: Do you feel masculine enough? Have you ever thought about that before?

Client: Um—probably not. Not really.

Therapist: Thinking about this is essential to your therapy. A lack of complete identification with masculinity can make a man sexually interested in other males. You don't look feminine, there's nothing about your looks that *says* you don't feel masculine . . . but on the inside you say you have doubts. Did you have problems finding male friends when you were growing up?

Client: . . . In school I had a couple of guy friends but the problem with that was—with most of the guys I hung around with when I was little, it always ended up kind of sexual.

Therapist: When you were having a sexual relationship with the boys, I think you were really trying to get close to them emotionally, trying to bond to them. I think you were short-circuiting your need for male identification and intimacy by having sexual contact [Nicolosi, 1991, pp. 224–225].[5]

Ambiguities between exploration and suggestion are endemic to any psychoanalytic psychotherapy, and often the treatment takes a long time to sort them out. Here, however, the therapist has set an agenda with great forcefulness. One might ask whether he has created a climate for exploration, or whether he is testing the client's compliance with a certain style of interpretation. If it is the latter, we would expect issues of compliance to emerge in the transference as treatment proceeds. But for this therapist, the parameters for transference exploration are pre-set. And more disturbingly, they not only involve issues of gender, but also entail as a prerequisite the actual gender of the therapist:

Most homosexual men tend to anticipate nonacceptance from men and therefore feel more relaxed and comfortable with women. For this reason, many choose a female therapist when first beginning to deal with their problem. However the healing of homosexuality through reparative therapy comes out of work with men. A female therapist may help in general ways, but only a male can stimulate reenactment of the conflictual feelings experienced with males, particularly problems with trust and the need for male acceptance. Only through men can masculine identity be found.

As a framework, we should recall the developmental model of the boy's gender-identity formation. The boy's first and primary identification is with mother, from whom he must later disidentify in order to develop an emotional bonding with the father; then he must move on to male peer relationships. Reparative therapy is a reenactment of this developmental sequence.

The female therapist can set the emotional groundwork for the task that lies ahead. She teaches the client about self-esteem, identification and expression of feelings, and trust in therapeutic relation-

---

5. If knowledge about the unconscious were as important for the patient as people inexperienced in psychoanalysis imagine, listening to lectures or reading books would be enough to cure him. Such measures, however, have as much influence on the symptoms of nervous illness as a distribution of menu-cards in a time of famine has upon hunger. The analogy goes even further than its immediate application; for informing the patient of his unconscious regularly results in an intensification of the conflict in him and an exacerbation of his troubles" (Freud, 1910b, p. 225).

ships. Within the framework of reparative therapy, her role will be to act as a bridge to surrender the client to a male therapist [Nicolosi, 1991, pp. 179–180].[6]

Not surprisingly, such attitudes have drawn criticism. Mitchell (1981) views reparative therapies as "exploitations of the transference" and criticizes their "directive-suggestive approaches" for evoking a "false-self compliance." Although he recognizes that some gay men may exhibit compliant transference constellations related to paternal figures, Mitchell strongly criticizes the apparent indifference of reparative therapists to the way they exploit that fact:

> One would imagine that an understanding of these dynamics would alert authors writing about treating such patients to the obvious dangers of such compliance manifesting itself in the transference, resulting in the patient adapting his surface appearance and behavior in conformity with what he perceives to be the therapist's goals and values. On these grounds alone, one might argue that the therapist ought to take a position only of extreme non-directiveness, to remain carefully alert to the state of the transference, and to be suspect of behavioral changes in the direction of what the patient takes to be the analyst's values. The authors in question [Bieber et al., 1962; Socarides, 1968; Ovesey, 1969; Hatterer, 1970] obviously do not reach such a conclusion, but what is most striking is that despite their understanding of the original dynamics, they seem either naively unaware, or else, simply unconcerned about the extent to which the approach they urge makes behavioral changes motivated by a compliant transference likely, and the extent to which their own illustrations strongly suggest this possibility [Mitchell, 1981, p. 69].

Interpersonal relationships can either inhibit or permit the emergence of a patient's inner struggles into consciousness. Reparative therapists buttress just one side of the patient's conflict and, in so doing, they appeal to certain moral values. A compliant patient uses the therapist's moral stance to suppress same-sex feelings. Gay men who anecdotally report "successful" reparative therapies, often return to homosexual activity (White, 1994; Isay, 1996). Their inhibitions are not permanent because their inner conflict was never fully explored. Rather, it appears to have been repeatedly and interpersonally enacted with the reparative therapist. These therapists have learned that continued repetition of etiological theories of immaturity or

---

6. In his later work, Nicolosi (Nicolosi and Freeman, 1995) reverses himself on this position and says women can complete a reparative therapy.

pathology help patients suppress homosexual attractions or keep them out of conscious awareness. The patient retains his forbidden desires and the therapist performs and reinforces the prohibitive role. Some reparative therapy patients learn to suppress their homoerotic desires and to create the appearance of a heterosexual identity. Wives may also be enlisted into the treatment (White, 1994). A knowing wife can help the ex-gay husband's ongoing need for social reinforcement, even after his therapy has terminated.

Reparative therapy enactments are not necessarily limited to the psychoanalytic session. As some former patients like prominent gay historian Martin Duberman painfully recount, their therapists took strong positions about the conduct of their outside lives:

> From the first [my analyst] Weintraupt advised me to give up the relationship with Larry. Until I did, he warned, any real progress in therapy would prove impossible. The drama of our interpsychic struggle, Weintraupt insisted, had become a stand-in for the more basic intrapsychic conflict I was unwilling to engage—the conflict between my neurotic homosexual "acting out" and my underlying healthy impulse toward a heterosexual union.
>
> I resisted—not so much Weintraupt's theories, as his insistence on a total break with Larry. I accepted the need, but could not summon the will. I spent therapy hour after therapy hour arguing my inability to give up the satisfactions of the relationship—neurotic and occasional though they might be, and though my future happiness might well hang on their surrender. I resisted so hard and long that Weintraupt finally gave me an ultimatum: either give up Larry or give up therapy [1991, p. 33] .

To repeat: whatever their good intentions, when therapists take sides in the struggle to establish a patient's sexual identity, they are likely to reinforce dissociative, rather than integrative tendencies. This is not only true in reparative treatments, but in some gay-affirmative ones as well. One gay man described his group therapy experience with a previous therapist who believed that gay relationships, when monogamous, were spiritually acceptable. Attracted to this philosophy, the patient agreed to follow the therapist's prescriptions for dating and proscriptions on cruising. However, during his many years in this treatment, the patient never told the therapist he was still having anonymous, compulsive sex. He felt the therapist and fellow group members would judge him harshly and so he kept this aspect of his feelings and his behavior out of the treatment setting.

The patient's attitudes in that treatment illustrate a general problem with psychotherapies, among which one would have to include reparative therapy, that encourage patients to use an external authority and the opinions of others to dictate their life decisions for them. The first therapist, in employing a coupled model of gay relationships toward which patients could aspire, implicitly communicated a critical judgment of non-monogamous relationships that did not measure up to this ideal. The patient, who was critically judgmental of his own anonymous sexual activities, hoped that by adopting the therapist's attitudes, language, and beliefs, he might change his sexual activities. The patient acted as if he believed that presenting himself to others as if he were trying to have a committed gay relationship might get him one. A similar "as if" quality has been reported by some gay men who, regardless of their true sexual feelings, tried to live as if they were heterosexuals in the hopes that doing so might make them heterosexuals (Buxton, 1994; White, 1994; Isay, 1996).

Although the actual motives of the previous therapist were unknown, he appeared to be providing his patients with a gay role model. Paralleling this approach, the reparative therapy literature places an emphasis on the therapist as a role model of heterosexuality toward which the patient can aspire. Reparative therapy also prescribes certain behaviors, like dating women and getting more involved in nonsexual male camaraderie, and proscribes others like viewing pornography and engaging in homosexual activity.

As many analysts know, many patients also want their therapists to provide them with goals and direction. That was certainly the case with this patient, who felt guilty about his compulsive forays to pornographic bookstores. In treatment with an analytic therapist some years later, the patient tried to persuade the new therapist to lecture him on the correct way to behave, and to discourage him from continuing his anonymous sexual activities. The therapist might have directly interpreted the patient's transferential longing for an omnipotent authority figure who would take control of the patient's behavior. However, it was the therapist's impression that such an interpretation might be heard as a criticism of the patient for having such longings. Making an indirect interpretation instead, the therapist pointed out that the previous therapist's discouragement had not seemed to stop the patient's anonymous sexual activities, so what purpose would it serve to use discouragement again? The patient became increasingly annoyed that the therapist would not play the role of authority figure as obligingly as the previous therapist had done. Frustrated by the therapist's unwillingness to participate in the enactment, the patient then angrily informed the therapist that it was the latter's job to stop the patient from engaging in "meaningless behavior." The therapist was intrigued by the patient's concept of meaningless behavior. He mused aloud that all behaviors had meanings, including those the patient wished to define as meaningless. By labeling his sexual behaviors as "meaningless," the patient was actually judging them to be "bad," rather than trying to understand them. This interpretation, which was not heard as the criticism he anticipated, disoriented the patient who replied, "What? Of course, I see what you mean. That makes sense. Of course what I'm doing sexually must have a meaning."

Variations of this interaction were repeated again and again over the sessions that followed. Once he ceased trying to make the therapist stop his anonymous sexual activities, the patient began talking about the anxious and lonely feelings that prompted him to search for human contact in that arena. As he came to understand the sources of his anxiety, and to tolerate those feelings as well, the patient felt a greater sense of control. This feeling increased his own sense of authority and, over the course of his treatment, he went less frequently to the bookstores. If he felt like going, he would tell himself why he didn't want to go and often he did not. On those rare occasions when he did feel compelled to go, he was able to look at his actions, talk about them more openly with himself, and then later with the therapist.

Because the therapist declined the projected role of moral guardian, the patient gradually came to understand that he had to deal with his own reservations about going to the bookstore. This increased the patient's awareness of his own internal struggle over his sexual behaviors. The solution he gradually arrived at, going less often, felt satisfactory to him. However, a different patient might have resolved a similar struggle by giving himself permission to go cruising. And finally, belying reparative therapy claims that equate homosexuality with sexual compulsivity, although this patient experienced a reduction in what was previously felt to be a sexual compulsion, he did not change his sexual orientation.

Conclusion

Some patients come into treatment thinking they are going to solve a mystery. The patient will provide the clues and the therapist will tell them who or what made them the way they are. When the culprit is found and his or her selfish motives explained, the patient's original potential can be recovered. Unfortunately, even when the detective finds the criminals, the victim's property is not always recovered.

Regardless of the etiology of homosexuality, reparative therapies will always exist as long as people have moral beliefs prescribing heterosexuality. This does not necessarily mean that such treatments will be successful. Bieber (et al., 1962) claimed a 27 percent success rate for psychoanalytic conversions of sexual orientation. Socarides (1968; 1995), a reparative therapy veteran, has had similarly sparse results: a 35 percent conversion rate of the homosexually-identified patients he treated since 1967. Thus, 73 percent of Bieber's patients and 65 percent of Socarides' did not, could not, or would not change into heterosexuals. Socarides' (1995) interpretation of his unsatisfactory treatment outcomes implies that the method is sound, but that the patients who do not change were either noncompliant or unmotivated:

Some simply had to move away because their jobs took them elsewhere. Some ended treatment because of their fears that emerged from their unconscious—fears that were responsible for their homosexual needs, and which they didn't have the courage to face, and try to conquer. Some may have simply been reluctant to change their lifestyles. This is true of some alcoholics. If they give up drinking, they have to start looking for a whole new set of friends [p. 102].

Any physician performing a risky medical procedure is faced with the difficult task of helping a patient feel confident. One way they do this is by being honest about what the physician does and does not know. Therefore, ethical physicians obtain a patient's informed consent before performing a medical procedure. The patient is told what are the known risks and benefits of undergoing the procedure. In this way, the patient will ideally have as much understanding of what he is getting into as does the physician.

Reparative therapists' beliefs can create unreasonable expectations in their clients. Some of them are people who are desperately attempting to conform to heterosexual normativity. They are willing to make major sacrifices of time, effort, and money to achieve that goal. Anecdotal reports from former reparative therapy patients indicate that when the treatment fails, the patient often blames the failure on himself. An unsuccessful outcome can leave an "unrepaired" patient feeling ashamed and depressed, and sometimes in worse condition than when treatment began. The implication that it is primarily the patient's motivation to change that determines the success or failure of reparative therapy only reinforces feelings of failure and incompetence in those who cannot change.

A review of reparative therapy practices raises many questions (Drescher, 1997b). Do reparative therapists obtain informed consent and routinely tell potential patients of the two-thirds probability that they won't change? Should they warn patients that if they don't change, they might feel worse about themselves than when they started? Are there ethical problems when a therapist's attitudes and values are played out with patients who enter treatment having been exposed to similar values that have profoundly affected their capacity to accept themselves for who they are (see Haldeman, 1991, 1994; Brown, 1996)? These are questions worth considering, not only by reparative therapists, but by anyone concerned about the social, professional, ethical and moral practices of psychoanalysis and psychotherapy.

7

THE THERAPIST'S STANCE

Personality is made manifest in interpersonal
situations, and not otherwise.

Harry Stack Sullivan,
The Data of Psychiatry (1938)

If one can really show people what they are doing they
become less frightened, they feel more secure about
themselves, so that when they are genuinely in doubt
or genuinely know that they are ignorant they seek not
advice but information.

D. W. Winnicott, *Talking to Parents* (1957)

Thus . . . man is the founding principle and woman
the excluded opposite of this; and as long as such a distinction is tightly held in place the whole system can
function effectively. "Deconstruction" is the name
given to the critical operation by which such oppositions can be partly undermined, or by which they can
be shown partly to undermine each other in the
process of textual meaning.

Terry Eagleton, *Literary Theory* (1983)

Psychotherapeutic work with gay men draws attention to aspects
of the therapy process sometimes overlooked in doing psychotherapy with
nongay patients. In fact, just as Freud found the category of homosexuality

to be a useful construct in illuminating his theories of bisexual libido, psychosexual development, and identification, so too, psychotherapeutic work with gay men offers insights into some general principles of psychoanalysis, as well as basic psychoanalytic beliefs and practices. These include but are not limited to: the nature of the psychotherapeutic frame; the values and risks of therapist self-disclosure; the limitations of psychoanalytic data to support theories of etiology; how adherence to theoretical preconceptions will restrict or inhibit a therapist's clinical listening; experience-near versus experience-distant responsiveness from the therapist; the therapist's embeddedness in cultural preconceptions and how they have an impact upon treatment; the role of the patient's and the therapist's subcultural identities and how they co-construct narratives in treatment; and the meanings and therapeutic uses of countertransference.

This chapter discusses some of the factors that go into a therapist's stance when treating gay patients. Developing one's own therapeutic stance depends upon specialized training in psychotherapy, continuing education, the therapist's own personal analysis, and ongoing self-analysis. Furthermore, the therapist's stance does not just entail what one knows, it also includes what the therapist does not know, and requires an ability to allow a dynamic interplay of knowing and not knowing in the patient, in the therapist, and in the transitional space between them. Bion (1967b) described such a state of mind as being "without memory or desire" and it is essential to creating what Schafer (1983) refers to as an "analytic attitude."

The therapeutic stance presented here draws upon Winnicott and defines a therapeutic holding environment as a space in which all of a patient's feelings and ideas are allowed to emerge. In the atmosphere of the holding environment, meanings are discovered, created, and deciphered. All patients, not just gay ones, can benefit from a therapeutic holding environment based on respectful principles. Respect for the patient is essential. But by itself, it may not be enough. As shown in earlier chapters, the subject of homosexuality often evokes uncomfortable feelings and denigrated meanings. When these emerge in treatment, they certainly need to be tolerated and respected by the therapist. However, it is a prerequisite in doing psychotherapy with gay men that therapists themselves be able to accept their patient's homosexuality as a normal variation of human sexuality, and that they value and respect same-sex feelings and behaviors as well. It should be noted that for some gay men, being treated with such respect by a therapist would constitute a novel experience:

> **B:** The idea of respect. That's the piece. The lack of self-respect and the degree to which I denigrate myself, and you ask me to challenge that

thinking. It's hard but it makes a lot of sense. The idea of the respect with which I go out of my way to treat other people and the lack of respect that I treat myself with is so obvious to me now. And mysterious. Part of the motivation is I don't want to treat anybody the way I treat myself. But I feel this rigidity, the priest wagging his finger inside me. That hammering away at myself, I think you referred to it as self-hatred, it's almost palpable. It has somehow taken over and overshadowed the other parts of me.

In addition to respect, the therapeutic stance presented here focuses on the meanings, rather than the origins of human sexuality. The therapist who enthusiastically searches for the causes of homosexuality will ultimately fall prey to a gay patient's etiological defenses (see below) and consequently mistake the meanings of sexuality for something else. It therefore follows that this therapeutic stance attends to the affective meanings of the language of the patient, as well as those of the therapist, and to their transferential and countertransferential implications. To broaden the understanding of a gay man's subjectivity, this chapter explains how the traditional concept of a sexual orientation is ambiguously derived from multiple frames of reference. The interchangeable and unexamined uses of these different meanings of sexual orientation, as seen in much of the scientific and psychoanalytic literature, makes the concept's clinical utility questionable. Alternative concepts—sexual attractions, sexual identities, and sexual hierarchies—are more flexible and therefore, more clinically meaningful. The chapter then concludes by discussing countertransference and self-disclosure by the therapist as they pertain, not only to issues of sexual identity, but to therapy in general.

The argument in this chapter hinges upon a paradoxical injunction to the therapist. In some ways, a nongay therapist working with a gay man is working with someone from a different culture or subculture. But the treatment of gay men is, in most respects, no different than the treatment of other patients. Therefore, it should be kept in mind that there are equal risks to the patient arising from a therapist's using specialized knowledge to make unwarranted, albeit affirming, presumptions about a patient's sexual identity and issues pertaining to it, as there are from a therapist's ignorance about or latent devaluation of that identity.

The Etiological Defense

Patients entering treatment are often searching for deeper explanations of themselves. One consequence of their demands upon the therapist for insights is a psychoanalytic literature replete with case studies by therapists attempting to use the data of psychoanalytic treatment to arrive at etiological theories. Contemporary psychoanalytic theory, however, has clarified the limits of psychoanalytic data in this regard, generally accepting that etiological formulations can only be supported from extra-clinical and longitudinal research. Furthermore, at least since Peterfreund (1983), it has occurred to thoughtful clinicians that the therapist's own etiological assumptions and hypotheses can pose a risk to the clinical process insofar as they lead to stereotyped interpretations and inhibit open exploration. In addition, a patient's own search for etiological explanations may be used to bind anxieties, and can limit more helpful psychotherapeutic exploration. In fact, a patient's etiological ruminations can be part of a character structure that seeks to maintain stable, dissociative mechanisms.

What is true generally is also true for the gay patient. A patient entered treatment with anxiety and confusion about his sexual identity. In his first session, he recalled a childhood attraction to men, but was quick to reassure the therapist that he also found "some women" attractive. He then sheepishly added that his heterosexual desires were not as strong as those he had toward men. He presented his sexual history spontaneously, in a rapid, pressured way, almost as a monologue in which he provided his own questions, answers, and rebuttals: "If I see a good-looking guy and a good-looking woman, who do I look at? You want to know who I look at? I look at the guy."

The therapist soon learned that embedded in these monologues were memories of an earlier treatment in which a previous therapist had not argued with the patient's belief that homosexuality was caused by a "smothering mother" and an "absent father." According to the patient, they both agreed the patient's "unhealthy" relationship with his mother made him feel uncomfortable around women and that the father's abandonment of the family "made me look for love in the arms of a man. That man then takes the place of the father I never had." Despite an endorsement of this pathological theory, the previous therapist also assured the patient that "It was OK to be gay."

The insights of that previous treatment notwithstanding, the patient never formed a close emotional attachment to either a man or a woman. He associated his loneliness with feelings of shame and discomfort. He ended the previous treatment without coming to any definitive conclusions about his sexual identity, but he found himself thinking more often, "I might be gay." He told a friend he was gay, and was considering telling others as well. He was not prepared to tell his parents, however, and was terrified that they would find out.

In the first session, the patient repeatedly quizzed the new therapist, "Do you think that what I told you makes sense? Do you think that's the reason that I might be gay?" The therapist said he did not know why anyone was gay. The patient repeated his etiological theories again and persisted in his wish to know the therapist's opinion of them: "So you don't think I might be gay because my mother smothered me? You don't think I might be gay because my father left me when I needed him?" The therapist pointed out that it was their first meeting and that he really didn't know much about the patient. Furthermore, the therapist knew nothing definitive about what caused either homosexuality or heterosexuality. This evoked the following response: "So you're telling me then, that people are born gay?" Again, the therapist said he didn't know. The patient responded in an annoyed tone: "I can't believe you don't think I'm gay because of my smothering mother. You can't even tell me if we're born gay. How can a psychiatrist not know what causes homosexuality? Are you sure you don't know? Now I'm all confused."

These interchanges occurred repeatedly as the evaluation proceeded over the next few sessions. The patient would anxiously interrupt himself in the middle of a vignette about his personal or family history and once again raise the question of why he was gay. At the beginning of their fifth session, the patient said: "You know what happened last week? Remember how you told me that you didn't know why I was gay and that nobody knew why anyone was gay? After I left here, I was thinking about that. Then I had this strong feeling of sexual excitement for another man. It was like I said to myself, 'It's all right to be gay.'"

It should be noted here that this last statement was as much a surprise to the therapist as it was to the patient. Up until then, the therapist thought it was an open question whether the patient was gay. Although the patient kept referring to himself as "gay," it was clear that he was not entirely comfortable with the appellation. He appeared to be trying it on, seeing how it fit him, and to see how the therapist thought it fit him. And, later during the session, the patient once again asked the therapist if he was gay because of his smothering mother. It was not the last time the patient returned to this question. As therapy progressed, the question's obsessional quality became clearer as it emerged each time the patient was anxious about discussing his interpersonal difficulties.

In terms of the subjectivities outlined in the previous chapter, one could say that the patient presented himself as a homosexually self-aware man who thought he might be gay. The therapist heard his struggle in the following way: If the patient was talking about coming out to a relative, that indicated the possibility of accepting himself as gay. However, his fears that his parents might find out indicated his own fears of being gay. These contradictions increased his anxiety.

The therapist tried to hear and respect both sides of the struggle. He communicated that the goal of treatment was not to judge or denigrate either possibility, but to talk about and understand both of them. Despite the patient's many invitations to do so, the therapist deferred from making genetic interpretations. "It is very important . . . that the analyst shall *not* know the answers except in so far as the patient gives the clues" (Winnicott, 1960a, p. 50). This is the only way to acquire more detailed knowledge about a specific patient. However, the patient wanted the therapist to use his professional authority to settle an internal debate. The therapist did not cooperate, replying honestly, and to the best of his knowledge, the etiological "facts" as he understood them and did not provide definitive answers to the patient's questions. What the patient experienced was that the therapist didn't say it was "OK to be gay," but he didn't say that it was not.

The therapist's stance undermined the patient's own prohibitions and made him feel more anxious. This anxiety fueled his efforts to elicit an authoritarian response of any kind from the therapist. Thus he turned to the belief that people are born gay. The therapist declined to throw his authority behind that argument as well. Instead, he used his authority to defend a position of uncertainty regarding the origins of homosexuality. The willingness to maintain a position of uncertainty is one of the things that distinguishes a psychoanalytic approach from a reparative therapy.

Initially, the patient was too anxious to pay attention to his inner struggle. Defining his homosexual feelings in the language of pathology partially inhibited them. He had asked the therapist to agree with his pathologizing theories in order to shore up his antihomosexual inhibitions. This is what occurred in the previous treatment when the first therapist said "It was OK to be gay," while endorsing a pathological theory of homosexuality. In effect, the patient heard the therapist say, "It is OK to be gay, even if it means you are sick." After leaving that therapist, the patient's sexual inhibitions gradually diminished, and he took tentative steps toward coming out. However, this made him more anxious since his internal struggle to define his sexual identity had never been addressed. He once again sought therapy to help restore the shaky inner truce that was now in danger of falling apart. The new therapist respectfully disagreed with the patient's etiological theory and the condemnatory, moral framework in which it was embedded. The patient heard this as the therapist saying "Since we don't know what causes homosexuality, we don't necessarily know that it is a bad thing to be gay."

In the sessions that followed, the therapist's stance increasingly annoyed the patient. The lack of definitive responses led the patient to question the therapist's competence. However, the therapist withstood the assault. Gradually, the patient began to experience the therapist in the paradoxical role of the authority who will not be judgmentally authoritarian. This distracted the patient from his usual internal struggles and he became disoriented. This surprisingly led to an increase in his homosexual desires and freed up his feeling that he indeed was gay.

It is important to remember that these interactions were only the first step in a long treatment in which other concerns eventually emerged, not specifically having to do with the patient's sexual identity. The clarification of these concerns, in turn, roughly coincided with a clearer understanding of the patient's obsessional style. In other words, the patient had begun with the most pressing issue on his agenda: whether or not he was gay. His etiological concerns, as reasonable as they were at face value, were also linked to his defensive structure. The previous therapist tried to address the question of etiology posed to him but neglected to see the defensive purposes which the question served. In this regard, gay men are not fundamentally different from other patients whose etiological theories about themselves are part of their character style. Patients of all kinds may seek to have their etiological theories ratified by therapists, and in the process may lure their therapists into unwitting enactments that serve to bolster the patient's defenses.

Talking Sex

A knowledge of etiological theories of homosexuality and the defensive purposes they may serve is one aspect of developing a therapeutic stance for treating gay patients. Another important area of specialized knowledge is a familiarity with the sexual practices of gay men. A therapist would do well not to assume anything about the sexual practices of a particular gay patient, or of any patient for that matter. Furthermore, when gay patients do reveal their sexual selves, they may evoke a range of countertransference responses, even from a seasoned therapist, regardless of the therapist's sexual identity. How a therapist feels about homosexuality in general, and even more, how one feels about homosexual behaviors in particular, will inevitably be manifest in one's therapeutic participation in one way or another. This could include the therapist's choice of words, in the kind of topics explored, or in where one chooses to remain silent. It is one thing to define oneself as accepting homosexuality in the abstract. But it is another thing altogether to feel sufficiently comfortable to pursue an inquiry in a way that is maximally close to the patient's experience. And it is in the therapist's language that one often finds unspoken, countertransferential attitudes toward what the patient presents of himself:

> **C:** I left work today early. My fantasy was to go to the [Greenwich] Village, go to a bookstore, get sucked off, get some poppers. The fucking train was so delayed I barely had enough time to get here. (Laughs) Clearly the level of frustration I'm feeling is getting greater and greater.

> **Th:** What is the connection between going to the Village, getting sucked off, and your level of frustration?

The therapist responded with an approximation of the patient's language, that included a graphic description of a sexual wish. The patient's explicit language, in this case, was affectively charged and experience-near. In general, this is a reasonable therapeutic approach with any patient, irrespective of sexual identity, and should not just be confined to questions about sexual wishes or fantasies.

> **C:** I have it in my head that I want someone to give me a blowjob and I'm not going to get it from my lover. Our sex isn't even erotic, and at least being able to do that is erotic to me. I feel the way I felt when I was single on a Saturday night, and just wanted to get laid in those happy carefree days.

> **Th:** What will the erotic experience in the bookstore provide you with?

In the therapist's second comment, something changes. Ideally, the therapist might have continued to stay close to the patient's experience and said "What will getting a blowjob in the bookstore provide you with?" Instead he spoke of the patient's "erotic experience." Although the patient did use the word "erotic," the therapist may have been made anxious by the discussion and unconsciously chose to use that word rather than the available alternative:

> **C:** It would provide me with a great way to come. Something different from my hand. Even when I tried to jerk off yesterday, I couldn't sustain the hard on. My mind started wandering. In my mind it would be this great orgasm. Then I would probably feel guilty and depressed and gross. Today that didn't matter. Today it was just what I wanted.

Did this gay man unconsciously hear the therapist's discomfort with the sexually explicit language? Although he began again by talking about "a great way to come," "jerking off," and his "hard on," his reference to "coming" was then sanitized and became a "great orgasm." Unconsciously encouraged by the apparent success of his previous intervention, the therapist's next remark, reasonable as it sounded, nevertheless continued to desexualize the conversation:

Th: Perhaps it is an action that allows you to address a number of different feelings.

C: Is that a leading question?

Th: Yes.

C: (Laughs) We work so well together.

The patient was communicating his sexual feelings in explicit language while the therapist resorted to terms that tried to reduce their intensity between them. This may account for the flirtatious quality of the patient's last remarks as the sexual feelings between them passed from the realm of language into that of enactment. The patient was not only being sexually rejected by his lover; in the transference and countertransference enactment, he was also being rejected by the therapist. However, the patient persistently tried to get the therapist to pay attention to his sexual feelings:

C: It would be an angry slap at my lover. Even though he wouldn't know, it's like saying "Fuck you, I'll get it somewhere." Maybe I want someone to look at me. I want someone to find me attractive. I want someone to say, "I want to have sex with you."

Th: What about the idea that the sexual act is a way to deal with many feelings?

"Fucking" and "sucking" became the "sexual act." By now, it was increasingly obvious that the therapist was having difficulty tolerating the feelings communicated in the patient's words:

C: I remember the last conversation we had about this. Somehow I was aware that the idea of being fucked was someone taking over, making the decisions, taking the power to take care of things. Somehow, being sucked off has made me aware of the word "pleasuring." Someone is taking some time to do something very intimate. When I was younger , I thought they were doing something for me, and not getting anything in return. As I've grown to like sucking more, I realize that is not the case. I get as much pleasure sucking my lover off as I do getting sucked. So I think that is part of sexual acts dealing with feelings. In some ways that is a bond, a bonding thing.

Th: A bond?

C: In the sense that there is an intimacy. If I view it as someone sucking me off is doing something for me, that is a greater level of intimate feeling and bonding.

Th: You lover will not suck you off?

Despite the therapist's unconscious resistance, the patient persevered in speaking frankly. He was rewarded as the therapist, who in the struggle between his countertransferential discomfort and his attempt to connect with the patient, once again returned to using the patient's language. When he did, the patient's narrative became even more explicit:

C: He can't. He tires. He's done a little bit with the tip of my cock, but I don't have the sense that he enjoys it. I did tell him I'm frustrated he didn't suck my cock. He knows that. I remember when I was younger and people would want to fuck me. Once I let someone fuck me. I remember feeling a loss of all sense of sexual pleasure. I thought, "I'm not putting up with this. This is not what I'm going to do to myself." I stopped him and I left. I went out with this guy 20 years ago who I allowed to fuck me, and I remember how good it felt. There were periods when I enjoyed being fucked. There have been times with my lover when I enjoy it, but in many ways I associate it with that early experience. Not letting somebody fuck me is a way to keep something closed up. I enjoy the idea of fucking someone else. My lover likes it, but I don't enjoy it because it becomes a certain production. As I tried to explain in the past, we jumped from the initial sort of foreplay to the fucking. The jump is too quick for me. Then there's all this preparation. He sort of takes over, he is too direction-oriented.

In intimate "fucking," one person gets inside another. The same is metaphorically true of psychotherapy. A patient's intimate feelings can get inside a therapist and conversely a patient can take something inside that comes from the therapist. As the patient spoke uninterruptedly, he experienced the therapist's silence as a detachment from their intimate exchange. Perhaps it was the hope of reengaging the therapist by reducing the level of sexual intensity between them that led him spontaneously to desexualize his own language:

C: We've talked about this. When we talked, we talked about how we masturbate. He masturbates and comes in a matter of two to four minutes. I can masturbate and it can take thirty to forty minutes. We are totally different in how we get to that end. I feel I've never gotten to the place where it is really a good orgasm. I'm not sure that hasn't been the case for a good part of my sexual life. I keep thinking of these women who fake the orgasm. I certainly didn't fake the orgasm when I was by myself and I had the video in. I'm perfectly content and I can have an orgasm that is fabulous. Why do I need anybody else?

The patient raised a transferential question: If the therapist could not tolerate the patient's sexuality, why did the patient need him? With still no response from the therapist, the patient's sexual feelings were increasingly accompanied by anger:

C: I was reading some article about S&M (sadomasochistic sexual practices), somebody getting men to come into a scene. He said S&M is a consensual thing. The two people agree on the level they would go to. I never knew that. My lover is now buying S&M videos and magazines. He's into this bondage, and I'm thinking, "Mr. Vanilla[1] is going in that direction?" If he likes to have sex, we have to close the blinds. Even when I do get turned on and I want him to fuck me, he loses his erection. Talk about taking the wind out of his sails. It happens almost all the time and yet he doesn't seem to deal with it. I want to say, "What about the act of fucking me causes you to lose your erection?"

Th: It feels like sex and anger are tied up with each other, no pun intended.

The therapist's interpretation included a spontaneous joke that attempted to link the relationship between the patient's sexual and aggressive feelings but that countertransferentially tried to diminish their intensity:

C: (Laughs) Yes, I can see that. In some ways sex is used that way. I can see it as a way to dominate somebody, as a way to punish somebody, use it as a way to get back. I think that is what I wanted to do today. Just do it. Get something you want. Fuck it.

As illustrated by the interaction above, talking sex can place demands on the treatment relationship. Fortunately for this therapist, the patient did not need a perfect analyst, just a good enough one who would make the effort of staying in contact despite his discomfort. In fact, the efforts made by a therapist to stay in contact are an important part of the holding environment.

Therapeutic Holding

Winnicott (1965), both pediatrician and psychoanalyst, was the most respectful of therapists. His theories, derived from his observations of the mother-child dyad, provide a model for a therapeutic holding environment. Infants do not require a perfect mother. A good enough mother will do. Maternal impingements are inevitable and necessary in the totality of the holding environment. Although impingements are painful for the child, they help him adapt to a world that, like the mother, cannot meet all of his needs.

---

1. Every sexual identity uses a subjective frame of reference to describe not-me identities. "Vanilla sex" is a term used by those who participate in S&M activities to describe non-S&M sex.

At times a therapist's interventions or interpretations can feel like holding. At other times, they can be experienced as impingement. Again, this is inevitable in psychotherapy with any patient. The therapist's job is to remain open to hearing the patient's complaints, sexual or otherwise. The experience of impingement can occur in a treatment expressly designed to be supportive. In fact, impingement can occur in a treatment based on principles of gay affirmation. The following patient was a quiet man, in general; in treatment, he was collaborative and productive. When he found himself in disagreement with others, he was reluctant to let them know:

> **E:** The whole thought of finding someone that I can really be physically and emotionally intimate with, it is just still hard to imagine that it could really happen. It has taken me so long to find a way to meet people. But I have to say that you have been very patient with me. My previous therapist couldn't have lasted through this. I am doing now what he wanted me to do three years ago.
>
> **Th:** What happened with your previous therapist?
>
> **E:** I resented him. He had all kinds of suggestions. He had advice and I didn't want advice.
>
> **Th:** What did the advice feel like?
>
> **E:** He was very authoritarian. He suggested that I put an ad in the Village Voice as a way to meet men. However, I knew it wasn't just a suggestion, because the next week I came in and he wanted to know if I had placed the ad. That was a problem.
>
> **Th:** You felt he was making demands of you?
>
> **E:** It was his agenda, how he would do it. I think how long it has taken me and how you let me go at my own pace. I appreciate that. I feel that it has to be my idea and that I have to be ready for it. It's taken a long time.

Despite his complaints, and an unsolicited testimonial to the current therapist, this patient was also identified with the previous therapist. In fact, he wanted the current therapist to push him harder, and was angry with him for not doing so. But in keeping within his character, he withheld his anger as a silent reservation. For the new therapist to criticize the former therapist would have been a mistake. It would have only delayed the day when the patient would be able to express his anger toward the new therapist in the transference. And here again, psychotherapy with a gay patient is not fundamentally different from the work with other patients.

Just as it is a mistake to take sides in discussing previous treatment, it is important to understand the consequences of taking sides in a patient's interpersonal struggles with family and friends. Ideally, everyone a patient discusses should be treated respectfully. This includes the people of whom he consciously disapproves. This therapeutic stance allows for a wider exploration of a patient's feelings and identifications:

> **F:** Part of me wants to understand my father more and accept the way he is. I know how much he means to me, but the notion that I still want my father's attention and approval is my ball and chain. It feels constricting, like I am tethered to him. I wish I didn't feel that demanding connection to him.

This man believed his mother was a saint who suffered at his hateful father's hands. His narrow view of his parents' relationship was stretched as he developed a wider view of himself:

> **Th:** Your affection for your father has always been affected by his behavior toward your mother. You get angry with the way he treats her and that makes it difficult to feel the affection.

> **F:** Right. But I also experienced my anger toward my mother this past weekend. Mixed with happiness and joy at seeing her. I was conscious of experiencing it. It all seems so fragile, trying to understand these things. It's almost as if I was waiting for the phone call telling me that my father has had a stroke, or that my mother has had a massive heart attack.

> **Th:** Your anger with your parents can be disguised by your concerns for their recently failing health. Your concern keeps you from knowing your anger.

> **F:** I can imagine being angry for many reasons, looking at the things they did and didn't do.

> **Th:** Your anger with your father is more accessible to you.

> **F:** I can justify my anger towards him. It's more difficult with my mother. She was the one who made life livable. He was inattentive and she was attentive.

From the transferential perspective, it should be noted here that the patient believed the attentiveness of the therapist would make it difficult for the patient to get angry with him as well.

> **Th:** You feel your mother was the victim of your father.

> **F:** That allows me to be more angry at him and to misdirect my anger. Instead of pointing the finger at her, and saying "You are weak. You let this happen. You allowed me to live a life of hell with this man." She was

an accomplished woman who had the means to live on her own. It's not as if she were tied to him financially. Maybe she was weak. He was authoritarian and maybe that was attractive to her. It could have been appealing and filled a need that she had. Maybe she was weak or afraid. Her actions seem selfish. These images are difficult to even consider together. I built her into one thing. To look at her any other way, to begin to see these things together in the same mindset is so difficult.

Th: Seeing things together generates anxiety.

F: It's like trying to push two magnets together, or grating stones.

Th: Your feelings divide people into saints and martyrs or devils and demons.

F: And angels. It's easier. It was something that I did in childhood. It's sad. It also takes me back. I was like a child living on a street, holding onto a box. The only thing the child had in this world was this box, to keep the frightening evil menacing world away.

Th: You've learned how your father is also like a child holding a box.

F: I'm aware of that. Part of me can understand that he worked with the tools that he had. It makes me think of the environment he grew up in. That thought makes me sick. I have these images in my mind of backbiting, lying, cheating, conniving, and abusing. It makes me want to puke. This is a family? It makes me sick that this is a family and that this has gone on for how many years? It doesn't seem it can possibly be real, and yet this is the environment I grew up in and I drag it around with me. I don't think things can change much. I guess what I'm looking for is a way to live with my parents the way they are. I could communicate better with my father if I understood better who he was. There's such a history of betrayal or lack of trust. To do something differently, to look at the situation differently is like learning a new language.

The exploration of the patient's multiple identifications with both of his parents and of his conflictual feelings toward them was a therapeutic task in its own right, one in keeping with general principles of analytic treatment. If the therapist inwardly harbors an etiological theory that demonizes binding mothers and sadistic fathers, it may be difficult to identify respectfully with the counter-currents in this patient's developmental history. In point of fact, this patient did have such an etiological theory and the foregoing exploration of his father's assets and his mother's deficits was not easy for him. In this man, the inner barriers against such exploration were connected to his sense of himself as gay. However, these defenses are not fundamentally different from the kinds of barriers against experiencing ambivalence found in many patients.

Furthermore, the direction of exploration need not be limited to an exclusive interest in issues related to the patient's sexual identity. Thus, it was eventually worthwhile to explore what "holding onto a box" was like for this man as a child, just as it was worth pondering how that experience was passed from father to son.

A patient may try to resolve inner conflicts about being gay by selectively inattending to his own antihomosexual identifications. This is sometimes seen in gay men who preach rigid doctrine to themselves in order to affirm their own homosexuality. Unable to tolerate conflictual feelings about homosexuality, these men sound as if they were trying to convince themselves that "It is OK to be gay." However, this solution only reverses the feelings and identifications of a former state of mind. In the subjectivity of a closeted identity, heterosexuality is idealized and homosexuality dissociated. After coming out, being gay can become idealized while disapproving feelings are denied. Therapeutic holding entails being able to contain both sides.

As has been previously shown, a patient's inner struggle for self-acceptance can present as an external struggle with an unaccepting family member. Acknowledging the interpersonal aspect of the struggles, and their pain, should not preclude exploration of the intrapsychic dimension of the conflict. Complicating matters, a patient's internalized attitudes are sometimes made up of rigid, moral absolutes and characterized by an intense disdain for compromise or relativism. The exploration of such internalized moral absolutes, and the identifications from which they stem, requires great tact. One often finds that a patient's dogmatic belief systems do not recognize the concept of respectful disagreement. This is true for a great many patients, gay and heterosexual, not just for the following gay patient who was wrestling with authoritarian, antihomosexual attitudes and identifications:

> **G:** I went to my brother's wedding but it was not as bad as I expected. His friends, a minister and his wife, approached me. I never met them before, but they were people with whom he had discussed my homosexuality. The minister's wife said, "You really love him, don't you?" It was so inappropriate. Why would people who I don't know be questioning my love for my brother? The minister kept staring at me when he shook my hand. He held it longer than he should have. It was like they believed that somehow they would heal me with Christian love. I said I had to go, and then I left.
>
> **Th:** What comes to mind about the experience?
>
> **G:** I think my brother has processed my homosexuality with a lot of these religious people. Even the gift I got for being in the wedding, I think it was

inappropriate. All the men in the wedding party got it. It's not appropriate for me. It's a book for straight men. I brought the book in to show you.

The book told how a man could find prayer, get married, and raise a family. The patient's complaint could be heard in at least two ways. He was indignant about his brother's treatment of him after much time, money, and effort were expended to participate in his wedding. He felt the brother was a terrible person who had betrayed him. However, although he was less aware of it, he also identified with his brother's position. The patient had previously discussed his conservative, religious upbringing and beliefs and how he tried to escape from them. In the session, the therapist returned to this line of inquiry:

Th: In your brother's world, there is no distinction between gay men and straight men. If you are a Christian, you choose to sin or you choose not to sin.

G: There's a chapter on sexual purity, having to do with sexual impulses when you are traveling away from home. You can hook up with other Christian men in the city of your travels so you can bond with them. I think it is so inappropriate to give that to me. They don't mention homosexuality at all, but the book talks about developing friendships with other men, getting in touch with their feminine or feeling sides. It was strange being at the wedding and knowing that attitude. I knew his position, but hoped at some level that he would understand mine. You know what kills me about these religious Christians? They feel they have the right to force their beliefs on other people.

Th: They believe they are going out and saving souls.

G: They feel they have this calling. He didn't go out of his way for me. It doesn't seem he spent any time considering me and my feelings. I think he believes he has a mission, this responsibility for saving me. Part of me says I have a lot of mixed feelings. This brought them all up again. This minister's wife is questioning my love for my brother. These people only talk to people they agree with. This makes me feel attacked.

Th: How does it feel like an attack?

G: It feels like a judgment. It feels like they are forcing their beliefs and values and ideas onto me.

The brother's beliefs, values, and ideals that he tried to ward off were also part of the patient's own life experience. There was a part of the patient that only wanted to talk to people who agreed with his assertion that religious people are bad:

G: Just thanking me for being in the wedding would have been better than this book. This book represents something to me. It makes my brother's position very real and it makes me see it as rigid. But there's no changing that. You cannot change what somebody believes. He's brainwashed.

Was the patient brainwashed because he had adopted a gay identity? Was his brother brainwashed for rejecting it? For the patient, both statements were true. The metaphor of brainwashing contemptuously dismissed the patient's unconscious identifications with his brother. The therapist next attempted to articulate the brother's position because he felt it was the patient's unspoken position as well:

Th: He probably feels you've been brainwashed.

G: I don't see how I can ever be close to my brother, knowing he has this position. That woman questions me if I love my brother? She should ask my brother if he loves me. I think it is hypocritical.

Th: Jesus loves you, but not unconditionally. He makes demands on you.

G: I was definitely raised with all of this. I don't believe it anymore. I don't believe any of it. If I believed it, I wouldn't have a strong repulsion or reaction.

Th: You may not act on the belief, but there is a part of you that still says it is wrong to be gay.

G: I'm sure there are parts of that inside me. But I can now see it in a different way. I can see the illogic of it. I can understand why people turn to religion. It makes things simpler. It makes life easier to deal with and explains things in simple terms. It gives you directions on what to do when you feel this or when you think this. It helps you control your life, is what it does. But religion makes things not OK that are OK. People that are religious present themselves as accepting and loving and they are not. They are the opposite. They are rigid and unaccepting. In being unaccepting, how can they be loving? My brother cannot see it.

Th: Their God is loving but He has rules. God loves you, but He wants you to behave in certain ways.

G: (Angry) That is his God. My understanding of God has changed.

Th: In what way?

G: I believe that if there is a God, He is not judgmental. He wouldn't give us feelings He didn't want us to feel. My brother's position is that He is testing me. Why would God do that? I can show my love for God with my interactions with other people. I can show my love for Him in that way, rather than being tested and giving me feelings and being attracted to men and denying it and not acting upon it. It doesn't make sense that God would give me feelings and not expect me to act on it. Homosexual feelings are not like homicidal feelings. They are not bad feelings.

Th: Aren't you interpreting scripture to suit yourself?

G: Sure, but that is what everybody does. My understanding makes more sense to me. These feelings are not evil, not sick, not bad.

Th: Who are you trying to convince? Me, you, or your brother?

G: I want to believe this and I think I do believe it. But when I am up against people like my brother, they fall back on it being evil and unnatural. I'm kind of a hypocrite. I want him to accept me, but I don't accept him.

Th: He feels your behaviors negate his beliefs. You feel that his beliefs negate your existence.

G: That's it exactly! They cannot be reconciled!

Th: You feel they cannot be reconciled inside you as well.

G: I don't have those beliefs anymore.

Th: I think you do.

G: (Silent) I wish I could get rid of them.

Space does not permit reproducing the latter part of the session in which the patient, with considerable sadness, began to feel his competing identifications as an internal conflict which he had yet to resolve. However, the session revealed that the patient's internalized religious beliefs were not limited to the condemnation of homosexuality. They also included moral and ethical beliefs that were integral to his adult self. He could not unilaterally rid himself of self-condemnation without severing his attachments to other important identifications. The psychotherapeutic challenge was to integrate his adult feelings and understanding of sexuality, ethics, and morality with his internalized childhood beliefs.

Another aspect to the session worth addressing was the kind of role-playing going on. That is to say, for part of the time, the therapist was assuming the role of speaking for the patient's internal, religious authorities and the patient was letting him. This had both witting and unwitting dimensions for both the patient and the therapist. Unwitting role-play is, of course, a recipe for unanalyzed enactments, and even knowing role play is tolerable only under certain circumstances. If the therapeutic environment can be compared to a play space (Freud 1914a, p. 154), role-playing constitutes perhaps the outer acceptable limit of rough and tumble play.

Role-playing is not the only way to play in psychotherapy. A therapeutic holding environment regards play as a serious business—and a serious responsibility for the therapist: "Psychotherapy takes place in the overlap of two areas of playing, that of the patient and that of the therapist. Psychotherapy has to do with two people playing together. The corollary of this is that where playing is not possible then the work done by the therapist is directed toward bringing the patient from a state of not being able to play into a state of being able to play" (Winnicott, 1971, p. 38). There may be any number of reasons for the inhibition of play between a particular patient and a particular therapist. Among these may be differences in cultural or subcultural backgrounds. A white therapist, for example, may simply not know how to "do the dozens" with an African-American patient. Similarly, "dishing" or "dishing the dirt" is a verbal form of rough and tumble play in some gay subcultures. A heterosexual therapist may not know how to dish or may feel uncomfortable engaging in it. Nonetheless, a therapist needs to find suitable ways to play with a patient. "If the therapist cannot play, then he is not suitable for the work" (Winnicott, 1971, p. 54).

A gay man had a dream and in the discussion of the dream, he and his therapist returned to a kind of word-play that had become an ongoing part of their work:

H: I had a dream about a pure white bat. It flew out of a couch with feathers. My boyfriend was there too, and maybe there was another bat. It was white, a symbol of purity.

Th: What comes to mind about bats?

Th: They are dirty and scary. They bite, supposedly. They get in your hair. Shadowy creatures of the night associated with evil.

Th: Was there a feeling in the dream?

H: Anxiety. The white bat was coming out of a couch with feathers flying up. It was hard to tell where the bat was and where the feathers were. What do you do with a bat? You don't want to touch it.

Th: And the couch with feathers?

H: It was reminiscent of couches we had at home when I was a kid. Very soft, and occasionally a feather would come out. I've not had the experience of a couch breaking.

Th: What if "couch" is a verb?

H: To spring forth, to couch things in a particular language. I'm very careful in the language I use.

Because they had played the game before, the patient picked up quickly on the therapist's invitation to play with the wording of the dream:

Th: In the dream, the bat comes out of the couch.

H: (Laughs) Yeah, transformed from a black animal into a white one. Like being put through a whitewash. It's certainly the way I feel about the delicacy and care with which I tell my boyfriend a cover-up story.

Th: You know the stories you tell your boyfriend are a whitewash and you have feelings about that.

H: Anxious feelings. The farther I get away from the experience of being unfaithful, the calmer I feel. But there is always a chance of a repeat event.

Th: There may be another bat in the dream. It doesn't matter how many times you go through the process, it may occur again.

H: Right. On the other hand, I had another dream on a different night. I came to a wonderful feeling of calm. A college dream again. Similar to my other college dream. The same geography, many rooms, dormitories. The insight of the dream was that I didn't have to study anymore. It was an incredible dream, You don't have to do this anymore. A dream about studying and preparing for exams and I was able to let it go. I think I'm a fearful person. Paranoid is too strong a word, but paranoids are afraid of things, afraid of people's reactions to things. Certainly I was terribly afraid of people's reactions when I was a kid. Very afraid about not doing anything that would give rise to the wrong reaction.

Fear of evoking a "wrong reaction" might be considered the antithesis of playful spontaneity. And by bringing up the second dream, the patient introduced the idea of inhibition and, in fact, the interpersonal schema underlying the interaction was about to change as the patient's sensitivity to criticism prevented him from continuing in the same vein. And yet some residual playfulness remained as the session turned into a peek-a-boo game in which the patient alternated between hiding from the therapist and inviting him to seek after him and recognize him. Hiding the truth is anxiety-provoking, but so is revealing it. Hiding and revealing are the rules of the peek-a-boo game. This man found the game anxiety-provoking. He was coming to understand that he was the agent who decided whether to hide or reveal himself. Later in the session, the therapist addressed this issue directly, but in the process upset the game:

Th: You are making a choice. You prefer to deal with the anxieties of covering up rather than deal with the anxieties of revealing.

H: Although I think you are right, that idea doesn't give me any comfort.

Like any traumatized individual, this patient's need for safety was a high priority, and his vulnerability to being disrupted by interpretation was great. He could tolerate word-play but the ensuing game of hide-and-seek became too rough for him. He could not tolerate this degree of verbal rough and tumble play, although other patients may find it stimulating, enlivening, and ultimately reassuring. The therapist was then left wondering if talking directly about hiding and revealing had poked at wounds related to the many humiliations this man had suffered by virtue of being gay, or whether it was related to other traumas. Although not every trauma stems from being gay, it is important for a therapist not to underestimate the extent to which a gay man may have been traumatized earlier in life. Many gay men have been assaulted, if not physically, then verbally, because of their sexual desires and identifications (DeCecco, 1985; Herek and Berrill, 1992). As a result, their lives may be characterized by an experience of not being accepted or respected for who they are. These experiences will be integrated into a patient's defensive system and, as a result, hiding and revealing may entail a matter of survival, not just a game.

From Sexual Orientations to Sexual Attractions and Sexual Identities

Some therapists believe they can treat gay men as they treat heterosexual patients without any additional special knowledge or training. This belief is based upon a lack of information about the cultural experiences that differently shape the sexual identities of heterosexual and gay people. Many therapists have a limited understanding of contemporary theories of sexuality that are not derived from analytic sources. However, understanding the meanings of gay patients' narratives requires sophisticated knowledge of the limits of contemporary knowledge about sexual development together with a willingness to question many cultural assumptions about human sexuality.

A *sexual orientation* is defined as the sum of an individual's sexual attractions and fantasies over a demarcated period of time. If the accumulated experiences of sexual attractions are toward the same sex, the orientation is *homosexual*, as in the man who always finds himself looking at or fantasizing about men, and does not feel any sexual attraction toward women. If the attractions are primarily toward a different anatomical sex, then the orientation is defined as *heterosexual*. A man who has always been attracted to women, but who absent-mindedly finds himself admiring another man's body on the beach, still has a heterosexual orientation. If one has significant periods of attraction to or fantasies about members of both sexes, one's orientation is defined as *bisexual*. Money (1988) reports of men who experience shifts in their sexual feelings from one gender to the other. These serial bisexuals report a period of homosexual activity and fantasy followed by a period of heterosexuality that may again "swing" back to homosexuality again.

A *sexual attraction* is an alternative concept that can be less ambiguously defined than a sexual orientation. Clinical practice shows that every human being is endowed with a broad repertoire of feeling states or affects. In the psychotherapy model presented here, sexual attractions are akin to affects, such as anger, shame, and sadness, in that they are subjective feeling states. Clinical psychoanalysis suggests that most feeling states have roots that go back to early development, begin organizing and reorganizing experience early on, and are always imbued with psychological meanings. Put another way, sexual attractions, like other feeling states, are part of the innate endowment of all human beings; what differs from one individual to the next are the meanings attributed to these states. As an adult, feelings in the present can be linked, consciously or unconsciously, to earlier meanings. This can be as true of anger as it is of a sexual feeling, as in, "When I get angry, I am just like my mother," or "When I am in my lover's arms, I remember the feeling of being held by my father."

Synecdoche, naming the part as a representative of the whole, narrows the field of observation (Magee and Miller, 1997, p. 96). Affects are a part of a person's identity, but one's identity is not defined by a single affect. One can characterize a person who displays anger all the time as "an angry person," or a person with same-sex feelings as "a homosexual," but in doing so, one potentially loses sight of the person's other feelings and qualities.

A *sexual identity* is a more flexible concept than sexual orientation or gender identity (see below). It includes all possible feelings and attitudes toward one's gender and sexual attractions. The people toward whom one is attracted do not define one's identity, although one's friends, acquaintances, spouses, and lovers do reveal something about a person. The sexual identity of a gay man is not the same thing as a homosexual orientation. Same-sex attractions are not the entirety of a gay identity. Four broad possibilities for thinking about sexual identities as they relate to same-sex attractions were defined in the previous chapter: closeted, homosexually self-aware, gay-identified, and nongay-identified. By contrast, heterosexual attractions or a heterosexual orientation are often used as a synonym for a heterosexual identity; this is expectable in a culture that defines heterosexuality as normative. Being called "a heterosexual" is not experienced as defining or as delimiting as being called "a homosexual," since being a heterosexual is frequently taken to mean being normal.

However, between the categories of a sexual orientation and a sexual identity, there is ample room for therapists either to insert their own culturally derived assumptions or to fail to hear the nuances in the assumptions that the patient has internalized. Often, these assumptions, for both patient and therapist, derive from binary oppositions that have become confused with one another (Ricketts, 1984). Thus, one common usage of "sexual orientation" is derived from a gender-based binary distinction between male and female. In this usage, a gay man's attraction for men is equated with a heterosexual woman's attraction for men, that is, as feminine. In other words, John's homosexual attraction to Bill (John >> Bill) would be considered the same thing as Mary's heterosexual attraction to Bill (Mary >> Bill). Thus John >> Bill = Mary >> Bill. But there is another commonly used meaning of sexual orientation that is drawn from an entirely different binary distinction between homosexuality and heterosexuality.[2] This binary distinction either infers or directly says that a woman's attraction to women means the same thing as a man's attraction to men: "The term Lesbian . . . has gained considerable usage within recent years. . . . Although there can be no objection to designating relations between females by a special term, it should be recognized that such activities are quite the equivalent of sexual relations between males" (Kinsey, Pomeroy, and Martin, 1948, p. 613). The homo/hetero distinction defines same-sex attractions, whether in men or women, as a deviant form of sexual expression. The natural state is an attraction to the other sex, regardless of whether one is a man or a woman. Thus John's homosexual attraction to Bill (John >> Bill) means the same thing as Mary's homosexual attraction to Sue (Mary >> Sue). Here, John >> Bill = Mary >> Sue. But if John >> Bill = Mary >> Bill, and if John >> Bill = Mary >> Sue, then Mary >> Bill = Mary >> Sue. Insofar as the two meanings of sexual orientation are unwittingly used interchangeably, one arrives at the peculiarly logical conclusion that

---

2. Historically, the homosexual pole of the continuum was created first (Bullough, 1979; Greenberg, 1988; Katz, 1995). Before then, heterosexuality had no official name because it was considered natural and self-evident. It did not require any name other than "normal." After the naming of same-sex attractions, science provided a new name for the feelings from which homosexuality was presumed to deviate. This led to the creation of the homo/hetero binary: the same (homo), the other (hetero), and the two (bi).

Mary's heterosexual attraction to Bill is indistinguishable from her homosexual attraction to Sue.

The political correctness of the above equation notwithstanding, few authors adequately contextualize these two different meanings of sexual orientation, and much of the research on human sexuality uses them interchangeably, grouping unrelated experiences and subjectivities (Ricketts, 1984; Haumann, 1995). In fact, a therapist is poorly advised if he or she expects that working with gay male patients automatically equips one with the cultural frame of reference needed to understand a lesbian patient (Drescher, 1996b), and vice versa. Considering cultural frames of reference further is only the prelude to considering the almost limitless variations possible in sexual fantasy. For example, how would one meaningfully define the sexual orientation of the man who is sexually attracted to the image of two women making love to each other?

A gay patient's confusion about the meaning of his sexual orientation often reflects the limitations of binary language to capture a wider range of subjectivities. Some gay men have spent considerable time contemplating these unquestioned cultural assumptions and have a sophisticated view of these matters. But others have not. And, regardless of their conscious understanding of these intellectual distinctions, at an emotional and unconscious level, they are often a good deal less clear.[3] While psychoanalytic therapies can provide important data about how meanings are attributed to feelings and may even suggest lines of research outside the field, psychoanalysis itself cannot provide definitive answers to many of the questions it raises. It can find out what an emotion means to a patient, but beyond that, cannot say what an emotion is. If there are conditions that favor developing one form of sexual attraction over another, that is also unknown. Although many gay men report early feelings of wanting closeness with a male figure, regardless of the absence or presence of a father, little is definitively known about the feeling states of children that later develop into adult sexual attractions. Freud (1905) believed one's sexual object choice was determined from biological and environmental variables, with factors that influenced one individual having a different impact on others (McWhirter, Sanders, and Reinisch, 1990; DeCecco and Parker, 1995). No one knows. Nor does anyone know how sexual feelings become integrated into a sense of personal

---

3. Many of these issues, as they pertain to lesbian subjectivities, have been discussed with great intelligence by Magee and Miller (1995, 1997) under the deliberately playful rubric of *lesbian rules*, defined as a set of flexible principles that "helps theory to accommodate to the individual variety of sexual possibilities, and to the effects of changing contexts" (1995).

identity. It is also not entirely clear why one man develops a closeted identity, another a gay identity, and still another identifies as non-gay. All the factors contributing to the construction of a sexual identity are not known, and they are, in all probability, highly complex. And contrary to most psychoanalytic theories, a person's sexual attractions tell a clinician nothing about his level of psychological function or integration (Morgenthaler, 1984; Friedman, 1988; Isay, 1989).

Further compounding matters, of course, is the ubiquity of gender polarities, whether or not these are further confused with biological sex. Stoller (1968, 1985) inched psychoanalysis toward greater theoretical flexibility by teasing apart the concept of *gender identity*, the subjective sense that one's own gender is male or female, from biological sex and, more germane to this discussion, from sexual orientation. The uncoupling of gender identity and sexual orientation, derived from Stoller's work with transgendered individuals, was only a step in a process that has yet to end. For example, a gay identity commonly includes the feelings of homosexual attraction, subjectively experienced within the confines of a stable gender identity, as in "I am a man who loves men but I know myself to be a man" However, there are some gay men who believe that homoerotic feelings define a man as feminine or womanly. This translates into, "Because I am attracted to men, I must be a woman or I am at least like a woman inside." Stoller's gender identity concept begins to falter here insofar as these men, at least, believe that one's sexual attractions do define one's gender. This is also a belief that is shared by many people in many cultures (Ulrichs, 1864; Chauncey, 1994). Transgendered individuals, on the other hand, subjectively experience their psychological gender as different from their anatomical gender. They, too, define their identities in terms of a masculine/feminine binary distinction: "I feel I am a woman trapped in the body of man." However this leaves hanging the question of sexual attractions. Further illustrating the limitations of binary distinctions, as well as the disorienting complexity of gender, all conventional categories are bent into a strange new shape by the transgendered individual who feels , "I am a lesbian woman trapped in the body of a man" (Bornstein, 1994; Brown and Rounsley, 1996).

Derived as they are from binary thinking, sexual orientations and gender identities are treated by many authors as immutable entities. This is still true of Stoller's (1985) psychoanalytic core gender identity as well as with various biological hard-wiring theories (LeVay, 1993; Hamer and Copeland, 1994). On the other hand, the concept of sexual identities grants that they are psychologically and socially constructed from what an individual's mind, body, and environment have to offer (Schwartz, 1993, 1995; D'Ercole, 1996; Drescher, 1996b; Kiersky, 1996, in press; Magee and Miller, 1996b, 1997). Therefore, a sexual identity may be subject to change. One way this can happen is when an individual experiences changes in his sexual attractions (Money, 1988), although it is not clear how this occurs or how commonly it occurs. More commonly, a sexual identity can change when an individual *changes his perspective about his sexual feelings*. Coming out is a common example of changing a sexual identity. The sexual attractions may not have changed, but how the person feels about them has.

Patients, regardless of sexual orientation, will vary in their readiness to examine the psychological complexities that may arise in relationship to their sexual attractions. One cannot rule out the possibility that sexual attractions, like other feelings, may entail compound meanings and involve conflict. For example, some men may be all too ready to assume that their sexual attractions to other men must have some other meaning. Others may assume that these sexual attractions have no other meaning than irrefutable evidence that they are gay and always have been. It should also be noted that, just as with other emotions, sexual attractions can exist and yet a person can be unaware of feeling them. Another way in which people differ is in their readiness to take responsibility for their feelings without feeling obliged to act on them. As a general rule, a therapist does well by approaching feelings of sexual attraction as one approaches any other feeling state. And what the therapist grants about the psychology of emotions generally, should also be granted in regard to sexual attraction. Thus, a person's emotions are never entirely subject to conscious control, though they may wish them to be, as in the common belief that, "I shouldn't be feeling embarrassed" or "I shouldn't be attracted to men." Furthermore, thoughts and feelings are not equal to the sin: "I was so angry, I was ready to kill my boss. But of course I didn't," or "I look at other women all the time, but I would never cheat on my wife." People can also be unaware of their own emotions: "People say I look depressed. Do I look depressed to you?" or "I was at work, staring at this cute messenger without realizing what I was doing, until he asked me if something was wrong." Feeling one emotion does not exclude the possibility of feeling another: "How can I love my father when I hate him for always being so hard on me?" or "How can I be attracted to men if the very thought sickens me?" Finally, one feeling can defend against another. In many people, anger is especially likely to be the wild card in the deck, either the affect that lies always closest at hand or else as the feeling that cannot be tolerated: "I don't care that he was 95 years old and in failing health, I'm going to sue the hospital for killing my father," or "I was so angry with my lover last night, I went out and picked somebody up just to get it out of my system."

Sexual Hierarchies

In addition to the concepts of sexual attractions and sexual identities, the clinician should be familiar with the notion of a *sexual hierarchy*. Briefly stated, sexual hierarchies refer to the ordering of sexual practices as better or worse in terms of some implicit or explicit value system (Schwartz, 1995). Despite what could be seen as an early social-constructivist approach to the question of the value of different sexual practices—in Freud's (1905) "Three Essays on Sexuality,"—psychoanalysts have in general perpetuated an ancient but official story that heterosexual genital sexuality (penile-vaginal intercourse) is the highest form of adult sexuality. To be sure, many contemporary analysts do not feel it is wrong to have sexual encounters outside of marriage, provided that they are heterosexual. Nonetheless, in psychoanalysis' hierarchy of sexual values, heterosexuality in a monogamous relationship is still preferred and idealized over and against other forms of heterosexual relatedness. Some analysts still use the categories of "perversion" to describe sexual behaviors that rank below their genital ideal. The primacy of heterosexual genital sexuality is also a popularly-held cultural belief. And on that account, the heterosexual ideal is consciously rejected in some subcultures. Thus, there are some gay men who celebrate their identities as "sexual outlaws" (Rechy, 1977). Others, however, may problematize their sexuality because it ranks low in a sexual hierarchy of values. Although some might argue that it would be preferable not to have such a hierarchy at all, as a practical matter everyone does.

When conducting psychotherapy, the therapist should be aware of his or her own value system, including the kind of sexual hierarchy to which he or she adheres. The therapist should also be aware of the extent to which the theory he or she has learned has embedded within it sexual, hierarchical judgments. And finally, most importantly, the therapist must be open to apprehending the patient's explicit and implicit sexual hierarchies. One could say it is all grist for the therapeutic mill. But in practice, it is often not an easy matter to disentangle these three different kinds of value judgments from each other, especially when the patient himself is in conflict about his own sexual practices. These conflicts emerge in the dream of the following patient who is still learning about his sexual likes and dislikes:

J: There are a couple of things on my mind. The shame that I feel as a gay man. I've talked about this before and it is still there. I had two dreams last night and I can't remember a lot about them except they both involved rimming [oral-anal sex]. Somehow or another there was a young guy's rear in front of my face and I kept burying my face in his ass. And I think there might have been some other people around or something and it was very matter of fact. In the dream I didn't feel any shame.

Th: What did you feel in the dream?

J: As I recall, in both cases it was good. It was exciting. It was a turn on, a fantasy. I wouldn't want my friends to know about my interest in rimming. It falls under the realm of kink. Kink or raunch. I do feel kind of ashamed about this feeling, of not being in the mainstream.

Th: What do you feel is shameful about rimming?

J: I've said it before, I think it is dirty. It's perverted. It's a perversion of my mother talking about sex being a beautiful thing. That is not a beautiful thing.

Th: Have you known sex as a beautiful thing?

J: I've seen pornographic films where it is very beautiful. Two beautiful guys are kissing each other and making love, and of course there are the genitals as well. It usually includes sucking and fucking.

Th: What makes rimming more shameful than other sexual activities?

J: It is because the anus is more dirty.

Th: More dirty than what?

J: Dirtier than the cock. (Pauses) Except urine comes out of the cock. . .

This man's sexual hierarchy was based upon a ranking of bodily products and secretions. The literal transcript cannot communicate or capture the way in which this man's self-presentation was quite straight-laced and his statements had an ingenuous, almost bewildered tone. He was truly puzzled by the question of which is dirtier: excrement or urine? Is it dirtier to swallow a sexual partner's semen, vaginal secretions, or saliva? How does one rank these activities in comparison with swallowing urine or feces? More generally, one is left pondering whether hygiene is the factor that ultimately determines the rankings of a particular sexual practice in the hierarchy. Such contemplation is the prelude to considering deeper questions such as what are the meanings of cleanliness and dirtiness? And further, what early and later object relations, real or desired, may have figured in making these meanings prepotent?

Th: It seems to be a trick of fate that our excretory functions have been connected to our sexual functions.

J: I believe rimming has fallen by the wayside because it is not a safer sex activity. But that only confirmed my feeling that the anus is dirtier than the cock. The bacteria, or the germs of whatever. That it is an aberration. I've seen spanking films, but I don't get a lot out of that. There is tickling and foot fetish and bondage and S&M, all sorts of variations. In my fantasy life, it is mostly anal.

Th: Oral-anal?

J: Or just visual anal. To look at a guy's anus.

Th: You find the anus attractive and that makes you feel ashamed.

J: Yes. A friend of mine said rimming is a "turn on" and that it added to his repertoire of sexual pleasures. He was matter of fact and up front about it. There was no shame when he told me. Another guy I met told me he is very much into rimming. I want to avoid him. He's really kinky, and besides he talks openly about it.

This man was amazed by his friend's capacity to discuss openly an unconventional sexual interest. He was also repulsed by another acquaintance who was open about his sexual preferences, pejoratively describing that person as kinky. By staying away from a kinky person, the patient interpersonally enacted his attempts to dissociate from his own unacceptable feelings. If he avoided the kinky person, maybe he could avoid the kinky feeling:

Th: The sexual activity that excites you the most also fills you with shame.

J: I would be afraid to tell someone. To be honest, I've never done rimming with another man and I'm not certain whether it is just a fantasy. I'm not sure I would want to do it in reality. However, the possibility of someone being interested in me brings up the anxiety of what will we do if we go to bed?

Th: One obstacle to being involved with another man is the shame you feel about your sexual fantasies.

J: I think I know why the shame is there. I blame it on my mother. It's not something I remember at all, but it's been reported to me. She used to give me enemas before I was two years old. I don't know how often she did that. I don't have any memory of that. I don't know if it was often or seldom.

Th: What is the relationship between shame and the enemas you had when you were two years old?

J: I guess it's a preoccupation with the anus.

This gay man had no memory of receiving enemas. And in fact, this was the first time he had brought up this reported history. His explanation had a tentative, intellectualizing quality that was different from his earlier, perplexed responses:

Th: Could there be other reasons for feeling shame that you do remember?

J: People would think less of me if they knew this.

Th: What makes you think less of yourself?

J: Partly because I don't think a lot of gay men are into rimming.

Th: Why is the numbers game so important?

J: I felt ashamed of being gay all of my life. When I finally came out to myself, I felt shame because I was in a minority of the population that society says is perverted and sick. Then I find out, as a gay man, that I am interested in men's anuses, and that seems to be a minority. It is not fucking that appeals to me. Sucking and fucking appears to be the main thing among gay men. It *is* a numbers thing. I think there is something wrong if only a minority of people are interested in it.

Statistical curves can create official stories: "infantile, frigid, sexually under-developed, under-active, excessively active, over-developed, over-sexed, hypersexual, or sexually over-active . . . can, in any objective analysis, refer to nothing more than a position on a curve which is continuous. Normal and abnormal, one sometimes suspects, are terms which [one] employs with reference to [one's] own position on that curve" (Kinsey et al., 1948, p. 199).

Th: Could you elaborate on that idea?

J: It's abnormal. The norm is what most people do and how most people are.

Th: So you are ashamed of being part of a sexual minority within a sexual minority?

J: Right. And then there's a risk of rejection if someone knew. That's kind of a theme in my life.

Th: If people knew what really turned you on, they wouldn't want to have anything to do with you.

J: That's the risk. I haven't actually tried rimming and I don't know if I would like it.

Th: You also don't know if your friends would be turned off if you told them about your interest.

J: In the few sexual encounters that I had, no one expressed any interest. I've had so few experiences that it is hard to generalize. The last guy I dated certainly wanted me to play with his ass. He wanted me to fuck him. I had trouble doing that. He made me nervous and scared. And trying to fuck him brought back memories of trying to have sex with women and the performance anxiety that came over me. I did feel like a failure.

Th: The shame seems to be connected to some feeling of failure or inadequacy.

J: Ever since I came out of the closet, I haven't been able to have sex with men to the point of orgasm.

This man had years of psychotherapy to try and change his homosexual attractions. An intelligent, scholarly man, he supplemented his therapy with readings where he was exposed to psychoanalysis's sexual hierarchies, embodied in concepts like "anal fixation" (Socarides, 1968, p. 75) or what he referred to as "anal-visual" attractions. He invited the therapist to voice the criticisms that he had long directed toward himself, namely that he could only find sex exciting if it was dirty and furtive. The therapist partially obliged:

Th: If I were a psychiatrist who claimed he could cure homosexuality, I would interpret what you said to mean that you weren't really gay.

J: (Laughs) Actually, I had very exciting sex with men before I came out of the closet.

Th: Perhaps coming out of the closet has made sex less exciting.

J: It is OK now.

Th: You dated women for years in order to conceal your sexuality. Issues of hygiene aside, now your shame prevents you from exploring your sexuality. You've come out of one closet and walked into another.

J: I hide my sexual interests from my best friend. Although I've told him that I'm turned on by it, I don't want him to get the idea that I am especially interested in rimming. I think he would look down on me and think I'm a pervert. I think I am a pervert.

As I have defined them, sexual hierarchies refer to bodily practices. However, they can merge imperceptibly into a different kind of ordering of relational hierarchies. For example, one may value enduring monogamous relationships over nonmonogamous ones, even though the latter may also endure for decades. There is also a hierarchy that values enduring relationships over transient ones. Here too a therapist needs to disentangle his or her own personal views, the views embedded in the theory he or she has learned, and the patient's own views.

A patient repeatedly came to sessions reporting what a failure he was for never having been in a relationship. In his view, people who had relationships were better than those who did not. One day, the therapist felt intensely unsettled by this repetitive self-reproach. Previously, the therapist had never directly responded to this particular criticism. He suddenly realized that he also shared this belief. The therapist searched inside himself to try and better understand the meaning of his own views. As he reflected upon his own training, the therapist realized that a vast psychoanalytic literature also endorsed the patient's self-critical point of view. In that moment, the therapist experienced a constricted feeling. The patient felt bad about himself because he had never been in a relationship. The therapist agreed that this was something to feel bad about. And finally, psychoanalytic theory also said this was something to feel bad about.

The therapist further reflected upon his own feelings about relationships. What was it that he valued about them anyway? Were his values based on his own actual experience with relationships? Did he, like this gay man, find relationships meaningful because so many people had them? Or did his own relationships provide something that gives life meaning? Were there compensations for not being in a relationship? As he silently pursued this self-analysis, the therapist's unconscious identification with the patient's self-denigration became clearer. It took the form of an idealized image of a heterosexual couple reaching their fiftieth wedding anniversary. Whatever the actual merits of that accomplishment, the therapist unconsciously felt that the golden anniversary was the gold standard of relatedness. Having clarified his own feelings to himself, the therapist also assumed that the patient might have a similar feeling.

The therapist said, "Sometimes, having a relationship can be overrated." The patient became angry with the therapist for daring to question his own fantasized ideal. Further discussion revealed that the patient himself was angry about having to conform to this ideal. His feelings of despair about never having had one, kept him from knowing how angry he was about being expected to have a relationship. Untangling these feelings led to further exploration of the patient's early and disappointing relationships and what they meant to him. He cried because he had no memory of being held by his mother. He associated to having to hide his sexual identity at work out of fear that he would be fired. He believed that letting people know how you felt inevitably led to the end of the relationship. He came to see how the social conventions that idealize relationships can be used to define a bachelor or old maid as deficient.

Having internalized those beliefs, he could only criticize himself. As his perspective on those beliefs shifted, he gradually became less self-critical.

Countertransference and Self Disclosure

In the above example, the therapist's constricted feelings were the result of a desire to be helpful to the patient in conflict with a critical judgment of him. This countertransferential judgment was based on the therapist's unconscious idealization of long-term marriages, which also made him feel both sorry for and contemptuous of this gay patient. These feelings had also been reinforced by the therapist's psychoanalytic and psychiatric training. Because feelings are given meanings by shared social beliefs, the therapist assumed this gay man might feel the same way. In this example, the specific meaning of the therapist's personal fantasy, that is his countertransference, was not directly revealed to the patient. However his interpretation did reveal the therapist's skepticism of the idealization of long-term relationships. Using the countertransference, defined as one's own feeling and subjectivity, is one way a therapist can make meaning of what a patient says.

The myth of the objective observer has been provocatively and convincingly deconstructed and challenged, from both inside and outside a psychoanalytic perspective (Foucault, 1978; Gould, 1981; Spence, 1982; Fausto-Sterling, 1992; Frommer, 1995; Levenson, 1995; Aron, 1996; Stern, 1997). Nevertheless, an official belief in neutrality asserts that the well-trained analyst does not bring personal issues into the treatment setting, except as undesirable countertransferences. This claim overlooks the many ways in which antihomosexuality is embedded in the cultures in which analysts are raised and educated, including the psychoanalytic training experience itself (Lewes, 1988; Drescher, 1995; Isay, 1996; Magee and Miller, 1997).

In recent years, the concept of neutrality has increasingly been questioned by psychoanalysts asking the epistemological question, "How does an analyst know what is going on?" The responses to this question increasingly focus on the way a therapist's subjectivity shapes the narratives that emerge in treatment (Spence, 1982; Greenberg and Mitchell, 1983; Schafer, 1983; Eagle, 1984; Stern, 1991, 1997; Langs, 1993; Spezzano, 1993; Frommer, 1994; Domenici and Lesser, 1995; Aron, 1996; Drescher, 1996a; Magee and Miller, 1996b). And although it can mean so much more, a sexual identity can sometimes be seen as a narrative about the meaning of one's sexual feelings. Consequently, the arduous path taken by therapists to define their own sexual identities makes it unlikely that they are neutral about sexual feelings or activities, either their own or their patients'. Acknowledging one's own subjectivity means knowing one's preferences and dislikes. Knowing and attending to them is an important part of doing psychotherapy. At times, it may even be necessary for a therapist to reveal to a patient what he or she is thinking or feeling. Yet, self-revelation contradicts the traditional model of neutrality, which urges therapists to say as little about themselves as possible:

> Young and eager psycho-analysts will no doubt be tempted to bring their own individuality freely into the discussion, in order to carry the patient along with them and lift him over the barriers of his own narrow personality. It might be expected that it would be quite allowable and indeed useful, with a view to overcoming the patient's existing resistances, for the doctor to afford him a glimpse of his own mental defects and conflicts and, by giving him intimate information about his own life, enable him to put himself on an equal footing. One confidence deserves another, and anyone who demands intimacy from someone else must be prepared to give it in return . . . I have no hesitation, therefore, in condemning this kind of technique as incorrect. The doctor should be opaque to his patients and, like a mirror, should show them nothing but what is shown to him [Freud, 1912, pp. 117–118].

A therapist may have the need to avoid having certain feelings toward patients. It is difficult for many therapists to admit they are sexually attracted to, hate, or are disgusted by their patients. Therapists may also be unwilling to talk about or admit those feelings to themselves. However, theorists in the Interpersonal and object relations schools of psychoanalysis believe that countertransference responses are not only inevitable in treatment, but when brought into conscious awareness, can also serve as a source of information about the therapist, the patient, and their relationship (Winnicott, 1947; Racker, 1968; Levenson, 1983; Bollas, 1987; Ogden, 1990).

> All contemporary interpersonalists . . . emphasize the transactive, interactive, and intersubjective nature of the analytic process. Transference and countertransference are seen as mutually created by both analytic participants, rather than as exclusively endogenous expressions of either's closed intrapsychic world. The analytic expressions of transference and countertransference are . . . variable amalgams of the unconscious of both patient and analyst. A central technical implication of this modern interpersonal approach is that understanding of the patient's personality inevitably involves an under-

standing of the analyst's personality. Countertransference analysis thus becomes an integral aspect of transference analysis. Interpersonal analysts focus variably on both their patients' and their own experiences of their analytic relatedness, often inviting the patient to do the same. . . . As Sullivan pointed out long ago, if analysts believe they can study their patients in some detached manner, their "data is incomprehensible" [Fiscalini, in Stern, et al., 1995, p. 7].

An asymptomatic HIV-positive gay man feeling depressed and anxious presented for an initial consultation. He was also using cocaine and engaging in unsafe sexual activity. When high, he liked fist-fucking, in both the insertive and receptive positions. He paid male hustlers, whom he knew to be crack addicts, and fellated them without taking safe-sex precautions. As the patient blandly described his other unsafe activities, the therapist felt a growing sensation of horror. However, he said nothing about his inner reactions during their initial encounter.

At their next meeting, the patient started the session by reporting a sense of dread and horror that had kept him awake the night before. He attributed his feelings to beginning psychotherapy, as he remembered a previous treatment experience being both difficult and painful. However, the patient's revelation surprised the therapist. He told the patient that he had experienced feelings of dread and horror during the previous session. The therapist wasn't entirely sure what had provoked his own feelings and had attributed them to a sense of helplessness. In listening to this gay man's account of his potentially self-damaging activities, the therapist felt frightened and out of control. He said this directly to the patient, wondering if his own feelings made sense to the patient. The patient thought about what the therapist told him. He said that he was also horrified by his own behavior but was unable to stop what he was doing. He too felt out of control. However, as a child he had learned that if he told himself he felt nothing, and presented an inscrutable facade, he could survive his alcoholic parents' physical and verbal abuse. Expectably, this pattern created problems in living and were doing so now. Being diagnosed HIV-positive in the early days of the AIDS epidemic had been traumatic. Pretending he had no feelings about his serostatus meant he selectively inattended from any activities he engaged in that might remind him of HIV. The therapist's revelation demystified and thus reduced the intensity of the feelings they both shared. Together they discussed ways of introducing some measure of control into the patient's life.

At times, directly revealing the therapist's countertransference can be helpful. In the above case, the therapist did not know the patient well, nor did he fully understand the meanings of his countertransferential response. He could offer no indirect or direct interpretations based upon countertransference analysis. He had not planned to reveal his emotional responses in the first session. In the second session, however, the therapist was surprised to hear the patient's spontaneous report of similar feelings. The patient's blasé presentation in the previous session had lulled the therapist who had not considered the possibility that there had been an indirect communication of the patient's feelings to the therapist. The therapist realized that he had pretended to feel nothing in front of the patient and that doing so served the interest of appearing to be a sympathetic but detached listener. The therapist's appearance of neutrality was mirrored in the patient's seeming detachment in the first session. In fact, the therapist countertransferentially enacted the patient's own defensive strategy. The therapist dealt with his own feelings of horror by giving the appearance that nothing he heard disturbed him. This enactment was, in part, supported by the therapist's analytic training which cautioned against spontaneous revelations.

> We do not make direct reference to whatever affects may have been integrated into our comments or interpretations. It is a critical part of our tradition that we do not generally identify our own affective states in the course of therapy. In fact, the phrase "self-disclosure" seems to be specifically reserved for the revelation of our affective states. . . . We imply that affects are the most private type of information and that telling a patient what we feel would burden them in some way that telling them what we think does not. Clearly, this is a theory about how affects operate in an interpersonal situation. And, as a result of our having this theory of affects, we want patients to "get at theirs" during analysis, while we do not say much about ours [Spezzano, 1993, p. 43].

In the second session, the therapist assumed that the patient's neutral facade covered over an increasingly dangerous situation. The therapist's revelation surprised the patient. However, it also freed the patient up enough to make a revelation of his own. The therapist's perspective on his own feelings demystified the process of living with uncomfortable feelings by hiding them, a tactic that the patient had learned in childhood. In this way, a frightened and self-destructive patient began to learn a new and different way to introduce some measure of control into his own life.

Despite its clinical utility, the revelation of a therapist's subjectivity to a patient is still a controversial subject in some psychoanalytic quarters. As Freud's concept of neutrality became enmeshed with his concept of abstinence, it led to the creation of a blank-screen paradigm of the psychoanalytic relationship. Regardless of what the patient might inadvertently perceive about the analyst, this approach discouraged any overt admissions about the analyst's subjectivity, let alone his or her sexual identity. Seen from this perspective, the openly gay therapist could only exist as a countertransferential enactment that would interfere with effective treatment. Yet trying to remain neutral does not mean that the therapist can be a blank screen, anymore than it means that the therapist can be magically free of countertransference. And trying to remain neutral does not mean that the therapist is without his or her own values.

In fact, cultural changes have led to new psychotherapeutic relationships that were unimaginable to psychoanalysts of earlier generations. Today, lesbian analysts treat lesbian and gay male patients and gay male therapists treat lesbians and gay male patients. Lesbian and gay therapists now treat heterosexual men and women, intersexed individuals, and transgendered people as well. The intersubjective possibilities of therapist/patient combinations increase as binary categories of gender and sexuality continue to unravel. One consequence of these changes is the question of whether therapists should tell patients about their own sexual identities.

This kind of self-revelation has been inadequately discussed for several reasons. Historically, the psychoanalytic position was that all therapists were heterosexuals. If they weren't, they had to pretend that they were. Gay therapists had to hide their true sexual identities or risk professional ostracism and disgrace (Drescher, 1995; Isay, 1996; Magee and Miller, 1997). With respect to the issue of the sexual identity of the therapist, the blank screen model suited heterosexuals who didn't want to know anything about gay therapists, as well as gay therapists who did not wish to reveal themselves. These historical conditions eventually led to the modern phenomenon of gay patients seeking treatment with gay therapists.

It would be an error to assume that a therapist, by virtue of being gay, will automatically have greater insight into the issues that bring gay men into treatment. For example, being gay is not a substitute for being trained to do psychotherapy or for undergoing an analysis. And a therapist's sexual identity may not necessarily be the most meaningful way to gauge a therapy's efficacy. One does not need to be gay to treat gay patients any more than one needs a heterosexual identity to treat heterosexual patients. This is also true of gender, race, religion, or any of the categories that therapists and patients use to identify themselves. A psychotherapy's effectiveness is not necessarily determined by the presumed similarities between a patient and therapist. A better way to evaluate a psychotherapy's effectiveness is by how the similarities and differences between two people are handled in the therapeutic relationship. Nevertheless, in many cities, gay men have the option of finding well-trained therapists, heterosexual or gay, who are comfortable with and knowledgeable about gay people's lives. A curious, beginning therapist who knows little about the lives of gay men will sometimes find patients who are willing to share that information. Other patients may feel that their time should not be used to educate a naive therapist.

Although there may be times when directly revealing the therapist's sexual identity can be helpful to a patient, this is not be an issue that stirs many heterosexuals. Living in a world that naturalizes their sexual identities, heterosexuals are often unaccustomed to the need for directly declaring them. Heterosexual therapists can assume that if they do not directly reveal their sexual attractions, the patient cannot determine their true sexual identities. However a sexual identity, gay or heterosexual, is more than just an orientation, and therapists always provide indirect clues about their own identities, even when they will not provide direct confirmation. Because gay men have grown up in a world where revealing their sexual identities is fraught with dangers, some of them develop an acute sensitivity regarding the sexual identities of others. This radar, or "gay-dar" as some call it, may help determine who it is safe to pursue sexually, with whom they can be honest and reveal their own identities, and who may be a potential tormentor. At other times, it may simply be a way to order securely their surroundings into a binary world of gays and straights.

Self-revelation can have other meanings when a therapist is gay. A gay therapist may deliberately ask naive questions about what goes on in a gay patient's social milieu, even when he already knows the answers. This is presumably out of a desire to maintain a blank screen. A heterosexual therapist may not want a patient to know they have frequented the same vacation spot for technical reasons. A gay therapist can consciously seek anonymity for technical reasons, but may also not want the patient or anyone else to know the therapist has gone to a gay resort. Gay therapists who live closeted, professional lives have a particular need to hide. They also experience their own homosexuality as something secretive and shameful. Isay (1991, 1996) believes that gay and lesbian analysts should always come out to their patients lest they countertransferentially perpetuate a patient's feelings of secrecy and shame. However this is not the only meaning of coming out, nor does coming out prevent other enactments in the transference and countertransference of secrecy and shame. Any therapist, regardless of their own sexual identity, should evaluate a patient's need for them to come out on an individual basis, and be prepared to do so when necessary.

8

DEVELOPMENTAL NARRATIVES OF GAY MEN

The history of an individual is not a fatalistically determined progression.

Simone de Beauvoir, *The Second Sex* (1952)

I was far from girlish, physically or in my nature; there were no marks upon me as I matured from which my father could have suspected the sort of son he had sired; I did not lisp, I could throw overhand, and I could whistle. True I disliked football and cricket and thought them dangerous recreations, but I was good at hockey and an accurate marksman.

J. R. Ackerly, *My Father and Myself* (1968)

In development, we are not seeing an inborn femininity or masculinity gradually unfold itself according to some prearranged plan, but rather a complex set of exchanges between self and other in which gender can take on a rich variety of meanings and gender performances can be put to a variety of usages.

Susan Coates, "Is It Time to Jettison the Concept of Developmental Lines?" (1997)

What are little boys made of? To date, the ways in which men's sexual identities can vary are not yet fully understood, nor have the developmental paths that lead to individual differences been well demarcated. Although the mechanisms that lead to these outcomes still remain unclear, one usually finds, in the normal process of acculturation, that a boy's sense of his male gender may come to be linked first with expectations of heterosexuality, and then later integrated with his emerging sexual attractions. When a young boy announces that he plans to grow up and marry his mother, he will probably have the facts of life, or rather of kinship, explained to him. He is likely to be told that he cannot marry his mother, although he may be encouraged to wait until he grows up so he can marry a woman like her. Psychoanalysts refer to this as the positive resolution of the oedipal complex and regard it to be the *sine qua non* of a male, heterosexual identity. Whether that is so may be debatable, but the oedipal narrative, as it emerges in the child's fancies about himself and his future, is but one of many ritualized and sanctioned ways in which linkages between anatomical gender and heterosexuality are supported and encouraged by cultural forces.

But what of the boy who expresses the desire to one day marry his father? Unfortunately for him, the negative resolution of the oedipus complex has never had the same cultural resonance as its positive counterpart, not even among analysts. In fact, for almost a century, developmental narratives of psychoanalysis, embedded as they were within heterosexually normative and teleological assumptions, did not account for a maturational line leading to normal, adult homosexuality. Psychoanalysts treated heterosexuality as nature's default setting and gay men as "oedipal wrecks." And in adherence with their theoretical constructs, they all too often misunderstood, underreported, dismissed or ignored many of the poignant meanings found in the developmental narratives of gay men, save perhaps for the limited sense they could make of them through the "negative oedipal" line of development. Their psychoanalytic theories, of course, reflected the values of the culture in which they were put into practice. In this culture, for example, the gay child will not only learn that boys don't marry their fathers, he will also discover that boys cannot marry other boys. It would be a gross understatement to say that he will not have the benefit of the sanctioning rituals that are available to the first boy. And without the ritualized support available to his heterosexual cohort, the desires of the second boy can acquire an aura of the forbidden, or of the immoral. And although these kinds of linkages are not unique to gay men, they can take on the additional coloration of social opprobrium that is attached to being gay.

With all that in mind, one still might ask what little gay boys are made of. An etiological question is never without a subtext. That is why for many analysts, "the idea of developmental line [is] heir to the assumption of psychoanalytic theorizing of an earlier time that psychopathology could invariably be traced back to particular developmental epochs and particular stage disturbances" (Coates, 1997, p. 43). In other words, regardless of who asks the question, it is often motivated by a wish to know why a gay man did not become a heterosexual.

Furthermore, there is another special problem related to narratives of gay male development. They almost always begin with cultural stereotypes. So although some gay children may have been "sissies" (Green, 1987) or simply gender non-conforming (Corbett, 1996), others were indistinguishable in both their physical appearance and overt behavior from heterosexual children (Bell, Weinberg, and Hammersmith, 1981). Nevertheless, a gay man is forced to come to terms with cultural beliefs about homosexuality. Consequently, a gay man's sexual identity must include a process of learning about what he is not, as well as what he is. The different pathways that lead to this knowledge can be thought of as the cultural markers of a modern gay identity.

For these and other reasons, hypothesizing a developmental line that would fit all gay men is not particularly relevant to the clinical work with an individual gay patient. None is offered here because a unitary approach can obscure the myriad psychological frames of mind, interpersonal experiences, and cultural beliefs from which the diversity of modern gay identities are constructed. For although a man can look back at his life and know that he was gay, no one knows how to predict, with any certainty, that someone else will grow up to be gay. Freud understood how difficult it was to make any general predictions from retrospective accounts in the psychoanalysis of an individual patient:

> So long as we trace the development from its final outcome backwards, the chain of events appears continuous, and we feel we have gained an insight which is completely satisfactory or even exhaustive. But if we proceed the reverse way, if we start from the premises inferred from the analysis and try to follow these up to the final result, then we no longer get the impression of an inevitable sequence of events which could not have been otherwise determined. . . . The synthesis is thus not so satisfactory as the analysis; in other words, from a knowledge of the premises we could not have foretold the nature of the result [Freud, 1920, p. 167].

Although it is both impossible and undesirable to delineate a single maturational line leading to a gay identity, there are developmental themes that do recur in the narratives of gay men. These stories have been told in literature, theater and movies as well as in psychotherapy. But the absence of these stories from traditional analytic discourse is noteworthy. This chapter attempts to address that omission by arguing that gay men's developmental narratives can be psychoanalytically meaningful even though they do not fit into the storylines of psychoanalysis' traditional developmental theories. Succinctly stated, the stories of boys who grow up to be gay tell of their attempts to integrate their desire and affection for other boys and men into their identities. For many, this integration is obstructed, to various degrees, by cultural conventions which say that boys *qua* boys shouldn't feel that way about other boys. These inhibitions do have an impact and one finds, in psychotherapy with gay men, evidence of a struggle to make sense of the interactions that surround their lifelong attempts to come to terms with familial and cultural definitions of their same-sex interests and feelings.

Same Sex Attraction and Otherness

A common theme in the lives of men who, in adulthood or adolescence, come to define themselves as gay, is an early memory of a same-sex attraction which they recall as a feeling that set them apart from others. It has even been hypothesized that a feeling of otherness may actually cause the feeling of same-sex attraction (Bem, 1996). However, there may also be independent variables in the case of those gay men who only become aware of their homoerotic feelings in adult life (Rist, 1992). Some patients can remember an attraction to men or other boys from as early as four years of age (Isay, 1989). In this chapter, they are referred to as boys who grow up to be gay. It should be again emphasized that this appellation is a retrospective description of a certain life experience. It is not an attempt to define prospectively a child's future sexual attractions, interests, or identity, nor is it intended to offer a prescriptive formula that presciently determines who will grow up gay and who will not. This approach offers no chronological sequence to account for the appearance of these feelings in all gay men. It cannot be said with any certainty that at age six, the boy who grows up to be gay feels "such and such." Instead, it can only be said that a patient recalled feeling "such and such" at age six.

Because all boys are taught that they are only supposed to be attracted to girls, boys who grow up to be gay must come to terms with cultural beliefs regarding masculinity and femininity. This is also true for children who grow up to be heterosexual. All children must contend with a gendered binary code that divides the broad range of human expression into two categories intended to fit all. In traditional American culture, for example, boys are not supposed to cry and girls are not supposed to be aggressive (for discussion see Macoby, 1980). Andrew Sullivan, a senior editor of *The New Republic*, recounts an early childhood recollection of his exposure to gender categories:

> I was around the age of ten and had succeeded in avoiding the weekly soccer practice in my elementary school. . . . I loathed soccer, partly because I wasn't very good at it and partly because I felt I didn't quite belong in the communal milieu in which it unfolded. . . . I found myself sequestered with the girls, who habitually spent that time period doing sewing, knitting, and other appropriately feminine things. . . . I was happily engaged reading. Then a girl sitting next to me looked at me with a mixture of curiosity and disgust. "Why aren't you out with the boys playing football?" she asked. "Because I hate it," I replied. "Are you sure you're not really a girl under there?" she asked, with the suspicion of a sneer. "Yeah, of course," I replied, stung and somewhat shaken.
>
> It was the first time the fundamental homosexual dilemma had been put to me so starkly. It resonated so much with my own internal fears that I remember it vividly two decades later. Before then, most of what I now see as homosexual emotions had not been forced into one or the other gender category. I didn't feel as a boy or a girl; I felt as me [1995, pp. 3–4].

Psychoanalysts are all too familiar with the trauma that rigid gender-labeling inflicts on all patients, regardless of sexual identity. However, boys who grow up to be gay must contend with these categories in a different way than do children who become heterosexuals. One difference between the two groups is that the other-sex interests of future heterosexuals are naturalized and taken for granted as normal, although acting on those feelings may be discouraged until they reach a certain age or until they marry. In contrast, a boy who grows up to be gay usually lacks any explanations for his same-sex feelings other than disparaging ones. For some, it is only when they become adults that they may see their own lives portrayed in a growing number of biographies, autobiographies, journalistic reports, and novels written by and about gay men. These books appear to fulfill an important need in shoring up a gay identity because they treat the gay man as someone to be understood sympathetically rather than denigrated:

> **A:** I started reading a book that was written by a man who is exactly my age. He talks about his childhood. This autobiography seems to be touch-

234 • Chapter 8

ing me closely. He is dressed in a photo that looks like me as a little boy. There are descriptions of being 5 or 6 years old. I feel I am looking at myself in the way he is talking or describing the emotions. It is sympathetic to my own feelings but it makes me uncomfortable, too. In the chapter I'm reading, he is only 12. His father has just died [A's father died when he was an adolescent]. I'm reading this man's life and experiencing it as my own. He felt there was something about him that he couldn't share with anyone else. Feeling that he was two little boys, the one that people perceived and the real one. The real little boy, the one who couldn't go to confession and couldn't be redeemed and saved. Did I feel that there were two little boys? One that nobody knew? I probably did. I probably felt that there was something that I had to keep hidden from people. It was under the heading of "infantile gayness," if there was such a thing. I think I had a sense of that difference before I knew what it was.

Th: What do you remember?

A: I remember having a great sexual curiosity about other males, about their bodies. A fascination, an imagination. I can remember being curious about both men and women, but there was a certain kind of guilt I felt because of my curiosity about other boys or men. I would get a feeling in the pit of my stomach when there was any suggestion of sexuality with other boys or men. It was a feeling I would get even if I did something wrong that wasn't sexual. A feeling that it was wrong, although I don't remember anyone saying anything to me. I don't know how I knew that I wasn't supposed to be curious about my uncle or my father, about what they looked like without their clothes on. As I got older, this feeling never went away and I probably became more aware of something to keep hidden, something that might go away. I told myself I wouldn't think of this anymore. When I grew up, I told myself I would start to find women attractive. I must have been 12 when it suddenly dawned on me that this wasn't going to go away. I was one of those people. Homosexuality is what it was, and I was one too. I got very upset and even said something to my mother about it. I said to her, "I think I like boys," or "I'm afraid I don't like girls." She said, "What makes you think that? Do you think about boys without their clothes on?" I said, "No." "Do you think about having sex with boys." I said, "No." She said "You're OK." I dropped the subject immediately. What could I have said? I was ashamed. When she asked specific questions about sex, I think I was embarrassed to say, "I think about boys without their clothes on." I was embarrassed to discuss sexual things about myself with her or with anyone. So I told myself I was not going to do this. That it was disgusting. That I was not going to be like those people and if I was, I was not going to act like them. I'm sure it's not easy for anyone in that situation to confront that position. Reading this guy's autobiography, it almost seems that childhood was a different place then than it seems to be now. I wonder if it is possible to heal this?

The patient's sense of "infantile gayness" is a powerful and recurrent theme in the lives and histories of many gay men, although what they felt as children may not have necessarily been an attraction of a sexual nature. Nevertheless, many gay men retrospectively connect their adult sexual feelings to their childhood curiosity about and affection for men, to the desire for closeness with another boy, to the desire to touch another boy, or to a desire for intimacy that somewhere along the way was labeled "inappropriate." Further complicating matters, there are many ways in which these feelings first emerge and they may even appear at different ages. Boys who hug each other at age two will be treated differently than boys who do so at age six. And those hugs will have different meanings if the boys are sixteen. As a boy grows older, he will learn that certain demonstrations of affection between himself and members of his own sex are no longer socially acceptable, and will have to learn why that is so.

Surprisingly, psychoanalysis has hardly addressed the subjectivity of these boys, although some analysts have provided analogous ways to think about their experiences. Stern (1985), for example, describes how angry feelings between a mother and child can be relationally coded in either language, action, silence, or some combination of the three (p. 181). One might wonder how a boy who grows up to be gay senses which feelings can be expressed to his parents and which cannot? How is he to interpret the meaning of parental silence on the subject of homosexuality? Or the discomfort he may evoke in them if he raises the subject of liking boys? Or the contempt he may experience if he persists in raising the subject too often? It is not altogether unreasonable to presume that the result of having feelings for which there is no acceptable name can foster an early sense of *otherness*. Many gay men who report this feeling as adults are likely to recall its first appearances in either childhood or adolescence, and link the feeling to their same-sex attractions.

Otherness is certainly not a feeling that is unique to gay men, and its meanings can also be organized around other aspects of the self having nothing to do with one's sexuality or gender. But in gay men, otherness often becomes linked to their sexual identities. In that process, other linkages may occur as well. One often finds that the complex social cues regarding appropriate intimacy and closeness become inevitably intertwined with the complex interactions that lead to constructions of gender. Again, these kinds of linkages are not unique to gay men. In fact, they may, in part, reflect the ways in which all children learn cultural values regarding sexuality, intimacy, and gender. That is why it is necessary to return to the subject of how any child integrates gender concepts into his or her identity if one is to understand the developmental narratives of gay men.

> Children appear to be programmed from the start to categorize in binary dichotomies. For example, big/little, male/female, bad/good, pretty/ugly. Kohlberg (1966) has suggested that the first concept that children learn is big/little and the second is male/female. Children create concepts by abstracting from multiple instances of perceptually salient characteristics. At this early stage of categorization, concepts are grossly overgeneralized and stereotypic. When you ask a 2-year-old how to tell the difference between boys and girls, you typically hear variations of the following: girls wear dresses or have long hair, and boys fight (Kuhn, Nash, and Brucken, 1978). For young children, outward appearance (haircut and clothes) and aggression (fighting) are the principal subcategories subsumed under the boy/girl categorical distinction. "Boys fight" is a stereotype that children learn early on. Indeed as Fagot and Leinbach (1993) have indicated, in girls the development of the ability to classify according to gender leads to a marked decrease in their levels of aggression [Coates and Wolfe, 1995, p. 21].

Further research (de Marneffe, 1997) has also shown that acquiring a sense of gender, both one's own and that of others, and linking it to a positively valued body schema, can be a much more complex process than is accounted for by the static concept known as "core gender identity" (Stoller, 1985). A gender identity may be better understood in terms of the processes in which the mind engages, rather than as a concrete structure that it contains. In what has been termed the performative aspects of gender, gender is not defined as what one thinks, but as what one does (Butler, 1990; Goldner, 1991; D'Ercole, 1996). And if clinical work with children with gender identity disorder is any guide, the gendered self can be seen as shaped within an interactive, relational matrix (Coates, 1990, 1992, 1997).

Some have hypothesized a causal relationship between gender identity disorder and homosexuality (Dörner, 1986; Friedman, 1988). But what if same-sex feelings do not originate in an already formed, gendered self? The early, emerging feeling of same-sex attractions in boys who grow up to be gay generates a thorny developmental problem for them. The early feelings that later develop into adult same-sex attraction may actually cause a child to question the authenticity of his male gender. In other words, a boy does not have to grow up gay because he was first confused about his gender identity. Instead, growing up gay may have led him to question the veracity of his assigned masculine identity. In fact, the ways in which gender concepts are taught to children can be quite confusing to a boy who grows up to be gay. It may be difficult to be comfortable about his masculine identity if he possesses a trait that is supposed to belong to the other gender. How do boys who feel attracted to members of their own sex make sense of their male gender while they are in the process of learning the family and culture's restricted definitions of boy? One possibility is a fantasied solution such as "if I want a boy, like a girl does, I will turn into a girl" (Benjamin, 1996, p. 34). Although these thoughts and fantasies may begin early in child-hood, they can either persist or first emerge in adolescents who fear that their same-sex attractions will lead to a "gender reversal: automatically wanting to dress and act like the opposite sex" (Herdt and Boxer, 1993, p. 110).

Children who grow up to be heterosexuals also experience difficulties in acquiring a sense of themselves as masculine or feminine. This should be further distinguished from the sense of themselves of being anatomi-cally male or female, which is increasingly appearing to be a different cognitive acquisition (de Marneffe, 1997). A boy longing for closeness with other boys has no explanation for that feeling other than the hetero-sexual constructions of sexuality to which he has been exposed. He is likely to define the feeling as feminine, and in some boys this labeling may interfere with its subsequent integration into the child's emerging identity as a boy. Boys and girls, like many other categories a young child must learn, are at first rigidly defined: "The [child's] universe is domi-nated by the idea that things are as they ought to be, that everyone's actions conforms to laws that are both physical and moral, in a word, that there is a Universal Order. The revelation of the rules of the game, of 'the real game' as played by his seniors is immediately incorporated into this universe" (Piaget, 1965, p. 89). And because heterosexuality is one of "the real games" that all children are expected to play, a frequent feeling in boys who grow up to be gay is that of personal failure for being unable to conform to the gender roles expected of them. In any patient, a feeling of failure can be linked to early feelings of being different or of having failed to measure up to others' expectations. In some gay men, their inability to conform to gender roles raises self-doubts about whether they can adequately conform to any of the social roles they may be required to play. That was the case with one patient who questioned his motives for doing his research in an unnecessarily isolated way, link-ing his behavior to other ways in which he felt different and isolated from others:

B: I do like learning but I turn in. Part of it comes from habits learned when one is growing up gay, it turns in upon oneself.

Th: What do you mean?

B: It was my experience. Part of my way of dealing with being gay was turning into myself. I always did things alone. Music when I was young; my studies when I was in school. My universe was an inner universe. I think it's a hard habit to break. There is an outer world in which one is not comfortable. One retreats into oneself. But it is certainly no longer necessary in Chelsea, in New York, in most places in Manhattan. But it is still a habit. Life doesn't come with a road map. Perhaps I'm a little too cerebral about the whole thing. I don't need to be so hard on myself.

Th: Why are you so hard on yourself?

B: I don't know, as long as I can remember I've been very demanding of myself. Could that be guilt or something? Could it be guilt at being gay?

Th: How would that work?

B: My upbringing was suburban gay. It's not that it wasn't tolerated. It wasn't even in the realm of thought. The feeling of being gay was something to be ashamed of.

Th: When were you aware of those feelings?

B: I knew that from the time I was nine or ten years old. From people's comments or their lack of comments. It wasn't talked about. I remember my mother making a comment about homosexuals masturbating in groups in a judgmental tone. But I knew I was gay. I knew I had an attraction to men. I knew it was there.

Th: How did you know?

B: I would see a guy's body and say, "Isn't he cute?" Flipping through a magazine, seeing a half-naked man and thinking, "Isn't it exciting?" From an early age, I knew I was different. I had these desires and feelings that were not ordinary and not accepted.

Th: Was your mother's comment the first thing you heard that let you know it wasn't accepted?

B: It's one of the first things that sticks in my mind. The family is not comfortable with sex and I think that is why, in part, I turned in.

The patient believed that his tendency to isolate himself was a function of knowing he was gay since preadolescence. Some patients can recall a feeling of otherness that started even further back; others have no such early recollections. Did being gay lead to this patient's tendency to isolate himself? Could his growing awareness of same-sex feelings compound an already-existing tendency to withdraw? The actual chain of events may never be known, although psychotherapy may permit the impact of this linkage on his ongoing life narrative to be understood. As it turned out in this case, the patient's isolation was consciously experienced as a joyful relief from the demands that others made on him. Alone, he could do as he pleased and he often did. Yet, unconsciously, he also experienced this isolation as a source of shame. He believed that if he didn't withdraw from the public arena, he would be humiliated. The therapeutic work allowed him to explore the unconscious linkage between being alone, "I get to do what I want," and the meaning of being gay, "I have to hide or I will be made fun of." As the exploration decoupled the two meanings, it allowed him to take greater pleasure in his solitary pursuits while he came to understand how his adult self still felt the need to hide his sexual identity.

The patient's need to hide was linked to his childhood expectation of parental censure and disapproval. Here again, a situation that may be commonly found in any patient is associated with the individual's gay identity. However, this linkage often makes many gay men anticipate rejection and disapproval in a variety of settings, either personal, professional, or both. And as associations to the following dream illustrate, a gay patient may even expect rejection if he reveals his sources of sexual pleasure to his therapist:

C: In the dream, I'm in my apartment with this guy. He rests his hand on mine while we are talking, and I make no effort to move it. I reestablish a connection with him. His mother is sitting right across the coffee table from us. The next thing we are both in our underwear. He is coming over the armrest to be next to me and he's on his back, kind of arched, and he's sliding over across my lap and then down next to me and sits close to me. I have my arm around him and then he says to me, "Not yet, because my mother is here." But I do have a sense that we are going to connect and we are going to be sexual and physical together but he said "Not yet." It wasn't proper to have sex with her watching.

Th: Mother is always watching.

C: I hadn't been aware of that. Part of me really wants to go ahead, sort of like she was there and I couldn't do anything about his mother sitting there. But then I did stop. If I keep saying "Not yet," how long is it going to be before I can be intimate with a man?

Th: That might be a question you are asking yourself in waking life.

C: That reminds me of something that I didn't want to tell you. I had such a nice time with my date last night. Then I thought about the transference. I always heard about transference but never believed much about it.

Th: It's always interesting to discover the transference from a position of skepticism.

C: I don't want to diminish what happened last night. But I feel you are watching. If I tell you, then you're observing. I don't want you to know about how pleasurable last night was.

Th: Because I'm identified with mother?

C: It's private. It's my business. And I hadn't thought of this before but my mother would be judgmental about that. It's safer not to tell her what is going on.

Th: It would be safer not to tell me what is going on.

C: I can tell you anything that is bad or that I would identify as something wrong with me. I can tell you that. I give you a certain status. I don't see us as equal or peers.

Th: How do you see our relationship?

C: Doctor and patient. Therapist and a sick person. I mean healing pre-supposes some kind of illness or sickness.

Th: Pain is not necessarily an illness.

C: But I think I felt like a sick person or there is something wrong with me and therapy is to fix it.

Th: And what is broken?

C: Well, even though I intellectually say it's OK to be gay, I don't think I feel it.

Th: Is that your identification with your mother?

C: As being sick or broken? Right. I do feel that I wasn't allowed to express my feelings as a child and I certainly wasn't allowed to fall in love with guys. I didn't even know that was an option, even though I did any-way. Or had crushes. But even to be sexual was unacceptable. I don't know how I could have had a positive attitude toward myself, I bought into all the messages I was getting.

Peer Relationships

Some gay men report a sense of otherness that they associate with their inability, as children, to engage in "rough-and-tumble" play with other boys:

Young boys are more aggressive than young girls and roughhouse more. When two- to three-year-olds were observed in an indoor free play setting, boys were more aggressive toward their peers. They also showed more rough-and-tumble play. Observations in such diverse cultures as the Philippines, India, Okinawa, Mexico and Kenya generally confirm these findings.

Are these differences innate or learned? The comprehensive review of the development of sex differences by Macoby and Jacklin (1974) discarded nearly all nonanatomical sex differences and saw sex-role socialization as the overarching principle. However, the researchers also concluded that greater aggression and rough-and-tumble play among young males has a "biological foundation" [Green, 1987, p. 31].

Although avoidance of rough-and-tumble play is not a universal experience among all boys who grow up to be gay (Ackerly, 1968; Rist, 1992), many gay men do report memories of displeasure associated with this form of activity. It is unclear if a feeling of otherness can lead to an inhibition of rough-and-tumble play, or vice versa, or even whether dislike for rough-and-tumble play is in any way related to feelings of same-sex attraction.

> **G:** There are certainly little boys who are more bookish, and not necessarily interested in rough and tumble sports who aren't necessarily gay. I've had extensive conversations with my gay friends about their childhoods. While in my immediate circle more people are aesthetic, I know gay people who are interested in sports and their personalities are more traditionally masculine. I'm not sure how much what we are talking about is especially part of being gay or part of being something else.

When boys do experience problems with these everyday rituals of masculine camaraderie, their difficulties are usually attributed to some perceived hypersensitivity (Green, 1987) with the presumption being that this is a constitutional factor which manifests itself at an early age. These explanations all too often resonate with cultural beliefs about "sensitive boys." An alternative explanation might be that some boys who grow up to be gay come to find rough-and-tumble play so stimulating later on in development that the unspeakable feelings it evokes in them may be too overwhelming:

> But he began to grow increasingly uncomfortable with wrestling . . . because he began to be aware of sexual feelings that were stimulated by the physical contact with other boys. Fearful that he would not be able to "control his penis," he fashioned a hard plastic liner for his jock-support, hoping that the device would suppress his desire. His

anxiety did not abate, and so he added another layer of plastic, and took to wearing two pairs of underpants over the device. Arnie eventually left the wrestling team and joined another after-school activity. But he recalled how his teacher "made an example of him in front of the whole class" by labeling his withdrawal as a "failure of will" [Corbett, 1996, p. 447].

Another patient goes on to compare rough-and-tumble-play to the way the business world works. He feels his lifelong aversion to that form of activity has had a detrimental impact on his professional life. At the same time, he idealizes his heterosexual colleagues whom he perceives to be immune from any harm:

I: In the business context of the white heterosexual males I know, they all get subjected to a fair amount of verbal abuse, either directly or behind their backs. It doesn't seem to bother them. It doesn't seem to wound them. Some of that may have to do with building up a certain amount of security and self-assurance over time. There is resentment on my part that some people are just able to slough off abuse or attacks or confrontation and not let it affect them and just move on. When I'm negotiating or in one of these confrontations that I shrink from, what happens is not just frustration at the situation. I ask myself "Why am I letting this happen?" and I often feel anger at the person on the other side who is being aggressive and confrontational. It's a combination of being angry with them for creating the situation and resenting the fact that they are able to handle this and I am not. One of the fellows on the other side of a deal I'm working on wanted something additional. It wasn't unreasonable but it was at the eleventh hour. My straight boss' reaction was "I don't want to deal with it. As far as I'm concerned, the transaction is done." I got on the phone with the other side who is arguing back and forth about what he wants. My boss told him, in a friendly way, "I'm not going to do this," and the other guy backed down. After it happened, I thought "I'd like to sit on my boss' knee and figure out how he was able to do that." It's not something I'm able to do. Tell somebody to go away. Then let's go play squash later and it's all OK. I admire those people who can. When I have an argument or a debate it becomes an emotional experience and very personal.

Th: You can't brush it off. You imagine that heterosexual men bounce off each other, then brush themselves off, and continue as if nothing had happened.

I: That's true. Growing up, I would prefer to sit and read a book. Those interactions were not something I wanted to do. In the straight male world, it's more than just exercise, it's sort of a socializing process. It's why so many people who are successful in business are people who were athletes in high school and college. It prepared them for the skills of communication and technique that men use in the world.

Th: Something made that difficult for you.

I: Yeah. I'm not sure how to describe what that difference in temperament is. It's not an avoidance of challenge. In the intellectual arena, I certainly like a challenge or two. I was competitive. It was important for me to get straight A's, to be the smartest kid in the class. It wasn't a universal shrinking from being challenged and competing. It has more to do with the form of competing.

Th: You don't want to butt up against somebody in the competition.

I: Not physically, not even verbally. In the academic setting, you compete but you don't even have verbal rough-and-tumble. It's very civilized.

Although the patient began by constructing a dichotomy between straight, that is heterosexual, men who enjoy the rough-and-tumble, and gay men who don't, he subsequently points out that the latter can play the game just as well:

I: Where I would like to be, and where the people I respect the most are at, they can do that without thriving on it. There are a lot of people in the business community, gay and straight, who thrive on that sort of conflict and confrontation. It's one of the things that drives me crazy in negotiations, even with people who are on the same side as I am. Even when I'm not on the receiving end of it. This is why I like my boss so much. He can be an aggressive negotiator but doesn't take it personally, doesn't internalize the conversation and doesn't start bad-mouthing people. There are people that I came across in my career who can do that. They are usually the people that I would describe as very secure. That's where I want to get myself. I have no desire to get myself to that point where I thrive on the battle. By temperament I'm not equipped to be that type of person. But I certainly would like to get more to the point where I can effectively represent my positions.

Rough-and-tumble play is a form of activity that some gay men associate with boys who grow up to be heterosexuals, rather than with themselves. But there are certainly men who grow up to be heterosexual who did not participate in this activity just as there are gay men who did enjoy the rough-and-tumble. However for many of his peers, a child's unwillingness to engage in the rough-and-tumble ultimately defines him as effeminate:

H: I think everyone knew I was gay then.

Th: How would they know that?

H: You wouldn't know it to look at me now but I was different. Although I'm normal height now, I was probably the smallest kid in my junior high. I hated sports, particularly team sports. One of my friends said about me that I had my own sense of humor. I found things funny that other people didn't, mostly word things. I was never one of the boys. I never got together with the boys and talked dirty. I was a very sincere kid. I thought there were words you shouldn't say. I was pretty much of a prude: not liking sports, doing well in school. During the football season I worked in the canteen selling popcorn. I used to take a book with me to read at away games. Instead of watching the game, I'd read until people made a lot of noise, look up from my book, then go back. Sort of an abridged football game.

This patient, a quite burly man, felt compensated for his lack of interest in athletics by his intellectual pursuits. Sometimes, being proficient in school, as opposed to sports, is presented as a source of shame rather than an accomplishment. This may be a common experience among men who, regardless of their sexual identity, grew up in working-class environments where intellectual or aesthetic interests were rigidly associated with effeminacy while athleticism was defined as masculine. For many, "nerdiness" is the antithesis of masculinity:

J: From the time I was a kid going to the school, the kids made fun of me all the time. I was placed in the first row, first seat. The teacher said it was based on a high test score. Being there was a stigma in itself. It was not cool. The people who were the bully types over in the last row came after you.

Th: By putting you in that row the teacher stigmatized you.

J: She had no sense of what that might do to somebody. I'm sure in her own warped little brain it was a way to motivate people, to keep them performing. Being good in school was what I could do. I didn't know who I was. Because I was smart, there were schoolmates I didn't hang out with. That was me. I hated it.

Th: You felt you were not accepted.

J: Not just "not accepted," but tormented. I was ridiculed, made fun of all the time. When they were doing those things I thought, "Why can't I just disappear? That might be better than what they are doing to me." Way back then I wanted to be dead. I couldn't stand it. Being the good little boy was not paying off but there was nothing else I knew how to do. I always felt my life was a waste. How many times I wished I was dead, over and over. In high school, I tried to get on the yearbook staff and they wouldn't let me in. I wasn't the right type of kid. If you get that kind of message from people, you believe it. I am a jerk. I am a nerd. The candid photograph of me in the yearbook shows me sitting at a desk in the library where I spent all my free time. I'm looking down at a book. You can't even see my face. My head is down, my cheek in my hand, my other arm across the desk. I see that picture, see the yearbook, and think "What a way to be remembered."

Because of his discomfort with peers, a boy may go out of his way to seek approval from adults. Yet, it is not uncommon to find that he may have experienced the qualities so admired by adults as scant compensation for the lack of acceptance from his peers:

K: Looking back at my teenage and high school years, it certainly hurt to not be accepted. It hurt to be rejected, to feel out of the mainstream. One of the ways I managed to get through that was to tell myself that the qualities I had and that I was comfortable with would win out in the end.

Th: In a way, you never believed that.

K: In a way, I never believed that. At the time, I don't think I would have admitted that.

There is one child more despised than the nerd or the teacher's pet, and he is the sissy. In his autobiography, the late Paul Monette (1992), an award-winning author and poet, described a brutal assault by four sixth-grade boys against another child that they had designated a "homo":

One of the brute lieutenants pushed Austin's face along the brick, scraping it raw. And now Austin, broken, surrendered whatever dignity was left. His tongue lolled out, and he licked up the phlegm while the bullies cheered. "Swallow it!" Vinnie commanded. From where I stood by my locker, I saw in a daze of horror, the self-disgust in Austin's face as he got it down without retching.

Vinnie and his boys sprang away, shrieking with laughter. Instantly I busied myself with my lunchbox, terrified they would notice me. As they swaggered away, neither I nor anyone else made a move toward Austin—slumped in the corner as if it would have been easier to die than to survive this thing. We all went hurrying away to eat our waxed-paper lunches. I never, never talked to Austin again. But, as I hastened to assure myself, we hadn't been friends anyway [p. 35].

What Monette learned from that experience was to try and avoid giving anyone the impression that he might be a "homo" himself. The treatment of sissies by their peers serves as a warning to anyone considering a transgression of gender boundaries. Another gay man described how his classmates reacted to his overt effeminate behavior:

L: In high school, a group of football players once picked me up in my chair in the lunchroom and carried me bodily to their table. I felt humiliated. They judged me and based their judgment of me on my appearance, on my being effeminate, on my being gay. I imagine that other people are going to do that. Just talking about it makes me angry. It's exhausting to go through this every day. I was miserable in high school. People were mean to me and I was never mean to anyone. I really didn't deserve to be treated the way I was treated.

Th: People who are treated badly do come to believe that they deserve to be treated badly.

L: It didn't make sense to me. I used to read the Bible to find passages, like "Turn the other cheek." If only someone had said, "You don't have to take this. You don't deserve this." I couldn't talk about it because I was ashamed.

Th: You couldn't talk about it to your parents?

L: I thought they would be ashamed. No, I didn't want them to know what people were saying. I'd walk around each day waiting for the next attack. It didn't matter where, it was just a matter of when. There was one guy who would pass me in the hall and mouth "Faggot." I used to be anxious just changing classes. I'd walk with my head down so if he were in the hall I wouldn't make eye contact. But he would always speak to me. It seemed like he was everywhere, every time classes changed, he would be there. That was the first time I heard that word, "Faggot." I knew it was bad but I didn't know what it meant. I tried to ignore it. I didn't deserve it. I was not an unkind person. I did not call people names. It made me so angry then but I couldn't be angry at school, so I would be angry at home. That would manifest myself as being depressed and withdrawn or I would lash out at my family. Sometimes I just coped with it by being the clown, always laughing, always making the joke. This happened so many years ago, it's amazing to me that I am still stuck with it. I guess talking about it helped a little. I feel a little calmer. I couldn't talk about it when I was younger. It left me feeling crazy. It wasn't about anyone else, it was about me. I figured I must be doing something that made me abnormal. There was something wrong with me.

Th: If people treat you as defective, you may also come to believe that you are.

L: (Silent) That's what happened. How does one undo that? I don't want to feel defective anymore.

Where do children learn to hate sissies? Some may learn this attitude from other children while others may learn it at home. In fact, the family of the boy who grows up to be gay will often join in his public shaming:

M: I remember Christmas when I was ten or eleven years old. My grandparents were there and we were taking pictures with a Polaroid. There was a picture of me, and my hands were in a strange position, clasped against my chest. I didn't like the way picture looked at all. It looked funny. I went to my grandmother, who I always thought of as supportive, and said, "Grandma, I don't like that picture. Could we get rid of it?" She said, "What did you expect? We've told you to stop acting like a sissy." Then she walked away. I felt even worse.

Gay Adolescents

Winnicott said of adolescence that

> Young people can be seen searching for a form of identification which does not let them down in their struggle, the struggle to feel real, the struggle to establish a personal identity, not to fit into an assigned role, but to go through whatever has to be gone through. They do not know what they are going to become. They do not know what they are, and they are waiting. Because everything is in abeyance, they feel unreal, and this leads them to do certain things which feel real to them, and which are only too real in the sense that society is affected [quoted in Davis and Wallbridge, 1981, p. 83].

When the boy who grows up gay becomes an adolescent, the difficulties he encounters will further intersect with the ordinary adolescent concerns about being or becoming real. Reality may be validated through a process of consensual validation (Sullivan, 1954). But what if one's desires are regarded as invalid or unreal?

The period of adolescence is characterized by an increase in sexual feelings. This is a problem for any adolescent, regardless of sexual identity, particularly in cultures that discourage sexual activity among teenagers. However, the powerful emergence of same-sex feelings in adolescence brings problems of a unique sort:

> A sixteen-year-old boy recalled his transition around puberty: "I just started having a feeling . . . I was more interested in men. It scared the hell out of me! I kind of forced myself to be interested in girls at the time. It felt very bad. I guess at the time it freaked me out. I thought, 'I can't be like that—no, I can't be'" [Herdt and Boxer, 1993, p. 180].

Such moments are routinely described in gay autobiographies. Bawer (1993) writes of a similar experience:

> It was during my early years that I first began to notice another difference between myself and my male classmates. . . . Many of those

classmates were beginning to be attracted to girls; I, on the other hand, found myself preoccupied with certain boys, my absence from whom during summer vacations upset me so much that I was incapable of enjoying myself.

. . . My father was a doctor and a medical editor, and since by the age of fourteen I had secretly read every word in his extensive medical library that related to the subject of adolescent sex, I knew very well that most boys experience during puberty a period of attraction to other boys. Thus I decided that I must simply be going through a "phase."

Yet as time went by and the "phase" didn't come to an end, that excuse came to seem less and less tenable. . . . I had another theory—namely, that my interest in boys was a lingering effect of the same sex play in which I'd engaged regularly for several months with a junior high school classmate (who is, I might add, now a husband and a father). Yes, that must be the answer; at times I was convinced of it. To be sure, my medical reading had also taught me that sex play between adolescent boys was extremely common; so this explanation, over time, likewise became less convincing.

Yet I remained undaunted, for I had plenty of other hypotheses at the ready, all of which I ran through in my mind every time I found myself drawn to a good looking boy. The first of these hypotheses was that I wasn't really attracted to other boys; rather, I was just curious about their bodies. (After all, I told myself, I was an extremely inquisitive boy.) The second hypothesis was that my attraction to other boys was a manifestation of my inordinately sensitive and sentimental nature. If, in other words, I was fascinated by another boy, it was not because I was sexually attracted to him but because I had exaggerated and romanticized my own quite natural feelings of friendship for him. The third hypothesis was that what I imagined to be an attraction to other boys was in reality an envy of their looks, their grace, their poise: I was, after all, a terribly insecure boy. The fourth hypothesis was that my interest in these boys was essentially not sexual or romantic but aesthetic. By nature and vocation, I told myself, I was an admirer of beauty; and if I could admire the beauty of a poem or a landscape or a piece of music, why not the beauty of another boy? [pp. 225–226].

If the adolescent Bawer was to maintain his sense of reality, that is if he was to feel a part of something larger than himself, he had to make sense of his desires. He did so by taking what he had been taught and by extrapolating from those teachings. The heterosexual environment, although acknowledging the existence of homosexuality, communicated to him that usually it is just a phase. That explanation satisfied him for a while, but then the phase didn't end. But if his homosexuality was not a phase, he had to make sense of his feelings any way he could. He kept trying to understand why he had not yet become the heterosexual he hoped he would become. And as his inner feelings failed to coincide with his expectations, each of his theories about his homosexuality had to be abandoned. The experience of having one's assumptions or rationalizations undermined can be quite overwhelming to a young person:

> Individuals come to a certain age with a body of what I suppose one might describe as implicit assumptions about themselves and the universe. We all depend upon a large number of things that we are really not justified in depending upon, but we have never had any reason to suspect them. The sun rises pretty regularly and our alarm clocks work if we give them a chance, and so on and so forth. A great body of assumptions is the foundation upon which our life processes rest. In a remarkable number of adolescents, however, there comes a time when their faith in this background of implicit assumptions about their own abilities or the consistency of the universe, and so on, is abruptly shattered. Then, instead of building the rationalizations as we do when someone points out that we have been an ass, these individuals go on feeling terribly upset about things. From that time on, instead of building the sort of rationalizations with which we heal the wounds to our self respect and all that sort of thing, these people are different from what they were before [Sullivan, 1962, p. 243].

Rist (1992), describing his own experience as a 15-year-old in Puerto Rico, illustrates a rather typical scenario in which the understanding that comes with unwanted knowledge can lead to dramatic shifts in one's identity:

> I walked home for lunch. The Arecibo Sport Shop was on the way. To be sure, it vended sports equipment, but it also carried such pornography as was available in Puerto Rico then. Each noon I stopped and, mesmerized, gazed at the colorful pages of "muscle magazines." The models all wore G-strings, the soft Victorian folds of the pouch concealing the sexual outlines. In the lower outside corner of every page, there was a small pencil drawing of the model naked. I studied these sketches closely, then panicked with desire, ran two blocks home to lock myself in the bathroom. . . . One day, as I stood in the sultry air of the sport shop, a young clerk took the magazine from my hands and held it up for his customers. "¡Mira!" He laughed. "¡Un pato!" ("Look! A duck!"—a feather-tailed swish, a faggot.) And for the first time in my life, I intimately understood how identities could change. I'd been given a new one that strangled me—that wholly contained me like a locked airless room. I learned I was "queer" [p. 8].

In this culture, adult prohibitions of adolescent sexuality tend to color those activities with a furtive feeling. Even heterosexual kids must be secretive about their sexual activities or face social opprobrium, reprisals, or punishment. Money (1986) believes that sexually inhibited societies create sexual problems for their citizens by inhibiting spontaneous, childhood sexual play. He cites primate studies showing that monkeys require youthful sexual role playing as "an essential precursor of male-female breeding in adulthood. The play of juveniles includes sexual rehearsal play with age mates" (p. 15). However, there are socially sanctioned, albeit sublimated outlets for heterosexual children that do serve the purpose of modeling or role playing the part of future, heterosexual adults. For example, teenage dating and supervised coeducational activities such as high school dances are useful in developing the interpersonal skills required for later life and relationships. In these interactions, an adolescent's confidence may be reinforced through his ability to conform with conventional gender roles. However, while the rituals of conventional adolescence teach lessons about future, adult heterosexual roles, those same rituals generate confusion, shame, and anxiety in the adolescents who grow up to be gay (Hunter and Schaecher, 1995). And because they are unable to integrate the assumptions of heterosexual culture, young gay men can sometimes become anxious, superficial, or detached at a time when their heterosexual peers are learning the social skills they will need for adulthood. The process of heterosocialization pervades daily life, with few alternatives available to gay teenagers. An exception is the small but growing number of social service agencies reaching out to lesbian and gay youth, such as the Hetrick-Martin Institute in New York City and Horizons in Chicago:

> Dating the same sex is an odd and perfectly unfamiliar idea to the youth of Horizons. Learning how to date and what to do erotically with the same sex are not only "unnatural" in the heterosexual socialization of these youth; they are completely foreign. How does a boy ask another boy to go out for a date at a movie or to have a Coke? If you have hidden your desires from your parents, how do you arrange such a romantic outing? Should you kiss and caress, and when is it the right and "natural" thing to initiate sexual advances or to make love? [Herdt and Boxer, 1993, p. 141].

Although these kinds of discussion can be helpful to gay adolescents, opportunities to have them are limited. It is usually a very precocious or a very troubled child who will avail himself of these services. Most gay adolescents delay such conversations until they are older and some may never have them at all. The delays and omissions that follow the secrecy imposed upon gay adolescents do have developmental consequences. "The gay male has lacked the proper anticipatory socialization for entrance into full adulthood" (Kooden, 1994, p. 51). In many ways, young gay men in their twenties may appear to some as "adolescent." They form cliques, in-groups and out-groups. There is a strong emphasis on style, conformity to standards of dress, a hierarchy of popularity based on looks, athleticism and affability, as well as opportunities for experimentation with sex and drugs. For some men, this "delayed gay adolescence" is a chance to catch up, in a manner of speaking. It provides them with opportunities to learn peer and social skills they may not have acquired while denied the chance to experiment with public demonstrations of their sexuality in adolescence. Furthermore, the discovery of other gay men after a prolonged period of hiding is a very powerful moment. Consider the account of a gay man discussing how the expressions of his sexual desire evolved through high school and his mid-twenties:

> **N:** All Catholic kids knew there were things called impure acts and impure thoughts before they knew what sex was. You knew it was a sin before you even knew what it was about. We were taught in parochial school that anything outside of procreation was a sin. I guess I felt that masturbation was a sin because it was pleasurable. I knew it was sexual and it wasn't marriage. It wasn't procreation. So, almost by definition it had to be wrong. Until I got to high school, my parents never sat down and talked to us about sex. A man and a woman got together and they produced children and breasts and penises were irrelevant. But even learning the biological aspects of it isn't learning about sex. I guess if you are heterosexual and you are coming out of that background you have a relationship with somebody of the opposite sex where, even short of actual intercourse, you get some pleasure out of it. As a straight man that is sanctioned in some way. Maybe you can sort of put it in that context. When I was in high school, I didn't realize I was gay. I did go out on dates with girls, movies and a prom or something like that. I never felt anything for those girls other than good companionship. That continued into my college years. When there was a special occasion, I would go out on a date with a woman but it was more companionship, or a particular occasion that called for having a woman companion. But my gay sexual activity was furtive and shameful. I would meet people in a movie house or bookstore or something like that. The only sex I had in my hometown was in parks that were known to be gay hangouts. When you start going to a public spaces, especially in a place like my hometown which is very conservative and there is an aggressive law enforcement situation in regard to gays, it is not only the fear of sin but also the fear that the police are going to pick

you up and something is going to happen there. I remember there were a couple of parks in the city and a couple of spots where it was known that "the gays" met and the police would periodically pass by those areas. I remember being afraid, not only that it was wrong, but because the police were passing by and taking down license plate numbers. I remember meeting somebody that way. We talked a while. I really liked him. For the first time I actually thought about seeing somebody beyond one quick sex act. I had his phone number and his name and knew he worked in town. A friend of a friend worked in the same store. But the next week, as I was thinking about calling this guy, I thought, "Oh God, I might be exposed if I followed through on this!" and so I didn't do anything. In fact, because I really hadn't accepted the fact that I was gay at that point, I'm not sure I wasn't actively considering options other than just dealing with some sort of immediate sexual outlet. I knew there were some gay bars in town but in my mind the risk of exposure was so high that I knew I was never going to do that. The potential to meet someone who knew you was always there. Growing up, we would always kid about the fact that we would run into people and that everyone had a connection back to our parents. I looked at my homosexuality as something to fight, something to try and overcome, or to bring under control. And it was certainly not something I was looking to provide me with a social life. When I went to live in New York City, I was afraid that if I went to a bar, I'd be exposed. So any encounter I had would be in a movie house or a bookstore, pretty furtive. For a long time every sexual encounter was filled with fear and shame. As I tell you about this, I feel a little anxious but I'm also feeling shame that I was reduced to meeting my sexual needs like that. That is what I was doing: struggling, meeting someone, feeling shamed. That was the source of my sexual pleasure for such a long time, and the sole source. At the time I didn't see any alternatives. I eventually started going to gay bars. But until I moved to New York, I don't think I knew any gay people. And when I got to New York and had friends here and started to socialize here, I continued to go to movie theaters and back rooms and things.

When the patient left his hometown and moved to a city where more open expressions of his sexual identity were possible, for a time he still continued to act as if that were not the case. The social opprobrium to which he had been exposed was integrated into his sexual life. As it turns out, for some gay men, furtiveness and the forbidden become essential components of their erotic lives (Rechy, 1997). However, this is a phenomenon that is not limited to gay men. The clinical utility of regarding feelings of attraction as affects, like anger or shame, has been previously stated. If that is the case, then normal maturational processes involve connecting these feelings with multiple fantasies, behaviors, and relationships. "At a very early age the child learns that there are social values attached to [sex play] activities, and his emotional excitation while engaged in such play must involve reactions to the mysterious, to the forbidden, and to the socially dangerous performance, as often as it involves true erotic response" (Kinsey, Pomeroy and Martin, 1948, p. 164). Kinsey also described the erectile stimulation of pre-adolescent boys as being nonspecific to both sexual and nonsexual situations. For example, a young man may have been aroused when, for the first time, he let himself get really angry. "The picture is that of the psychosexual emerging from a much more generalized and basic physiologic capacity which becomes sexual, as an adult knows it, through experience and conditioning" (p. 165). Bem (1996) refers to this as the *extrinsic arousal effect* and suggests that "autonomic arousal, regardless of its source or affective tone, can subsequently be experienced cognitively, emotionally, and physiologically as erotic/romantic attraction" (p. 326). The heightened physiological arousal associated with early, forbidden sexual experiences may explain why some gay men continue to seek their sexual pleasures in furtive places, even when hiding is no longer necessary. When homosexuality is banished from everyday life, there is an eroticization of environments (Schwartz, 1995) and secretive rituals evolve in a hidden, but public arena (Rechy, 1977):

> **P:** When I was a little boy, my curiosity was about men. I was interested in what was going on underneath people's clothing. But I had little opportunity to find out. There was a lot of prudery in my family, and if I showed any interest in looking at a medical book or at an art book, I would be teased by my brother and my parents. There was a lot of teasing about that. Those things don't go away. Here I am as an adult and I feel that my sexual appetites are shameful. I shouldn't let on how I truly feel. Not that it is immoral, although there is an element of that, but my sexual feelings are laughable. What makes you think you can function in this way? That's why anonymous sex is great. No one can see you except the person you are with. You can walk away from it and they can walk away from it and you don't have to be faced with humiliation on a daily basis. I was in my late twenties before I began having these anonymous experiences.

> **Th:** How did they start?

> **P:** I used to go to work on the subway and it would get very crowded. I noticed that some of the men were squeezing each other and fondling each other. There was no way of telling what was going on because we were all packed in like sardines. I did that for a few years. Then I discovered pornographic theaters and I would go sit there and do nothing. Once I finally relented and let somebody blow me. I was sitting there and a guy sat next to me. Instead of getting up and leaving, which I would have done

normally, I let him give me three separate blowjobs. I came three times. It was amazing. It was like the dams busted. Periodically, I would go back to that theater. That is how that began. But I feel cheated of this relationship thing that everybody else is doing. I don't picture myself in one. Relationships are a foreign language that other people speak. I think I can get by in it but I don't understand it and I haven't had the practice or the opportunity to practice. I feel like it's too late. I'm going through a whole thing now, a journey of the hero so to speak, which I should have done twenty years ago. That frustrates me and angers me and I don't know who to be angry at. I've always been able to blame myself for my confusion or depression, but it wasn't entirely my own weakness and my own situation that caused it.

As the above patient described it, having to hide his true desires discouraged any psychological linkage between sexuality and emotional intimacy. Monette described a similar split:

I wanted to kiss Richie. I never came close to verbalizing that, let alone acting on it, because I understood that all romance was forbidden. We could dick around as much as we liked, but a kiss would have bordered on love. And yet I was aware of feeling tender as well as carnal. I would summon up Richie's face in my mind when I wasn't with him. The one crooked tooth in his lopsided grin, the porcupine brush of his waxed crewcut. He was a couple of inches shorter than I, bursting with energy and a raucous smutty laugh. Half Armenian, half black Irish, a mongrel just like me [Monette, 1992, p. 52].

Monette and his friend could be sexual, but not intimate. With other boys he shared a different kind of anxious intimacy:

Totally inappropriate then, my fleshly worship in the locker room. How small I felt beside them. This intersect would have never happened in a public high school, where a wimp like me would've had no business being in the gym at all. It was Andover's stubborn insistence that every one of us have a go at the ball—wimp and Olympian alike—that dragged me wincing into the showers, me who hated the soft androgyny of my body, which somehow managed to be both scrawny and plump at once.

Add to that my fear, eyes fixed on the floor, not to be caught staring. Then jerking off every night in the dark thinking about them, summoning them in their nakedness, but without the least desire to fuck with them. That's the oddest thing. The gods were too far above me for me even to think of touching. I lay cocooned beneath the covers and whacked my meat in solitude, running the video over and over in my head, that antic frieze of demigods at play. This was like saying my prayers before bed, a lowly and humble offering to their greatness. Then, by way of *Amen*, I'd wipe up the marrow with a Kleenex [Monette, 1992, p. 70].

The cultural construction of heterosexual normativity separates boys and girls during public disrobing. A gay male adolescent can be sexually overstimulated by his everyday environment and may never openly acknowledge it to himself or to others. Yet he is no more responsible for his sexual responses than a heterosexual boy would be if he were required to change in the girls' locker room. For some gay adolescents, this fosters connections between sexual and anxious feelings: "We were terrified of being naked in the showers with other guys. Fearful of having an erection. . . . What do we do then!" (cited in Herdt and Boxer, 1993, p. 79). The terror of potential exposure can lead to defensive responses. A patient recounts his patchy recollections of his anxious college years:

> **Q:** I can barely remember being a college student but I spent four years of my life there. I don't remember leaving my room in my freshman year. I was very shy. Other than to go to class, I don't know what I did. I was very lonely then. Very scared, very uncertain. There must have been a sexual fear there as well. I don't remember ever taking a shower (Laughs). I must have but I don't remember doing it. It's completely blocked out. The shower was way down the hallway. I had to go out of my room and risk running into people in order to go there. In a sense there is a connection, a little bit of scaredness to do things.

Social isolation and awkwardness are not unusual in children who feel they have to hide their sexuality from family and peers. The impact of hiding on an adolescent's identity is recounted in a gay teenagers support group:

> If a single generalization about the ritual approach to Horizons holds true, it is this: all the youth, even the ones who have clandestine contact with other gay youth before they come to the group, are secretly terrified. The youth say they have to fear harassment and violence. But their most profound fears are perhaps closer to home: the fear of exposure to family and friends. "I'm scared to tell my parents," one girl confessed in an emotional interview with us. Parents sometimes react with anger to the knowledge of their children's sexual desires. In our study, seven youth reported that they were kicked out of their homes after their parents learned of their same-sex desires. While this was exceptional for the group, it conveys the strongest dread of the mythology of the homophobic reaction: fear the worst in what your parents will do if they discover that you are "homosexual" [Herdt and Boxer, 1993, p. 104].

Herdt and Boxer further report that almost one-third of the teenagers who attended the groups they studied had tried to take their lives at least once. In fact, gay teenagers may be at high risk for suicide. Bell and Weinberg (1978) reported that almost 20 percent of the men they interviewed had seriously considered taking their own lives. A later study of runaway lesbian and gay teenagers found "one third of the clients had suffered violence because of their sexual orientation; 49 percent of this violence was at the hands of the family. A related but separate finding was that 20 percent of our clients had either attempted suicide or had strong suicide ideation. The incidence was higher for those who had only telephone contact with the Institute" (Hetrick and Martin, 1988, p. 33). More recently, Remafedi et al. (1998) found that gay male adolescents were three times as likely to have suicidal intentions as their heterosexual peers. Although not every gay adolescent is suicidal, these statistics are a sign of how desperate they can feel.

Conclusion

This chapter explored childhood and adolescent experiences recalled by adult gay men. For many of them, a pervasive sense of otherness became intimately linked to their sexual identities. Some gay men firmly believe that their same-sex attractions led to the feeling of otherness as antihomosexual bias and expectations of heterosexual normativity wreaked havoc on a their self-esteem and promoted a sense of alienation. Therapists need to proceed with caution here. Psychotherapy with gay men is a much broader experience than one might expect if a therapist were to address only the issues related to having a gay identity. In clinical practice, these issues may only account for a fraction of the time spent in treatment. Nevertheless, it is not possible to define or delimit the role of a particular kind of life experience in the development of boys who grow up to be gay. Although a gay identity need not be reductionistically constructed from the role of victim, some patients will present themselves as if that were the case. Therefore, a therapist will find it helpful to remain cognizant of the ways in which growing up gay in a heterosexual world can add to the burdens of everyday life and complicate them. If and when these distinctions are made, a therapist may more fully investigate with a patient how he attributes the cultural bias against homosexuality as contributing to his difficulties, and to what degree. And in many cases, a therapist can help a patient put those experiences in perspective so that he can get on with his life.

9

THE CLOSET

Beginning at about age ten, Amethyst boys learned to
use the word "cocksucker" as the worst imaginable
epithet, and a fear of being called cocksucker kept
everyone in line; to actually *be* a cocksucker was too
scary to think about.

> Steven Saylor, "Amethyst, Texas" (1991)

I think I should call this "a letter from prison,"
because this is what it feels like. I have a real urgency
about writing this because for the moment, a little bit
of light is coming into my "cell."

> William Carrol, "On Being Gay and an
> American Baptist Minister" (1997)

This is what the closet is all about—translating one's
natural impulses into a heterosexual language.

> Vito Russo, *The Celluloid Closet* (1987)

Some gay men compare themselves to members of stigmatized minority groups. They feel they share with other minority group
members the experiences of being outnumbered, feared, denigrated, or
hated. Such experiences play a significant role in the developmental narratives that lead to a gay identity, just as racism or antisemitism play a
role in shaping the developmental narratives of racial or religious
minorities. A stigmatized group member can either reject the majority's
perspective or assimilate its values. Among racial or religious minorities,

it is the family and its community that teaches its members how to cope with the majority's disparagement. Gay men, unsurprisingly, rarely get their families' support in learning how to deal with the majority's prejudices. On the contrary, many gay men find themselves subject to antihomosexual attitudes from their own families and communities:

> I was isolated, not by iron bars or guards in uniforms, but by fear. I was surrounded by my loving family and close friends, but there was no way to explain to them my desperate, lonely feelings even when we were together. I wasn't tortured by leather straps or cattle prods, but my guilt and fear kept me in constant torment. I wasn't deprived of the basic necessities, in fact I lived a life of plenty, but I was starving for the kind of human intimacy that would satisfy my longing, end my loneliness, and at least calm if not fulfill my unrequited passion [White, 1994, p. 123].

The prison in which a gay man may grow up is a heterosexual environment that is rarely tolerant of manifest expressions of same-sex feelings or intimacy and often punishes them. As a child or adolescent, a gay man may have been traumatized for either revealing he was gay or for having been perceived as gay (Hetrick and Martin, 1988; Herek and Berrill, 1992):

> At nine, I was caught in bed with Gavin—thrown onto the floor by the headmaster's wife, lectured publicly and whipped. Frightened by this unexpected outburst, I was to have no physical contact for thirteen years. I lived my adolescence so demoralized I became reclusive. The physicality of sport, particularly the changing rooms, were an agony of deception. I was desperate to avoid being the sissy of my father's criticism, terrified of being the Queer in the dormitory. . . . My work also suffered. I dropped behind. At puberty my reports said "more concentration needed." You see I was distracted [Jarman, 1992, pp. 36–37].

As a result of these external attitudes, a gay man's personal history often includes a time of difficulty in acknowledging his homosexuality, either to himself or to others. Constant fear of discovery can interfere with developing a sense of self-worth. Consider the plight of one young man who allowed another athlete to anally penetrate him:

> To the boy's horror, the boxer promptly went to the gym and told everyone what he had done; the boy, humiliated, concluded he could never go there again. A man who allowed himself to be used sexually as a woman, then, risked forfeiting his masculine status, even if he

were otherwise conventionally masculine; in this case, the boy's shame clearly derived from his perception that he had been made a fairy in the eyes of his comrades. The story also illustrates the belief among men in this world that so long as they played the "man's" role, they remained men. The most striking aspect of this story is the confidence the boxer felt that reporting the encounter would not endanger his status among his friends, that, indeed, having sexually subordinated the boy would enhance it [Chauncey, 1994, p. 81].

Gay men commonly report an accretion of interactions in which they were either denigrated or rendered invisible. Repeated experiences of public humiliation can have a powerful impact, lower self-esteem (Cohler and Galatzer-Levy, 1996), and subsequently cause a gay man to hide important aspects of himself. The trauma of being discovered, punished, and humiliated for showing or acting on one's feelings can lead to hiding behaviors that persist long after the traumatic event is forgotten. Even in the absence of a specific traumatic event, repeated, unsuccessful attempts at closeness with unreceptive boys or men can cause a gay man to develop techniques for hiding that often persist into young adulthood, middle age, and sometimes even into senescence. One of the closet's underlying theses is that a secret revealed will lead to disaster. And consequently, a proficiency in hiding one's sexual feelings can also become a generalized approach to life in which one may learn to hide all open expressions of emotion or intimacy. Although hiding is a salient characteristic of those gay men who marry and have children in order to disguise their homosexuality from themselves and others (Buxton, 1994; White, 1994; Isay, 1996), even unmarried men may remain hidden well into later life. Hiding inevitably affects the developmental narratives of some boys and men. As this chapter reveals, their narratives tell of the impact that the need to hide can have upon a gay man's self-esteem as well as his interpersonal relationships.

In the jargon of contemporary gay culture, those who hide their sexual identities are referred to as "closeted" or are said to be "in the closet." Some readers may simply assume that being in the closet refers to a discrete state of hiding one's homosexuality. However, in clinical work with gay men one encounters a wide array of related behaviors that deserve to be differentiated from each other. Thus, there is not *a* closet, or *the* closet, but a whole panoply of closets. This chapter, in offering a glimpse into some closets where gay men hide their spontaneous feelings and impulses, tries to illuminate psychological mechanisms and interpersonal maneuvers used to maintain the closet's secrecy.

In thinking about the array of behaviors and attitudes that maintain a closeted state, it is useful to think in terms of dissociative defenses, particularly as they were conceptualized by Sullivan. Sullivan was himself a closeted gay man (Chatelaine, 1981; Perry, 1982; Ortmeyer, 1995), though it is not entirely clear how central this sexual identity was to his formulations about dissociation. Nevertheless, his formulations of these defensive operations are extremely useful in clinically understanding and therapeutically working with gay men and, for that reason, this chapter will repeatedly refer to Sullivan's writings about dissociation.

In line with his famous maxim that "everyone is more simply human than otherwise" (1953, p. 32), and as part of his general approach of linking everyday phenomena with clinical observations, Sullivan believed that dissociative acts took place along a continuum. Thus, the terrors and dread associated with severe dissociation—with the possible emergence of the not-me—is of a piece with other, less dramatic, psychological phenomena. And in Sullivan's view of defensive operations, anyone, regardless of sexual identity, can construct a "closet" of dissociative defenses. However, the reader should not extrapolate from this chapter's focus on dissociative gradients to infer that being closeted necessarily occurs on a continuum as well. In fact, the myriad ways of being closeted are complex, multi-dimensional, and may also involve other defenses. Thus, it should be emphasized that Sullivan's approach to dissociation is only a part, albeit an integral one, of what ought to be involved in treating a gay man (see chapter 7).

Dissociation

In contrast to repression's intrapsychic, or one-person, model of the mind, Sullivan (1938, 1956, 1972) sees dissociation as an interpersonal process that is accessible to observation. In Sullivan's two-person psychoanalytic model, rather than inferring metapsychological interactions between psychic structures and drives, a therapist hears a patient avoiding certain subjects and topics. It is Sullivan's belief that this avoidance is intentional, although the patient's motive to avoid is out of conscious awareness.

The degree to which a person knows they are avoiding something can vary from topic to topic or from individual to individual. For Sullivan, there is a continuum of dissociative phenomena and *selective inattention* is a nonpathological process in which one is "keeping the attention on something else—in other words by *controlling awareness* of the events that impinge upon us" (1956, p. 37). "It seems to me that the hierarchy of things that can happen about awareness of events begins with selective inattention and goes on to dissociation of events, with various degrees of awareness between, controlled largely by substitutive processes" (Sullivan, 1956, p. 63).

Dissociation is "as basic as repression to human mental functioning and as central to the stability and growth of the personality" (Bromberg, 1994, p. 517). In other words, dissociative operations are ubiquitous. They help an individual cope with life's daily routines. Selective inattention makes life more manageable, analogous to tuning out the background noise on a busy street. Unlike repression, in which thoughts, feelings, and memories are totally inaccessible to consciousness (Freud, 1915b), "selective inattention performs the function of preserving the separation of the dissociated experience by preventing attention being paid to anything that would tend to bring that dissociated material closer to awareness . . . *it screens experience rather than actively deleting it*" (Stern, 1995, p. 122, emphasis added). According to Sullivan, "Selective inattention is the classic means by which we do not profit from experience. . . . We don't have the experience from which we might profit—that is, although it occurs, we never notice what it must mean" (1956, p. 50). Through this mechanism, a whole double life can be lived and yet, in some ways, not be known:

> As half of me babbled on, more and more desperate to impress [my interviewer] and to get the job, my other half seemed to be observing me operating. It was a strange sensation, this being divided and still functioning. My pattern of lying, of hiding the things I knew to be the truth, was beginning to become an integral part of me [Liebman, 1992, p. 82].

At the other extreme of Sullivan's dissociative continuum is what he terms *dissociation of events*. He describes this as "impulses which are choked off in large measure very early in our education. . . . But they are not choked off utterly—it is probably impossible to do so. Like the trees growing at the edge of the Grand Canyon, something happens, however terribly distorted" (p. 66).[1] In dissociation, "the patient simply hasn't any of this business of being aware of events. You know from his subsequent behavior that an event has simply sidetracked itself, for it was part of his life, even though it is not part of his known experience" (p. 76). In

---

1. Sullivan's own life experience as a closeted gay man (Chatelaine, 1981) may have given him insight into the mechanisms of selective inattention. A psychiatric hospitalization in his youth may have also given him clinical insight into the power of severe dissociative experiences (Perry, 1982).

Sullivan's continuum, dissociation comes closest to Freud's repression (Stern, 1995). The clinical presentations of being in the closet may lie somewhere in severity between selective inattention, most commonly seen in the case of a patient thinking about "the possibility" that he might be gay, to severe dissociation, in which any hint of same-sex feelings resides totally out of conscious awareness.

In Sullivan's theory, there is no self without an other, and hiding from the self is tantamount to hiding from others. Many gay men had some sense of their same-sex feelings years before acknowledging them. But homoeroticism is an aspect of their selves that got "very little social attention" (Sullivan, 1956, p. 66), and was therefore not incorporated into the self system. These men learned to dissociate knowledge about themselves. And they also have to prevent other people from being able to recognize the quality of their sexual impulses. These more severe forms of dissociation are commonly observed in married men who are homosexually self-aware but who do not wish to think of themselves as gay (Buxton, 1994).

A middle-aged woman sought couples treatment because she believed that her marriage was over. She said she knew her husband was attracted to other men, and in recent years they shared no physical intimacy. She explained "I always knew my husband was gay, but I tried to ignore it." She hoped couples therapy could amicably bring their relationship to a close. However, she was ambivalent about her decision. Although she was angry with her husband, she still had affectionate feelings for him. She hoped he would "come out and find his true gay self. I want him to be happy, for his own sake, and for our children's sake."

The husband, on the other hand, was appalled by his wife's position. He had told her years ago that he had homosexual feelings. He referred to them as his "evil thoughts," and had never thought of himself as gay. He denied having ever acted on those feelings during their marriage. He insisted that she misinterpreted several affectionate interactions between him and other men. Those men were just friends. He did not want to end their marriage, and was opposed to couples therapy. He also did not think that their lack of sexual intimacy was a problem for the marriage. However, he was willing to grant his wife's request for a divorce because he was tired of fighting with her. During the session, he expressed hopelessness about his future and gave the therapist the impression that he was thinking about taking his own life. Although he refused to discuss suicidal feelings openly, he did not deny having them. Before a scheduled second session, the husband called, and said they had decided to stop coming for treatment and were pursuing "other options." He had left the impression that the marriage would continue as before, with the wife selectively inattending what she knew, and with the husband continuing to severely dissociate from what he had no wish to know.

Detailed Inquiry

Regardless of sexual orientation, a patient who presents for treatment with severe dissociative operations raises an important issue regarding analytic listening. Here we find that Sullivan's technique for dealing with dissociative phenomena—detailed inquiry—takes the treatment in a different direction than other relational techniques. For example, Winnicott, envisioned the therapy setting as a holding environment that created room for a patient's spontaneous gestures. Bion (1967b) stressed the importance of the therapist being without memory or desire. From this relational, analytic perspective, the therapist approaches a session without a fixed agenda, acts as a container, and allows the patient to fill up both the session and the therapist. However, when patients severely dissociate, it is sometimes necessary for the therapist to be more than the repository of their feelings and memories. Although a therapist usually waits for the patient's memories to emerge spontaneously over the course of a session, sometimes it may be necessary to assist the patient in reconnecting with forgotten memories and feelings. This requires activity:

A: My mind is a blank.

Th: What's it like to be blank?

A: It's exciting. I look at this as a new lease on life. I can try and do the things I truly want to do. If one had Alzheimer's, you couldn't remember basic things. But what am I forgetting? Whatever I was thinking of, I just processed and got rid of it so I don't have to deal with it. It has gone behind the screen. There are negative things I have to deal with. As I come to accept what they are, and how to deal with them, it's something I can't forget and I have to face.

Th: We were discussing your parents last time.

A: Oh, were we? I don't remember what it was we talked about. I find myself looking at your books. I wonder why you have all those psychiatry books? Then I see your art books, and then a family therapy book.

Although this might sound like free association, the patient was actively moving away from the troubling subject he had raised two days earlier in the previous session:

Th: The family therapy book reminds me that we were talking about your family.

A: My mother called me this week. She tried to get me to come home on Saturday, so the whole family can be together. Being together is her issue, not mine. While I can understand her need, she can't understand my indifference. I never noticed the clock ticking in this office until now.

Th: It's the way your mind focuses on other things to avoid focusing on yourself.

A: On the way over here, I thought, "Maybe when I fall asleep he will hypnotize me." Could this be related to sleeping? Did I talk about feeling I couldn't love anyone? The thought that came to mind is "I don't deserve it." I can't imagine why I think that. All I worry about is taking care of others.

Th: In our last session, we spoke about whether you deserved to be loved and who will take care of you. Do you remember that?

A: No.

Sullivan maintained that a patient's free associations alone were sometimes inadequate to the therapeutic task (Sullivan, 1938, 1954, 1956; Shawver, 1989; Cooper, 1995). Although listening to a patient's free associations is what a therapist does much of the time, the detailed inquiry can be helpful in those moments when a patient's dissociative defenses are in ascendancy:

E: I can't remember what we talked about last week.

Th: What do you remember from last week?

E: Not much.

Th: Forgetting is one way to deal with troublesome issues.

E: I must be running into a lot of troubling stuff. I can talk about how little I remember from my childhood. I'm sure it's something I used to avoid stuff.

Th: I rarely get the sense that forgetting troubles you.

E: I think you are right. I experience it as not-a-problem. When I think about the forgetfulness, I feel frustrated. I feel I'm running on a treadmill. I'm talking about stuff for forty-five minutes, and I sort of remember it, things keep up, but it takes longer than it has to because I've forgotten so much.

Th: In part, you feel better and don't want to get into troubling issues. This week you are doing fine. So perhaps you feel there's nothing to talk about?

E: Right. I hear you. That brings up a memory from last week. We talked about my lover and I poking each other and that poking needs to be talked about. The thing I was confused about is how to bring the subject up with him.

As the therapist focused on forgetting, the patient remembered the previous session. He wondered how his relationship would survive its ongoing bickering, described in the metaphor of "poking each other." Detailed inquiries can be experienced as impingements, and the patient was also making a transferential reference to the experience of being "poked" by the therapist. The subject of the detailed inquiry can, at times, be made quite anxious, irritable, and angry by its intrusiveness. Yet anxiety, irritability, and anger, among other things, were exactly what this particular patient would not allow himself to feel. The ultimate goal with any patient, when doing a detailed inquiry, is to take them into places where they do not wish to go—and yet not let the patient's anxiety reach intolerable proportions. In the case of the psychotherapeutic work with gay men, the detailed inquiry can elicit the painful affects they associate to being gay and from which they may have dissociated.

The Closet

In contemporary gay culture, revealing one's gay identity to others is referred to as "coming out" or "coming out of the closet."

> Given the ubiquity of the term today and how central the metaphor of the closet is to the ways we think about gay history before the 1960s, it is bracing—and instructive—to note that it was never used by gay people themselves before then. Nowhere does it appear before the 1960s in the records of the gay movement or in the novels, diaries, or letters of gay men and lesbians. . . . Like much of campy gay terminology, "coming out" was an arch play on the language of women's culture—in this case the expression used to refer to the ritual of a debutante's being formally introduced to or "coming out" into, the society of her cultural peers. . . . Gay people in the prewar years, then, did not speak of *coming out of* what we call the "gay closet" but rather of *coming out into* what they called "homosexual society" or the "gay world," a world neither so small, nor so isolated, nor, often so hidden as "closet" implies [Chauncey, 1994, pp. 6–7].

Although the everyday meaning of putting something into the closet implies that one is merely hiding something, or putting it away until later, there are actually various combinations of openness and hiding in different people's closets. A closeted man can completely isolate his homosexual feelings and activities from himself, his acquaintances and his family. Or he may move to an urban gay ghetto without letting anyone back home know anything about him.

> **C:** I called a couple of my college friends, all of whom are straight, and we've gotten together. I miss not getting together with them more often. It is a little strange, how I never told them that I'm gay. I honestly don't know if they suspect or not. On one occasion, I thought about telling them, but it never came close to entering into the conversation. They either assume that I don't date or that I'm not going to get married. Or they've figured out I'm gay and don't think about it. Or they don't want to talk about it. I sometimes wonder about what they do and don't know.

From an intrapsychic perspective, a gay man may be closeted to himself. This is captured in a repeated refrain among many gay men who report, "I always knew I was gay, but I didn't want to admit it to myself." Being able to reveal one's sexual identity only in certain arenas while having to hide it in others can foster dissociative splits in everyday life. The subjective and interpersonal experience of splitting one's identity is sometimes referred to as multiple presentations of the self. In this model of the mind, an individual can potentially experience himself in the present as the helpless child he once felt himself to be, as the unhappy adult he is today in his relationship, as the feared authority figure he may be to his employees, and so on (Bromberg, 1994). Although such presentations of the self can be adaptive, when the dissociative activities that separate one's self-states are more severe, they may prevent a gay man from paying full attention to the full consequences of his hiding activities. For example, divorcing sexual and intimate feelings from the objects of one's desire is bound to occur if one is to keep one's sexual identity hidden from the rest of one's life. As one gay man wrote, "The men I had sex with were quick encounters, men I met at the beach or on the subway, at the library or in cafes. I never attempted to see these people again or to have a conversation of any depth with them, because I was afraid of getting involved, afraid that it would mean I was a homosexual" (Signorile, 1993, p. 33). To develop a fleeting relationship more fully would require an unacceptable, to the closeted gay man, integration of his everyday and sexual identities. In fact, the closeted gay man can go to great lengths to prevent others from knowing who he is. Consider, for example, the patient who explained why he often made out-of-town sexual forays as a younger man, despite the fact that he lived relatively anonymously in the gay enclave of New York City's Greenwich Village:

B: When I was coming out in the 60s, my whole life was closeted. As a college student, I couldn't go to bars in New York. I was paranoid that people from school might see me. I would fly to Ft. Lauderdale. That's where I came out. So, the first time I went to gay bars and had love affairs, I had to go out of town to do it. I was too paranoid to do it where I lived.

Th: What did you fear?

B: Being spotted as a homosexual. I was afraid of being known as a homosexual. I didn't want people to know I was gay. I was ashamed of myself. I had this fear that if the other students saw, they wouldn't like me or they would laugh at me. I would walk a block or two out of my way and take a roundabout route to the hot, Greenwich Village hangout. It was later, when I'd been to bars in Ft. Lauderdale, and I felt a little more comfortable, that I eventually started going to New York bars in a more direct way. In those days, all of my homosexual relationships were purely sexual. No socializing, no speaking.

Th: Why was that?

B: I couldn't admit I was homosexual. The sexual impulse was very strong, but if I didn't act on the social impulse, then I could deny I was gay. That was the feeling I had. And in those days, I was thinking about getting married and having a family and having children. Doing what my family expected of me, what society expected of me and what I expected of myself. I could have been one of these sad married guys who got caught in the basement of the White House having sex. But if I didn't talk about it, and if there were no social involvements, then I didn't have to admit I was gay.

To the closeted gay man, "not talking about it" can appear to be a solution. This is because dissociative operations attempt to exclude from consciousness those words, symbols, or sensations that might induce anxiety. "Paradoxically, while language vastly extends our grasp on reality, it can also provide the mechanism for distortion of reality as experienced. . . . It is for this reason that so much of what is clinically important when language emerges is invisible and silent. It includes everything that is not expressed verbally and involves the choices about what is being left unspoken as well as what is being said" (Stern, 1985, p. 226). Subjectively, a person's identity is, in part, constructed of affectively laden markers that are embedded in both the language he uses as well as the language he avoids. In the autobiographical *Becoming a Man* (Monette, 1992), the author was nine years old when he and a friend were showing their genitals to each other. The author's mother unexpectedly walked into the bedroom and asked, "What are you boys doing?" He replied, "Nothing." Nothing more is said about the incident for three days:

On the third day, I came home from school and found her brooding at the kitchen table, smoking a cigarette. Right away I started to talk, changing the unspoken subject, strewing the table before her with A's. She finally looked at me grimly and upped the ante: "What were you doing with Kite?"

No deal. "I told you—nothing," I flung back, skittering away to the living room door. Then tossed it again with bitter emphasis. *"Nothing."*

She looked down at the cigarette in her hand, tapping it into the ash tray, and said no more.

I was right, of course—it had been nothing. Yet I knew as I walked lead-footed to my bedroom that the high-wire act of passion was over, because it was somehow wrong [pp. 28–29].

As the following patient recalled, in a developing child, self-states of good-me, bad-me, and not-me (Sullivan, 1953) derive their meanings from the labels attached to interpersonal encounters:

> F: When I was a child, I didn't know what was good or what was evil. I had feelings for other males. I acted on those feelings and it was perfectly innocent. It wasn't until I learned it was wrong that it became a problem. I was perfectly OK with it until the point where I was told it was wrong to hold another guy's hand or to have these feelings.

If an early behavior was tinged with interpersonal anxiety or shame, an individual might inattend later experiences or relationships that re-evoke those feelings. The dissociative act prevents the person from re-experiencing feelings remembered from earlier encounters. Another gay man, who came out in middle age, experienced his religious convictions as good-me, that is his religious faith was felt to be a valuable part of his identity. When he was aware of his sexual feelings and desires, they had elements of bad-me, that is to say they represented aspects of his identity that he didn't like. Although he could never entirely dissociate from the dreaded feeling that he might be gay, at times his sexual feelings were so threatening to his self-image that they verged on the not-me:[2]

---

2. Uncanny emotion [is] Sullivan's term for the most primitive type of *anxiety* experienced in the form of feelings such as awe (the most commonly occurring), dread, horror, or loathing. Uncanny emotions result from sudden, intense, and overwhelming experiences of anxiety produced by significant others when they disrupt the child's activity because of their own unusually intense anxiety about, and very strong disapproval of, the activity. The child's intense anxiety obliterates the capacity to form clear, causal connections between events, so that the activity elicited the dramatic and noxious interference and the feelings associated with the activity are relegated to the completely out-of-awareness *not-me*. Since not-me experiences are unavailable to awareness, they are not modifiable by subsequent learning or experience (Brown, 1995, p. 875).

G: I spent much of my life feeling suicidal. I dated women. I got no support from my church but stayed involved for many years. I had to use denial, to say "I was not gay." But as soon as I turned 18, I was finding male physique magazines, buying them, masturbating to them, and hiding them. But I was still telling myself, "I am not gay." The denial part was not to know about it. I didn't want to read anything about homosexuality or anything gay-affirmative. If something like that came on the television, I would leave the room or turn it off. I was afraid. Down deep I knew, but I didn't want to know. I had two or three books on homosexuality, but I didn't read them. I thought homosexuality was an illness, a disorder. I thought I was blocked, that my mother had done it to me, and I didn't like women because of my mother. I believed that. When I took abnormal psychology in college, and I still have that book, the entire chapter on homosexuality was lumped together with other types of pathology. So I read that, and knew I had those feelings. I prayed about them too. I remember, in high school, going out on my bicycle with my bible. I was trying to get healed, or cured, on my own, without telling anyone. But it wasn't happening.

This patient's attempts to dissociatively ward off knowledge of his same-sex feelings is not uncommon in the developmental narratives of many gay men. In Gore Vidal's *The City and the Pillar* (1948), the novel's gay protagonist, Jim, is a teenager. While on a camping trip with his best friend, Bob, they playfully begin wrestling:

They clung to one another. Jim was overwhelmingly conscious of Bob's body. For a moment they pretended to wrestle. Then both stopped. Yet each continued to cling to the other as though waiting for a signal to break or to begin again. For a long time neither moved. Smooth chests touching, sweat mingling, breathing fast in unison.

Abruptly, Bob pulled away. For a bold moment their eyes met. Then, deliberately, gravely, Bob shut his eyes and Jim touched him, as he had so many times in his dreams, without words, without thought, without fear. When the eyes are shut, the true world begins.

As faces touched, Bob gave a shuddering sigh and gripped Jim tightly in his arms. Now they were complete, each became the other, as their bodies collided with a primal violence, like to like, metal to magnet, half to half and the whole restored.

So they met. Eyes tight shut against an irrelevant world . . . and the moment was gone. In the fast beat of a double heart, it died.

The eyes opened again. Two bodies faced one another where only an instant before a universe had lived [p. 29].

Many gay men report similar sexual experiences before they came out to themselves. Like Jim, some spend many years fantasizing about their childhood lovers. In Vidal's novel, the adult Jim moves away from his hometown but eventually reunites with the object of his adolescent crush. Although Jim has idealized their love for years, Bob had apparently forgotten their shared adolescent experience. Forgetting one's homosexual experiences is a recurrent theme in gay literature. As one member of Mart Crowley's The *Boys in The Band* (1968) describes it, forgetting while under the influence of drugs and alcohol can also help maintain the illusion of being in the closet:

> Michael: I know I didn't come out til after I'd graduated [college].
>
> Donald: What about all those week ends up from school?
>
> Michael: I still wasn't out. I was still in the "Christ-Was-I-Drunk-Last-Night Syndrome." You know, when you made it with some guy in school and the next day when you had to face each other there was always a lot of shit-kicking crap about, "Man, was I drunk last night! Christ, I don't remember a thing."
>
> Donald: You were just guilty because you were Catholic, that's all.
>
> Michael: That's not true. The Christ-Was-I-Drunk-Last Night Syndrome knows no religion. . . . Yes, long before Justin or I or God-only-knows how many others *came out*, we used to get drunk and "horse around" a bit. You see, in the Christ-Was-I-Drunk-Last-Night Syndrome, you really *are* drunk. That part of it is true. It's just that you also *do remember everything* [p. 23].

Dissociative operations probably account for numerous reports of unusual sexual encounters that took place between friends or acquaintances under the guise of one or both of them being asleep. Sullivan (1956) describes a dramatic example of this behavior as a severe form of dissociated homosexual impulses. Sullivan gives the example of two houseguests who are forced to share a room. One of them, Mr. A, has only been consciously aware that he finds Mr. X disagreeable. Nevertheless, as Sullivan tells it:

> What is apt to happen in the course of the night—what, in fact, has in many such instances happened—is the following: During the night Mr. A gets out from under his cotton precaution and goes around and tenderly fondles Mr. X, and then goes back to bed under his bottom sheet. There is considerable evidence of his being in a curiously foggy state of mind, which so impresses Mr. X that he does not say anything about the incident the next morning. Mr. A acts as if nothing on earth like that could conceivably have happened, and Mr. X just says to himself, "Well, this bird is a funny one." Mr. A leaves the house with a feeling that, considering that he had had to share a room with this extremely

disagreeable person, he has had a remarkable good night's sleep. He feels fine, and has no trace of any information about what has happened [p. 176].

As in the case of the following patient, pretending to be asleep while engaging in homosexual activity may reduce anxiety and shame in men who are loathe to integrate homosexuality into their identities:

I: An old friend from college called me at work the other day. He is still with the same woman he married when we were in college. I wasn't terribly turned on to him, but we did have sex three times. It started in our senior year on a school trip. We were in a double bed together and I pretended to be asleep. His hand started coming over toward me gradually. I knew exactly what was happening, because I had done it myself to other guys. It was very exciting to be on the receiving end. He gradually worked his hand across to my cock, which was hard, and he took a hold of it. I kept pretending I was asleep. Somehow, I took off my shorts, but still didn't acknowledge what was going on. He put his cock between my thighs and started humping me. He was moaning his wife's name. In fact, he had recently gotten married. He came between my legs, calling her name. I recall whipping back the covers and going down on him. While masturbating, I sucked him until I came.

We didn't acknowledge that it happened and both of us acted as if it never happened. Later, on one occasion, he came over to my place at night and crawled into bed with me. The first time, I didn't acknowledge he was there, but we played out this little dream scene. He sucked on me and I sucked on him. He masturbated and came, put his clothes on, and left. We didn't talk about that. By that time, I was planning to marry myself. I had already bought the engagement ring. And here he was in my bed!

The last time he came over was when I was leaving town to get married. He sat on my bed. The light was on and we talked. We talked about all sorts of things, but not sex. All the while we talked, he was running his hand up my leg and up to my cock. We kept talking without acknowledging that. I started to stroke him through his pants. He pulled out his cock and started to masturbate, and came on my blanket. As long as I had that blanket, I could always see that spot where he came. The experience left me with the feeling that I had failed in some way. We haven't seen each other or talked to each other since then.

It is also worth noting the severity of the dissociative operations that this man's married sexual partner was using. Married gay men do raise another of the closet's recurrent themes, that of double lives. But there is no monopoly on secrecy. Isay (personal communication), for example,

reports that several gay men he treated had a prolonged, childhood interest in comic books. Comic book super-heroes, in fact, offer models on
how to live double lives. Their "secret identities" protect them from
exposure to enemies. Certainly, the theme of double lives is not unique
to gay patients. However, a closeted gay man, like Superman's Clark
Kent, may need a secret identity to feel safe in the work environment:

> The U.S. government's policies regarding lesbians and gay men who
> serve in the armed forces were infamous and atrocious. The Pentagon
> relentlessly conducted witch hunts year after year; since 1982, these
> had netted almost 13,000 queers, all of whom were discharged because
> they were "incompatible" with military service. People were interro-
> gated and tormented after their homosexuality was revealed, while
> their superiors demanded to know who else in the service might be
> gay. They were threatened with having their children taken away, their
> families informed, and their lives ruined. Whether they cooperated or
> not, the queers were kicked out of the military and branded with a
> mark on their discharge papers that stigmatized them forever. Some,
> demoralized by their treatment and shaken by the disclosure of their
> homosexuality, were driven to suicide. While a handful of lesbians and
> gay men fought back and went public with their stories, most retreated
> into obscurity, humiliated and afraid [Signorile, 1993, p. 98; also see
> Shilts, 1993; Jones and Koshes, 1995; Purcell and Hicks, 1996].

Although military service has its unique dangers, there are often risks
associated to coming out in other work settings as well (Woods and
Lucas, 1993). Another patient believed he had to decide between remain-
ing closeted at work or satisfying his growing desire to integrate his gay
identity into his larger life:

H: The personal side of me is in ascendancy right now, although I'm sure
I still have my professional ambition. I tell myself, "If I want that ambition, maybe I should suppress my personal side.

Th: You feel that keeping these two sides of yourself separated is a
necessity.

H: It has to do with being gay. Maybe it's OK to be gay, but don't bring it
into the workplace. My emotional side is very connected to being gay. I've
always believed you can separate your professional life and your personal
life. I'm not sure that's true. My emotions follow me everywhere. A large
part of my emotional life, for the last two years, has been sorrow and hurt
over the break-up of my previous relationship. I can't and shouldn't bring
that fact into the workplace. It would be inappropriate and no one does it,
at least not where I work. You are not supposed to think or talk about

those things when you are working. But I thought about it all the time. I just didn't speak about it. Part of what I was trying to do in taking this job was to drown out the emotions about my relationship breaking up. Of course, the fact that I'm gay made me more reticent to speak about it. If a straight person had a divorce and broke up, you can imagine talking about it at work. I can't deal with that anymore. I refuse to feel like I can't say anything. For me, it is not psychologically healthy.

Th: Being unable to speak may not be healthy, but it is familiar.

H: It is familiar. Many of my friends in this profession do the same thing. They lead two lives. I don't know a single person who's out at work. I'm about as out as they come in my circles. All the role models I've had are very closeted, and they think *I'm* pushing the limits. Then there's always the fear of being judged. I don't want to be judged, so I don't volunteer information. I won't go in and say, "I'm seeing this new guy" or "Me and my boyfriend broke up." You don't say certain things. You don't say where you went for the weekend. You don't say where you have the beach house. You don't tell the details of your life. You don't say, "I went to the doctor for an HIV test." I resent that, and I resent myself because I think it's inauthentic. It grates on my nerves. I feel so sad right now.

Maintaining a closet can lead to an intuitive understanding of postmodern theories of gender and sexuality. A lifetime spent hiding his true sexual and emotional desires sensitizes a closeted gay man to the binary linkage of language and gender. He may learn to speak reflexively without revealing the gender of the person being discussed, or without providing any gendered details of his personal life. He might say "she" instead of "he," without any conscious thought at all. Or he might avoid references to gender altogether: "I went out last night with *someone* I've been dating for the last few weeks. *We* went to a movie in *their* neighborhood. *We* talked about the possibility of going to the beach next weekend." A heterosexual listening to a man speaking these words might automatically assume he was discussing a relationship with a woman. In fact, that is what the gay man wants a heterosexual listener to assume. The feeling of urgency to conceal his sexual identity and relationships can remain with a gay man, even if it is no longer necessary to hide, and create the false impression of detached isolation, withdrawal, or asexuality:

K: Last night my new boyfriend wanted to have sex, but for some reason the thought made me uncomfortable. I'm waiting for someone to break in and arrest me for having sex, someone to be critical and punishing of gay sex. That is the most powerful experience of the shadowy nature of gay sex. It is not a loving thing. It has to be secret. It has to be shameful.

Th: What is shameful?

K: What came to mind about shame, is when I first began to masturbate, at age 12. It left terrible stains on my pajamas. I feared they would be discovered or commented on when the laundry was done, but they never were. That is what came to mind. Shame today would probably come from being caught looking at a man who was good looking in an office or someplace.

Th: Shame about being sexual and being known by others as sexual?

K: Very much so. The recognition of being gay at some unconscious level makes one act asexually as a form of protection.

Th: What does it mean to "act asexually?"

K: To hide sexual feelings, to deny them. To not participate in them. I didn't have a clue until I was 24 what it meant to be sexual.

Th: What was your first clue?

K: As my furtive gay sexual experiences mounted, I began to gradually accept the possibility of acting upon my sexual desires, or giving in to them. Before that happened, I was so ashamed and embarrassed that I would just shut down. That shutting down attitude still persists as the wall that separates other parts of my life and my sexual life. A lack of integration. As long as my sexuality was kept hidden, it was OK.

For another patient, hiding had become a way of life as he continually tried to keep from being known by others:

J: I think relationships with people, when they are not family, are conditional upon your behavior. If you misbehave in the other person's eyes, there's a price. If you stake out your own course of action and be yourself, you will not have a relationship.

Th: You said earlier you don't want to be lied to, but now you sound like you think not being yourself is necessary to maintain a relationship.

J: A lie is when you went to "so and so" and you said "such and such." No, I don't think it's a lie if you don't mention something.

Th: You never heard of a lie of omission?

J: (Laughs) Yes, but I can live with that.

The therapist experienced confusion in this interpersonal exchange. He revealed this feeling to draw attention to the impact that the patient's line of reasoning had on others:

Th: I feel the slope is very slippery here. I'm not sure how to proceed.

J: I'm glad to hear that. It means I've come up with a successful means of deflecting questions, a smoke-screen.

Th: It evokes a feeling of wanting to throw up my hands, rather than trying to clarify how you think and feel.

J: That's probably what it was developed for. To discourage unwanted inquiries.

This exchange underscores how "'Closetedness' is itself a performance initiated as such by the speech act of a silence—not a particular silence, but a silence that accrues particularity by fits and starts, in relation to the discourse that surrounds and differentially constitutes it" (Sedgwick, 1990, p. 3). The interpersonal construction of the closet was noted by another patient after he saw the television episode in which *Ellen* came out:

Th: What was your experience of the episode?

L: I think it was real. That's what the homophobes were afraid of. That we're too mainstream. The network news did a good job afterwards of interviewing Ellen's real mother, talking about teenage suicides. It was a good feeling. Ellen was on *Oprah* and a guy was going on about how it is a sin and it's a choice. But *how* can you choose it? That's a concept I can't get. The next day at work, I was at lunch with some lesbians and I brought up the show. I said, "I don't understand why people think this is a choice." They were all uncomfortable talking about it in the cafeteria. Nobody said anything, it just lay there.

Th: It is not just heterosexuals who don't want to talk about it. When the subject of being gay begins to be talked about publicly, there are also many gay people themselves who don't want to talk about it.

L: That's true, and that's the reason why *Ellen* needs to come out. It is important to be out there so it doesn't become this gargoyle of an event. That is what the homophobes are afraid of, that it's too normal.

The Impact of Being in the Closet on Self-Esteem

The following man was not gay, although like gay men he had an unconventional sexual identity which he hid from himself and others. In order to hide, he tried to accommodate the needs of others as a way to increase his self-esteem through reflected appraisals (Sullivan, 1972). This was not an entirely successful strategy:

M: Oedipus at Colonnus is one of my favorite plays. There is a battle for the city of Thebes going on. A political battle, or one that could be won by persuasion. Even though he wants to wander blind, Oedipus has withdrawn from the world. He doesn't want to participate. Essentially, he wants to die, but he can't bring himself to take his own life. He finds himself an icon of both political groups in their struggle for supremacy. Each one kidnaps him to claim, "We have him on our side. We have the magic." He doesn't want any part of this, but allows himself to be used this way. His daughter, Antigone, also insists on it. He allows himself to be a representation of what the other people want him to be. He plays a role for them. He ends up dying in a strange way. He finds a peaceful tree. He realizes that if he ascends the tree, he will go into the afterworld, the heavens, and he will escape this life. And that is what he does. He climbs up the tree and disappears into the heavens. People may applaud him and he could be many things. He is offered many things in order to be their magic person. But he doesn't want them, because he is essentially sad. He was an active participant in a tragedy and knows that those tragic events were the major events of his life and that all other events are inconsequential to his soul. His life is dictated by what has happened in the past, and there is no way to overcome that except to die. He can't die until he comes to that place.

Th: You are looking for a peaceful tree.

M: I am. When will I be free enough of work so if I'm not in the office, they can manage? When will my children have had enough of my guidance to manage on their own? When will my wife not be upset if I am not there? When will my parents be dead?

As any patient, gay or otherwise, can attest, it can be painful to keep significant aspects of the self hidden, or to vigilantly separate aspects of the self from each other. And maintaining self-esteem through reflected appraisals calls for a great deal of mental activity that can interfere with spontaneity:

N: As spontaneous as I try to be, I censor and rehearse everything I say. It is not without a filter. I don't know how to *not* think before I speak.

Th: It may be dangerous to speak spontaneously.

N: It is losing a great deal of control. Fearing what will pop out. The princess who opens her mouth and out comes a frog.

Th: What are you afraid of here?

N: I don't really know, other than I'm still trying to preserve control over what other people think of me. It is built into my circuitry.

Th: What is your earliest memory of this circuit?

N: Of trying to behave? That is what it feels like. My earliest memory would be to project something into someone else's perception. It is interpreted by how they react to it. My life is defined by other people's reflections of it. That is an extreme way of putting it. But as I said that, I was wondering, "Does a tree falling in the forest make a sound?" What would happen if I were all by myself? That is a scary thought. I dismiss it very quickly. Totally by myself; what would that be? Would that be in a box? Could you be by yourself and be unconcerned? I say that, and I hear that I am totally defined by coming across as the right thing to other people.

This patient found that constant hiding created difficulties in accurately assessing other people's perceptions of him as well as recognizing his own strengths. Dissociation's impact on self-esteem can also make an individual unable to feel his actual accomplishments as reflections of his own abilities. That was represented in the dream of the following patient, a successful gay businessman:

P: At the beginning of the dream, I was at my competitor's new factory trying to see what it looked like and what he was doing. I didn't want to be recognized. Then I went back to my factory. There was a parade of people walking past me and going up to his factory. Then people in my factory started to leave and to join the parade going to my competition. Somebody at the other factory said something like, "This is a big new operation and we're going to promote the hell out of it. We are going to market the hell out of it." Which is also my waking fear. I was trying to stop people from leaving my factory. I woke up and couldn't go back to sleep. It was a nightmare.

Th: What comes to mind about the dream?

P: I have anxieties about being put out of business. I've never had such a literal dream in my whole life. I'm absolutely obsessing that I will go out of business. My competitor already steals a lot of my marketing ideas and even some of my employees. Instead of making realistic business plans about this, I am panicking. I feel like saying, "I need help with this anxiety I feel about my competitor." If I continue this way, it will be unhealthy. I don't want to have these dreams and I don't want to have this anxiety.

Th: This dream appears to be based on your feeling that you are not a viable contender.

P: One hundred percent! We were talking about my not having achieved Forbes 500 status. So why bother? There's a sense of futility. It's about my own inadequacy. I feel I'm not going to be able to compete, that no one will give me support, and an underlying feeling that I won't have any success. Under that is the feeling of being persecuted, of being inadequate, of being different, of always being an underdog. I'm not supposed to have any luck in business.

As stated elsewhere, the impotent contender is a common cultural stereotype of the gay man. Although this man was very ambitious, he was also uncomfortable with his own competitive feelings. He linked them to his envy and aggression, other feelings that he found intolerable.

Th: The dream is not just about your feelings toward your competitor.

P: He has become a symbol that my success is fleeting and undeserved. Why haven't I done anything in the last few years to expand my own business? I haven't done anything to make it grow, or to find another location, or to find new markets. He has been successfully expanding, and now I'm worried he will knock me out of the ring forever. Realistically, I know there is room for both of us. I shouldn't covet his success. I have my own success. But I don't feel successful. I either feel stagnant or I feel I'm not making progress. I'm taking it too easy. All of that is somewhat true, but emotionally I feel it more strongly. I can't relax and enjoy my success. The level of success I've achieved may be taken away from me. I still feel I'm a fraud in my work.

Th: What do you believe is fraudulent about you?

P: I never got an MBA. My business experience is street-wise. I'm afraid I don't know all the details.

Th: Anything else?

P: Being gay. When I was in the closet, I always felt I was a fraud who would be found out one day. My recent meeting with several potential investors fed into my own sense of inadequacy. I did get a vague sense that I have the potential resources of this powerful investment group. If I were better, I would marshal those resources and do something to feel better. I feel inadequate, because I don't know what to do. I have anxiety about doing anything. I don't know how to make the business more successful.

Transparency, invisibility, losing one's voice, being stuck behind walls or other barriers are some of the terms used to describe the subjective experience of dissociative detachment. The following man felt shamefully transparent. He believed that people could see his imagined defects through his clothing:

Q: I was thinking about how I grew up feeling there was something wrong with me, and how things happened to me that reinforced that. I thought, "Maybe there isn't something wrong with me. You know how I spend all this time worrying if my behaviors are healthy or unhealthy. Maybe I'm not that bad, but then maybe I am.

Th: What do you feel is bad about you?

Q: I've always been ashamed of my body. As a child I would wear heavy sweatshirts, even in the summer, to cover up my body. I don't know where that comes from.

Th: What comes to mind?

Q: I'm bad because I'm effeminate. I'm bad because I'm skinny. I'm ashamed of my body. I feel that even you can see how deformed I am through my clothes. I feel embarrassed. When I listen to myself, it all sounds like self pity. It sounds ridiculous. I'm an adult and I should have come to peace with this. But when I look in the mirror, I still think I'm deformed. It doesn't matter what I wear. It's almost like my body doesn't look good. I feel horrible. I hate that. There's a feeling of shame. The other day I thought, "Is this what I see? Is that what other people see? Is my perception an exaggeration?" A friend of mine said he doesn't know who I am. I said, "Ask!"

Th: Do people have to ask who you are?

Q: Sometimes I feel I have many personalities. They are not distinct but there are so many different components to me. If you follow me into different situations, you will see a different part. I wish I could be the person that I am when I am by myself. Although not all the time, there are times when I am by myself when I feel calm, centered, and very rational. I would like to be more of that person when I am around other people. I am not. I am pulled off center. I am anxious. At times, I am almost paranoid. Imagining that people are thinking, "Who knows what?" Anticipating what I will say and what I will do. It's exhausting, completely exhausting. It keeps me stuck.

Th: When you said people don't see all of you, I was reminded of the sweaters you used to wear to hide your body.

Q: I have this wall around me. Each time something painful happened, I put up a brick. Eventually I had this wall. The wall is all about shame. I have to do something about it. I have to stop feeling ashamed. It's easy to say that, but to not feel ashamed is not easy. I anticipate that people are going to judge me in some way. I try to protect myself from that. The other day, I had to walk past a group of male coworkers. Instead of being friendly and saying "Hello," I became very angry, very tight, very nonapproachable. I was like that on the subway today. There are people with whom you can make eye contact, that you can smile at or give an angry look. I gave an angry look. A look that means "Don't look at me." It's not that I am angry. That is how I protect myself, with an angry look.

Th: What was your concern when you passed your coworkers?

Q: They might have wanted to say "Hello" to me. Some of the men have this macho mentality. But they are not all like that. Some are very macho, but they are open and friendly. Especially when they are in a group. But they remind me of high school and being humiliated by the jocks. I don't know what the point was then, except to humiliate me, to watch me squirm, to watch me turn red.

Invisibility is another metaphor that a gay man may use to communicate difficulties in regulating self-esteem, as was seen in the following patient's account of his high school travails:

R: I have always felt like blending in, not being noticed. I was surprised at how ineffective that was. I can remember lots of time wishing that I wasn't there physically; that I wouldn't be the object of derision. I remember not responding to my tormentors at all, just to lessen the ordeal. I guess my only strategy in high school was to disappear.

Th: How did you disappear?.

R: I was always picked on in high school, especially in gym because I wasn't athletic. So I stopped going to gym, and instead went to play with the orchestra. That is an example of my actually disappearing. I would never fight back. Once I got so angry, I hit back. That seemed to give the guy permission to hurt me even more. So I disappeared by not hitting back. I disappeared into silence by becoming a punching bag. Letting people hit me. I was talking to someone the other day who told me how many friends he still had from high school. I don't have any. Not even from college. I disappeared by not holding onto friendships. I guess I was preoccupied with protecting myself, not saying anything that would expose myself or leave me to ridicule, to a situation that might lead me to surprise and embarrassment.

Closeting oneself does not only hide one's sexual identity. For some, it also conceals traumatic memories of not fitting in, or of being attacked and harassed in childhood. Such linkages were seen in another patient's recollection of a dream:

S: I had a dream in which my boss caught me shitting on my desk. I'm sure the dream ties in with the whole gay thing. It relates to the fact that mother made us keep secrets from my father. My father wouldn't allow us to order take-out food. But when he left the house, Mom would order it for us. We would get a treat but she would say, " Don't tell Dad we did this."

Th: It was a secret pleasure.

S: It wasn't out in the open. There were lots of times she said "Don't tell your father, don't tell your father." The good things had to be kept secret.

Th: If they are not kept secret, it is like shitting on the desk.

S: My view is dirty. Oh my god, this feeling I'm having is so sick. It's sick. It feels awful.

Th: You feel you are sick and dirty.

S: But it also makes me mad that people made me feel like that. They trained me to feel like that. It was many years before I came out and realized I was gay. "Poor me." That is what I feel, "Poor me." Why did people do that to me? That's why I pick the wrong people for me. It's related to that. I feel nobody took care of me when I was growing up. (Begins to cry) I was like a little kid in the middle of traffic, with nobody there to help him. That makes me sad.

In *Stranger at the Gate* (White, 1994), a religious gay man who frequently tried dissociating his sexual, aggressive, and anxious feelings draws attention to another of the closet's recurrent themes, that of "the good boy":

For me, arriving on the Mt. Tabor campus of Warner Pacific College was "turning my face to Jerusalem." I wanted more than anything in the world to serve Jesus and His church with my whole heart, mind, and body. I knew my heart and mind were pointed in the right direction, but that first night in that little dorm room with my handsome, new roommate, I was terrified again to learn that my body just didn't want to go with the program.

That men's dormitory, with shared room, shared showers, and shared halls filled with young men in various stages of undress was a real challenge. Still, not once in those four, long years was any one of them, even the most vulnerable, in any kind of danger from me. I hated when my body responded naturally to the beautiful young men in that place. I felt guilty that I was attracted to them in spite of my discipline and determination to the contrary. I was constantly afraid that they would see the conflict in my eyes. I lay awake at night, praying that God would take away my unwanted, unworthy passion. And in the daytime, I worked to prove myself a good person in spite of it [p. 68].

Good boys do not openly express their anger, they do not challenge authority directly, and they frequently experience the rough and tumble of everyday life as excess aggression. As one gay man's angry feelings emerged from a closet constructed of his unwillingness to draw attention to himself, he was less willing to be demeaned by others:

W: I've been paying attention to how I beat up on myself. I made a conscious effort not to do it a couple of times, and I stopped doing it. You had asked, "What do I get out of participating in it?" I don't get anything out of it. My ex-boyfriend called me to go to the movies. We had a big argument on the way. Because I'm down on myself, I realize how much I let him berate me. We got to the point where he began criticizing me. I said to myself, "I won't talk to myself like this anymore and I'm not going to let him talk to me that way." I told him, "I'm not going to the movies with you." I turned the car around and went home.

Struggling to rid oneself of unwanted affects often leaves a person feeling inadequate, incomplete, or less than whole:

U: I'm enraged at my life, enraged.

Th: What enrages you about it?

U: It's been too good, too goody-good. Mr. Goody Two Shoes has done everything by the rules. He went to the college his parents wanted. He didn't do the drugs and drinking. As a kid, he put a lid on it. That's what angers me. I did everything by the book. My mother was watching, the teachers were watching, God was watching. If I didn't do right, I would go to hell. All those years saying I wasn't gay, instead of trying to make it part of my life. Maybe I would have been happier as a kid. At least I would have been able to explore my sexuality to some degree. There's nothing I can do about it now. I'm tired, just tired. I think about everybody and I get angry at them.

This patient's time in treatment led him to feel more comfortable with his anger and he subsequently explored the sources of his original uneasiness with that feeling:

Th: That anger used to be directed at yourself. You would tell yourself that you are not good. You are not satisfying. You are not who you should be.

U: That's true. I guess that's an improvement. (Sigh) But my interactions with people have become so erratic and volatile now. Sometimes I think I'm behaving like a bastard when I get angry.

Th: Feeling like Mr. Goody Two Shoes or feeling like a bastard represent extremes. Neither one of them represents the whole person that you are.

U: I know what you mean.

This gay man continued to feel discomfort with his own anger. Ironically, just as he went to great lengths to ward off his same-sex feelings before he came out, now he used similar dissociative operations to keep himself from feeling angry.

Th: What's making you angry?

U: Somehow this has to do with being a gay person, living in a society where people are battered for being gay. Somehow it gives the feeling of anger so much more intensity. It seems like it was worsened because you were gay. You were sick, perverse, slimy. Maybe what it did was taint everything.

Th: You mean it was not just your affectionate feelings that were perverse. All your feelings were perverse.

U: It's bizarre. How could you be normal? Everything you feel is warped.

Some people may experience their sexual desires as a compulsive force, outside their conscious control. Their sexual activities can take place in a reverie state, a severe dissociative phenomenon that significantly interferes with developing a sense of self. The following gay man was severely traumatized in childhood, and had great difficulties integrating many of his feelings into his self-image. The pleasures associated with his early experiences of furtive sexual activity led to his defensive pattern of dealing with uncomfortable emotional states by engaging in anonymous sex. When he entered the sexual underworld, he deliberately lost sight of the rest of his identity:

V: I had gone out with friends and I suddenly got that overwhelming sex drive when I got home. Although I knew it was stupid, I got dressed and went to a porno theater. It was the most awful one I've ever been to. No, I've been to another theater that was more awful. But this was a stage set for sleaze. There were homeless people and people who were on drugs there. I asked myself, "What did you expect?"

The patient described both surprise and annoyance with himself after he arrived at the pornographic movie theater and then "suddenly" remembered what he might find there.

Th: Had you been to that theater before?

V: Months ago. Upstairs, there are two bathrooms where people sit in the stalls waiting for guys to come by and blow them. Downstairs, they have an awful basement with corridors. That felt unsafe. This was a dirty and sleazy set. If a set designer created it, it would be almost too much.

Th: You experienced going there as a piece of theater?

V: Yes.

Th: What role were you playing?

V: Maybe I would meet someone who would blow me or I would blow them. But no one was interesting. I've been there several times, and nothing ever happens. I tell myself, "You know more efficient ways to get sex. I saw an ad in the *Village Voice* that said, "Blond hunk looking to meet successful older man."

Th: Had you thought about calling the blond hunk instead of going to the movie theater?

V: That would be too serious a commitment. The movie theater is less committing. But answering the ad, that's a commitment. When I was younger, I loved the idea that these guys wanted to suck me. I felt like I was sort of powerful. I liked that. It felt like I had a scenario or a scene, that I could fall into. That I didn't have to be concerned with what I really wanted.

Th: What you describe feels a little like a daydream.

A reverie state can be solely confined to one's imagination, like a daydream. It can be subjectively experienced as a private, psychological space where the inflexible circumstances of everyday life do not apply. However, in this case, the patient's reverie took place in a sexual arena where other men were actors in his fantasy while he played a role in theirs:

V: Yeah. There was an understanding that I had some kind of power. That somebody would get on their knees and I would say, "Suck that dick boy." I think they felt sort of lucky. I think that's what I should have now.

Th: Are you saying you feel powerless and you need to feel powerful?

V: (Laughs, and then yells angrily) I would say that! Yes! I'm not even happy talking to you about it now. I feel like I'm pushing myself into making sense of how I live my everyday life. This is a stupid way of living!

The patient became angry as his attention was drawn to something he did not wish to attend. Nor did he wish to integrate the enacted fantasies of his reverie state into his ongoing experience of himself. He was also angrily judgmental of his own behaviors when he and the therapist talked about them openly:

V: Yes, I feel powerless, no question, no question. I don't have too many friends anymore, just the same old friends, thank goodness. It would be terrific if I had one very special friend. There wouldn't have to be any sex at all. I just want to know that he'll be there and be encouraging.

Th: In the past, these sexual experiences made your feelings of helplessness go away. That no longer seems to be the case.

V: I still hope I can meet someone who might want to suck my dick. I hate talking about this!

Th: You don't want to talk about this?

V: I'll talk about it! But it's hard for me to say why I go back to the porno theater. There's a possibility that something might happen, like years ago, somebody sucking me.

Th: How do you tell yourself that it might happen?

V: I'll throw myself in there. Part of it is that you don't have to think. This is blind habit.

Th: I'm trying to draw your attention to how you are not thinking in those moments. It's almost as if you went there in a trance.

V: I'll admit it. There is a trance-like state.

Th: You don't want to understand your trances?

V: I think the function they serve now is a desperate attempt to recapture the person I used to be. But I always had a little trance. It used to be more satisfying. It was somebody sucking my dick. It was a definite interest. People were interested. They were after me. Definitely trance-like. It was like jumping into a pool and not having to think about how to swim. There would be a certain kind of—something that would feel OK for that time. Then it is over. You get out of the pool and you go home. I do not think I was ever excited about the attractiveness of other people. Attractiveness didn't matter if they were going to blow me. Come on you nameless people, "Blow me!" Right now, when I go to the porno theater, its like throwing myself in the pool. It's going to be like a wave.

The patient's experience of riding on a wave was accompanied by a surge of feeling. Yet as the emotional wave crested, his tone became more subdued:

V: You know, the porno theater doesn't work. It doesn't give me what it gave me before, and yet I do go. The trance thing is a good image, like someone in a trance. "Go!," and I'll be in this atmosphere. It was very much a part of my life. Getting blowjobs anonymously was very much a part of my life. It was really like hiding, going into the pool.

The Closet and Anonymous Sex

The above patient used anonymous sexual activity to shore up his self-esteem. There are other reasons why some gay men feel drawn to anonymous sexual activities. Few families, even non-puritanical ones, will sanction a gay teenager's search for physical or close emotional intimacy with a member of the same sex. Hiding his sexuality during important developmental years may lead a gay man into prolonged periods in which he furtively expresses his need for sexuality and intimacy. Forbidden sexual activities, often taking place during critical times in adolescence and young adulthood, can impede linkages between the need for intimacy and sexual feelings. The following gay man's dream illustrated how he never connected sexuality and emotional intimacy during his early developmental experiences:

> **Y:** I had an interesting dream last night. It was at a department store in the video equipment section. Actually my equipment is on the blink, which makes it hard for me to watch my porno videos. Here I am at this middle class department store, and it turns out they have porn video rentals. I ask to look at the book that listed the available rentals. The first section is heterosexual, and the back section is gay. I don't see any films that excite me, so I have to go behind the counter where it is more sleazy and rundown. I'm back there and looking, and then I see boxes under the counter in the back. I think there are more videos in there. I ask if I can look through them and they say, "Sure." I start looking and it turns out they are not videos, but valentine cards. It wasn't porn. I was kind of disappointed. I thought there were going to be more videos and there weren't. Part of what I felt in the dream was "I don't have any use for these." When I woke up, I thought of love and sex being in two different places. I didn't have any use for or any need for these valentine cards because I don't have a lover. Of course the symbolism of being behind the counter and in a sleazy area has to do with porn videos. That is not uncommon in my dreams. Sex is behind the counter. It is hidden.

> **Th:** What was the feeling in the dream?

> **Y:** I was disappointed with the selection. I was disappointed that there weren't more. Maybe there was a little sense of shame. I would have to go behind something. I don't know if there are any other feelings. I think it is not a feeling but the separation of sex and love. If anything, the valentines were more remote and hidden than the videos were. When I don't have any love, all that is left is sex.

A year later, after ending a brief relationship, this gay man returned to the theme of connecting his sexual desires and his need for emotional intimacy:

> **Y:** He was really the only man that I spent much time with. In fact, he's the only one, since I came out, that I really developed a relationship with and slept with.

> **Th:** You were very anxious about that relationship.

Y: I think I got used to that kind of anxiety in some ways. I came out of that relationship feeling better about myself. After those three months with him, I know how much I like cuddling and holding. I know I can connect loving and sexuality.

Many patients, regardless of gender or sexual orientation, struggle to integrate a need for emotional intimacy in a long-term relationship with a need for sexual contact outside the relationship.

Z: I guess I still have some of my early experience of gay sexuality in me, which is "the more the merrier." As I get older, I think at some level it is a confirmation that I can still do it. I can still attract the bees. I have very mixed feelings. We talk about integrating all facets of myself. This is an aspect of me. Last week I told you I thought I could make a choice. The strong feeling I have about the stability in my home life is something worth preserving and that might mean giving up something. I don't see a way to reconcile these two feelings. Sometimes I feel there is an element of my religious upbringing here. The element of sin and redemption, sin and forgiveness.

Th: What are the feelings that are at odds with each other?

Z: Good question. I think it would be hard to locate the feelings. One word that came to my mind is resentment. I feel my freedom impinged, restricted. There is a connection here to compulsivity, a feeling of being in the grip of some compulsion that actually satisfies some need.

Th: Compulsion in what sense?

Z: The sexual hunt, when it takes over, is a compulsion. It practically obscures everything else. It becomes very strong. I don't have a strong sexual feeling for my lover. What I get from him is a feeling of security that is different from a sexual encounter. A feeling of protection. A very nice feeling of being taken care of.

This gay man called his wish to stray from his primary relationship a sexual compulsion. He also wished to feel exciting, attractive, free and unburdened by any commitments. He could not integrate these two self-images.

Z: My lover had to work very late the other night. I was angry about that. I felt he should have stayed home with me. So before he came home, I went out and had a sexual encounter.

Th: Was there any relationship between how you were feeling when you went out and your sexual encounter?

Z: It was like a license. He was going to be out late and I thought, "I don't have to report to you now." I saw it as an open window of opportunity.

Instead of feeling my anger and disappointment, it was a sudden feeling of being freed. I'm also in a relationship because I'm afraid of suddenly being freed. If I wasn't in a relationship, I'd be compulsively out every night. Being in a good relationship, where I feel protected and cared for, protects me from my own compulsive feelings.

Th: You almost describe your lover as if he were your baby-sitter.

Z: In a sense, he is. He is an element of stability. He is a check. When I step out, he gets angry. My unspoken response was, "Be angry. So we won't live together." Then my anxiety kicks in and I think, "What if he wasn't here?"

This patient designated the lover as the guardian of the couple's commitment who, at the same time, obstructed the patient's desire for outside contact. When they struggled over his freedom of movement, the patient's internal struggle was enacted interpersonally. He dissociated from those feelings and only then did he feel freed up. He then proceeded to have a sexual encounter that fulfilled his need for variety but also served to enact the anger that he could not directly express toward his lover.

Regrettably, psychoanalysis' countertransferential idealization of monogamy has been inadequately studied. Consequently, many therapist's may not respect a patient's wishes for sexual diversity. This is unconsciously expressed by pejoratively labeling a patient's non-monogamous sexual behaviors as "compulsions," "acting out," or "resistance" (Drescher, 1997a). Therapists may privilege a patient's wish for monogamous relationships over his other sexual and intimate desires. In this case, the patient also wanted the therapist to play the part of baby-sitter. However, it was preferable to avoid being drawn into that enactment and instead to accept both the patient's desire for sexual novelty and excitement, as well as his longing for a protected, monogamous relationship. This stance ultimately helped the patient to acknowledge his own contradictory wishes. If the patient's contradictions were experienced as acceptable to the therapist, then the patient did not have to dissociate from his feelings and could derive some insights about them.

Z: Then I feel the allure of something that is dangerous. Something that is not controlled. Sexual compulsivity. Somehow I don't make a connection between sexual conduct and love.

Th: What you call "sexual compulsivity" is a behavior that emerges when you can't tolerate your feelings of anger, disappointment, resentment, or deprivation. You don't connect those feelings with love, but with sex.

Z: (Silent) That's true. That's like opening a trunk. It gives a new slant on why I can feel so close to my lover, and yet I don't feel sexually interested. I don't make a connection between loving someone and having sex with them. I've never really felt expressive in that way. You said "deprivation." Yes, sexual compulsivity is triggered by feelings of deprivation. One is lonely and sex can assuage that feeling. I don't equate love with sex.

The Closet and Gay-Bashing

For some gay men, "Hiding and passing as heterosexual becomes a life-long moral hatred of the self; a maze of corruptions, petty lies, and half truths that spoil social relations in family and friendship" (Herdt and Boxer, 1993, p. 21). One writer recalls:

> I was not about to accept the fact that I was gay. . . . I pursued what I thought was "normal" with a vengeance in high school, determined that, if the spirit was weak, the flesh would be more willing at the prospect of heterosexuality. I dated every girl I could literally get my hands on, earning a well-deserved reputation as a jerk who tried to see how far he could get on the first date. I attacked anyone who suggested that gay people might be entitled to some rights, too, and was the biggest teller of fag jokes at Radford High. But what I really hated was myself, and this I couldn't escape from, no matter how drunk or stoned I got, which I was doing on an almost daily basis by senior year [Jennings, 1994, p. 4].

There are many gay men who, before they came out, were either gay-baiters or gay-bashers themselves:

X: In college there were two guys living together, who I guess were gay. Even though I had bought my first gay porno magazine at age 14, I heckled them. I yelled, "Faggot."

Th: What was that about?

X: I was attracted to one of them, and scared to approach him. My reaction was to harass them.

Classically, this defense was defined as "identification with the aggressor" (A. Freud, 1966). However, the dynamics underlying this behavior are better explained by Sullivan's (1953) concept of the "malevolent transformation":

> A child may discover that manifesting the need for tenderness toward the potent figures around him leads frequently to his being disadvan-

taged, being made anxious, being made fun of, and so on, so that according to the locution used, he is hurt, or in some cases he may be literally hurt. Under those circumstances, the developmental course changes to the point that the perceived need for tenderness brings a foresight of anxiety or pain. The child learns, you see, that it is highly disadvantageous to show any need for tender cooperation from the authoritative figures around him, in which case he shows something else; and that something else is the basic malevolent attitude, that attitude that one really lives among enemies—that is about what it amounts to [p. 214].

Attacking those perceived to be gay serves several functions. Interpersonally, it may represent an effort to control perceptions of the gay-basher's own sexual identity. This would translate into "If I attack gay people, no one will think I am gay," or "Being gay is not-me." Intrapsychically, this is an attempt to maintain a psychological distance from one's own homoerotic feelings.

Th: If you were attracted to one of them, why did you harass them?

X: I wanted to have sex with them, but I couldn't. I was scared of who I was, of my sexuality.

Th: What scared you about it?

X: Rejection by my family. (Silent) Now I'm getting angry at the comments my family members made about gays. My father once said, "What do they do? Sit down to pee, as a woman does?" I have this image that all the males in my family are anti-gay. I guess I feel a teeny bit of anger in that I never had anyone to talk to. I didn't feel I could talk to the people around me. All I could remember was the negative comments. I'm feeling like a kid who only wanted to be heard, somebody to listen. I guess harassing those guys was about trying to meet other gay people. I wanted to, but I didn't know how. So I felt alone.

Conclusion

The dissociative operations that create an individual's closet are ubiquitous. Unfortunately, the very real factors that exacerbate these defenses in gay men are underreported in the analytic literature. This too is an example of selective inattention worthy of a detailed inquiry in itself. It is also important to emphasize again that a person's sexual attractions are not pathognomonic of any defensive style. This chapter's focus on the way gay men may dissociate to maintain their secret, sexual identities should not obscure the fact that gay men are a heterogeneous group. Denial, intellectualization, rationalization, and other defenses are as likely to be found in gay men as they are in heterosexual patients. Having noted this, however, many gay men do have a history of being subjected to events, traumatic or otherwise, that exaggerated the normal tendency to screen anxiety-provoking and shameful memories.

Psychoanalysts know that traumatic experiences that heighten dissociative operations can also lower an individual's self-esteem. Consequently, the patient who comes to understand his own self-hatred, and the dissociative maneuvers used to defend against it, can obtain a wider view of himself. This can occur if a patient feels increasingly visible and heard in the therapeutic setting. The closet, however, is a victim's hiding place and some people will hide in it, even when it is no longer necessary to do so. To gain a more accurate view of his adult self, the gay man in psychotherapy need not embrace the victim's role. Although a patient may have been victimized in the past, and perhaps is also being victimized in the present, he may need to learn how he may be actively participating in his own victimization. A therapist's consensual validation of past victimization can help a patient put his current emotional and interpersonal participation in perspective. A patient's need to hide in the present may be based on reasonable concerns about being found out, as in the case of gay men who serve in the military. But in order to help a patient determine the accurate assessment of danger in other settings, the therapist needs to understand the defensive purpose of the dissociative operations that maintain the gay man's closeted state of mind. By helping the patient become more comfortable with his own feelings, a process of self-awareness may ensue that can increase a gay man's self-esteem and the quality of his relationships.

10

COMING OUT

The rituals of coming out are so distinctive of
American culture that they deserve a special status in
the archives of anthropology.

> Gilbert Herdt and Andrew Boxer,
> *Children of Horizons* (1993)

I've come to believe it's better to be hated for what you
really are than loved for what you pretend to be.

> Darrell Yates Rist, *Heartlands* (1992)

I felt that I had stepped over a threshold, through a
door that suddenly opened from the shadowy darkness
to a brighter technicolor world filled with possibilities.
What do I do about it? Do I say, "Listen, I am one of
them. Look at me. I am still one of them—a faggot, a
newly born and lucky faggot." Although I didn't say
any of that, I experienced a very real sense of joy and
liberation in the knowledge that I could if and when I
wanted to.

> Marvin Liebman, *Coming Out Conservative* (1992)

"Coming out" may be the most commonly shared cultural
experience defining the modern gay identity. It marks the beginning of
openly transgressing heterosexually constructed categories of gender and
sexuality. In its everyday usage, coming out or "coming out of the closet"

means telling another person that one is gay. There is quite an extensive literature of coming out stories that includes novels (Vidal, 1948; Rechy, 1963; Warren, 1974; Holleran, 1978; Kramer, 1978; Maupin, 1978; Leavitt, 1986), plays (Crowley, 1968; Fierstein, 1983; Kushner, 1992a,b), autobiographies and biographies (Ackerley, 1968; Crisp, 1968; Brown, 1976; Kantrowitz, 1977; Duberman, 1991; Preston, 1991; Jarman, 1992; Liebman, 1992; Monette, 1992; Bawer, 1993; Hooven, 1993; Mass, 1994; Singer, 1994; White, 1994; Goldman, 1995; Isay, 1996), histories, journalistic documentaries, and social commentaries (Silverstein, 1981; Shilts, 1982, 1993; White, 1991; Rist, 1992; Signorile, 1993, 1997; Woods and Lucas, 1993; Browning, 1994; Duberman, 1994; Sullivan, 1995; Eskridge, 1996).

Spending many years in the closet can make the prospect of revealing oneself an emotionally charged experience. However, the process is not just about revealing oneself to others. For in coming out, a gay man integrates, as best as he can, the dissociated aspects of the self. In Sullivan's terms, the not-me becomes me. Anthropologists and social scientists such as Herdt and Boxer (1993) classify coming out as a ritual *process of passage* that requires a gay man to (1) unlearn the principles of natural or essentialist heterosexuality, (2) unlearn the stereotypes of homosexuality and (3) learn the ways of the lesbian and gay culture they are entering. Coming out is rarely given much attention in the psychoanalytic literature, although the following remarks are a thoughtful exception:

> The [act of] coming out represents a process of consciousness in which the homosexual recognizes himself and presents himself as such. The process reveals whether or not homosexuality is consistent with the internalized image of one's own person and with societal reality. . . . If this step is successful, a reorientation in the life of the homosexual takes place. It is no longer primarily a matter of whether and how to be recognized and whether one feels socially accepted or discriminated against. For homosexuals it becomes increasingly a matter of striving for the arrangement of a love life free from the socially delineated modes of behavior, even though they follow them in all other matters of daily life [Morgenthaler, 1988, p. 67].

This chapter explores some intrapsychic and interpersonal aspects of the coming out process. There are many kinds of coming out stories and a range of temporal relationships between a gay man's first sexual contacts, his coming out to himself, and his coming out to others. For a gay man, coming out will not only involve his sexual identity, but will include other aspects of his personality as well. And when one is gay in a heterosexual world, one repeatedly faces moments in which one has to decide whether or not to reveal himself. Consequently, coming out is an ongoing process that potentially never ends.

True and False Selves

Sullivan (1956) would say that anxiety causes the infant to dissociate from his own needs. Winnicott would say the infant hides his true self (1960b). These experiences lead to the development of an interpersonally compliant infant. The infant's true self, or what Sullivan referred to as authenticity, is felt to be unacceptable to the maternal holding environment. Winnicott says this leads to a pattern of hiding one's needs from both the self and the other. Sullivan would say that traits or desires that cannot be revealed to others cannot be acknowledged or integrated into the self.

The early, compliant false self can serve as a template for organizing a child's later experiences. A need to hide in childhood and adolescence can intensify the defensive mechanisms acquired during an earlier developmental epoch. In other words, as a child matures, he may learn that some of his emotions are unacceptable to others. In the experience of gay men, dissociative defenses are stressed by a greater than average need to hide their feelings. And because young children do not know how to distinguish their different emotional states from each other, dissociating from one feeling can lead to dissociating from others as well. Thus when a gay patient does decide to come out, he will likely find that other feelings, hitherto kept in various states of dissociation, will also emerge. Consider the following patient who has yet to come out:

Bill: That's how I've lived most of my life. If somebody wants to do something, I go "OK, OK." Other people go first, I go second.

Th: What makes it necessary that other people go first?

Bill: I don't feel comfortable being the one out front. In some things I do, but in my personal life I don't. I can be out front by myself, but not with a group. I can do what I want if I'm by myself, but when I'm with people, I will go with what the group says. I am not going to assert myself with the group. It's uncomfortable for me to do that. I don't know why. I'm not going to say what I want. I think what difference does it make what I want if "It's only for Bill?"

Th: This feeling that "It's only for Bill" is painful.

Bill: It's a sense of being abandoned, a sense of not counting. It's lonely. It's sad. Empty.

Th: Are there any images that come to mind?

Bill: An image of me as a young boy, sitting on the side of the road in the desert, sitting on a curb.

Th: What is the boy doing on the curb?

Bill: He has his legs together and his knees turned in. He is hunched over, chewing a fingernail, looking around, feeling abandoned.

Th: How did he get there?

Bill: I don't know. His parents put him there.

Th: They left him there?

Bill: That's what it feels like. All I can see is my mother. I don't even see my father. I see my parents when they were much younger. My mother looking for my father who is not there. She was very lonely. The household I come from was about a lot of loneliness and abandonment. I think my parents abandoned us. My mother was so lonely, she was always chasing after my father. She couldn't give to us, and my father couldn't give to anybody. Even at that time, I wasn't a person who was out and around. I played with the kids in the neighborhood, but something kept me from being in the core of the group. I'd do things with them, but I wasn't the core. That is how my life has been. I've never been the one they rallied around. This feeling of being abandoned. Something about that feeling keeps me from jumping in.

Th: You say to yourself that you are "only Bill."

Bill: Why do I treat myself that way? Maybe I don't treat myself well. I tell people, "You don't have to treat me well." Do they do it to me or do I do it to myself? I kind of think that is how my parents treated me. My brother was so obnoxious and someone had to be the good one, the quiet one. For the sake of my mother.

In a Winnicottian narrative, the compliant false self puts others' needs before one's own. The patient's feeling that he was "only Bill" was linked to a childhood idea that he had to take care of his mother. However, no matter what he did, he always felt her attention was constantly focused elsewhere:

Bill: My brother graduated from high school and didn't get any awards. My mother said, "When my Bill graduates, he'll get something." So I joined a couple of extracurricular groups. I gave the awards to her and said, "Are you happy?" Her needs were more important.

Th: They weren't your awards, they were your mother's awards.

Bill: I figured out how to do it. Then, I got them and I gave them to my mother. But when I got those awards, nobody else celebrated that with me.

(Angrily) Nobody celebrated me. Why was I celebrating anyone else? That is a lot of the abandonment feeling. Now I'm angry. Now I'm mad. I'm very angry. I was always doing for others. I was there for them all the time, but nobody was there for me. People who treat me that way leave me with a feeling that "I was only Bill."

The only thing inevitable about the process of coming out is the need to break with expectations that all sexual identities be heterosexual ones. Coming out, in the broadest sense, can be integrative and lead to greater acknowledgment of the patient's affective range. But individual variations in defensive structure, as well as internal and family dynamics will play themselves out in different ways, if and when a particular gay man decides to come out. A therapist needs to sort out the different levels involved. For example, a patient can use coming out as a vehicle for maintaining compliant defenses, for expressing anger, or for other purposes as well. That is to say that declaring one's sexual identity as gay, in and of itself, does not necessarily have to lead to integration. It can, instead, express compliance, anger, or resentment. Thus, for the above patient, coming out will not only be complicated by his compliance, embodied in his wish to win awards for his mother, but by his underlying anger and resentment which he does not wish to reveal. He will presumably learn, if he does come out further, that unwanted feelings, sexual or otherwise, will not disappear and that if they are not integrated into his emerging gay identity, they may nevertheless emerge in other ways.

First Contact: Coming Out to Oneself

Coming out to oneself is described as a subjective experience of inner recognition. It is a moment that is sometimes charged with excitement and at other times with trepidation. It is a realization that previously unacceptable feelings or desires are part of one's self. As illustrated by the following, self-awareness can sometimes be a frightening prospect:

B: In the dream, I'm some sort of secret agent and I'm looking down from the sky, at what I perceive to be a French park. It's deserted except for a *gendarme*, and this fellow who turns out to be Captain Hastings. He's Poirot's right-hand man, an affable upper-class Englishman who is not real bright. Suddenly, instead of looking from on high, I'm driving a limousine up to Captain Hastings in the park. He gets in the car. I become Captain Hastings and he becomes the driver. I become aware that he might not be a trustworthy confederate in the spy business. We keep changing places. I become him and he becomes me. Then he drops me off at a building which turns out to be a geriatric home. I have been given a pill or some sort of treatment to make me age quickly. Too quickly. I have to go here for a cure.

The scene shifts and Captain Hastings and I are at some sort of bar or lunch counter. Suddenly these FBI types, or the opposing secret agency forces pretending to be FBI, rush up on me. Behind them are newsmedia people, or people pretending to be newsmedia people. They are acting as if I was caught doing something wrong. They slap this gadget on me. It electronically reads your fingertips, like a glove, and they go, "Ah ha! You are my man." Suddenly there is an earthquake. The glove falls off and the FBI guys run off. The building at this point does something to guard itself. It has locked itself shut. Plate glass walls go up to prevent you from getting out. I do some secret agent thing. The building is on the top of a hill and all the land slopes down from it. I roll down a hill to a ravine and go up another hill to the hideout. You can see the building so well from the hideout that you think anyone can see you.

The themes of the dream illustrate many of the issues in the struggle to come out: hideouts, secret lives, who can or cannot be trusted, an unwanted identification with the fop, changing identities, anxieties about getting old, finding a cure, foes disguised as friends, the fear of being either caught, found out, publicly exposed or arrested, a feeling of impending disaster if discovered, a wish to escape from one's own self, a sense of fragility about one's identity, and uncertainty if one's hiding place is safe.

Th: What comes to mind about the dream?

B: It seems obvious to me. It's about the things we've been discussing. The idea of being gay; the question of exposing that; the question of keeping a secret place in yourself that does not seem to be growing and the connection of that experience with childhood. Without really knowing it, you end up back there. My straight life can be maintained. The association to the bar is to drinking which also brings up the subject of gayness. Being drunk is the only time when I had gay sex. The Captain Hastings character is a gay character, he's not at all trustworthy. He's me, other people seeing some reflection of me. It is not a trustworthy image. The foppishness of Captain Hastings. He's a dandy, almost a cartoon character. That is how I look at a lot of gay men, this dandy image and nothing behind it that would be desirable to know.

Although he may not think of himself as gay, a homosexually self-aware man can engage in sexual activities well before he comes out to himself:

A: I remember my first kiss from a man. I felt shame, even though that kiss had gone right to my very soul. I was in a men's room in the suburbs.

This guy came in and it started out just as a sexual encounter. Then he kissed me and it was a passionate kiss, a French kiss. Something just clicked, and when I came out of it, I was dazed. When he left, I went out looking for him. This man had shown me something. It scared me so much, I got out the yellow pages and started looking for a therapist.

Th: What scared you?

A: I had my first blowjob years earlier in a men's room. That kiss meant that it wasn't just sex, it was also affection. It was connecting in a way I'd never connected with anyone before.

Th: Before the kiss, you told yourself it was just about sex.

A: That was what I hoped. I had to bury the idea that I might be gay. To suppress it further, I had to get in therapy. I felt something happened in that men's room with that kiss. A truth that I saw but didn't want to see. There was that moment of recognition. I thought, "This is what really turns me on. This is where my sexual energy connects." Recognition was powerful and it was scary and I immediately got into therapy.

Among other possible responses, discovery of a previously hidden or dissociated aspect of the self may cause a flight into therapy. Patients often want a therapist to put the genie back into the bottle. This was the case of another patient, a thirty-year-old married man and father, who sought treatment for his anxiety. During the six months before the initial consultation, he had become increasingly involved, both sexually and emotionally, with another man. He had a history of anonymous sexual relations with other men since adolescence, and all through his eight-year marriage. Although he was no longer sexually interested in his wife, he was not prepared to end their marriage because he wanted to keep his family intact.

At the initial consultation, he reported that two years earlier, he began thinking of himself as "bisexual." But he was seeking help at this time because he wanted to stop obsessing about a man with whom he was becoming increasingly involved. With a great deal of embarrassment, he told the therapist he was beginning to think "I might be gay." When the therapist asked how he had previously understood his many years of same-sex activities, he sheepishly replied "I thought I was just fooling around."

This is one man's way of defining his sexual identity; after engaging in homosexual activities for more than a decade, he was only beginning to think of himself as gay. He initially defined his same-sex interests and activities as "fooling around." By this he meant that he had thought of himself as normal and believed that a normal man will seek out any sexual outlet he can find. These sexual contacts with other men preceded his coming out to himself. Only after many years did he begin considering the possibility that he might be "bisexual." Bisexual men are often neglected and misunderstood in the psychoanalytic literature (but see Friedman, 1988; Money, 1988). However, some men adopt a bisexual identity as a transitional one. "Bisexual" is an accurate description of this man's behavior since he was having sex with his wife and other men during the same period of time. However, he was not bisexual in his sexual attractions and fantasies. He told the therapist he always thought about men when having sex with his wife or when masturbating. In retrospect, calling himself bisexual kept him from thinking that he might be gay.

This man's dilemma illustrates how culture and language shape sexual identities. Coming out is, in part, a verbal process, that puts into words one's previously inarticulated feelings and ideas. "The false self becomes established as a semantic construction made of linguistic propositions about who one is and what one does and experiences. The true self becomes a conglomerate of disavowed experiences of self which cannot be linguistically encoded" (Stern, 1985, p. 227). Coming out is a process of recapturing disavowed experiences. This is done through an ongoing process of linguistic coding that gives what were once unacceptable feelings new meanings. The patient's progression toward a gay identity is shaped by the linguistic markers he had previously learned, as well as the new ones he is contemplating. For example, he previously treated his same-sex attractions as if they meant, "I'm not gay. I'm just a normal, horny guy." Then their meaning changed to "I am bisexual." Now, two years later, his perceptions are changing and he thinks those same feelings mean "I am gay."

Different cultures, using different linguistic markers, produce different sexual identities. Chauncey's *Gay New York* (1994), a work we have previously cited in this text and an important study of cultural definitions of homosexuality, provides a picturesque view of the homosexual scene of the late 19th and early 20th century. In that world, sexual identities were more likely to be based upon what are now called gender roles, rather than upon sexual attractions. Fairies and pansies were men who acted effeminately. Outwardly, queers were conventionally masculine in dress and manner, but they too desired other men. A third category was the normal man. Under certain circumstances, a normal man would have sex with other men, although he did not "really" desire them. It was understood that a normal man only had sex with another man as a matter of convenience, or when he was drunk, or for money, and that his primary sexual interest was in women. And regardless of what went on behind closed doors, it was publicly understood that a normal man would only perform as an inserter with another man.

In that culture's frame of reference, the married man discussed above was never a fairy or pansy. Until two years ago, he thought of himself as a sexual inserter and would have been defined as normal in *Gay New York*'s frame of reference. In fact, in the ethnic enclave in which this particular patient lived, a normal man could "fool around" and still avoid being called gay. In that community's cultural frame of reference, two men could engage in homosexual behaviors but only one of them had to be gay. Sex between a normal man and a gay man was understood to describe their performative gender roles, not necessarily their sexual attractions. However, the married man noted above sought treatment because he now had begun to think of himself as "a queer," from Chauncey's frame of reference. From this patient's cultural perspective, gay meant he was becoming like a woman and developing affectionate feelings for a man. To him, this meant he was taking on a feminine gender role. His anxiety was partially provoked by what he experienced as a lowering of his masculine status. The patient was not experiencing a change in his sexual orientation, rather he was undergoing a significant change in what his sexual feelings meant to him.

Coming out to himself may precede a gay man's first sexual contact. In those cases, men report a long-standing fear that they might be gay or "homosexual." Their fear prevented them from acting on their feelings. Sometimes, the moment of coming out to oneself is a sexually exciting one. Some gay men describe it as a switch being turned on. They may experience it a powerful realization of "who I really am:"

> **C:** I had fucked women all through high school, college and graduate school. It was an ordeal, since half the time I couldn't get it up. I pretended to have girlfriends all this time. And I was closeted for the whole time. Then one day I went to another town on business. I went to a gay bar. I loved that gay bar.
>
> **Th:** What did you love about it?
>
> **C:** The feeling of freedom. I didn't feel I had to hide anything. I loved it. I was working for an ultra-straight firm at the time that was hinting that I should get married. I moved to that other town, moved to the gay neighborhood and went to gay bars every weekend. Then I moved to New York where I essentially went out all the time.

Frequently, a sexual contact in an unfamiliar setting can trigger the process of coming out to oneself. A man had been involved in homosexual activities throughout adolescence, but only in his late teens did he think of himself as gay:

> **E:** The first time I had gay sex with another gay person knowingly [sic], I felt "This is what I want and this is the way I want to live." It was in the town where I grew up. I don't know how I found out, but I found out there was a place where gay men went and had sex with each other. That was my introduction to gay sex.

> **Th:** What happened?

> **E:** I was walking around the block looking for the place. A guy came up to me and put his hand on my ass. He introduced himself and we walked off and had sex. I found it absolutely thrilling! It was like coming home sexually. Here was somebody who wanted to do what I wanted to do. I had discovered these people and it was like coming home. I had sex with a woman a few years later, but I felt there was no spark. It just wasn't there. I never felt it was a choice, once I discovered sex with men. It was home. Whatever I thought was wrong about doing it, this was still me. For better or worse, at least I knew what it was.

Statements like "coming home" or "discovering who I really was" are how gay men frequently describe coming out to themselves. In Winnicott's terms, perhaps it is the moment in which they make contact with what they experience as their true selves.

Coming Out to Others

Coming out to oneself is often followed by coming out to others. A gay man may come out to a friend, a family member, a mentor, a coworker or to a stranger. His revelation is not always greeted with enthusiasm. That was certainly the experience of Darrel Yates Rist, a popular gay writer and social commentator:

> My mother cried all night when I told her I liked men and so might someday fall in love with one. Stricken, I listened until dawn to her muffled sobs through the wall of my bedroom. I had asked her not to talk to my dad about it until I'd talked to him myself. It was a cruel, selfish request, insisting on her vow of silence while she hurt. But I had not known that she would mourn my homosexuality [sic] like a death. She reneged. At breakfast my father was sullen. Over the weeks phone calls came for me from men he did not know. Shortly he confronted me. We fought viciously. Did I wear a dress when I met these men on weekend nights? he asked. He disowned me and banished me from his house [Rist, 1992, p. 415].

The false self is the mannered self. Consequently, the phenomenon of gay people coming out in growing numbers has raised new questions about what constitutes proper public decorum:

> If a person's sexual orientation is so private a matter that a mention of it in a newspaper article about gay civil rights constitutes a breach of decorum, then the same should hold for gender. For if sexual orientation is strictly a matter of what one does (or desires to do) in bed, gender is, according to the same narrow logic, strictly a manner of what is in one's pants. In reality, of course, both gender and sexual orientation have to do with much more than private parts and bedroom business. The only difference between the two is that we are all used to discussing men and women as such without thinking automatically about their distinguishing genitalia; most heterosexuals, however, are not yet accustomed to references to an individual's sexual orientation and consequently, when told that so-and-so is gay, tend to conjure up the indecorous bedroom images. This is not a good enough reason for requiring homosexuals to keep quiet about who they are [Bawer, 1993, p. 115].

There was a time when homosexuality was not a subject that came up in polite company. Even today, some heterosexually-identified individuals feel that talking about being gay is a *faux pas*. Their discomfort is captured in the question, "Why do you have to talk about it?" Heterosexuals often do not wish to have this information, nor do they want their children exposed to it, the premise being that knowledge is contagious and might lead to putting unwelcome ideas in impressionable young minds. When a gay man comes out to a heterosexual friend or family member, the latter may experience this as breaking a social taboo. In a way it is. Although heterosexual identities are publicly enacted, they are usually not named:

Q: What aspects of yourself make up your identity?

A: Let me put it in terms of identifying information, as if I were writing a case report about myself. I am a forty-five-year-old white Catholic American psychiatrist, father of two.

Q: Anything else?

A: Committed, loving husband, also an involved son and son-in-law. Northeasterner, Ivy Leaguer. My college is important to my identity.

Q: Anything else?

A: Jogging! Unless I jog twenty-five miles a week I get crazy. In the past ten years being a jogger has become an integral part of my identity.

Q: Are you a heterosexual?

A: Of course.

Q: Would you have mentioned it if I hadn't asked you?

A: Probably not, I take it for granted [Friedman, 1988, p. 8].

It is normal to bring a spouse to the company picnic or to a business dinner, to keep a picture of the family on the desk at work, to wear a wedding band while working, to take time off from work to go on a honeymoon or to care for a sick spouse. A gay man coming out is saying "I want you to understand who I am because my life will unfold differently from yours."

F: Our family doesn't talk. It took me to thirty-three years to tell my mother I was gay.

Th: What prompted you to tell her?

F: Coming here. That is, my decision to start therapy. I needed financial help and told her, "Mom, I need therapy. And the reason I need therapy, not because I'm gay, but let's discuss the fact that I'm gay." My mother said she had figured it out and that it was no surprise to her. She knows a lot of gay people from work and I knew it wasn't going to be traumatic. I said, "I can't believe I'm telling you." However, I remember the entire time I talked to her about it, she had trouble looking me in the eye. She found it uncomfortable talking about it.

Th: You were not so sure you wanted to talk about it.

F: Why open a can of worms that was closed for thirty years? It's my own reluctance. If I can get past my own reluctance, she will accept it.

The patient's difficulty coming out to his mother reflected, in part, his difficulty coming out to himself. He said telling his mother was an event of no great consequence. However, in the material that followed, he associated to the difficulties he has in revealing any of his feelings. First, he worried that his being gay would be used against him in situations of ordinary conflict. Then he associated to a memory of being unfairly punished by his mother. This childhood memory parallels his unconscious fears about coming out. If he comes out and declares himself, he reexperiences a childhood fear that he will be unjustly punished for expressing an authentic feeling:

F: If I feel I want to criticize or reprimand someone, I find that hard to do. I think, "Oh my God, what are they going to say behind my back now? They are not going to like me anymore." The list goes on and on. I may open something up that gives them power in a situation. It is something I always had. I'm sure that comes from my mother. When I was a kid, my mother would scream and yell at the top of her lungs. I would take it, and then I'd go into my bedroom and wish she were dead.

Th: You've never talked about that before.

F: I never mentioned that? When I was young, I felt that way a lot. It was not what she said, I think it was the yelling itself. I didn't do anything wrong to deserve the yelling.

Th: What made her yell?

F: It was for stupid things. Once, when I was in eighth grade, my sister was teasing me, but of course when we got caught, she said I was doing it to her. My mother made me leave the room. I explained that my sister had started it. I really had just been minding my own business. My mother yelled, "Leave the room." I said, "Fuck you." Then she said, "Young man, get back here right now." I stormed and stomped and walked up right in front of her. She said say, "Say you are sorry!" I said "I'm sorry" without meaning it. She said, "Go to your room" and I marched into the room and slammed the door. I probably cried.

After coming out, a close relative may accept the gay man's sexual identity, but then suggest that he shouldn't tell anyone else. A man in the early stages of coming out, grateful for not being immediately rejected or punished, was initially unaware that he had made a devil's bargain:

J: After I came out to him in my late teens, I got a lot of pressure from my father not to tell anyone else. He was always saying. "Don't wear an earring." We couldn't tell my aunt for years. I was always close to my aunt. It turns out, she didn't have a problem with it.

Th: Why did your father say you shouldn't tell your aunt?

J: He didn't think my aunt could handle it. That she'd be really upset and that it would take a long time for her to get used to the idea.

In projecting a lack of acceptance onto the aunt, the father communicated that he himself couldn't completely "handle it." This was, in fact, understood at the time and then selectively inattended by the gay man. Relieved that he wasn't totally rejected by his father, and not wanting to push his acceptance any further, the patient accepted his advice. In effect, he widened his hiding space to include his father. He inhibited his own coming out process with the hope that his father would come to terms with his own:

J: My father kept me from telling my aunt for years. I finally told her two weeks ago. The fact of the matter is I did my aunt and myself a grave injustice. I told her, "I'm only telling you this because I want to be closer to you, and that can only happen if you know who I am." She was wonderful about it. I was so angry about it, because I had waited so long in order not to make waves.

Th: You kept your personal life secret from your aunt to avoid making waves?

J: It's true. I'm sick of the whole thing. I now have this real quest for authenticity. I want to be who I am to everyone in every situation I care about. I had to tell my aunt. I told my father that part of the reason I didn't come home for Thanksgiving is because I'm not out to my aunt. I'm not welcome for who I am. And now, miracle of miracles, I'm looking forward to Christmas.

Th: What kept you from telling your aunt?

J: I didn't want to be rejected by her.

Fear of rejection often plays a significant role in the gay man's decision about who to tell or whether to come out. The father's warning about the aunt evoked his own fears:

Th: What made you think your aunt would reject you?

J: She's a sweet person, not at all cosmopolitan. She hasn't traveled abroad. She married her high school sweetheart. My father said she couldn't deal with it. I sensed she could handle it. She's a very kind person, a fundamentally kind person. I have a sense for feeling kindness in people that is rarely wrong. I felt it in her. And I was absolutely right. Part of me is mad at my father. He's a good man, but it would have been nice to have a father who said, "I love you for who you are." Instead I got, "You can't tell the family."

Th: You couldn't tell anybody in the family?

J: Nobody. I never told my grandmother, never told my other aunts and uncles. I respected my father's judgment, respected his wishes. I think doing so did me a big disservice. He should have had better judgment and realized that it is damaging to a child. Especially a child who is as sensitive as I am. He should have known better. I never had this anger until a year ago, and now it's there. Maybe I'm expecting too much of my father but he should have been willing to make waves for his son.

It is worth noting that although at first he was defensively compliant with the father's wishes, his compliance did not keep him from living a gay identity. It did, however, leave him feeling inauthentic, detached from his aunt, and resentful of his father. Coming out, in this context, had almost nothing do with his sexuality. Instead, it was about his attempt to create an identity for himself that would allow him greater emotional freedom as well as authenticity in his relationships.

Th: It makes you question where his priorities lie.

J: Maybe a little bit. It makes me question how much does he really accept it? How much does he accept me? It's frankly a little disappointing.

Th: You sound sad.

J: Yeah, a little. It would kill him if I said these things directly to him, but I'm wondering if they need to be said.

Th: You are so angry, you imagine you can kill him with your words.

J: I don't know what good it would do. It would probably make me feel worse to tell him. But there's real anger, no doubt about it. And none at my aunt.

Th: You allowed your relationship with your aunt to be mediated by your relationship with your father.

J: It's time to come out.

Th: That can be stressful too.

J: Yeah, but it's a real emotional payoff. What I'm after now is an emotional payoff.

For some gay men, coming out to others starts with telling long-time acquaintances and family about themselves. However, when a gay man senses that he cannot come out at home, moving to another city offers him opportunities to come out among strangers. Sexual opportunities, freed from the surveillance of family and friends may be a motive. But often, the move generates other surprises, no less important:

> I moved to New York on July 19, 1962 in pursuit of someone I later captured and lived with for five years. That first night he took me to dinner at a gay restaurant in the Village. Washington Square and the streets surrounding it were so filled with people I was both frightened and exhilarated. And the very words together, "gay restaurant," struck me as a delightful impossibility. I had heard of gay baths and been to gay bars, but a gay restaurant sounded unexpectedly civilized, as though there were something to gay life beyond sex and cruising for sex [White, 1991, p. 251].

It is often an exhilarating experience to come out in new and faraway places where one is not known to either family or friends. After making his move, a gay man may completely sever his relationships with people he has known previously. And in the case of the following patient, the strategy used to accomplish this may provide a gay man with opportunities to express varying combinations of personal resolve and unresolved feelings:

> **K:** I have an old friend from back home who is married with four children. He said, "The person I knew you as back then is not the person I know now." When his mother died, I wrote a letter of condolence to him which he really appreciated. I have spent so many years avoiding all those people back home. I am ashamed about my lack of forthrightness with them. That is why I don't want to go back and face them. To go back and say, "Yes I pretended all those years." I've read coming out stories and most gay people did that. I was a coward. If I went back, they probably would think I am such a fraud. I was rude to my hometown friends when they came up to visit me in New York. I sent them to a straight club. Although I didn't know it when I sent them there, it happened to be "gay night." They were mad about it. They said, "Is everyone in this town queer?" But after they said that, I deliberately sent them to the snootiest restaurant I could find. It had a gay overtone to it with a lot of snobbery. They had a miserable time. They've never really gotten over that. I sent them to that restaurant on purpose. It was all calculated to get them to fuck off.

> **Th:** You were afraid to openly tell them you were gay?

> **K:** Right. Burning bridges is what I was doing.

> **Th:** What was the purpose of burning bridges?

> **K:** I wouldn't have to go through the uncomfortable process of being honest with them. And possibly having to listen to their complaints about my behavior. I was a good faker before I came out, a hard-drinking, hell-raiser. That's how I dealt with it. I got drunk. I remember before I came out, there were some openly gay people in town. I heard the straight guys talk horribly about them. I was never going to subject myself to that. A gay guy could be nice and smart, but it didn't matter. He was still just a faggot. Why even try? Instead, I made them think that there was something wrong with them. Like, "You don't fit in New York. You are a bunch of hicks. Stay away." Rather than having them make me uncomfortable, by trying to get into their heads and thinking what do they think of me, I did it that way. I heard their comments when we were all a bunch of straight guys. I knew the way they thought.

> **Th:** You felt you had no choice but to let them feel something that you had experienced. The feeling of not fitting in.

K: I know, but I'm not proud of the way I handled my being gay vis à vis my friends. I never told them nor gave them the chance to deal with their own feelings and say whatever they wanted to say to me. What I did was send them to the meanest places in New York without me, in the hope that they would leave me alone and I would never have to deal with those uncomfortable feelings.

Sometimes, a gay man's reluctance to come out reflects his accurate assessment of the potential reactions of friends and family members. At other times it does not. Moreover, what one friend may do does not predict what another will do:

K: But I have one hometown friend who still likes me and calls me from time to time. We've known each other since elementary school. He is still straight and married. He says, "I can't believe you are gay." He then reminds me of some of the carousing that we did together. Another friend I grew up with since second grade is a reborn Christian. Recently he called me up and said, "Please stop whatever sexual activity you are engaged in. Please stop. Seek out Pat Robertson to help you." He called another time and wanted to talk about old times. I said, "No. I know the way you feel about me. It would be very false." His father died a few months ago. I sent a nice note and got a perfunctory, cold note back. "Thank you for your condolences."

Th: You feel you're damned if you come out and damned if you don't.

K: Right. But I'm thinking, "I'd rather be damned if I do. Damned if I don't is the meaner way of doing it even though that is still the way I handle it."

When a family has more than one gay child, they may not necessarily come out at the same time, or even to the same family members:

L: My sister is a lesbian. They're going to her lover's, Sheila's parents on the day before Christmas. Sheila will stay there and my sister will come down to my parents for Christmas Eve. It will be fun having the family together. But my sister will probably leave midday on Christmas to go pick up Sheila and then head back to their own home. My family is accepting of the relationship, and it doesn't faze them. They treat them as a couple. It's interesting that they are splitting their holidays between families. I'm a little disappointed.

Although his sister has come out to their parents, this gay man has not. The therapist questions the gay man's description of his family's acceptance:

Th: Nobody minds that they don't come together to spend the holidays?

L: I think my mother is relieved that they don't come together, because when they do, they bring two large dogs.

Th: Your parents aren't offended that Sheila doesn't come with your sister?

L: I think they would like her to come. They bought Sheila presents. But they realize that she wants to spend some time with her own family.

Th: I'm trying to imagine how the two families would feel if a wife were to spend the holidays with her family and the husband spent them with his.

L: That's coming at it from a different angle. An interesting point.

This gay man entered treatment wanting to explore his difficulties in finding a relationship. His explanation of his sister's holiday plans has a disingenuous quality. It made the therapist wonder why did two people in a long-term relationship choose to spend their holidays apart and to act as if they were not a couple?

Th: It's interesting to think how couples make choices about spending the holidays with their families.

L: I have friends at work who are newly married. They have lots of difficulties in arranging how to spend the holidays.

Th: Holiday social engagements are rarely arranged in a way that treat a married couple as divisible.

The patient does, in fact, know something about the social obligations of heterosexual couples. Married couples have to sort out their responsibilities and priorities to each other and to their families. But without the kind of social conventions that define heterosexual marriage, the same expectations do not hold for gay couples:

L: For me, where I'm coming from, its wonderful that they are thought of as much of a couple as they are. Since they got together two years ago, I've been less hesitant to mention them as a couple to my parents. I have even begun to talk to my parents about things that I do with my friends, and I am less reluctant to mention my friends' names. I never specifically told my parents that I'm gay. That's an interesting point. I should ask my sister if my parents know I'm gay. I don't know if they do know. I assume that they must. Under that assumption, I've been discussing things with them as if that were the case.

Coming out to others highlights the interpersonal enactments that perpetuate the invisibility intrinsic to being closeted. A gay man received a phone call from a relative living in another city:

M: It's been years since we last spoke. I only hear about the goings-on in that part of the family from my parents. He was calling to invite me to his son's wedding. I've always received invitations for his kids' Bar Mitzvahs and other occasions. I would always send a gift and a polite note of regret. To tell you the truth, I was avoiding that part of the family because my mother told me she didn't want them to know I was gay. I didn't want to go anywhere where I had to be closeted and present a facade. Last year my sister was there for another family function and told them that I was gay, which was fine with me. My cousin was calling because he said he hadn't seen me in many years and he wanted me to come to his son's wedding. I was very touched. I told my cousin I would speak with my partner and let him know if we could make it. There was a moment of silence and he said, "Anybody you want to bring is welcome." I said, "Let me give you the spelling of his name for the invitation." He said, "Oh yeah, that makes sense." I said, "It would certainly make him feel welcome." There was a pause and then he said, "You know, I think the invitations are already addressed. Let me check." He got back on the phone a few seconds later and said, "It's too late. The envelopes are already being stuffed. But if you want to bring anybody, that's fine with us."

Th: And what was your reaction?

M: Mixed. I was touched. I felt like I was being treated like a full member of the family. But I had the impression he had never had a conversation with an openly gay person before. After so many years of my being silent on the subject, I think he was surprised by my sudden directness. When I thought about it later, I felt sad because he never asked me my lover's name, even if it was too late to put it on the invitation.

Th: Did you offer the name?

M: No. In my own way, I participated in the silence. I didn't refer to my lover by name but called him "my partner." What is the right word to use? "Lover" is too sexualized but "partner" seems so formal. "Friend" is too vague and "roommates" are for college students. "Significant other, long-time companion, spousal equivalent?" They remind me of ad copy or bureaucratic jargon. "Spouse" comes closest, but of course, we can't get married. My cousin was making a good faith effort, but he didn't quite know how to handle it. Maybe I didn't either. I also noticed something else as I ran the conversation over and over in my head. As soon as I spoke openly about my gay self, referring to my partner as "he," my cousin's speech became neutral. He said, "Anybody you want."

Th: Usually it's the gay person who hides behind neutral or genderless speech.

M: For the first time in my life, I realized that heterosexuals can also play closet games.

Outing

Up until this point, the discussion has focused on an individual's private experiences of being closeted and coming out to himself, to family, and to friends. However, one gay journalist and social commentator has observed that social conventions help maintain a public closet, in the sense that they render ordinary gay life invisible. Michael Signorile (1993) points out that until very recently, newspaper editors would not mention an individual's gay identity if it did not seem immediately relevant to a story's subject. In general, editors only felt the subject was relevant in stories pertaining to gay rights activism, gay sex crimes, gay sex scandals, child custody cases involving a gay parent, or illnesses that affected the gay population. In this way, Signorile notes, television and print journalism perpetuate society's view of the homosexual as misfit and outsider or political radical. The politically uninvolved, healthy, law-abiding gay man who lives with his children is invisible. His life, like his equally unnewsworthy heterosexual neighbor's, does not make good copy. As a result, his gay life and the lives of people like him do not enter the public consciousness nor do they have an impact on homosexual stereotyping. For Signorile, a solution to this problem is "outing," a radical way to create visibility, a revolutionary act intended to overturn social conventions that maintain the closet. He had an opportunity to put his ideas into practice in the early 90s as a writer for *OutWeek*, a now-defunct lesbian and gay newsmagazine. He explains:

> What came to be called outing—declaring closeted public figures to be gay—was not a preconceived program on the part of [*OutWeek*] magazine or its editors. It just happened. Contrary to popular perception, outing was a *by-product* of a revolution rather than a conscious invention of that revolution. At *OutWeek*, there were sharply divergent views on outing, but everyone agreed that the closet was an ugly institution that had to be broken down [Signorile, 1993, p. 70].

One often finds that social revolutionaries are individuals with a highly developed penchant for moralizing. Like religious moralists, they can zealously frame the issues about which they feel strongly in the language of right and wrong:

> Many people say outing is wrong under any circumstances. Others see it as a weapon and a tool, something that should be used only against those queers who are closeted and harming others. For me, outing has a far larger scope. I agree hypocrisy should be exposed: If gay people

are party to hurting other gay people, that fact should be made public [Signorile, 1993, p. 77].

Can one find a balance between Signorile's social activism, however well-intentioned, and the purely personal needs of individual gay men? Signorile, like many radicals, sees a solution for a social problem in the unwilling sacrifice of others. But a gay or homosexually self-aware man may not be ready to come out to everyone he knows. And his fear of being revealed is likely to be based on realistic concerns. Yet Signorile would justify violating the privacy of a closeted gay man if he thought it served a greater good, that is the destruction of the public closet. Yet revealing someone else's sexual identity, even inadvertently, can sometimes have tragic consequences. A nineteen-year-old student was seen by his father, who lived in another city, in what became a nationally televised gay march. The father, an Orthodox Jewish rabbi, flew to San Francisco with his wife, both of them Holocaust survivors, where their gay son was studying in preparation for entering the rabbinate himself.

> "Are you a sodomite?" [the father] demanded when he got to his son's apartment. Steve allowed that he was. "Either you get on the next plane home with us or we no longer have a son," the rabbi ordered. The parents left without their only surviving child. Two years later, Steve's friends would call him from Toronto to see why he had not attended his own mother's funeral; that's how Steve learned his mom had died. Gays have long been disowned by irate parents, but the story of Steve Hollonzine's estrangement carried an extra twist since both his parents knew that he was suffering from a malignant brain tumor that was slowly spreading cancer throughout his body. They had left their nineteen-year-old son to face his early death alone [Shilts, 1982, p. 290].

To some, deliberately exposing a closeted gay man to potential personal or public humiliation is a revolutionary act, perhaps even a righteous one. But it can have other meanings as well. Sometimes, it is done as an act of revenge committed by vindictive acquaintances or spurned lovers. Blackmailers will keep a gay man's secret for an unspecified amount of financial or political remuneration. Economic rivals might deliberately expose a closeted gay man's identity for financial gain. Historically, some politicians have tried to discredit an opponent's credibility by exposing him as gay.

Some gay men live conservative lives, hold conservative political views and may sometimes have a small circle of equally closeted and equally conservative gay friends. Such a man may even privately identify himself as gay, but have no interest in integrating his gay identity into a wider sphere of living. And as Signorile (1993) notes, "Some, pathetically trying to mask their identities, publicly speak out against lesbians and gays" (p. 106). According to some gay activists, these closeted individuals should not be allowed to abuse their positions of power in the newsmedia, in the entertainment industry, in the government, or in politics. Abuse of power is defined as abetting antihomosexual, social, and political structures that oppress gay people. This was the rationale for *OutWeek's* outing of a closeted gay spokesman for the Pentagon in 1991 whose job required that he publicly defend the military's discriminatory policies against homosexuality (Signorile, 1993).

Outing as a moral act must be judged, at least in part, by considering the sensibility of the person being outed. The following patient has recently begun asking whether he might be gay. He does not welcome the therapist's suggestion about possibly joining a gay support group. The patient, on hearing the tentative offer, experiences it as if he were being outed. He does not wish to reveal himself to others before he can accept the possibility of being gay himself:

> **N:** I have a date with another banker next week. I met him through the personal ads. I'll see how it goes. I have to be careful, I might meet someone from work. I've also been hoping, through friends, to meet other gay people. The process is kind of slow. But once I get something in my noggin, I follow through.

> **Th:** Would you have any interest in joining a gay professional group for bankers?

> **N:** No. It's not a good idea. I've only stopped being depressed for the last month. Each day is reinforcing the notion of accepting myself. I'm not ready to be a gay person in public. I work in a professional environment that is not tolerant of that. It's an environment that hates gay people. There are lots of gay people in the office, but not overtly. Nobody gives a damn, but you don't bring it into the office. I'm not ready for professional organizations. I have to be concerned about my children. I have to be a normal father.

> **Th:** There are groups for gay fathers.

> **N:** No thanks. I have led dual lives my whole life, and I find it quite the natural thing.

A severe dissociative split between one's sexual identity and one's internalized antihomosexual attitudes may explain how politically and religiously conservative gay men are able to support individuals and organizations that publicly condemn homosexuality (Liebman, 1992; White, 1994). What Signorile calls "hypocrisy" may actually reflect differing self-states that permit a closeted gay man to live with his own contradictions. However, the dissociation can be a defense against profound anxiety and shame. From the subjective experience of the outed person, revealing his sexual identity can be a form of psychological violence.

It is beyond the scope of this book to address all the implications of outing, or of allowing antihomosexual gay men and women to operate with impunity from positions of power. It is unlikely, however, that the ubiquitous social conventions that maintain the closet as a public space can easily be surmounted. It is also not clear how a policy of widespread outing can be implemented without doing great harm to many gay or homosexually self-aware individuals. Some see no moral ambiguity in outing, and justify the predictable unleashing of antihomosexual forces against the outed individual because the survival of other gay people may depend upon it. However, sacrificing others to achieve one's own political survival is also a favored activity of antihomosexual demagogues who seek political gain by appealing to society's fears and prejudices. To out someone is to expose that individual to the very social forces that gay activists oppose. If the ultimate political goal of the gay rights movement is to reduce and eliminate the power of such forces to adversely affect the lives of gay people, it is not entirely clear how exploiting those same forces and using them as a weapon against closeted gay individuals will achieve those ends.

The Ongoing Process of Coming Out

Coming out is an ongoing process that never ends. A therapist who is fluent in the idioms of coming out can point out both obstacles to and inhibitions of the process. To some patients, this might appear as if the therapist was encouraging, coaching, implicitly controlling, or directing the patient toward that end. A patient can hear a therapist's fluency in discussing this issue as tacit encouragement to hurry up and come out. If the therapist is gay, a patient might even experience this as recruitment or even a seduction. In fact, when treating compliant patients, therapists need to be aware of the possibility that their interventions may be heard this way. On the other hand, a less compliant patient will often call a therapist on what he perceives are efforts to force movement in that direction. These possibilities, of course, need to be openly talked about and they provide grist for the psychotherapeutic mill. Having said that, however, it is worth reiterating that to be gay, in contrast to being homosexually self-aware, is to claim a normative identity. From this perspective, coming out to oneself is an integrative process that serves to affirm one's sense of worth. Every situation in which a gay man comes out may be associated with anxiety, a sense of relief, or both:

> **N:** We went to the opera last night. I haven't been there in years. This guy I'm dating is very outgoing and has a strong physical presence. We were having a great time. Then, at one point during the intermission, as we were talking, he put his arm around me. I became very anxious and started looking around to see if anyone was watching.
>
> **Th:** What made you anxious?
>
> **N:** I told him, "Don't do that. We're in public."
>
> **Th:** What were you afraid to reveal publicly?
>
> **N:** I've been out for many years. My family knows I'm gay. My friends know. But I was worried that we would be looked at or judged by people in the audience. We were sitting in the orchestra where almost everyone could see us.
>
> **Th:** And who did you imagine was sitting in the audience of the Metropolitan Opera House that was going to be surprised by or critically judge a man putting his arm around another man?
>
> **N:** (Laughs) When you say it out loud, it sounds irrational, even to me. Of course, there were lots of gay men in the audience. I'm sure no one was bothered by it, one way or the other. I guess I felt uncomfortable revealing myself in an unfamiliar setting. It's like coming out all over again.

In the above exchange, when the therapist wondered who the patient thought could see him as an openly gay man, a question with multiple meanings was being asked. One of these meanings was a question about the patient's inner world. What internalized aspect of the patient found it unacceptable to be seen as gay in public? This part of the question focused on integrating the patient's own lack of inner acceptance with his stated wish to live as a gay man. The patient did not directly respond to this question, although it was later addressed in the session.

In addition, the therapist's inquiry was also a reality-based question about who the patient actually thought was in the opera house that might be offended. However, the question was asked in a way that spontaneously took account of the therapist's and patient's shared language and experience of living in a gay community. Seen from this perspective, the therapist was being sarcastic. And this is exactly how the patient immediately heard it, responding by labeling his feelings as irrational because, as he put it, "Of course, there were lots of gay men in the audience." Although humor, irony, and sarcasm play an integral part in gay culture, as they do in the cultures of other denigrated minorities, exchanges of this sort can sting a patient. However, the patient could hear and brush off the sarcasm without offense because he had gone a certain distance in his coming out process. It is very likely that the sarcasm might simply not be heard by a different patient who was only beginning his coming out process, because the latter would not yet be fully acquainted with either the social realities or the idioms of the gay world that he was thinking about entering.

A therapist might decide that it would be preferable not to take a position on whether or not the patient came out, and might even define that stance as a neutral one. That position, however, confuses the process of coming out to oneself with that of coming out to others. Coming out to others is fraught with dangers that no therapist can predict. It would certainly be unwise to advise a patient to come out to anyone if the therapist does not personally know the intended target of the patient's revelation. And even then, a therapist cannot fully predict the consequences of such a revelation on the relationship of those two people. Coming out to others needs to be addressed with each patient in a way that recognizes individual differences. And if the patient chooses to come out, it needs to be carefully explored. The same is true if the patient decides not to come out.

Consider the example of a patient who was anxious about coming out to his father. He described his father as an overbearing man who always yelled and complained. He was labeled as an ultra-conservative, Roman Catholic bigot who hated Jews, hated blacks, hated gays, etc. The patient repeatedly talked about letting his father know he was gay. He had already told his mother he was gay and she had warned him that it would kill his father if he knew. The patient would return from weekends with his parents feeling brutalized by his father's casual expressions of bigotry. Dwelling on these weekends usually precipitated a wish to write a coming-out letter. But when the therapist asked how the father would react to such a letter, the patient acknowledged his wish to use the communication as a weapon to pay his father back for the hurtful comments he endured. Accordingly, the therapist repeatedly interpreted the wish to come out as a symbol of his anger and hostility toward his father, above and beyond a wish for openness and dialogue with him. Ultimately, the patient never wrote the letter. Instead, he withdrew from his family.

This withdrawal provoked curiosity in his father who began to ask his wife why their son no longer came home to visit. After much evasion, the mother finally told him the truth. One day, as they spoke on the phone, the father asked his son why he was avoiding him. He said there was nothing anyone could tell him that would make him stop loving his son. The patient excitedly came into his session but was also confused about his feelings. His father's reaction surprised him. It was not what he had expected and it was not what the therapist, who shared the patient's surprise, had expected either. The therapist had countertransferentially accepted the patient's pejorative construction of the father. But upon regaining his analytic balance, or at least some of it, the therapist said if the father was not the intolerant person that the patient had painted him out to be, perhaps the patient had to locate the feelings of intolerance within himself. This led to associations and explorations of the patient's own continued lack of acceptance of his homosexuality, despite his conscious attempts to live an openly gay life.

The above account illustrates how coming out to others contains a story about coming out to oneself. And therapists must recognize that it is the gay patient's struggle to define himself that should be the important therapeutic focus. It also needs to be emphasized that this is not a typical struggle for those who claim a heterosexual identity. To repeat, the gay patient faces a whole set of decisions quite unlike anything a heterosexual person faces. Hiding from oneself depends upon dissociative defenses while coming out to oneself holds the possibility of psychological integration. Of course the particular needs of any patient to find a balance between dissociation and integration will vary, depending on the specifics of his life situation and personality. Nevertheless, an implicit value of psychotherapy is that integration is ultimately more psychologically meaningful than dissociation. Although one need not take a position about coming out to others, it is not possible for a therapist to be neutral about coming out to the self. Unsurprisingly, however, one usually finds that as patients feel more comfortable with themselves, they may begin to feel more comfortable with others:

> **P:** I had a dream. I was in a meeting and there were two sides, two groups of people in negotiations. I had a sense of a group of people on both sides. They had no specific qualities except there was a young MBA type on the other side of the negotiations who was disdainful of everybody else, very arrogant. I had this image of him with a suit and tie, no sense of anybody else. I remember starting the dream with the feeling that I was part of a group. In the process of the dream, I got the sense that whatever negotiations we were preparing for, I was going to be handling those negotiations for our side. I remember people talking about numbers, financial restructuring, and feeling lost in those discussions. It was all sort of gibberish to me. And that's about it.

Th: What comes to mind about the dream?

P: Although it's a business-related dream, it's easy to initially apply it to my life. In comparison to a number of meetings and situations where I felt very anxious and very much wanted to hide within myself, this was one where I was being pushed out in front and the people who were with me were comfortable with me being pushed out in front. And I was comfortable with it. In trying to relate it to feelings of the last week or so, I told you that I had taken on this volunteer job at the Gay Community Center. In the last few weeks, I've had more time to devote to that. I'm finding that not only do I get satisfaction out of it, in many cases, these people have the potential for developing new programs. I was reflecting on this yesterday and it makes me feel much more comfortable with being gay. Even though it is a sort of controlled audience in some respects. Being out front like that on a continuous basis seems to be making me feel I enjoy it. It's out front, you get good feedback, and then it spills over into other things. We've been doing work with some city agencies. I didn't realize it would mean identifying myself as gay to someone who is not gay outside the organization.

Coming out includes ongoing efforts to make contact with other gay men. A patient was interested in another gay man, but was anxious about letting him know. He resorted to an old but reliable method of hiding his feelings:

Q: My sense was that it didn't feel like he was receptive. I didn't want to be rejected.

Th: But you ended up feeling rejected anyway.

Q: I was feeling rejected before I started fishing for a sign that he was receptive. I left it in such a way that now it's up to him to call me. Part of me is thinking, "I don't know if I want to do anything with him."

Th: Sometimes you feel that way, other times you don't.

Q: OK, let's explore that. I get very lonely and I get very needy to be in touch; to be in touch with him, to be in contact with him. The other part is I feel scary and I want to keep my distance from him. I have ambivalent feelings about everybody.

Th: Let's look at the ambivalence.

Q: Relationships with people are very threatening. They create anxiety in me. I don't know if I can call someone because I'm lonely and I want to go out to a movie or dinner. If I've never gone with a person before, they may think it is a date and I may not want it to be a date. I stayed around after my men's group ended the other day. I saw someone I used to be attracted to, but I never let him know. Even though I was interested in some of the other people there, I ended up leaving. I went home and masturbated.

Although he had come out to some degree, this man continued to isolate himself. This was the same way he behaved when he was in the closet. In the current situation, he was no longer pretending to be heterosexual, but he was not comfortable making contact with other gay men. He hid within a private space where he felt defeated:

Th: You must have been feeling pretty nervous.

Q: Masturbation is a way to calm my anxiety. I think what made me anxious at the meeting is that I've gone through all this upheaval of coming out of the closet, Now I'm a gay man and I'm having trouble connecting with gay men. To be honest, part of the reason is I don't want to connect. I think of the gay men I have turned away. I can think of seven who showed interest in me, maybe more. Men who showed some interest in me in terms of dating or getting better acquainted and I totally brushed them aside.

This gay man had shown little interest in the men who were interested in him. He was saying he would never join a country club that would have him for a member:

Q: I'm trying to be honest here. I'm really trying. I've never had friends, close friends. I don't think I've ever wanted close friends. When I was pretending to be straight, there were all kind of connections and connecting to people. More than enough to fill up any kind of social calendar. I was there by virtue of being straight and now I don't have that.

Th: You didn't have to be yourself. You just had to be the role you were playing.

Q: It was a role I knew how to play. But coming to New York alone, that was the real me. Being gay, fearful, isolating. Keep one's distance, just keep your distance. I don't know if its the real me.

Th: The real you is a mystery.

The therapist heard the comment about "the real me" as a metaphor for the patient's uncertainty about his own needs and desires:

Q: Yes, I have barriers up, and I'm keeping people away from me.

Th: You've always kept people away from you. By living as if you were a straight man, you kept people from looking too closely.

Q: My life was too much of a secret. I had to hide my sexual interests because they didn't fit with being a straight man. I hid them because they were not OK with my religion, my society, and my culture.

Th: Now that you are in a culture where it is OK to be gay, you are still hiding. You are searching for a person or group of people that will define what kind of gay person you are. You want to be part of something larger than yourself, but you also want to hide from others.

Q: Part of it is retreating, part of it is getting away. Have you treated other people who have hidden out? Have you had other people hide after coming out?

Th: Learning to hide becomes deeply ingrained and it is hard to give up.

Q: It's like going to the security blanket. I think, there was a point in my life when I would have been much more social in adolescence and I wasn't allowed. I wasn't encouraged. I wanted to be with other people, wanted to be with friends, go to things. I got squashed. The question is what do I do about it? I would rather be alone, but there is an impulse to want to come out of hiding.

This gay man was caught in an anxious game of peek-a-boo:

Th: You come out and you go in, you come out and go in.

Q: Yes, and in all these years since I came out, it isn't getting any easier. I think I have improved. Although I stopped attending the gay church services, I'm sticking with the reading and support groups. When I hear other men talking about isolating and withdrawing from people, I know I'm not the only one who does that. Then I see people hugging each other and making friends and it looks good. I don't do well once the structured parts of the groups are over.

Two years later, this gay man had come out further. He felt more comfortable with himself, and had gradually widened his gay identity. Now he considers another discussion:

Q: I wouldn't have said this two or three days ago, because I was feeling pretty depressed, but now I don't feel as depressed. And, I've been seriously considering the possibility of coming out at work. Being outed couldn't be worse than suicide. One reason I avoided an old friend is because he said, "Being in the closet is part of the problem." I didn't want to hear that.

Th: That's a difficult concept to understand when you actually are in the closet.

Q: My son is getting married. His girlfriend works and the two of them will be able to pay their own way. If I lose my job and have to take a big cut in salary, I won't have any financial responsibilities for them. I wouldn't have said this two or three days ago.

Here the holding environment is maintained by a therapist's respect for a gay man's indecision about staying in or coming out of the closet. In this case, the therapist appreciated the patient's difficult but pragmatic decision to remain closeted in a thankless job. Because of the nature of the patient's position, there were professional risks in coming out at work. The therapist also respected the patient's identity of a supportive father, notwithstanding the fact that the patient also had resentments about it. Anticipating his son's impending financial autonomy reduced the intensity of this gay man's feeling that he had to stay in a difficult work environment. Having done the job he set out to do, his paternal identity felt secure. Because he felt more secure, he wanted to come out even further.

> **Q:** I'm having dinner with a man who is just coming out of the closet. He is married 30 years and has children. After we were introduced, he wanted to talk to me about how I handled coming out. He's not sure how he feels about his new gay relationship. He is in such a transition, he can't be sure what is going to happen to him. I feel good about his wanting to speak with me. I certainly listen to him and understand what he is facing. I also decided that I might be interested in leading a gay reading group in my apartment. I'm just thinking about it and I feel I can do a good job of that.

Another patient, a middle-aged man, had come out in his early twenties and in fairly short order had done many things that for him were quite daring. He told his family and close friends he was gay. Although they made him uncomfortable, he had regularly gone to gay clubs and made gay friends. He had even lived with another man and had continued to do so throughout his thirties. However, he had never come out at work. Moreover, he had always been reluctant to express his anger overtly; being able to acknowledge it openly represented a new level of coming out to himself:

> **R:** My mind just went back to the situation at work. I have a tightness in my chest. I am thinking of cutting loose, not giving a damn what people think. Wearing an earring. I wanted to scream, "I am gay" to this loudly homophobic woman at work. Part of me wants to be outrageous. There was a point where I thought, "I should come out at work." This is why people come out. Making a clear statement about being out is pushing the envelope. I can feel it rising in me. The anger I feel in me. Why do I have to hear this kind of crap from people? Why do I have to hide? It is this unspoken thing that pisses me off. Then my mind says, "You have to wait until you retire or the people at work will make fun of you. Your tires will be slashed. The fear of retaliation is what keeps people in the closet. I'm angry too. There is anger in addition to the feeling that I missed some-

thing. I want to let my hair down. I blame my lover for how I live. But I chose him because he is as conservative as he is. I'm sure that is part of it.

After a gay man comes out to some people, he may feel he does not want to go beyond that step. "Even at an individual level, there are remarkably few of even the most openly gay people who are not deliberately in the closet with someone personally or economically or institutionally important to them" (Sedgwick, 1990, pp. 67–68).

S: I had a crazy dream. My father was ironing shirts downstairs, and came up to put them in my closet. My friend Sam was staying over. My father opened the door, hit Sam in the face, and broke his glasses. My father ran away. I told my mother and she started yelling at me. My sister is in the corner, smirking. I found my father who started blaming me. He began chasing me with a knife. People started to calm down and began to understand what happened and I woke up.

Th: The feeling in the dream?

S: The feeling of frustration, the old feeling of, "I'm gone, I'm leaving, fuck you." An incredible frustration that no one was believing me, no one was listening. When I was awake and thinking about the dream, what I found troubling, was why did I have such a dream?

Th: What does the dream bring to mind?

S: My college reunion is coming up but I have no intentions of going. There is a huge chunk of me that would love to go. You could ask, "Why don't you want to go?" I can tell you why I don't want to go. It means I have to leave my gay life behind. Go there and live a lie. Or I go and I have to integrate the two lives together. I can't get myself to do it. So I let it go. There's a piece of me that is sad over it.

Th: There's also a piece of you that is angry in the dream.

S: Yeah. Angry at who? Angry at me? It has to be directed toward me. Is it because I haven't handled the situation well? I haven't integrated all the pieces of my life together? Is it because of the lifestyle I have finally chosen? In some of those settings you have to be phony, you have to play a role.

Th: You associate to being gay and having to hide that. Coming out means giving up a pretense. If you go to your college reunion as yourself, you have to give up the pretense of people imagining you are someone else.

S: Looking back at the dream, my father slams into the pretense and knocks it down.

Th: The dream shows you arguing with yourself about whether or not to maintain the facade.

S: I can remember the first time when I took my lover to meet my sister and my niece. The two of them were walking behind us, and my lover and I were walking together. I glanced back at the two of them. I saw my niece roll her eyes at my sister who did the same back. That was sort of the feeling in the dream.

Th: And what is the feeling exactly?

S: I've got people around me who will tolerate my being who I am, but they obviously have hidden feelings about my being gay. Just the roll of an eye. It says a lot. Fortunately or unfortunately, I captured that moment. Here was the first time the four of us were getting together. My sister was being two-faced.

Th: She is smirking in the corner in your dream.

S: She's always smirking in all my dreams. Going to the reunion would be going into a situation where I have a hundred rolling eyeballs. Why go into a situation that will hurt me?

Th: You are also rolling your eyeballs at yourself.

S: The people I basically hung around with in college were not gay. One friend who is now divorced has been trying to get together with me and I won't do it.

Th: You don't want to come out to him?

S: You're right. I don't want to deal with him. We went our different ways after college. Last year his wife divorced him, and he surfaced again. I can't get myself to tell him. I would like to do it, in the perfect world, to have him treat my lover and me as his best friends. In my own home, I have no qualms about introducing my partner to new people and I've done it. But I look at my old college friend and he has a totally destroyed life right now. And you and I know I have this perfect life. (Laughs) If I have to compare the two, I have a better life than he has. We have our problems, but I go home and laugh. I like to go home. I can't wait to go home. My lover gets up early in the morning to put the coffee on for me. If I have to compare my life with my college friend, he is living alone. His wife has custody of the two children and she moved far away. It's hard for him to get to see the kids without a major trek. He's at square one, having to create a new life.

Another therapist might have handled this dream and its associations differently. It is worth repeating that what is presented here is not a textbook approach to doing psychotherapy with gay men. The patient's feelings and associations that emerged in this session, and the therapist's responses to them, resulted, in part, from the fact that both patient and therapist had a shared cultural identity, albeit both of them looked at being gay from very different perspectives. But flying in the face of cultural stereotypes about the transience of homosexual coupling (McWhirter and Mattison, 1984, p. xiii), this man's gay relationship has been more enduring than his heterosexual friend's marriage. Both of them implicitly understood how internalizations of that stereotype undermined self-esteem. The therapist and patient shared a subcultural joke that turned the stereotype on its head:

> **Th:** I guess your friend's experience proved that heterosexuality doesn't work as a lifestyle.
>
> **S:** I guess I could have told him that a long time ago.

Once a gay man opens the closet door, or rather the doors of his various closets, he risks revealing aspects of himself that he has always kept hidden. A gay man who never pursued his artistic interests when he was deeper in the closet, began doing so as he came out. His brother was designated the family artist and his parents never expressed any interest in the patient's work:

> **U:** It's so hard to make decisions on what I want and I need.
>
> **Th:** Perhaps that's because you've spent so much time hiding who you are?
>
> **U:** Is that what it is? Sometimes I feel so estranged from my family. They don't love the idea of me being gay, but it is OK.
>
> **Th:** It took many years to tell your family something you've known about yourself all along. Once you come out, it's hard to stop the process.
>
> **U:** It's scary. I'm learning bits and pieces about myself all the time. I'm feeling things I've felt before but never acknowledged. Like not allowing myself to know my fantasies. I never allowed myself the possibility of having a fantasy that might not come true because it would have been potentially dangerous.
>
> **Th:** Without our fantasies, we cannot create.
>
> **U:** I wonder if my anxiety is associated with coming out, not just in terms of my sexual orientation, but all the parts of me.
>
> **Th:** Officially, your brother is the artist in the family. It might be dangerous to usurp his role.
>
> **U:** I fantasized about telling my parents how much artwork I sold this weekend. People kept coming in and asking, "Who's the artist?" That's not a definition I had of myself. My business cards are blank. I mean they just have my name and address on them.

Th: Who defines the artist? His family? His public? The artist himself? His critics?

U: I guess the person himself.

Th: You don't trust your own definitions.

U: That's true. I would have considered anybody else at that craft show an artist, but not me. The criteria have always been different for me.

Conclusion

Given the social stigma attached to homosexuality, the severity of anti-homosexual attitudes in the culture, and the difficulties associated with revealing one's sexual identity, why would a gay man come out at all?

> Coming out is not simply a statement made to combat discrimination nor is it usually a disclosure of private sexual experiences. Most frequently coming out involves choices about how to handle moments of ordinary, daily conversation. Even less than other social markers such as gender or "race" (whose supposedly "identifying characteristics" are thought to be discernible) that which is currently called "sexual orientation" is not self-evident. The invisibility of homosexuality forces choices about secrecy or disclosure in all social interactions that go beyond the superficial: A [person] must decide whether to reveal; when and how to reveal; how to weigh the consequences of the disclosure; how much time and energy to allocate to the responses in self and others set off by the disclosure; or, if deciding not to disclose, how to manage relationships with family members, friends and work colleagues while keeping such significant information hidden [Magee and Miller, 1994, pp. 483–484].

Given the dangers, why should a gay man come out? A man makes the case for coming out to his parents:

> **Z:** The reason that I came out is that I thought not having said I was gay, not to have it open, presented a significant barrier to us expressing our love to each other. I said it was something I could go on not telling them, but it would be as if I had left home and not let them know where I had moved. I could have continued to communicate with them without telling them where I was, but I would have to continue censoring things. It's not that I wanted to share with them anything inappropriately intimate. I just wanted them to know who I was, who my friends were, where I traveled and what causes I got involved in. Those are things that are all affected by my being gay. Not saying anything was closing them out of all those pieces

in my life. If they thought about my life, if in their minds they questioned whether they had given me anything that was useful in the life I was leading, they most definitely had. Although I love New York, there isn't a day that goes by where I don't say I am glad I was raised in our hometown. That is an expression of how they had raised me. One of the things they had given me was a definite sense of ethical conduct. There was a way in which one dealt with other people. There were rules. While sometimes they got in the way, I was grateful for having gotten that sense of integrity from them. As I got older, I realized how important that was. They had also given me a sense of requiring some sort of contribution to the community. I told them about my volunteer work in the gay community.

Th: What prompted you to tell your parents?

Z: It felt like something I needed to accomplish. It was a piece of becoming much more comfortable with my sexual orientation. It felt like the natural thing to do. I guess coming to that point makes some indication that I am becoming more comfortable with myself and not agonizing over the reaction of people who may find out or may suspect that I am gay. If my family knows that I'm gay, and I can feel comfortable with talking to them, not just about being gay, but talking without censoring what I say, it's a big piece of getting comfortable with who I am. To know that the family is a place where my sexual orientation is known, and no one has a major hang-up with it, then it's a place where I can feel comfortable and feel that there is support there. I think it also goes a long way for me, making me comfortable with other people in other situations. As I was thinking about it, it is not necessarily making an announcement. It is a matter of not censoring what you say. The anxiety that comes from watching what you say with a lot of people is corrosive. It feels like, your body producing some kind of bile or acid. This feels more like a sense of relaxation that another hurdle has been crossed.

As there are many closets, there are many different ways a gay man can come out. There is no correct way to do so, a fact that may be overlooked by a therapist in a well-intentioned effort to affirm a patient's homosexuality. A therapist's recognition and respect for individual differences will allow a multiplicity of possibilities in the coming out process. In this way, a gay man may find his own way to define his gay identity.

> The closet, as presented here, is not easily defined. What does it mean to be "in the closet" or "out of the closet?" Every gay person—and every straight person—has a different answer to those questions. The closet has many levels, depending on how many people one has told about one's sexuality and who those people might be. Does being "out of the closet" mean that you've got to tell everyone you run into you're queer? No [Signorile, 1993, p. xvii].

And yet there is an aspect of the coming out process that does engage the therapist's support regardless of whether the therapist is heterosexual or gay. Early and painful hiding experiences either induce for the first time or exacerbate existing dissociative tendencies, preventing the integration of unacceptable feelings into the self. A person's comfort with his own feelings are integral to his social and psychological development. Coming out offers a gay man the possibility of integrating a wider range of his previously split-off affects, not just his sexual ones. Greater ease in expressing them, both to himself and to others, can lead to an enormous enrichment of his work and his relationships. This, in the final analysis, is a reasonable definition of "mental health."

REFERENCES

Abelove, H., Barale, M.A. & Halperin, D., eds. (1993), *The Lesbian and Gay Studies Reader*. New York: Routledge.

Abraham, K. (1924), A short study of the development of the libido, viewed in the light of mental disorders. In *Karl Abraham: Selected Papers on Psychoanalysis*. London: Maresfield Library, 1988, pp. 418–501.

Ackerley, J. (1968), *My Father and Myself*. London: Poseidon.

Allport, G. (1954), *The Nature of Prejudice*. Boston, MA: Beacon.

Altman, D. (1982), *The Homosexualization of America, The Americanization of the Homosexual*. New York: St. Martin's Press.

American Psychiatric Association (1968), *Diagnostic and Statistical Manual of Mental Disorders, 2nd ed.* Washington, DC: American Psychiatric Press.

—— (1980), *Diagnostic and Statistical Manual of Mental Disorders, 3rd ed.* Washington, DC: American Psychiatric Press.

—— (1987), *Diagnostic and Statistical Manual of Mental Disorders, 3rd ed., Revised.* Washington, DC: American Psychiatric Press.

—— (1993), *The Principles of Medical Ethics: With Annotations Especially Applicable to Psychiatry*. Washington, DC: American Psychiatric Press.

—— (1994) *Diagnostic and Statistical Manual of Mental Disorders, 4th ed.* Washington, DC: American Psychiatric Press.

Aron, L. (1996), *A Meeting of Minds: Mutuality in Psychoanalysis*. Hillsdale, NJ: The Analytic Press.

Bailey, J. & Pillard, R. (1991), A genetic study of male sexual orientation. *Arch. Gen. Psychiat.*, 48:1089–1096.

Bauman, R. (1986), *The Gentleman from Maryland: The Conscience of a Gay Conservative*. New York: Arbor House.

Bawer, B. (1993), *A Place at the Table: The Gay Individual in American Society*. New York: Poseidon.

Bayer, R. (1981), *Homosexuality and American Psychiatry; The Politics of Diagnosis*. New York: Basic Books.

—— (1989), *Private Acts, Social Consequences: AIDS and the Politics of Public Health*. New York: Free Press.

Bell, A. & Weinberg, M. (1978), *Homosexualities: A Study of Diversity Among Men and Women*. New York: Simon & Schuster.

—— —— & Hammersmith S. (1981), *Sexual Preference: Its Development in Men and Women*. Bloomington, IN: Indiana University Press.

Bem, D. (1996), Exotic becomes erotic: A developmental theory of sexual orientation. *Psychol. Rev.* 103:320–335.

Benjamin, J. (1996), In defense of gender ambiguity. *Gender & Psychoanal.*, 1:27–43.

Bergler, E. (1956), *Homosexuality: Disease or Way of Life*. New York: Hill & Wang.

Berzon, B. (1988), *Permanent Partners: Building Gay and Lesbian Relationships That Last*. New York: Dutton.

Bieber, I. (1976), Psychodynamics and sexual object choice. I: A reply to Dr. Richard C. Friedman's paper. *Contemp. Psychoanal.*, 12:366–370.

—— Dain, H., Dince, P., Drellich, M., Grand, H., Gundlach, R., Kremer, M., Rifkin, A., Wilbur, C. & Bieber, T. (1962), *Homosexuality: A Psychoanalytic Study*. New York: Basic Books.

Bion, W. (1967a), *Second Thoughts*. New York: Aronson.

—— (1967b), Notes on memory and desire. In *Melanie Klein Today, Vol. 2: Developments in Theory and Practice*, ed. E. Spillius. London: Routledge, 1988, pp. 17–21.

Blechner, M. (1993), Homophobia in psychoanalytic writing and practice. *Psychoanal. Dial.*, 3:627–637.

—— ed. (1997), *Hope and Mortality: Psychodynamic Approaches to AIDS and HIV*. Hillsdale, NJ: The Analytic Press.

Blos, P. (1962), *On Adolescence: A Psychoanalytic Interpretation*. New York: Free Press.

Bollas, C. (1987), *The Shadow of the Object*. New York: Columbia University Press.

Bornstein, K. (1994), *Gender Outlaw: On Men, Women and the Rest of Us*. New York: Vintage.

Boswell, J. (1980), *Christianity, Social Tolerance and Homosexuality: Gay People in Western Europe from the Beginning of the Christian Era to the Fourteenth Century*. Chicago, IL: University of Chicago Press.

—— (1994), *Same-Sex Unions in Premodern Europe*. New York: Villard.

Bowlby, J. (1969), *Attachment and Loss, Vol. 1: Attachment*. New York: Basic Books.

Bradley, S. & Zucker, K. (1997), Gender identity disorder: A review of the past 10 years. *J. Amer. Acad. Child & Adolesc. Psychiat.*, 36:872–879.

Breuer, J. & Freud, S. (1895), Studies on hysteria. *Standard Edition*, 2. London: Hogarth Press, 1955.

Bromberg, P. (1994), "Speak! that I may see you": Some reflections on dissociation, reality, and psychoanalytic listening. *Psychoanal. Dial.*, 4:517–547.

Brown, H. (1976), *Familiar Faces, Hidden Lives: The Story of Homosexual Men in America Today*. New York: Harcourt Brace Jovanovich.

Brown, L. O. (1995), A glossary of Interpersonal psychoanalytic concepts and terms. In *Handbook of Interpersonal Psychoanalysis*, ed. M. Lionells, J. Fiscalini, C. Mann & D. Stern. Hillsdale, NJ: The Analytic Press, pp. 861–876.

Brown, L. S. (1996), Ethical concerns with sexual minority patients. In *Textbook of Homosexuality and Mental Health*, ed. R. Cabaj & T. Stein. Washington, DC: American Psychiatric Press, pp. 897–916.

Brown, M. & Rounsley, C. (1996), *True Selves: Understanding Transsexualism*. San Francisco, CA: Jossey-Bass.

Browning, F. (1994), *The Culture of Desire: Paradox and Perversity in Gay Lives Today*. New York: Random House.

Bullough, V. (1979), *Homosexuality: A History*. New York: Meridian.

Butler, J. (1990), *Gender Trouble: Feminism and the Subversion of Identity*. New York: Routledge.

———— (1993), *Bodies that Matter: On the Discursive Limits of Sex*. New York: Routledge.

———— (1995), Melancholy gender—Refused identification. *Psychoanal. Dial.*, 5:165–180.

Buxton, A. (1994), *The Other Side of the Closet: The Coming-Out Crisis for Straight Spouses and Families*, 2nd ed. New York: Wiley.

Byne, W. (1994), The biological evidence challenged. *Scientific Amer.*, May, pp. 50–55.

———— (1997), Why we cannot conclude that sexual orientation is primarily a biological phenomenon. *J. Homosexual.*, 34:73–80.

———— & Parsons, B. (1993), Human sexual orientation: The biologic theories reappraised. *Arch. Gen. Psychiat.*, 50:228–239.

———— & Stein, E. (1997), Varieties of biological explanation. *Harvard Gay & Lesbian Rev.,* winter, pp. 13–15.

Cabaj, R. & Stein, T., eds. (1996), *Textbook of Homosexuality and Mental Health*. Washington, DC: American Psychiatric Press.

Carrol, W. (1997), On being gay and an American Baptist minister. *The InSpiriter*, spring, pp. 6–7, 11.

Chatelaine, K. (1981), *Harry Stack Sullivan: The Formative Years*. Washington, DC: University Press of America.

Chauncey, G. (1994), *Gay New York: Gender, Urban Culture and the Making of the Gay Male World, 1890–1940*. New York: Basic Books.

Chodorow, N. J. (1992), Heterosexuality as a compromise formation: Reflections on the psychoanalytic theory of sexual development. *Psychoanal. Contemp. Thought*, 15:267–304.

———— (1996), Theoretical gender and clinical gender. *J. Amer. Psychoanal. Assn.* (Suppl.), 44:215–238.

Coates, S. (1990), Ontogenesis of boyhood gender identity disorder. *J. Amer. Acad. Psychoanal.*, 18:414–438.

———— (1992), The etiology of boyhood gender identity disorder: An integrative model. In *Interface of Psychoanalysis and Psychology*, ed. J. Barron, M. Eagle & D. Wolitzky. Washington, DC: American Psychological Association, pp. 245–265.

———— (1997), Is it time to jettison the concept of developmental lines? Commentary on de Marneffe's paper, "Bodies and Words." *Gender & Psychoanal.*, 2:35–53.

———— & Wolfe, S. (1995), Gender identity disorder in boys: The interface of constitution and early experience. *Psychoanal. Inq.*, 51:6–38.

———— & ———— (1997), Gender identity disorders of childhood. In *Handbook of Child and Adolescent Psychiatry, Vol. 1*, ed. J. Noshpitz, S. Greenspan,

S. Wieder & J. Osofsky. New York: Wiley, pp. 452–473.

Cohler, B. & Galatzer-Levy, R. (1996), Self psychology and homosexuality: Sexual orientation and maintenance of personal integrity. In *Textbook of Homosexuality and Mental Health*, ed. R. Cabaj & T. Stein. Washington, DC: American Psychiatric Press, pp. 207–223.

Coleman, E., ed. (1988), *Psychotherapy with Homosexual Men and Women: Integrated Identity Approaches for Clinical Practice*. New York: Haworth.

Coleman, G. (1995), *Homosexuality: Catholic Teaching and Pastoral Practice*. Mahwah, NJ: Paulist Press.

Cooper, A. (1995), The detailed inquiry. In *Handbook of Interpersonal Psychoanalysis*, ed. M. Lionells, J. Fiscalini, C. Mann & D. Stern. Hillsdale, NJ: The Analytic Press, pp. 679–693.

Corbett, K. (1993), The mystery of homosexuality. *Psychoanal. Psychol.*, 10:345–357.

――― (1996), Homosexual boyhood: Notes on girlyboys. *Gender & Psychoanal.*, 1:429–461.

――― (1997), Speaking queer: A reply to Richard C. Friedman. *Gender & Psychoanal.*, 2:495–514.

Crisp, Q. (1968), *The Naked Civil Servant*. New York: New American Library.

Crowley, M. (1968), *The Boys in the Band*. New York: Samuel French.

Darwin, C. (1859), *The Origin of the Species*. Ontario, Canada: Mentor, 1958.

Davis, M. & Wallbridge, D. (1981), *Boundary and Space*. New York: Brunner/Mazel.

de Beauvoir, S. (1952), *The Second Sex*. New York: Vintage, 1978.

DeCecco J., ed. (1985), *Bashers, Baiters and Bigots: Homophobia in American Society*. New York: Harrington Park Press.

――― ed. (1988), *Gay Relationships*. New York: Harrington Park Press.

――― & Parker, D., eds. (1995), *Sex, Cells and Same-Sex Desire: The Biology of Sexual Preference*. New York: Harrington Park Press.

de Marneffe, D. (1997), Bodies and words: A study of young children's genital and gender knowledge. *Gender & Psychoanal.*, 2:3–33.

D'Ercole, A. (1996), Postmodern ideas about gender and sexuality: The lesbian woman redundancy. *Psychoanal. & Psychother.*, 13:142–152.

Dickemann, M. (1995), Wilson's Panchreston: The Inclusive Fitness Hypothesis of Sociobiology Reexamined. In *Sex, Cells, and Same-Sex Desire: The Biology of Sexual Preference*, ed. J. DeCecco & D. Parker. New York: Harrington Park Press, pp. 147–184.

Dimen, M. (1991), Deconstructing difference: Gender, splitting, and transitional space. *Psychoanal. Dial.*, 1:335–352.

――― (1995), On "our nature": Prolegomenon to a relational theory of sexuality. In *Disorienting Sexualities*, ed. T. Domenici & R. Lesser. New York: Routledge, pp. 129–152.

Domenici, T. & Lesser, R., eds. (1995) *Disorienting Sexuality: Psychoanalytic Reappraisals of Sexual Identities*. New York: Routledge.

Dörner, G. (1972), *Sexualhormonabhängige Gehirndifferenzierung und Sexualität*. Vienna: Springer Verlag.

———— (1986), Hormone-dependent brain development and preventive medicine. *Monogr. Neural Sci.*, 12:17–27.

———— (1989), Hormone-dependent brain development and neuroendocrine prophylaxis. *Exp. Clin. Endocrinol.*, 94:4–22.

———— Rohde, W., Stahl, F., Krell, L. & Masius, W. (1975), A neuroendocrine predisposition for homosexuality in men. *Arch. Sex. Behav.*, 4:1–8.

———— Poppe, I., Stahl, F., Kölzxch, J. & Uebelhack, R. (1991), Gene- and environment-dependent neuroendocrine etiogenesis of homosexuality and transsexualism. *Exp. Clin. Endocrinol.*, 98:141–150.

Drescher, J. (1995), Anti-homosexual bias in training. In *Disorienting Sexualities*, ed. T. Domenici & R. Lesser. New York: Routledge, pp. 227–241.

———— (1996a), Psychoanalytic subjectivity and male homosexuality. In *Textbook of Homosexuality and Mental Health*, ed. R. Cabaj & T. Stein. Washington, DC: American Psychiatric Press, pp. 173–189.

———— (1996b), Across the great divide: Gender panic in the psychoanalytic dyad. *Psychoanal. & Psychother.*, 13:174–186.

———— (1997a), From preoedipal to postmodern: Changing psychoanalytic attitudes toward homosexuality. *Gender & Psychoanal.*, 2:203–216.

———— (1997b), What needs changing? Some questions raised by reparative therapy practices. *NY State Psychiat. Soc. Bull.*, 40:8–10.

———— (1998), I'm your handyman: A history of reparative therapies. *J. Homosexual.*, 36:19–42.

———— (in press), Start spreading the news: Book review of *Chauncey's Gay New York*. *Arch. Sex. Behavior*.

Duberman, M. (1991), *Cures: A Gay Man's Odyssey*. New York: Dutton.

———— (1994), *Stonewall*. New York: Plume.

Dunlap, D. (1995a), Shameless homophobia and the "Jenny Jones" murder. *The New York Times*, March 19.

———— (1995b), An analyst, a father, battles homosexuality. *The New York Times*, December 24.

Eagle, M. (1984), *Recent Developments in Psychoanalysis: A Critical Evaluation*. Cambridge, MA: Harvard University Press.

Eagleton, T. (1983), *Literary Theory: An Introduction*. Minneapolis: University of Minnesota Press.

Eissler, K. (1953), The effect of the structure of the ego on psychoanalytic technique. *J. Amer. Psychoanal. Assn.*, 1:104–143.

Ellis, H. (1938), *Psychology of Sex*. New York: Harcourt Brace Jovanovich.

Eskridge, W. (1996), *The Case for Same-Sex Marriage: From Sexual Liberty to Civilized Commitment*. New York: Free Press.

Fagot, B. (1974), Sex differences in toddlers' behavior and parental reaction. *Development. Psychol.*, 10:554–58.

———— (1977), Consequences of moderate cross-gender behavior in preschool children. *Child Devel.*, 48:902–907.

————— & Leinbach, M. (1985), Gender identity: Some thoughts on an old concept. *J. Amer. Acad. Child Psychiat.*, 24:684–688.

————— & ————— (1993), Gender-role development in young children: From discrimination to labeling. *Devel. Rev.*, 13:205–224.

Fast, I. (1984): *Gender Identity: A Differentiation Model.* Hillsdale, NJ: The Analytic Press.

Fausto-Sterling, A. (1992), *Myths of Gender: Biological Theories about Women and Men*, 2nd ed. New York: Basic Books.

————— (1993), The five sexes: Why male and female are not enough. *The Sciences*, March/April, pp. 20–24.

Ferenczi, S. (1914), The nosology of male homosexuality (homoerotism). *In First Contributions to Psycho-analysis.* New York: Brunner/Mazel, 1980, pp. 296–318.

Fierstein, H. (1983), *Torch Song Trilogy.* New York: Random House.

Ford, C. & Beach, F. (1951), *Patterns of Sexual Behavior.* New York: Harper.

Foucault, M. (1978), *The History of Sexuality, Vol. 1: An Introduction.* (Originally published as *Histoire de la sexualité, 1: La volonté de savoir.* Paris: Gallimard.) New York: Vintage, 1980.

Fraiberg, S. (1961), Homosexual conflicts. In *Adolescents: Psychoanalytic Approach to Problems and Therapy*, ed. S. Lorand & H. Schneer. New York: Paul E. Hoeber, pp. 78–112.

Freud, A. (1966), *The Ego and the Mechanisms of Defense.* New York: International Universities Press.

Freud, S. (1896a), Heredity and the aetiology of the neuroses. *Standard Edition*, 3:142–156. London: Hogarth Press, 1962.

————— (1896b), The aetiology of hysteria. *Standard Edition*, 3:191–221. London: Hogarth Press, 1962.

————— (1899), Screen memories. *Standard Edition*, 3:303–322. London: Hogarth Press, 1962.

————— (1900), The interpretation of dreams. *Standard Edition*, 4 & 5. London: Hogarth Press, 1953.

————— (1905), Three essays on the theory of sexuality. *Standard Edition*, 7:130–243. London: Hogarth Press, 1953.

————— (1908), "Civilized" sexual morality and modern mental illness. *Standard Edition*, 9:181–204. London: Hogarth Press, 1959.

————— (1910a), Leonardo da Vinci and a memory of his childhood. *Standard Edition*, 11:63–137. London: Hogarth Press, 1957

————— (1910b), The future prospects of psycho-analytic therapy. *Standard Edition*, 11:139–151. London: Hogarth Press, 1957.

————— (1911), Psycho-analytic notes on an autobiographical account of a case of paranoia. *Standard Edition*, 12:1–82. London: Hogarth Press, 1958.

————— (1912), Recommendations to physicians practicing psycho-analysis. *Standard Edition*, 12:109–120. London: Hogarth Press, 1958.

————— (1914a), Remembering, repeating and working-through. *Standard Edition*, 12:145–156. London: Hogarth Press, 1958.

—— (1914b), On the history of the psycho-analytic movement. *Standard Edition*, 14:7–66. London, Hogarth Press, 1957.

—— (1914c), On narcissism: An introduction. *Standard Edition*, 14:73–102. London: Hogarth Press, 1957.

—— (1915a), Instincts and their vicissitudes. *Standard Edition*, 14:117–140. London: Hogarth Press, 1957.

—— (1915b), Repression. *Standard Edition*, 14:146–158. London: Hogarth Press, 1957.

—— (1917), Mourning and melancholia. *Standard Edition*, 14:243–258. London: Hogarth Press, 1957.

—— (1919), Lines of advance in psycho-analytic therapy. *Standard Edition*, 17:157–168. London: Hogarth Press, 1955.

—— (1920), The psychogenesis of a case of homosexuality in a woman. *Standard Edition*, 18:145–172. London: Hogarth Press, 1955.

—— (1923a), Some neurotic mechanisms in jealousy, paranoia and homosexuality. *Standard Edition*, 18:221–232. London: Hogarth Press, 1955.

—— (1923b), The infantile genital organization. *Standard Edition*, 19:141–145. London: Hogarth Press, 1961.

—— (1924), The dissolution of the Oedipus complex. *Standard Edition*, 19:173–179. London: Hogarth Press, 1961.

—— (1925), Some psychical consequences of the anatomical distinctions between the sexes. *Standard Edition*, 19:248–258. London: Hogarth Press, 1961.

—— (1926a), Inhibitions, symptoms and anxiety. *Standard Edition*, 20:87–175. London: Hogarth Press, 1959.

—— (1926b), The question of lay analysis. *Standard Edition*, 20:183–258. London: Hogarth Press, 1959.

—— (1927), The future of an illusion. *Standard Edition*, 21:5–56. London: Hogarth Press, 1961.

—— (1935), Anonymous (Letter to an American mother). In *The Letters of Sigmund Freud*, ed. E. Freud. New York: Basic Books, 1960, pp. 423–424.

Friedman, R. C. (1976a), Psychodynamics and sexual object choice. *Contemp. Psychoanal.*, 12:94–108.

—— (1976b), Psychodynamics and sexual object choice, 3: A reply to Drs. I. Bieber and C. W. Socarides. *Contemp. Psychoanal.*, 12:379–386.

—— (1988), *Male Homosexuality: A Contemporary Psychoanalytic Perspective*. New Haven, CT: Yale University Press.

—— (1997), Response to Ken Corbett's "Homosexual boyhood: Notes on girlyboys." *Gender & Psychoanal.*, 2:487–494.

—— & Downey, J. (1993), Psychoanalysis, psychobiology, and homosexuality. *J. Amer. Psychoanal. Assn.*, 41:1159–1198.

—— & —— (1994), Special Article: Homosexuality. *New Engl. J. Med.*, 331:923–930.

———— & ———— (1995), Internalized homophobia and the negative therapeutic reaction. *J. Amer. Acad. Psychoanal.*, 23:99–113.

———— & Lilling, A. (1996), An empirical study of the beliefs of psychoanalysts about scientific and clinical dimensions of male homosexuality. *J. Homosexual.*, 32:79–89.

Frommer, M. S. (1994), Homosexuality and psychoanalysis: Technical considerations revisited. *Psychoanal. Dial.*, 4:215–233.

———— (1995), Countertransference obscurity in the treatment of homosexual patients. In *Disorienting Sexualities*, ed. T. Domenici & R. Lesser. New York: Routledge, pp. 65–82.

Gagnon, J. (1990), Biomedical theories of sexual orientation. In *Homosexuality/Heterosexuality: Concepts of Sexual Orientation*, ed. D. McWhirter, S. Sanders & J. Reinisch. New York: Oxford University Press, pp. 177–207.

Gay, P. (1987), *A Godless Jew: Freud, Atheism and the Making of Psychoanalysis*. New Haven, CT: Yale University Press.

Glassgold, J. & Iasenza, S., eds. (1995), *Lesbians and Psychoanalysis: Revolutions in Theory and Practice*. New York: Free Press.

Glover, E. (1957), Book review of Rado's *Collected Papers. Psychoanal. Quart.*, 26:251–258. Reprinted In *Heresy: Sandor Rado and the Psychoanalytic Movement*, ed. P. Roazen & B. Swerdloff. Northvale, NJ: Aronson, 1995, pp. 201–208.

Goldberg, S., Muir, R. & Kerr, J., eds. (1995), *Attachment Theory: Social, Developmental, and Clinical Perspectives*. Hillsdale, NJ: The Analytic Press.

Goldman, S. (1995), The difficulty of being a gay psychoanalyst during the last fifty years: An interview with Dr. Bertram Schaffner. In *Disorienting Sexualities*, ed. T. Domenici & R. Lesser. New York: Routledge, pp. 243–254.

Goldner, V. (1991), Toward a critical relational theory of gender. *Psychoanal. Dial.*, 1:249–272.

Gonsiorek, J. C. (1991), The empirical basis for the demise of the illness model of homosexuality. In *Homosexuality: Research Implications For Public Policy*, ed. J. D. Gonsiorek & J. D. Weinrich. Newbury Park, CA: Sage Publications, pp. 115–137.

Gooren, L. (1986a), The neuroendocrine response of leutenizing hormone to estrogen administration in heterosexual, homosexual and transsexual subjects. *J. Clin. Endocrinol. & Metabol.*, 63:583–588.

———— (1986b), The neuroendocrine response of leutenizing hormone to estrogen administration in the human is not sex-specific but dependent on the hormonal environment. *J. Clin. Endocrinol. & Metabol.*, 63:588–593.

———— (1990), Biomedical theories of sexual orientation. In *Homosexuality/Heterosexuality: Concepts of Sexual Orientation*, ed. D. McWhirter, S. Sanders & J. Reinisch. New York: Oxford University Press, pp. 71–87.

———— (1995), Biomedical concepts of homosexuality: Folk belief in a white coat. In *Sex, Cells, and Same-Sex Desire: The Biology of Sexual Preference*, ed. J. DeCecco & D. Parker. New York: Harrington Park Press, pp. 237–246.

Gould, S. J. (1977), *Ever Since Darwin: Reflections in Natural History*. New York: Norton.

———— (1981), *The Mismeasure of Man*. New York: Norton.

Green, R. (1987), *The "Sissy Boy Syndrome" and the Development of Homosexuality*. New Haven, CT: Yale University Press.

Greenberg, D. (1988), *The Construction of Homosexuality*. Chicago, IL: The University of Chicago Press.

Greenberg, J. & Mitchell, S. (1983), *Object Relations in Psychoanalytic Theory*. Cambridge, MA: Harvard University Press.

Greenhouse, L. (1996), Gay rights laws can't be banned, high court rules: Colorado law void. *The New York Times*, May 21, p. 1.

Group for the Advancement of Psychiatry (in press), *Homosexuality and Mental Health: The Impact of Bias*. Washington, DC: American Psychiatric Press, Inc.

Haldeman, D. (1991), Sexual orientation conversion therapy for gay men and lesbians: A scientific examination. In *Homosexuality: Research Implications for Public Policy*, ed. J. C. Gonsiorek & J. D. Weinrich. Newbury Park, CA: Sage Publications, pp. 149–161.

———— (1994), The practice and ethics of sexual orientation conversion therapy. *J. Consult. & Clin. Psychol.*, 62:221–227.

Hamer, D. & Copeland, P. (1994), *The Science of Desire*. New York: Simon & Schuster.

———— Hu, S., Magnuson, V., Hu, N. & Pattatucci, A. (1993), A linkage between DNA markers on the X-chromosome and male sexual orientation. *Science*, 261:321–327.

Hancock, K. (1995), Psychotherapy with lesbians and gay men. In *Lesbian, Gay and Bisexual Identities Over the Lifespan*, ed. A. D'Augelli & C. Patterson. New York: Oxford University Press, pp. 398–432.

Hanley-Hackenbruck, P. (1993), Working with lesbians in psychotherapy. *Rev. Psychiat.*, 12:59–83.

Hanson, G. & Hartmann, L. (1996), Latency development in prehomosexual boys. In *Textbook of Homosexuality and Mental Health*, ed. R. Cabaj & T. Stein. Washington, DC: American Psychiatric Press, pp. 253–266.

Harris, A. (1991), Gender as contradiction. *Psychoanal. Dial.*, 1:197–224.

Hartmann, H. (1958), *Ego Psychology and the Problem of Adaptation*, trans. D. Rapaport. New York: International Universities Press.

———— (1960), *Psychoanalysis and Moral Values*. New York: International Universities Press.

Harvey, J. (1987), *The Homosexual Person: New Thinking in Pastoral Care*. San Francisco, CA: Ignatius Press.

Hatterer, L. (1970), *Changing Homosexuality in the Male*. New York: McGraw-Hill.

Haumann, G. (1995), Homosexuality, biology, and ideology. In *Sex, Cells, and Same-Sex Desire: The Biology of Sexual Preference*, ed. J. DeCecco & D. Parker. New York: Harrington Park Press, pp. 57–78.

Hausman, K. (1995), AMA reverses stand on homosexual issues. *Psychiat. News*, 30:1, 18.

Helminiak, D. (1994), *What the Bible* Really *Says about Homosexuality*. San Francisco, CA: Alamo Press.

Hendin, H. (1992), Suicide among homosexual youth. *Amer. J. Psychiat.*, 149:1416–1417.

Herdt, G. (1994), *Guardians of the Flutes: Idioms of Masculinity*. Chicago, IL: University of Chicago Press.

—————— & Boxer, A. (1993), *Children of Horizons: How Gay and Lesbian Teens are Leading a New Way Out of the Closet*. Boston, MA: Beacon.

Herek, G. (1984), Beyond homophobia: A social psychological perspective on the attitudes towards lesbians and gay men. *J. Homosexual.*, 10:1–21. Reprinted in *Bashers, Baiters and Bigots: Homophobia in American Society*, ed. J. DeCecco. New York: Harrington Park Press, 1985, pp. 1–21.

—————— (1990), The context of anti-gay violence: Notes on cultural and psychological heterosexism. *J. Interpersonal Violence.*, 5:316–333.

—————— & Berrill, K. (1992), *Hate Crimes: Confronting Violence Against Lesbians and Gay Men*. Newbury Park, CA: Sage.

Herrn, R. (1995), On the history of biological theories of homosexuality. In *Sex, Cells, and Same-Sex Desire: The Biology of Sexual Preference*, ed. J. DeCecco & D. Parker. New York: Harrington Park Press, pp. 31–56.

Hetrick, E. & Martin, A. D. (1988), Developmental issues and their resolution for gay and lesbian adolescents. In *Psychotherapy with Homosexual Men and Women: Integrated Identity Approaches for Clinical Practice*, ed. E. Coleman. New York: Haworth Press, pp. 25–43.

Holleran, A. (1978), *Dancer from the Dance*. New York: Plume.

—————— (1988), *Ground Zero*. New York: William Morrow.

Hooker, E. (1957), The adjustment of the male overt homosexual. *J. Proj. Tech.*, 21:18–31.

Hooven, F. V. (1993), *Tom of Finland: His Life and Times*. New York: St. Martin's Press.

Hopcke, R. (1989), *Jung, Jungians and Homosexuality*. Boston, MA: Shambhala.

Hunter, J. & Schaecher, R. (1995), Gay and lesbian adolescents. In *Encyclopedia of Social Work*, ed. R. Edwards & J. Hopps. Washington, DC: NASW Press, pp. 1055–1061.

Hynes, W. (1997), Simply home: Integrity/Staten Island finds a seat at the table for lesbians and gays. *Staten Island Advance*, December 13, pp. B1,4.

Isay, R. (1989), *Being Homosexual: Gay Men and Their Development*. New York: Farrar, Straus & Giroux.

—————— (1991), The homosexual analyst: Clinical considerations. *The Psychoanalytic Study of the Child*, 46:199–216. New Haven, CT: Yale Universtiy Press.

———— (1996), *Becoming Gay: The Journey to Self-Acceptance*. New York: Pantheon.

Jarman, D. (1992), *At Your Own Risk: A Saint's Testament*. Woodstock, NY: Overlook Press.

Jennings, K. (1994), American dreams. In *Growing Up Gay: A Literary Anthology*, ed. B. Singer. New York: New Press, pp. 2–7.

Jones, E. (1961), *The Life and Work of Sigmund Freud* (abridged version). New York: Basic Books.

Jones, F. & Koshes, R. (1995), Homosexuality and the military. *Amer. J. Psychiat.*, 152:16–21.

Kantrowitz, A. (1977), *Under the Rainbow: Growing Up Gay*. New York: William Morrow.

Kardiner, A. (1955), *Sex and Morality*. London: Routledge & Kegan Paul.

Katz, J. (1995), *The Invention of Heterosexuality*. New York: Dutton.

Kerr, J. (1993), *A Most Dangerous Method: The Story of Jung, Freud, and Sabina Spielrein*. New York: Knopf.

Kertzner, R. & Sved, M. (1996), Midlife gay men and lesbians: Adult development and mental health. In *Textbook of Homosexuality and Mental Health*, ed. R. Cabaj & T. Stein. Washington, DC: American Psychiatric Press, pp. 267–288.

Khan, M. (1979), *Alienation in Perversion*. New York, NY: International Universities Press.

Kiersky, S. (in press), *Exiled Desire*. Hillsdale, NJ: The Analytic Press.

———— & Gould, E., eds. (in press), *Sexualities: Lost and Found*. New York: International Universities Press.

Kinsey, A., Pomeroy, W. & Martin, C. (1948), *Sexual Behavior in the Human Male*. Philadelphia, PA: Saunders.

Kirkpatrick, M. (1996), Lesbians as parents. In *Textbook of Homosexuality and Mental Health*. ed. R. Cabaj & T. Stein. Washington, DC: American Psychiatric Press, pp. 353–370.

Kohlberg, L. (1966), A cognitive-developmental analysis of children's sex role concepts and attitudes. In *The Development of Sex Differences*, ed. E. Macoby. Stanford, CA: Stanford University Press, pp. 82–172.

Kohut, H. (1971), *The Analysis of the Self*. New York: International Universities Press.

———— & Wolf, E. (1978), The disorders of the self and their treatment: An outline. In *Essential Papers on Narcissism*, ed. A. Morrison. New York: New York University Press, 1986, pp. 175–196.

Konrad, P. & Schneider, J. (1980), *Deviance and Medicalization: From Badness to Illness*. St. Louis, MO: Mosby.

Kooden, H. (1994), The gay male therapist as an agent of socialization. *J. Gay & Lesbian Psychother.*, 2:39–64.

Krafft-Ebing, R. (1886), *Psychopathia Sexualis*, trans. H. Wedeck. New York: Putnam, 1965.

Krajeski, J. (1996), Homosexuality and the mental health professions. In

Textbook of Homosexuality and Mental Health, ed. R. Cabaj & T. Stein. Washington, DC: American Psychiatric Press, pp. 17–31.

Kramer, L. (1978), *Faggots*. New York: Plume.

——— (1994), *Reports from the Holocaust: The Story of an AIDS Activist*. New York: St. Martin's Press.

Kuhn D., Nash S. & Brucken, L. (1978), Sex role concepts of two- and three-year-olds. *Child Devel.*, 49:445–451.

Kuhn, T. (1972), *The Structure of Scientific Revolutions*, 2nd ed. Chicago, IL: University of Chicago Press.

Kushner, T. (1992a), *Angels in America, Part 1: Millennium Approaches*. New York: Theater Communications Group.

——— (1992b), *Angels in America, Part 2: Perestroika*. New York: Theater Communications Group.

Langs, R. (1993), Psychoanalysis: Narrative myth or narrative science? *Contemp. Psychoanal.*, 29:555–594.

Laplanche, J. & Pontalis, J.-B. (1973), *The Language of Psychoanalysis*. New York: Norton.

Lauritsen, J. & Thorstad, D. (1974), *The Early Homosexual Rights Movement (1864–1935)*. New York: Times Change Press.

Leavitt, D. (1986), *The Lost Language of Cranes*. New York: Bantam.

Lesser, R. (1993), A reconsideration of homosexual themes. *Psychoanal. Dial.*, 3:639–641.

——— (1996), Category problems: Lesbians, postmodernism and truth. *Psychoanal. & Psychother.*, 13:153–159.

LeVay, S. (1991), A difference in hypothalamic structure between heterosexual and homosexual men. *Science*, 253:1034–1037.

——— (1993), *The Sexual Brain*. Cambridge, MA: MIT Press.

Levenson, E. (1983), *The Ambiguity of Change*. New York: Basic Books.

——— (1995), A monopedal presentation of Interpersonal psychoanalysis. *Rev. Interpersonal Psychoanal.*, 1:1–4.

Lewes, K. (1988), *The Psychoanalytic Theory of Male Homosexuality*. New York: Simon & Schuster. Reissued as *Psychoanalysis and Male Homosexuality* (1995, Northvale, NJ: Aronson).

Liebman, M. (1992), *Coming Out Conservative*. San Francisco, CA: Chronicle.

Lilling, A. & Friedman, R. C. (1995), Bias towards gay patients by psychoanalytic clinicians: An empirical investigation. *Arch. Sex. Behav.*, 24:563–570.

Lingiardi, V. (1997), *Compagni d'Amore: Da Ganimede a Batman: Identità e Mito nelle Omossesualità Maschili*. Milano: Raffaello Cortina.

Lionells, M., Fiscalini, J., Mann, C. & Stern, D., eds. (1995), *Handbook of Interpersonal Psychoanalysis*. Hillsdale, NJ: The Analytic Press.

Lorenz, K. (1953), *King Solomon's Ring*. London: Methuen.

MacIntosh, H. (1994), Attitudes and experiences of psychoanalysts in analyzing homosexual patients. *J. Amer. Psychoanal. Assn.*, 42:1183–1207.

Macoby, E. (1980), Sex differences in aggression: A rejoinder and reprise. *Child Devel.*, 51:1223–26.

———— & Jacklin, C. (1974), *The Psychology of Sex Differences*. Stanford, Cⱼ Stanford University Press.

Magee, M. & Miller, D. (1994), Psychoanalysis and women's experiences of "coming out": The necessity of being a bee-charmer. *J. Amer. Acad. Psychoanal.*, 22:481–504. Reprinted in *Disorienting Sexualities*, ed. T. Domenici & R. Lesser. New York: Routledge, 1995, pp. 97–114.

———— & ———— (1995), *Assaults and Harassments: The Violent Acts of Theorizing Lesbian Sexuality*. Presented at panel entitled "Psychoanalysis and Homosexuality: A Contemporary View," American Academy of Psychoanalysis, December 10.

———— & ———— (1996a), Psychoanalytic views of female homosexuality. In *Textbook of Homosexuality and Mental Health*, ed. R. Cabaj & T. Stein. Washington, DC: American Psychiatric Press, pp. 191–206.

———— & ———— (1996b), What sex is an amaryllis? What gender is lesbian? Looking for something to hold it all. *Gender & Psychoanal.*, 1:139–170.

———— & ———— (1997), *Lesbian Lives: Psychoanalytic Narratives Old and New*. Hillsdale, NJ: The Analytic Press.

Mahler, M., Pine, F. & Bergman, A. (1975), *The Psychological Birth of the Human Infant: Symbiosis and Individuation*. New York: Basic Books.

Marmor, J., ed. (1965), *Sexual Inversion: The Multiple Roots of Homosexuality*. New York: Basic Books.

———— ed. (1980), *Homosexual Behavior: A Modern Reappraisal*. New York: Basic Books.

———— (1996), Nongay therapists working with gay men and lesbians: A personal reflection. In *Textbook of Homosexuality and Mental Health*, ed. R. Cabaj & T. Stein. Washington, DC: American Psychiatric Press, pp. 539–545.

Martin, A. (1995), A view from both sides: Coming out as a lesbian psychoanalyst. In *Disorienting Sexuality: Psychoanalytic Reappraisals of Sexual Identities*, ed. T. Domenici & R. Lesser. New York: Routledge, pp. 255–261.

Martin, A. D. (1982), Learning to hide: The socialization of the gay adolescent. In *Adolescent Psychiatry, Vol. 10,* ed. S. Feinstein, J. Looney, A. Schwarzberg & A. Sorosky. Chicago, IL: University of Chicago Press, pp. 52–66.

Mass, L. (1990), *Homosexuality and Sexuality: Dialogues of the Sexual Revolution, Vol. 1*. New York: Harrington Park Press.

———— (1994), *Confessions of a Jewish Wagnerite: Being Gay and Jewish in America*. New York: Cassell.

Maupin, A. (1978), *Tales of the City*. New York: HarperCollins.

McDougall, J. (1980), *Plea for a Measure of Abnormality*. New York: International Universities Press.

McWhirter, D. & Mattison, A. (1984), *The Male Couple: How Relationships Develop*. Englewood Cliffs, NJ: Prentice-Hall.

———— Sanders, S. & Reinisch, J., eds. (1990), *Homosexuality/Heterosexuality: Concepts of Sexual Orientation*. New York: Oxford University Press.

Merlino, J. (1997), Support groups for professional caregivers: A role for the contemporary psychoanalyst. *J. Amer. Acad. Psychoanal.*, 25:111–122.

Metcalfe, R. (1991), Halifax, Nova Scotia. In *Hometowns*, ed. J. Preston. New York: Dutton, 1992, pp. 311–320.

Mitchell, S. (1978), Psychodynamics, homosexuality, and the question of pathology. *Psychiatry*, 41:254–263.

—— (1981), The psychoanalytic treatment of homosexuality: Some technical considerations. *Internal. Rev. Psycho-Anal.*, 8:63–80.

—— (1988), *Relational Concepts in Psychoanalysis: An Integration*. Cambridge, MA: Harvard University Press.

Moberly, E. (1983a), *Homosexuality: A New Christian Ethic*. Cambridge, UK: James Clarke.

—— (1983b), *Psychogenesis: The Early Development of Gender Identity*. London: Routledge.

Monette, P. (1988), *Borrowed Time: An AIDS Memoir*. New York: Avon.

—— (1992), *Becoming a Man: Half a Life Story*. San Francisco, CA: HarperCollins.

Money, J. (1986), *Lovemaps*. New York: Irvington.

—— (1988), *Gay, Straight, and In-Between: The Sexology of Erotic Orientation*. New York: Oxford University Press.

—— & Ehrhardt, A. (1996), *Man & Woman, Boy & Girl*. Northvale, NJ: Aronson.

Morgenthaler, F. (1984), *Homosexuality Heterosexuality Perversion*, trans. A. Aebi. Hillsdale, NJ: The Analytic Press, 1988.

Morin, S. & Garfinkle, E. (1978), Male homophobia. *J. Soc. Issues*, 34:29–47.

Moss, D. (1992), Introductory thoughts: Hating in the first person plural: The example of homophobia. *Amer. Imago*, 49:277–291.

—— (1997), On situating homophobia. *J. Amer. Psychoanal. Assn.*, 45:201–215.

Nagourney, A. (1995), Father doesn't know best. *Out Magazine*, February., pp. 75–77, 113–115.

National Association for Research and Treatment of Homosexuality (1994), New AMA Policy Statement. *NARTH Bull.* 2, December, p. 5.

National Conference of Catholic Bishops (1982), *Norms for Priestly Formation*. Washington, DC: United States Catholic Conference.

New York Times (1996), Excerpts from Court's Decision on Colorado's Provision for Homosexuals. *The New York Times*, May 21, p. A20.

Nichols, S. & Ostrow, D., eds. (1984), *Psychiatric Implications of Acquired Immune Deficiency Syndrome*. Washington, DC: American Psychiatric Press.

Nicolosi, J. (1991), *Reparative Therapy of Male Homosexuality: A New Clinical Approach*. Northvale, NJ: Aronson.

—— & Freeman, L. (1995), *Healing Homosexuality: Case Stories of Reparative Therapy*. Northvale, NJ: Aronson.

O'Connor, N. & Ryan, J. (1993), *Wild Desires and Mistaken Identities: Lesbianism and Psychoanalysis*. New York: Columbia University.

Ogden, T. (1990), *The Matrix of the Mind: Object Relations and the Psychoanalytic Dialogue*. Northvale, NJ: Aronson.

O'Leary, J. (1997), A heterosexual male therapist's journey of self discovery: Wearing a "straight"jacket in a gay men's bereavement group. In *Hope and Mortality: Psychodynamic Approaches to AIDS and HIV*, ed. M. Blechner. Hillsdale, NJ: The Analytic Press, pp. 209–220.

Orange, D. (1996), A philosophical inquiry into the concept of desire in psychoanalysis. *Psychoanal. & Psychother.*, 13:122–129.

Ortmeyer, D. (1995), History of the founders of Interpersonal psychoanalysis. In *Handbook of Interpersonal Psychoanalysis*, ed. M. Lionells, J. Fiscalini, C. Mann & D. Stern. Hillsdale, NJ: The Analytic Press, pp. 3–27.

Ovesey, L. (1969), *Homosexuality and Pseudohomosexuality*. New York: Science House.

Patterson, C. & Chan, R. (1996), Gay fathers and their children. In *Textbook of Homosexuality and Mental Health*, ed. R. Cabaj & T. Stein. Washington, DC: American Psychiatric Press, pp. 371–393.

Perry, H. (1982), *Psychiatrist of America: The Life of Harry Stack Sullivan*. Cambridge, MA: Harvard University Press.

Person, E. (1980), Sexuality as the mainstay of identity: Psychoanalytic perspectives. *Signs: J. Women Culture & Society*, 5:605–630.

Peterfreund, E. (1983), *The Process of Psychoanalytic Therapy: Models and Strategies*. Hillsdale, NJ: The Analytic Press.

Pezzana, A., ed. (1976), *La Politica del Corpo: Antologia del "Fuori" Movimento di Liberazione Omosessuale*. Rome: Savelli.

Piaget, J. (1965), *The Moral Judgment of the Child*. New York: Free Press.

Plant, R. (1986), *The Pink Triangle: The Nazi War Against Homosexuals*. New York: Henry Holt.

Poland, W. (1983), Review of Marmor's *Homosexual Behavior: A Modern Reappraisal*. *J. Amer. Pyschoanal. Assn.*, 31:775–777.

Preston, J., ed. (1991), *Hometowns*. New York: Dutton.

Pronk, P. (1993), *Against Nature: Types of Moral Argumentation Regarding Homosexuality*. Grand Rapids, MI: William B. Eerdmans.

Purcell, D. & Hicks, D. (1996), Institutional discrimination against lesbians, gay men, and bisexuals: The courts, legislature, and the military. In *Textbook of Homosexuality and Mental Health*. ed. R. Cabaj & T. Stein. Washington, DC: American Psychiatric Press, pp. 763–782.

Racker, H. (1968), *Transference and Countertransference*. Madison, CT: International Universities Press.

Rado, S. (1940), A critical examination of the concept of bisexuality. *Psychosomatic Medicine*, 2:459–467. Reprinted in *Sexual Inversion: The Multiple Roots of Homosexuality*, ed. J. Marmor. New York: Basic Books, 1965, pp. 175–189.

——— (1969), *Adaptational Psychodynamics: Motivation and Control*. New York: Science House.

Rechy, J. (1963), *City of Night*. New York: Grove.

———— (1977), *The Sexual Outlaw: A Documentary*. New York: Dell.

Remafedi, G., French, S., Story, M., Resnick, M. & Blum, R. (1998), The relationship between suicide risk and sexual orientation: Results of a population-based study. *Amer. J. Public Health*, 88:57–60.

Rich, A. (1986), Compulsory heterosexuality and lesbian existence. In *The Lesbian and Gay Studies Reader*, ed. H. Abelove, M. A. Barale & D. Halperin. New York: Routledge, 1993, pp. 227–254.

Ricketts, W. (1984), Biological research on homosexuality: Ansell's cow or Occam's razor? *J. Homosexual.*, 9:65–93.

Rist, D. Y. (1992), *Heartlands: A Gay Man's Odyssey Across America*. New York: Dutton.

Roazen, P. & Swerdloff, B. (1995) *Heresy: Sandor Rado and the Psychoanalytic Movement*. Northvale, NJ: Aronson.

Rotello, G. (1997), *Sexual Ecology: AIDS and the Destiny of Men*. New York: Dutton.

Roughton, R. (1995), Overcoming antihomosexual bias: A progress report. *Amer. Psychoanal*, 29:15–16.

Rubin, G. (1982), Thinking sex. In *The Lesbian and Gay Studies Reader*, ed. H. Abelove, M. A. Barale & D. Halperin. New York: Routledge, 1993, pp. 3–44.

Russo, V. (1987), *The Celluloid Closet: Homosexuality in the Movies*. New York: Harper & Row.

Saylor, S. (1991), Amethyst, Texas. In *Hometowns*, ed. J. Preston. New York: Dutton, 1992, pp. 119–135.

Schafer, R. (1983), *The Analytic Attitude*. New York: Basic Books.

———— (1995), The evolution of my views on nonnormative sexual practice. In *Disorienting Sexualities*, ed. T. Domenici & R. Lesser. New York, NY: Routledge, pp. 187–202.

Schaffner, B. (1986), Reactions of medical personnel and intimates to persons with AIDS. In *Psychotherapy and the Memorable Patient*, ed. M. Stern. New York: The Haworth Press, pp. 67–80.

———— (1990), Psychotherapy with HIV-infected persons. *New Directions for Mental Health Services*, 48:5–20.

———— (1996), Modifying psychoanalytic methods when treating HIV-positive patients. *J. Amer. Acad. Psychoanal.*, 25:123–141.

Schmalz, J. (1992), Gay politics go mainstream. *The New York Times Magazine*, October 11.

Schoenberg, E. (1995), Psychoanalytic theories of lesbian desire: A social constructionist critique. In *Disorienting Sexualities*, ed. T. Domenici & R. Lesser. New York: Routledge, pp. 65–82.

Schüklenk, U., Stein, E., Kerin, J. & Byne, W. (1997), The ethics of genetic research on sexual orientation. *Hastings Center Report*, July–August, pp. 6–13.

Schwartz, A. (1998), *Sexual Subjects: Lesbians, Gender, and Psychoanalysis*. New York: Routledge.

Schwartz, D. (1993), Heterophilia—The love that dare not speak its aim. *Psychoanal. Dial.*, 3:643–652.

———— (1995), Current psychoanalytic discourses on sexuality: Tripping over the body. In *Disorienting Sexualities*, ed. T. Domenici & R. Lesser, New York: Routledge, pp. 115–126.

———— (1996), Questioning the social construction of gender and sexual orientation. *Gender & Psychoanal.*, 1:249–260.

Searles, H. (1977), Dual- and multiple-identity processes in borderline ego-functioning. Reprinted in *My Work with Borderline Patients*, Northvale, NJ: Aronson, 1986, pp. 79–97.

Sedgwick, E. (1990), *Epistemology of the Closet*. Berkeley, CA: University of California Press.

———— (1991), How to bring your kids up gay. In *Tendencies*, ed. E. Sedgwick, Durham, NC: Duke University Press, 1993, pp. 154–166.

Segal, H. (1974), *Introduction to the Work of Melanie Klein*, 2nd ed. New York: Basic Books.

Shawver, L. (1989), Detailed inquiry. *Corrective & Soc. Psychiat.*, 35:78–82.

Shilts, R. (1982), *The Mayor of Castro Street: The Life and Times of Harvey Milk*. New York: St. Martin's Press.

———— (1987), *And the Band Played On*. New York: St. Martin's Press.

———— (1993), *Conduct Unbecoming: Gays and Lesbians in the U.S. Military*. New York: St. Martin's Press.

Siegel, E. (1988), *Female Homosexuality: Choice Without Volition*. Hillsdale, NJ: The Analytic Press.

Signorile, M. (1993), *Queer in America: Sex, the Media and the Closets of Power*. New York: Random House.

———— (1997), *Life Outside: The Signorile Report on Gay Men*. New York: HarperCollins.

Silverstein, C. (1981), *Man to Man: Gay Couples in America*. New York: Quill.

———— ed. (1991), *Gays, Lesbians, and Their Therapists*. New York: Norton.

Singer, B., ed. (1994), *Growing Up Gay/Growing Up Lesbian: A Literary Anthology*. New York: New Press.

Smith, B. (1990), Homophobia: Why bring it up? In *The Lesbian and Gay Studies Reader*, ed. H. Abelove, M. A. Barale & D. Halperin. New York: Routledge, 1993, pp. 99–102.

Socarides, C. (1968), *The Overt Homosexual*. New York: Grune & Stratton.

———— (1976), Psychodynamics and sexual object choice, 2: A reply to Dr. Richard C. Friedman's paper. *Contemp. Psychoanal.*, 12:370–379.

———— (1978), *Homosexuality*. New York: Aronson.

———— (1994), The erosion of heterosexuality. *The Washington Times*, July 5.

———— (1995), *Homosexuality: A Freedom Too Far*. Phoenix, AZ: Adam Margrave Books.

———— (1998), Letter to the Editor. *NY State Psychiat. Soc. Bull.*, 41, Spring, p. 2.

Sontag, S. (1989), *AIDS and Its Metaphors*. New York: Farrar, Straus & Giroux.

Spence, D. (1982), *Narrative Truth and Historical Truth: Meaning and Interpretation in Psychoanalysis*. New York: Norton.

Spezzano, C. (1993b), *Affect in Psychoanalysis: A Clinical Synthesis*. Hillsdale, NJ: The Analytic Press.

Stein, T. & Cohen, C. (1986), *Contemporary Perspectives on Psychotherapy with Lesbians and Gay Men*. New York: Plenum.

Stekel, W. (1922), *The Homosexual Neurosis*, trans. J. Van Teslaar. Brooklyn, NY: Physicians & Surgeons Book Co., 1934.

Stern, D. B. (1991), A philosophy for the embedded analyst: Gadamer's hermeneutics and the social paradigm of psychoanalysis. *Contemp. Psychoanal.*, 27:51–80.

——— (1995), Cognition and language. In *Handbook of Interpersonal Psychoanalysis*, ed. M. Lionells, J. Fiscalini, C. Mann & D. Stern. Hillsdale, NJ: The Analytic Press, pp. 79–138.

——— (1997), *Unformulated Experience: From Dissociation to Imagination in Psychoanalysis*. Hillsdale, NJ: The Analytic Press.

——— Mann, C. H., Kantor, S. & Schlesinger, G., eds. (1995), *Pioneers of Interpersonal Psychoanalysis*. Hillsdale, NJ: The Analytic Press.

Stern, D. N. (1985), *The Interpersonal World of the Infant*. New York: Basic Books.

Stoller, R. (1968), *Sex and Gender*. New York: Science House.

——— (1985), *Presentations of Gender*. New Haven, CT: Yale University Press.

——— & Herdt, G. (1985), Theories of origins of male homosexuality: A cross-cultural look. *Arch. Gen. Psychiat.*, 42:399–404.

Sullivan, A. (1995), *Virtually Normal: An Argument about Homosexuality*. New York: Knopf.

——— ed. (1997): *Same-Sex Marriage: Pro and Con*. New York: Vintage Books.

Sullivan, H. S. (1938), The data of psychiatry. *Psychiatry*, 1:121–134. Reprinted in *Pioneers of Interpersonal Psychoanalysis*, ed. D. B., Stern, C. H., Mann, S. Kantor & G. Schlesinger. Hillsdale, NJ: The Analytic Press, 1995, pp. 7–30.

——— (1953), *The Interpersonal Theory of Psychiatry*. New York: Norton.

——— (1954), *The Psychiatric Interview*. New York: Norton.

——— (1956), *Clinical Studies in Psychiatry*. New York: Norton.

——— (1962), *Schizophrenia as a Human Process*. New York: Norton.

——— (1972), *Personal Psychopathology*. New York: Norton.

Szasz, T. (1965), Legal and moral aspects of homosexuality. In *Sexual Inversion: The Multiple Roots of Homosexuality*, ed. J. Marmor. New York: Basic Books, pp. 124–139.

——— (1974a), *The Myth of Mental Illness: Foundations of a Theory of Personal Conduct*. New York: Harper & Row.

——— (1974b), *Ceremonial Chemistry*. New York: Anchor.

Tripp, C. A. (1975), *The Homosexual Matrix*. New York: Meridian.

Trop, J. & Stolorow, R. (1992), Defense analysis in self psychology: A developmental view. *Psychoanal. Dial.*, 2:427–442.

Tyson, P. & Tyson, R. L. (1990), *Psychoanalytic Theories of Development: An Integration*. New Haven, CT: Yale University Press.

Ulrichs, K. (1864), *The Riddle of "Man-Manly" Love*, trans. M. Lombardi-Nash. Buffalo, NY: Prometheus, 1994.

van den Aardweg, G. (1997), *The Battle for Normality: A Guide for (Self-) Therapy for Homosexuality*. San Francisco, CA: Ignatius Press.

van Naerssen, A., ed. (1987), *Gay Life in Dutch Society*. New York: Harrington Park Press.

Vidal, G. (1948), The city and the pillar. Reprinted in *The City and the Pillar and Seven Early Stories*. New York: Random House, 1995, pp. 1–207.

Warren, P. (1974), *The Front Runner*. Markham, Ont., Canada: Plume.

Weinberg, G. (1972), *Society and the Healthy Homosexual*. New York: Anchor.

Whalen, R., Geary, D. & Johnson, F. (1990), Models of sexuality. In *Homosexuality/Heterosexuality: Concepts of Sexual Orientation*, ed. D. McWhirter, S. Sanders & J. Reinisch, New York: Oxford University Press, pp. 61–70.

White, E. (1991), *States of Desire: Travels in Gay America*. New York: Plume.

White, M. (1994), *Stranger at the Gate: To Be Gay and Christian in America*. New York: Simon & Schuster.

Williams, W. (1986), *The Spirit and the Flesh: Sexual Diversity in American Indian Culture*. Boston, MA: Beacon.

Wilson, E. (1975), *Sociobiology: The New Synthesis*. Cambridge, MA: Belknap Press (Harvard University Press).

Wilson, J. (1996) Against homosexual marriage. In *Same Sex Marriage: Pro and Con*, ed. A. Sullivan. New York: Vintage, 1997, pp. 159–168.

Winnicott, D. W. (1947), Hate in the countertransference. In *Through Pediatrics to Psycho-Analysis*. New York: Basic Books, 1975, pp. 194–203.

———— (1957), Health education through broadcasting. In *Talking to Parents*. Workingham, England: Merloyd Lawrence, 1993, pp. 1–6.

———— (1960a), The theory of the parent-infant relationship. In *The Maturational Processes and the Facilitating Environment*. New York: International Universities Press, 1965, pp. 37–55.

———— (1960b), Ego distortion in terms of true and false self. In *The Maturational Processes and the Facilitating Environment*. New York: International Universities Press, 1965, pp. 140–152.

———— (1962), Ego integration in child development. In *The Maturational Processes and the Facilitating Environment*. New York: International Universities Press, 1965, pp. 56–63.

———— (1963), Communicating and not communicating leading to a study of certain opposites. In *The Maturational Processes and the Facilitating Environment*. New York: International Universities Press, 1965, pp. 179–192.

———— (1965), *The Maturational Processes and the Facilitating Environment*. New York: International Universities Press.

———— (1971), *Playing and Reality*. New York: Routledge.

Woods, J. & Lucas, J. (1993), *The Corporate Closet: The Professional Lives of Gay Men in America*. New York: Free Press.

Wortis, J. (1954), *Fragments of an Analysis with Freud*. New York: Charter.

INDEX

unconscious
  viewed as childish, 50
  viewed as phase, 247–9
  viewed as selfish, 50
homosexually self-aware men, 173,
    195, 298–9, 315–16
Hooker, E., 67–8
Hooven, F. V., 294
Hopcke, R., 154
Horizons, 250
Hu, N., 81
Hu, S., 81
humanistic psychology, 182
Hunter, J., 250
Hynes, W., 106
hypersensitivity, perceived, 241
hysteria, contrasted with perversion, 52

I
Iasenza, S., 154
identification(s)
  with the aggressor, 289
  Freud's theory of, 158
  multiple, complex/competing, 159,
    161, 208
  Nicolosi's drive-based theory of,
    157–8
  relational approach to, 159–62
identity development, 235–6
identity(ies), 212. *See also* bad-me;
    good-me; not-me
  affectively-laden markers of, 98
  as culturally defined, 4
  multiple, 7
illness. *See also* pathology
  conceptions of, 76
immaturity. *See* etiological theories,
    fixation/immaturity
impingement(s), 201–2
  detailed inquiry as, 264–5
individuality, 5
  curiosity about and respect for
    patients', 162, 169
infant, clinical *vs.* observed, 134
"infantile gayness," sense of, 235
infantile sexuality, 129

infantilism, theoretical, 122
insight, intellectual, 184n.
Institute for Human Identity, viii
Integrity, 106
internalized beliefs about
    homosexuality
  analytic exploration of, 149
  negative, 37, 223. *See also*
    homophobia, internal
interpretation(s), 11–12
  compliance with, 184
  stereotyped, 194
intersexuality, 22–3. *See also*
    Mary/Jack, case of
intimacy
  avoidance of, 81
  between boys, labeled inappropriate,
    235
  disconnected from sexuality, 254,
    266, 286–7. *See also* male
    intimacy
inversion, 96
invisibility, 278, 280n.
  adolescents, invisible gay, 143–5
Isay, R. A., vii, 12, 13, 46n., 72, 81,
    86n., 90, 122, 139, 144, 171,
    177, 180, 185, 187, 215, 223,
    227, 228, 232, 259, 271, 294
  experiences in psychoanalytic
    training, 177
  training analysis, 177, 179, 180
Issacharoff, A., ix

J
Jacklin, C., 241
Jacobson, L., viii
Jarman, D., 258, 294
Jennings, K., 289
Jenny Jones Murder Case, 114–15
Johnson, F., 16
Jones, E., 132
Jones, F., 272
*Journal of Gay and Lesbian
    Psychotherapy*, vii
Journal of Homosexuality, vii
Judaeo-Christian tradition, 97–8

reparative therapy *(continued)*
  directive-suggestive approaches, 185
  enactments
    vs. exploration of inner conflict,
      185
    outside therapy, 186
  as exploitation of transference, 185
  Freud and, 155–6
  informed consent and, 189–90
  moral values and beliefs in, 162–71,
    182–3
    expecting patient to adopt, 182
  Nicolosi's, 157. *See also* Nicolosi
  preoedipal explanations and, 138
  prognostic indicators, 176
  unacceptability of seeing homoerotic
    feelings as authentic, 180
  wives enlisted into treatment, 186
reparative therapy literature, stereotypes
  in, 170
reparative therapy patients, 171–81
  alleged change achieved by
    behavioral, motivated by
      compliant transference, 185
    celibacy, 180
    incomplete, 179–80
    marriage and fatherhood, 180
    rate of, 189
    return to homosexual activity
      after, 185
  creating appearance of heterosexual
    identity, 186
  learning to suppress homoerotic
    desires, 186
  must hide wishes not to change, 180
  reasons for seeking reparative ther-
    apy, 176–8, 180–1
    contradicted by unconscious
      desires, 181
    dissatisfaction with "gay
      lifestyle," 177–8
    expanding freedom of move-
      ment, 176
    fear, 177
    to live as heterosexual in hetero-
      sexual world, 177

nonacceptance of homoerotic
  feelings, 177
taken at face value, 179, 181
wanting approval, 177
who do not change, 221. *See also*
  Duberman; Isay
explanations regarding, 189
harmful effects experienced by, 189
pain and humiliation experienced
  by, 179, 180
sometimes blame themselves, 189
wish for reparative therapy, 176
reproduction, sexual orientation and,
  130–2, 148, 165–6
researchers, need to articulate feelings
  toward subject material, 3
Resnick, M., 144, 256
reverie state, 283. *See also* dissociation
  sexual activities taking place in,
    283–5
Rich, A., 94
Ricketts, W., 213, 214
rimming (oral-anal sex), 218–21
Rist, D. Y., 11, 114, 232, 241, 249,
  293, 294, 302
Rizzuto, C., viii
Roazen, P., 157
role-playing in therapy, unwitting,
  208
Romer v. Evans, 92n.
Rosen, M., viii
Ross, S., viii
Rotello, G., 40n.
"rough-and-tumble" play, 240–4
  childhood avoidance and dislike of,
    241, 243–4
    due to overwhelming stimulation,
      241–2
  compared with business world,
    242–3
  gay men's like or dislike of, 243
Roughton, R., viii, 2, 86n.
Rounsley, C., 215
Rubin, G., 85
Russo, V., 32, 33n., 257
Ryan, J., 154